PUBLIC ADMINISTRATION

AND THE

PUBLIC INTEREST

PENDLETON HERRING, president of the Social Science Research Council since 1948, has been a college professor, a foundation executive, a United Nations official, and a consultant to various governmental agencies. He received his doctorate in political science from Johns Hopkins and taught at Harvard from 1928 to 1946; for the first ten years of the Harvard Graduate School of Public Administration he held the post of secretary. He was for two years on the staff of the Carnegie Corporation (1946-48).

During the attempt in 1946 to negotiate an international control agreement he was head of the Secretariat of the United Nations Atomic Energy Commission. He has served the United States Government in the Bureau of the Budget and has been a consultant to the War Department, the Navy Department, the Air Force, and more recently, the National Science Foundation. He holds the Navy Department's Civilian Distinguished Service Award, an M.A. (hon.) from Harvard and an LL.D. from Princeton. He is an honorary member of the Harvard chapter of Phi Beta Kappa.

He was president of the American Political Science Association in 1953, and is currently president of the Woodrow Wilson Foundation and vice-president of the International Social Science Council.

He has been associated in an editorial capacity with the *Public Administration Review*, the *American Political Science Review*, and the *Public Opinion Quarterly*, and has served on the board of Franklin Publications and the Inter-University Case Program, Inc.

He is the author of *Group Representation Before Congress* (1929); *Federal Commissioners, Study of their Careers and Qualifications* (1936); *Public Administration and the Public Interest* (1936); *The Politics of Democracy* (1940); *Presidential Leadership* (1940); and *The Impact of War* (1941).

PUBLIC ADMINISTRATION

AND THE

PUBLIC INTEREST

BY

PENDLETON HERRING, Ph.D.

President, Social Science Research Council

NEW YORK / RUSSELL & RUSSELL

To
KATHARINE

Preface

UNDER democracy the public interest is based not upon the welfare of one class but upon a compounding of many group interests. We assume the possibility of achieving a balance of forces, social and economic. Whether this process becomes anything more than political jugglery depends upon the standards of justice that are accorded general acceptance by the community. Will social responsibility and loyalty to the democratic process outweigh opportunism and immediate self-interest? Intrinsically this is a question for statesmen, but officials can affect in some measure the turning of the scales.

The administrative branch of the government cannot maintain a balance in a dynamic society but it can do much toward clarifying and effectuating the purposes declared by our legislators. The caliber of our officials and the efficiency of their organization will largely determine the successful application of those policies designed to promote the general welfare. An able administrative service has much to offer. If the state is to carry its increasing burdens, the potentialities of officialdom must be realized to the utmost.

This book is offered as an inquiry into the functioning of our federal administrative machinery. The writer has spent many hours talking with officials in various bureaus and departments. He hopes to repay their courtesy at least in part by indicating some of the problems they encounter in actually applying the law. A better understanding of administration may be gained by noting the difficulties of federal officials in dealing with politicians and special interest organizations. This study attempts to analyze the relations between pressure groups and officials and to survey various efforts being made to adjust our bureaucracy to its heavy responsibilities. In this investigation one is tempted to ponder a theory as well as disclose a process. The evidence offered in this book suggests the question: what next? Upon what theory shall we proceed? What assumptions shall guide governmental action?

Economic laissez faire is gone; political laissez faire is passing. The government is undertaking the care of groups that are economically insecure; it is defending interests that are politically weak. Can a democratic government interpret in such positive and specific terms the meaning of the general welfare regardless of the strength of the underlying interest groups? In theory our government should strike a balance among these conflicting forces so as to promote the welfare of all. In fact some groups are placed more advantageously than others within our governmental structure and under our industrial system. The government draws its strength from the very elements it is supposed to regulate. Its officials both elective and appointive are subjected to constant pressures from these powerful interests. Complete objectivity is practically impossible for the elective official. Its exposes the administrative official to the charge of bureaucratic aloofness. Our government must be responsive if democracy is to survive. Yet the citizen in facing public questions seeks to promote his own immediate interests rather than the welfare of all. This attitude becomes the more dangerous as government extends its activities further into the social and industrial life of the nation.

What the final outcome of such tendencies will be no one can say. The authoritarianism of fascism and the dictatorship of the proletariat are the two alternatives persistently offered. Before granting the inevitability of either, the possibilities of our present democratic institutions warrant further exploration.

The administrative experience surveyed in this book gives cause for hope as well as fear. Weaknesses, abuses, and failures are frequently found. But experimentation continues. No logical a priori theory can embrace the flux of actual government. New laws, new administrative forms appear. There is a persistent search for some workable means of adjusting the forms of governance to the uneasy needs of men. The story of the federal bureaucracy today is kept in a looseleaf ledger. Revision is the only constant. In this lies the hope for the future.

The only suggestions for meeting its contingencies offered in this book are those taken directly from administrative experience. Our concern is in seeking present tendencies in the federal government that hold a promise of furthering administration in the public interest.

This volume is largely a collection of case studies. The work is exploratory rather than exhaustive. Were the volume several

PREFACE

times its present size much pertinent material would still remain untouched. The data presented here should demonstrate the importance of considering the tug and pull of economic and political forces upon our federal bureaucracy. To understand public administration we must know something of its general social context.

Ever since his survey of the activities of organized groups before Congress the author has been desirous of following a somewhat parallel line of investigation into the administrative process. Preliminary delving over a period of years suggested the fertility of the subject matter. Opportunity was offered during the past year to bring this project to fruition. First thanks must be given to President Conant's new plan of granting leave of absence for research and to those officers of the university who made it possible for the author to enjoy this privilege.

The author's colleagues and students make a contribution too profound to be particularized. Special mention, however, must be made of the help gained from presenting some of this research before the graduate seminar offered jointly by the writer with Professor C. J. Friedrich and Dr. George C. S. Benson. The critical scrutiny of this group aided the writer greatly in facing the baffling confusion of factual data. My colleagues Professor A. N. Holcombe and Dr. W. P. Maddox have read and commented helpfully on certain chapters. My wife has given many valuable suggestions as to style and arrangement.

To Mr. Philip Stone of Cornell, to Mr. W. M. Newton of Balliol, and to Mr. Wayne Woodmansee of Harvard, all of whom assisted in the collection of source materials at various times, and to Miss Dorothy Winthrop, who brought both intelligence and skill to the preparation of the manuscript, the author expresses his appreciation.

The author wishes to acknowledge his debt to Mr. W. F. Willoughby, who, while Director of the Institute for Government Research at the Brookings Institution, encouraged the initiation of this study. Professor W. Y. Elliott of the Department of Government at Harvard University gave the writer stimulus and aid in bringing it to completion. Mr. Laurence M. Channing very kindly read through the manuscript in its earlier stages and Dr. Merle Fainsod went through the entire study when finished. The criticism of these readers proved very valuable indeed.

PREFACE

Acknowledgments are due to The Macmillan Company and to Harper and Brothers for permission to quote from several books on their lists. Thanks are also given to the other publishers cited in the footnotes who were equally generous in granting leave to use various quotations.

The chapter headings in this book are taken from *Alice's Adventures in Wonderland* and *Through the Looking-glass*. The author is only one of several who have noted the relevance that Lewis Carroll's gentle classics can be made to have for present-day affairs. It may be Alice's readiness to try something new that makes her adventures seem so pertinent. She found that different experiments brought very different results. It was too big a bite of the mushroom from the extreme right that brought her to a state of collapse. She found that "her chin was pressed so hard against her foot, that there was hardly room to open her mouth; but she did it at last, and managed to swallow a morsel of the left-hand bit." The next thing she knew her head had shot above the trees and she was twisting her neck about in "graceful zig-zags." Politicians in their turn are alarmed at the difficulties of finding some point of equilibrium between extreme left and right influences.

Various chapters or parts of chapters in this book were originally published as articles and later revised. For leave to reprint such materials the author is indebted to the editors of the following journals: The American Political Science Review, Annals of the American Academy of Political and Social Science, Christian Science Monitor, Harvard Business Review, New Outlook, Political Science Quarterly, Public Utilities Fortnightly, Revue des Sciences Politiques, Social Forces, and the Southwestern Social Science Quarterly. For financial aid in conducting this research the author thanks the Milton Fund and the Committee on Research in the Social Sciences at Harvard University. The Brookings Institution most graciously extended its hospitality to the author during the months of 1933 and 1935 that were spent in the capital. This kindness proved a very substantial aid. The author's deepest thanks are given to those kind relatives and friends living in and about Washington who made his visits so pleasant and his work so agreeable that he fain would return for more.

DUNSTER HOUSE,   E. PENDLETON HERRING.
CAMBRIDGE, MASSACHUSETTS,
January, 1936.

Contents

CONTENTS

PUBLIC ADMINISTRATION
AND THE
PUBLIC INTEREST

Chapter I

BUREAUCRACY AND DEMOCRATIC GOVERNMENT

"I was thinking," Alice said very politely, "which is the best way out of this wood: it's getting so dark."

WHEN a democratic government undertakes to alleviate the maladjustments of the economic system, it stirs up a greed that it may lack power to control. The "voice of the people" sometimes suggests the squeal of pigs at the trough. The regulation that a democracy can enforce is based upon the self-discipline of its people, and this in turn demands the guidance of wise leaders who hold on high a clear vision of the public interest. But proper administrative tools are essential.

The part that the federal government shall take in the social and economic affairs of the nation will probably remain an open question for many years to come. It has been long argued as a question of "more" or "less" federal activity. At the present time the *kind* of role that the government should take is under critical scrutiny. Is it in the public interest that the federal government assume a positive responsibility for the security and welfare of its citizens? Or shall the government limit its efforts to stimulating competitive business activities and to encouraging the productive forces of the community?

This latter theory identifies the national welfare with a competitive economic order capable of providing for the needs of the people without political superintendence. The government is simply to police the obviously immoral and to assist those politically capable of securing federal aid. This view is based upon a faith in the inherent soundness of capitalism and in the generally benign working of political democracy in an industrial order. This view has in practice meant that the general welfare has been identified primarily with the prosperity of business and secondarily with that of agriculture. Federal administrative agencies might aid with statistical reports and scientific researches but they were not to attempt control. Federal regulation involved a mild policing

[3]

among the camp followers of the nation's business army. Seldom was a direct battle risked. Within the last few years new emphasis has been placed upon governmental responsibility.

Now it is argued that the public interest must be positively interpreted through political agencies and administered by appropriate governmental institutions. Economic forces, if unregulated and undirected, will not bring about a just distribution of the benefits of our technically advanced society. The inequalities resulting from capitalism must be compensated for by social controls that will ensure security for all. The federal government must undertake to direct economic forces toward providing a more equitable distribution of the national wealth.

Federal administrative bureaus are no longer assisting in the "natural" workings of economic enterprise. The government has assumed a general and positive responsibility for the management of industrial and social relations. The "general welfare" is no longer regarded as a by-product inevitably ensuing from the profitable operation of the competitive system. This means that the public interest cannot be left to chance but must be formulated in concrete terms. Or, to say the same thing in other terms, a plan for the general welfare must now be arranged by regulating or advancing the interests of particular groups in such wise as to produce a balanced and harmonious whole. A dynamic synthesis is sought with the federal government manning the controls.

There is no agreement as to which is the true gospel. These two views concerning the responsibilities of government have very different implications, yet they are being accepted concurrently in the federal government at the present time. Our administrative machinery must be based upon common agreement as to the general social responsibility of the federal government. Shall it initiate and lead? Shall it serve and follow? The law is administered on many fronts and under many conditions. Our thousands of federal laws are under the jurisdiction of scores of bureaus and commissions, involving myriads of interests, weak and powerful. How can administration be consistent without some broad agreement upon ultimate objectives?

At present the federal government cannot interpret all aspects of the public interest. Constitutional limitations bar the way in some directions. It is debatable as to whether all the social objectives of the Roosevelt administration can be implemented with appropriate constitutional agencies. Moreover, sectional differences would have to be discounted and economic influences counter-balanced before a federally ordained conception of the good life could be achieved. Can we build up within our administration a rallying point for effective opposition to the selfishly organized groups that terrorize our representative assemblies into granting them special favors? How can a balanced execution of law in the public interest result from an administrative service that is the product of the political aggressiveness of fortunately situated economic groups? A collection of federal bureaus created at the behest of aggressive minority groups cannot envisage the general welfare. There must be harmonious purpose and unified leadership. Is the scope and development of our administrative service to be determined by the urging of special groups for services and pro-tection? How can interests that are socially important but politi-cally weak be given a place in the federal administration?

To develop administrative services competent to meet these new demands is a unique task for a democracy. Our representative institutions were based upon a conception of the state whereby the government that governed least governed best. Increasingly economic classes are turning to the federal government to promote their interests. The area of conflicts is becoming central and political. Washington is today a national arena for class battles. Administration in the public interest necessitates general agree-ment as to the broad social objectives of the government.

President Roosevelt, in attempting to summarize his views, stated that the government must try

. . . to increase the security and the happiness of a large number of people in all occupations of life and in all parts of the country; to give them more of the good things of life; to give them a greater distribution, not only of wealth in the narrow terms but of wealth in the wider terms; to give them places to go in the summer time—recreation; to give them assurance that they are not going to starve in their old age; to give honest business a chance to go ahead and make a reasonable profit; and to give everyone a chance to earn a living.[1]

The bureaucratic machinery appropriate to such objectives differs radically from that needed to satisfy less comprehensive

[1] *New York Times*, June 8, 1935, p. 1.

[5]

aims. If the federal government is to carry burdens generally pertaining to national, social, and economic welfare, then the administrative services must be equally encompassing. The administrative organization must be adapted to the tendency that ultimately prevails. In any event, the federal government will undoubtedly continue to grow. The moot question is: how much direct responsibility will the federal government assume for directing and regulating economic activity? Democratic government must provide for all classes a degree of social stability and of economic security sufficient to keep these elements loyal to the community of purpose that makes the state possible. Democracy itself will collapse if it creates irreconcilable minorities.

Under the present economic order such groups will occur when in the competitive conflict they are dispossessed of what they regard as their minimum share of the national store of goods and of opportunities. Today these elements demand that the government provide not only freedom of opinion and association but likewise the conditions that make existence tolerable under its regime. The government must do so because it cannot refuse to do so and still retain the allegiance of those interests that see their existence threatened.

This necessarily implies that classes and sections must make concessions to other classes and sections. Unless this willingness exists, the democratic state is impossible. A toleration of different religions, or of philosophies, social or economic, is based upon a readiness to make concessions in the intellectual realm. As the government is forced into the economic realm by the need for order and control in these complex relations, a similar sacrifice is demanded. If it is denied, a bloody sacrifice may one day be exacted. We are here concerned, however, with exploring the possibilities of representative institutions.

It is in the legislature that the reconciliations essential to democratic government are expected to take place. Blocs in Congress bargain and logroll. Classes and sections there struggle for the privileges and appropriations they desire. Popular assemblies represent only too clearly the social and economic rivalries of the community. The task of arriving at a consensus of opinion regarding the general welfare is immensely complicated by the existence of organized minorities. Our representative legislative bodies have demonstrated their inadequacy for synthesizing group conflict into a unified conception of the public interest.

There seems to be a tacit recognition of the limitations of representative assemblies for accomplishing the purpose of the state. The democratic ritual is still observed, but certainly there is less faith in the outward forms of representative government. When obvious and gross injustices appeared under this system, efforts were made to improve the machinery of popular government. The theory was that, if the system were made more accurately representative, the public interest and general welfare would become clearer. When these political reforms failed to bring the improvement expected, legislative assemblies were discredited in the eyes of many people. The fundamental necessity of achieving a working compromise among class and sectional interests continues, even though the shortcomings of representative institutions have been demonstrated.

Congress has to an increasing extent escaped the onus of directly settling group conflicts by establishing under vague legislative mandates independent regulatory boards. The technical and complex nature of these conflicts has encouraged this trend. A parallel development within the past two decades has been the great increase in the service activities of the federal government. Bureaus have been established to aid special classes and sections and have thereby given all interests strong enough to demand it a share in public funds and services. Moreover, under emergency conditions, and where the political pressure has been very great, direct aid and subsidies have been distributed. Thus has the democratic process redressed the balance among conflicting interests and avoided arousing to the point of rebellion groups adversely affected by the ruthless force of a competitive society.

Upon the shoulders of the bureaucrat has been placed in large part the burden of reconciling group differences and making effective and workable the economic and social compromises arrived at through the legislative process. Thus Congress passes a statute setting forth a general principle. The details must be filled in by supplemental regulation. The bureaucrat is left to decide as to the conditions that necessitate the law's application. He is in a better position than the legislators to perform these duties. His daily occupation brings him into direct contact with the situation the law is intended to meet. He knows what can be enforced and he can better envisage the limits of legislative fiats. This increase in administrative discretion, while making possible the more understanding application of rules to concrete situations, nevertheless places a heavy duty on the administrator. The words of the statute delimit his scope, but within the margin of his discretion he must write his interpretation of state purpose.

The social and economic aspects of this process must be left to others. The political result has been the preservation thus far of the liberal democratic state as the agency of control and the transfer from Congress of much of the direct superintendence of reconciling the conflicting groups within the state. The governmental result has been the creation of a great bureaucracy with wide powers to carry on these functions. Great public services are needed all the way from the primary functions relating to police, sanitation, and the care of paupers to official enterprises that compete with private business. There are huge public-relief projects financed by taxing one class in order to alleviate the hunger pangs of another. The extent to which these activities are carried cannot be fixed but will vary in accordance with the character of the economic groups that have succeeded in attaining control of the government at any given time. There persists, nevertheless, a residue of responsibility no matter what combination is in control of the government. The mere existence of a great administrative organization necessitates a certain continuity that has little reference to political overturns. Groups must be willing to recognize that the state has a purpose which transcends their own immediate ends. The bureaucracy cannot assert a state purpose against the united hostility of groups that basically comprise the source whence authority springs.

In the United States the bureaucracy suffers for want of a hierarchical organization and a personnel united by a harmonious concept of state service. But a bureaucracy in these terms arouses the suspicion and criticism of interest groups, who regard the administration as designed to serve them or at least *not to interfere* with their group purposes. And it is these interest groups that wield political authority under a representative system. Such interests criticize "bureaucracy" as inimical to popular government. Yet only through developing a proper administrative organization can democracy survive.

We conclude, then, that the purpose of the democratic state is the free reconciliation of group interests and that the attainment of this end necessitates the development of a great administrative machine. Thus, paradoxical as it may seem to Jeffersonian Democrats, the liberal democratic state must be sustained by a huge bureaucracy. This viewpoint, however, has not won general acceptance.

Groups of citizens, seeking to advance their own interests or to protect themselves from the onslaughts of rivals, have turned to the government for aid. Yet the citizen distrusts the state at the same time that he appeals to it for help. He desires to use the facilities of the government; but he does not wish the government to direct or control his activities. As a result the federal administrative services have not been fused into a unified and responsible whole. They are a conglomeration of service agencies, independent regulatory commissions, and ill-proportioned bureaus and departments.

The present tangle of alphabetical monstrosities is not a new phenomenon. The confusion is greater because the variety of federal functions is greater. If the government is to become responsible for the economic security of various classes, the administrative machinery must be made adequate to the burden imposed. This does not mean creating more bureaus and commissions but rather reorganizing those that exist. The federal administration must be viewed as a whole: it must be developed into an institution for executing policy in the public interest and for promoting the general welfare. This will require a change in attitude on the part of most citizens. Groups have demanded special consideration from the federal government for themselves while condemning the general encroachment of the state into private affairs. The establishment of an adequate administrative structure and personnel must be undertaken if the state is to carry its ever-increasing load. The problem of bureaucracy must be faced directly.

No civil servant, however, wrapt in the bindings of official red tape, can regard himself as insulated from the currents of opinion generated by the groups with which his bureau comes into contact. The citizen for his part must feel that his experience and his special competence have some place in governance. How can a mutually advantageous connection be made?

The adjustment is not easy. "In every country," Herman Finer states, "the public is hostile to the official because at some time or other, as an inspector or a tax collector or a medical officer, or what not, he comes to take away, not to give—it is in the nature of his task to limit one's freedom and property."[1] The suspicion of bureaucracy is particularly keen in the United States, and not without just cause. "Political pull" remains the citizen's chief defense against officialdom in this country. This faulty resource is all the more necessary under a system where ministerial responsibility is lacking and public integrity is often wanting in official circles. Moreover, we have a tradition of distrust for government that harks back to Colonial and Revolutionary days. Official interference has long been regarded as irksome and unfriendly. Conditions of pioneer life doubtless intensified this feeling. We accepted bureaucratic incompetence as an inevitable characteristic of an institution from which little good was to be expected in any case. Our confidence was placed in the courts where the justice of the rule of law would protect us, we hoped, from the caprice of a government by men.[2]

The courts are often found taking the part of the citizen against the powers of officialdom. Their verdict time and again delimits or restricts bureaucratic competence. In the elected executive and legislature the citizen feels that some degree of control is attainable through political channels. The tradition of a rule of law gives him confidence in the courts. But how can he affect the course of administrative action?[3] Underlying such criticism is the uneasy

[1] Herman Finer, *Theory and Practice of Modern Government*, p. 1500, Dial Press, 1932.

[2] John Dickinson, "Administrative Law and the Fear of Bureaucracy, parts 1 and 2, *American Bar Association Journal*, October and November, 1928, and "The Perennial Cry of Bureaucracy," *Yale Review*, Spring, 1935. For recent discussions of interest, see E. Watkins, "Dangerous By-products of Bureaucracy," and S. E. Edmunds, "The Growth of Federal Bureaucratic Tyranny," *Lawyer and Banker*, January, 1933; Charles and William Beard, "The Case for Bureaucracy," *Scribner's*, April, 1933; Lawrence Sullivan, "The Dead Hand of Bureaucracy," *Forum*, January, 1933.

[3] The attitude of many businessmen is reflected in the following words taken down during a discussion at the annual meeting of an important association: "We can

feeling that the force of the government is turned to purposes contrary to those of his group. It often happens that a regulatory measure is enacted over the urgent protest of those thereby affected. The legislature, supported by a momentary public enthusiasm, discharges its duty in passing the law and turns to other matters. The bureaucrat is left to enforce the law over the disgruntled group thus brought under his jurisdiction. Governmental activity is unobjectionable to special interests when in accord with their aims, but when it is directed to other ends the cry of bureaucratic interference is raised.

The legislature, often because of a fortuitous combination of political factors, enacts a law. An administrative agency becomes responsible for its execution, and the legislative will is thus in a sense institutionalized and personified. Except for the relatively rare instances where a statute is rendered innocuous by non-enforcement, the legislative will is "frozen" until the law is changed. Meanwhile, a change of economic or political conditions may alter the alignment of social forces in the community and thereby bring the statute into disfavor, without necessarily forcing legislative amendment in response to criticisms. The legal responsibility of the official remains the same and the censure he incurs is the price of discharging his manifest duties.

Men, finding the state remote, unyielding, and huge when they attempt control, discover its powers to be only too intimate and encompassing when they offer resistance. These characteristics of unresponsiveness and oppressiveness are associated with the bureaucracy of the state. In this country the President is a representative-at-large as well as a symbol of national authority. But his responsibilities for political leadership receive more

hardly say that we today live under a government of law. We rather live under a government of bureaus and commissions. Personally I would prefer to have my rights fixed by law to having my interests always subject to the discretionary control of bureaus and commissions. Yet that is exactly what Government regulation means. The Government, of course, has certain functions like that of experimentation, the increase of human knowledge, with which we cannot quarrel, but when it comes to a proposition of regulating all business by people located in Washington it is time to protest. They proceed upon the assumption of omniscience on the part of these people and then wish to clothe them with omnipotence. They like to have the laws so formulated that there is no appeal from their decision." *Tenth Annual Meeting of the National Coal Association*, June 15-17, 1927, p. 63.

emphasis than his duties in law enforcement. He is often regarded as the people's champion. Congress is often derided, but it is seldom feared. The frequent lack of respect for its deliberations, if serving to emphasize its human failings, likewise reassures the citizen of its kinship to himself.

Officialdom embodies most concretely the concept of state coercion and control. Thus it falls heir to more than its share of the general human impatience with authority.

Much of the criticism of our administrative services is richly deserved though much of the condemnation of "bureaucracy" is emotional rather than rational. The word "bureaucracy" has become a stereotype.[1] It is employed most frequently, not to convey a meaning, but to evoke an emotional aversion to the situation with which the term is associated. This was well illustrated by the use of the word during the 1934 congressional campaign. On July 4, Senator Borah delivered an opening blast against "that meddlesome, irritating, confusing, undermining, destructive thing called bureaucracy." He stated that "of all the forms of government which has ever been permitted to torture the human family, the most burdensome, the most expensive, the most demoralizing, the most devastating to human happiness and the most destructive of human values is a bureaucracy."[2] The theme of Senator Borah, the liberal Republican and the champion of the little businessman, was echoed a few days later by the Honorable J. W. Davis, conservative Democrat and the spokesman for the big businessman. He warned the country against "the slow strangulation of an engirdling bureaucracy."[3]

An examination of the *Congressional Record* over the last decade or so reveals the free use of this word in the language of opprobrium. Senators and Congressmen apparently consider virulent attacks on the federal bureaucracy effective oratorically. In what other fashion can senatorial outbursts such as the following be taken: "With bureaucratic government growing by leaps and bounds at Washington, the battle is on and will continue until the American people themselves rise in their might and destroy bureaucracy and

[1] See A. N. Holcombe, *Government in a Planned Democracy*, p. 119, Norton, 1935; Luther Gulick, *Better Government Personnel*, pp. 57–60, McGraw-Hill, 1935.

[2] *Boston Herald*, July 5, 1934.

[3] *Ibid.*, July 11, 1934.

plutocracy to restore the Government to the people, where our fathers planned that it should always remain, as expressed by Jefferson.[1] If the Democrats have the unsuspecting Jefferson to fall back upon, the Republican critic of bureaucracy is not without his prophet. "I want to get away just as far as I can from commissions and go back to a government by law rather than a government by bureau, board or commissions," stated one such Senator. "I agree with the Harding philosophy."[2]

Bureaucracy is not only condemned outright and linked with the faults of the opposing party, but it is also joined with abuses in administration. One Congressman condemns the "spirit of haughtiness, of arrogance and of self-sufficiency that comes to control those that rule over" federal bureaus and departments.[3] Such spokesmen draw a stinging parallel between bureaucratic bumptiousness and business sense, between the rule of red tape and the rule of reason, and generally conclude with an attack upon the opposing party for its encouragement of paternalism in government.

Sometimes the motivation behind such denunciations can be even more clearly discerned. For example, one prominent Senator stated:

The tendency to increase and enlarge bureaucracy at Washington, with all its red tape, multiplications and duplications of offices, is regrettable. It is another effort to remove the Government from the people. It is a strike at local self-government. In a word, it is undemocratic.[4]

His remarks were occasioned by the debate on the proposed federal Department of Education. He concludes thus: "We have been drifting too rapidly toward bureaucracy; let us call a halt at nationalization of education." A distrust of bureaucrats may have been the Senator's genuine reason for opposing this bill, but certainly it was not the only reason. In his state a large, well-organized, and influential group was bitterly opposed to the measure under consideration. Whether one can fairly distinguish in this case between the reason given for opposing the federal

---

[1] *Congressional Record*, Senate, Apr. 21, 1926, p. 8015.
[2] *Ibid.*, Jan. 24, 1921, p. 1945.
[3] *Ibid.*, House, Feb. 19, 1926, pp. 4289–4291.
[4] *Ibid.*, Senate, Dec. 15, 1923, p. 309.

bureau and the reason underlying, the fact remains that the term "bureaucracy" has become encrusted with meanings that induce a dyslogistic response in the hearer and is hence used in argument to evoke such a reaction.

Private interests demand honesty in government and at the same time seek privileged treatment for themselves. They demand economy and efficiency in government, and yet a chance for "honest graft" is seldom neglected.[1] Neither red tape nor an inevitable tendency toward expansion can be regarded as a fundamental characteristic of bureaucracy. These attributes are scarcely compatible. They are by no means implicit in bureaucracy itself but arise, first, from the nature of the administrative responsibility of a given bureau and, secondly, from the character of the public confronting this bureau. Only in these terms can the characteristics peculiar to any one bureau be determined. One cannot damn all bureaucracy by condemning a tendency toward expansion or toward routine. The circumstances that distinguish one bureaucratic situation from another must be considered.

Contrast the Bureau of Home Economics with the Patent Office. Precision, order, and system should dominate the latter. The former is, however, a promotive agency. Its purpose is to advance the knowledge and practice of home economics. The measure of its success is the extent to which it is used. A tendency to expand is a healthy indication of a desire to fulfill its purpose by spreading information and enlisting interest in its work. Its *raison d'être* is justified only to the extent that its services are used.

Examples could be multiplied to stress the empty fashion in which this word "bureaucracy" has been used to cloak administrative or political developments held to be objectionable for other

[1] One writer finds organized business confronted with this dilemma: "First-rate government supposedly effects a reduction of taxes, a result ardently wished for by business at all time; but government that is too good encourages popular reliance in government, which in turn might result in the increase of governmental regulation of business, and possibly in new forms of government ownership and operation." Homer Ferguson, "A Plea for Inefficiency in Government," *Nation's Business*, November, 1928, pp. 21–22. See also Samuel O. Dunn, "The Practical Socialist," *Nation's Business*, November, 1928, p. 17, and Marshall E. Dimock, "Do Business Men Want Good Government?" *National Municipal Review*, January, 1931.

less obvious reasons. When a derogatory statement is to be made about the administrative authorities, the word "bureaucracy" is usually employed. As unfavorable connotations have become accepted, its usefulness as a stereotype has increased. Unless we are to define the term as that-aspect-of-administration-which-is-disliked-by-those-who-are-adversely-affected, this loose criticism of bureaucracy must be discounted.[1] A blanket denunciation of bureaucracy is not only unfair but positively misleading. The connotations generally associated with the term are not an accurate indication of the relations actually existing between administrative officials and special interests.

In all this eloquent denunciation of bureaucracy, the fact is overlooked that the despised bureaus are in a sense the creations of their critics and that, while bureaucracy is flayed in general, single bureaus are loyally supported by their congressional sympathizers. Congressional committees have certain bureaus in their charge and a strong bond develops between these bureaucrats and their committee. Powerful economic groups support both the committee and the bureau.[2] The abused bureau appeared because it was desired by groups with sufficient political power to make their demands effective. Our vast administrative development is eloquent evidence of the responsive character of popular government and of the effectiveness of pressure politics. The question now remains: can the democratic state cope with the child of its own creation?

[1] It is here that the analysis offered by C. J. Friedrich is invaluable. C. J. Friedrich and Taylor Cole, *Responsible Bureaucracy*, p. 18, Harvard University Press, 1932. He suggests these characteristics as the basic criteria for any type of bureaucracy: first, "a determinate distribution of offices or functions among the members of the organization"; secondly, "a determinate distribution of the powers of control and coercion attached to these offices"; and thirdly, "determinate qualifications required of officials for the fulfillment of those several functions." This statement stresses fundamentals applicable to bureaucracy generally, whether in the organization of great corporations or in the governmental hierarchy.

[2] Congressman Beck has written: "The bureaucracy of a department is keenly attentive to the supposed wishes of the members of the committee, having in charge its department and it is no unusual situation for a member of such a legislative committee to believe that it is his right and duty to support the demands of the bureaucracy of the department under his charge with little or no investigation." James A. Beck, *Our Wonderland of Bureaucracy*, p. 204, Macmillan, 1932.

[15]

PUBLIC ADMINISTRATION

If the bureaucracy dominates the groups, the state ceases to be democratic. But if special interests turn the bureaucracy to their own selfish ends, the purpose of the democratic state is denied. This Gordian knot in some countries has been cut by the sword of dictatorship. It can be unraveled under a democratic regime but only at the cost of compromise.

Chapter II

BRINGING DEMOCRACY INTO ADMINISTRATION

"How am I to get in?" asked Alice again, in a louder tone.
"*Are* you to get in at all?" said the Footman. "That's the first question, you know."

HOW to bring officialdom under the control of the people has been a persistent problem. Andrew Jackson was interested not only in rewarding his followers with the spoils of office, but in applying "democratic" principles to office holding. He wished to discourage a permanent civil service because he regarded it as unsuitable to democratic conditions. He stated his theory in his first message to Congress when he said:

There are, perhaps, few men who can for any length of time enjoy office and power without being more or less under the influence of feelings unfavorable to the faithful discharge of their public duties. Their integrity may be proof against improper considerations immediately addressed to themselves, but they are apt to acquire a habit of looking with indifference upon the public interests and of tolerating conduct from which an unpracticed man would revolt.

Old Hickory's fears were well founded, but his way of meeting the problem was merely to expel the appointees of his predecessors for the henchmen of a party machine. Jackson's mistake lay in identifying the public with his own great partisan following and in leaving the selection of public servants to the bargaining of politicians. The result of this effort to democratize bureaucracy was to remove public administration further from the range of those most competent to judge it on its merits. The public service in this country has been merely an adjunct to the more aggressive allegiance to party.

When Jackson nipped in the bud our federal bureaucracy, he sowed the seeds of party organization over the land and fertilized them with the bones of patronage.

[17]

The growth of the electorate necessitated systematic party organization. Popular government could hardly be made effective unless certain individuals were induced by the hope of reward to undertake the taste of arousing the voter. The spoils of office, however, tended to become the sole concern of professional politicans and the party came to be "represented by anyone stamped with the hallmark of its Organization."[1]

We exchanged a weak bureaucracy concerned with the public interest for a strong and often corrupt political hierarchy concerned with its own interest.

The political machine attempted to monopolize control of the governing process in all its phases. Before its untiring onslaught the citizen withdrew. "It does not pay to buck the machine" and "All politics is rotten" became political maxims substantiated by much bitter experience. A German observer viewing our political panorama concluded that our political party bureaucracy removed government from the people in much the same fashion that the governmental officialdom of imperial Germany dominated popular control.[2] Without raising questions as to the significance of patronage in our system or the importance of responsible party government, the simple conclusion can be made here that the citizen is not drawn closer into the administrative process via the political party. Jacksonian democracy at its best was an unsuccessful effort to fuse together ruler and ruled. How can this goal be approached today?

Does democracy under modern conditions mean nothing more than the doubtful duty of choosing at intervals between the ballyhoo of the "Outs" and the balderdash of the "Ins"? The citizen puts little faith in the ballot as a means of influencing the vast operations of government. His observation of the intricacies of nominations, elections, and legislatures discloses still less opportunity for what he has to offer. He does not want "to get mixed up in politics." Partisan battles may at times be interesting spectacles, but they share that element of unreality

[1] M. Ostrogorski, *Democracy and the Organization of Political Parties*, vol. 2, pp. 76–77, Macmillan, 1902.

[2] Charlotte Lütkens, "Über Büreaukratie und Parteimaschine in den Vereinigten Staaten," *Archiv fur Sozialwissenschaft und Socialpolitik* 60 (2), pp. 280–301, 1928.

and very remote attraction associated with murder trials, Hollywood scandals, and Chinese revolutions. How can the man in the street contribute whatever knowledge, experience, or skill he may possess toward meeting the problems of the state? Here is a great storehouse of expert opinion and genuine interest in concrete questions that might be contributed to the general welfare.

If politics is to mean anything to the average man, it must speak in terms that he can understand. He must be able to meet "government" upon his own level and speak to the "governors" in the language of his profession or business. If contact with the governing process is confined to the periodic casting of a ballot, democracy is sterile indeed. Any numskull can put his cross on a slip of paper and drop it in the ballot box. We have need of Aristotle's conception of citizenship wherein direct participation in government was the determining factor.

We have learned the limitations of direct democracy. Our experience with the direct primary, the initiative, the referendum and the recall, and the long ballot have demonstrated that the mass public cannot be treated as though it possessed a unified and responsible will. We have been largely preoccupied with manipulating the elective and legislative aspects of government. The election of representatives and the framing of laws by these spokesmen are but the initial phases in the process of popular control. It is in the execution of the laws that government assumes direct and concrete meaning for the citizen. Popular responsibility must then be broken down to conform with the relevant interest units of the community. The choice lies between this and either control by a political party or bureaucratic isolation.

These latter alternatives are the handmaids of dictatorship. There can be no responsibility of the mass of officials to the mass of the public. The chief executive is perhaps the only figure who can be thought of as holding a general mandate from the people. If the administration of laws is left in the hands of a bureaucracy that is not accountable for its actions, representative institutions become farces. The sporadic and tardy intervention of a legislative body in the affairs of the executive branch is inadequate as a check upon the bureaucracy. This is particularly the case under the presidential system in the United States where the independence of the executive and the remote relations of the Cabinet members to Congress render effective surveillance difficult. Speaking for the situation in Great Britain, Finer states:

. . . we are beginning to see, in fact, that it is difficult for any one but an expert fairly and effectively to criticize an expert; and it is one more sign of the governmental predominance of the Civil Service that in order that the member of Parliament shall be able to criticize effectively, he needs oral or written coaching by an expert from the Civil Service as to what points need criticism.[1]

No writer has presented our problem with greater clarity and authority than Leonard D. White in his monograph prepared for the President's Research Committee on Social Trends. He concludes his searching discussion of recent developments in public administration in the United States by raising this question:

Faced with the steady growth of technological operations in government, to what extent and in what way can citizen participation in administration be preserved? A century ago the distinction between citizen and official was slight, passage from one status to the other was easy. Now inexpert participation in whole blocks of administration has become impossible, the distinction between official and citizen is more definite and permanent, a bureaucracy has emerged out of the conditions of modern government. Democratic institutions presume that the bureaucracy must remain responsive to public opinion, and citizen training by participation in government remains an ideal not yet abandoned. The reconciliation of democratic institutions and a professionalized bureaucracy operating still in the retreating shadow of the spoils system is one of the major perplexities of the future.[2]

The problem is twofold: (1) to keep the bureaucrat responsive and uncorrupted; (2) to join the citizen with the administrative process in order to utilize his particular expertness or to gain the sanction of his consent. Herein lies the meaning of modern democratic government. It is in these terms that public administration must be faced if "popular control" is to have any meaning for this present age. If the democratic process is to continue, it must be guarded, not simply by exhorting the citizen to his duty, but by making guardianship part of the duty of officials. Opinion is

[1] Herman Finer, *Theory and Practice of Modern Government*, pp. 1178, Dial Press, 1932.

[2] L. D. White, *Trends in Public Administration*, McGraw-Hill, 1933, p. 340.

like water. Administrators must dig for it. In only a few instances does it rise spontaneously and even then the source may be tainted. A storm of disapproval may bring a downpour of protest upon officialdom, but flashes of indignation are as transitory as they are sudden. A sustained interest is more desirable.

The main rule, according to Laski, is that "officials should do their work in the atmosphere of a critical and competent public opinion. . . . " This is the only reliable safeguard against the dangers to which bureaucracy is prone. Competent and intelligent administrative services have conscientiously conducted the business of the state in other countries, but, when they have become remote from the opinions and concerns of those they governed, grave abuses have inevitably appeared. Even though the public service is directed by honest men endowed with *esprit de corps*, inflexibility and unimaginative routinism threaten when contacts with the public outside cease to be close and sympathetic.

Interest groups are here of great aid in showing Congressmen administrative needs and in convincing them of the "public" support behind such requests. These special-interest groups are much better acquainted with administrative problems and with the records of officials than are the legislators. Since the heads of administrative departments and bureaus hold no positions of power in the legislature, they must seek support outside. Owing to the lack of an integrating device, such as the ministry, it is difficult to obtain remedial legislation directly or to bring about a change in policy through statutory declaration without political assistance. By working hand in hand with pressure groups, officials immensely strengthen their position before Congress. "These same group forces must be looked upon," one authority states, "as furnishing a political check upon a powerful Executive with discretion to put into effect or to suspend laws in particular cases, to turn the purpose of Congress in directions not contemplated by that body, or to create privileges and rights as well as to take them away."[1]

Inescapably the bureaucrat becomes the target of pressure groups. He is, to be sure, in a more defensible position than the Congressman whose public career may be cut short by the

[1] J. P. Comer, *Legislative Functions of National Administrative Authorities*, p. 199, Columbia University Press, 1927.

powerful enmity of organized interests. Nevertheless, these groups, because of conditions peculiar to our present administrative system, are of great *personal* significance to public officials in this country. The future of many civil servants, particularly the ablest and most enterprising, lies not in the federal service but in the private employ of the groups with which their official duties bring them into contact.

Security of tenure for the administrator has been cited as a needed safeguard against political interference and group pressures. The official must undoubtedly be able to resist intervention when it is aimed at procuring privileged treatment. The bureaucrat, however, does not suffer so much from an inability to execute the law unhampered as from an uncertainty in direction. Where is the official to look for guidance on the broad plain of public interest? He is hemmed in by the immediacy of his own tasks. Within the system of which he is but a subordinate part, his contribution to the total administrative responsibility is left largely to his own judgment.

The wide margin of discretion given civil servants in carrying out the law has aroused criticism of rule by the bureaucracy, especially in Great Britain. Lord Hewart looks with a futile nostalgia to the rule of law as interpreted by the courts.[1] His confidence in the judicial hierarchy and distrust of the bureaucratic, while backed by the traditions of the past, must needs be qualified by the demands of the present. Despite abuses and defects in the administrative system, governance by civil servants under a system of administrative law has definitely won a place. As a means of control in the modern world it has demonstrated its utility and efficiency over the courts and legislative assemblies. The balance of power is shifting to this branch of the government. This means, moreover, that, not only in the execution of the law, but also in the framing of legislation, the bureaucrats are of greater importance. As the Webbs have pointed out, the determination of policy rests not so much with Cabinet and Parliament as with civil servants, balancing and counterbalancing the demands of interest groups and then framing the statutes for Parliament to act upon. In the United States the determination of policy arises from the bargaining between leaders in the administration and the

[1] Lord Hewart, *The New Despotism*, *passim*, Cosmopolitan Book Company, 1929.

representatives of special interests acting either directly or through their respective blocs in Congress. This oversimplifies somewhat a situation that is vastly more confused, but the essential outlines cannot be mistaken.

Government today is largely a matter of expert administration. Increasing authority and discretion are granted the executive branch. The state has undertaken a great number of services left in the past to private enterprise or scarcely attempted at all. These activities have given special interests a stake in the government. The actual point at which their right to pursue freely their own aims comes into conflict with the fulfillment of the broader aims of the community is a matter for judgment as particular cases arise. But the civil servant has no clear standard upon which to act. In a word, our present bureaucracy has accumulated vast authority but it lacks direction and coördination.

The President is nominal head of the "administration," but under present conditions the task of coördination is beyond the capacities of the transient occupants of this position. A system of administrative law might in time indicate the limits of bureaucratic responsibility and develop the conception of public interest. But the official today finds himself largely isolated except for the presence of those interests directly affected by the consequences of his action. These loom largest in the context of his administrative surroundings.

What criteria are to guide him? The *public interest* is the standard that guides the administrator in executing the law. This is the verbal symbol designed to introduce unity, order, and objectivity into administration.

This concept is to the bureaucracy what the "due process" clause is to the judiciary. Its abstract meaning is vague but its application has far-reaching effects. The radio commissioners were to execute the law in the "public interest, convenience or necessity." The trade commissioners are to apply the law when they deem such action "to the interest of the public." Congress has frequently authorized boards and quasi-judicial commissions to determine the public interest.

Although it is clear that the official must balance the interests of the conflicting groups before him, by what standards is he to weigh their demands? To hold out the *public interest* as a criterion is to offer an imponderable. Its value is psychological and does not extend beyond the significance that each responsible civil servant must find in the phrase for himself. Acting in accordance with this subjective conception and bounded by his statutory competence, the bureaucrat selects from the special interests before him a combination to which he gives official sanction. Thus inescapably in practice the concept of public interest is given substance by its identification with the interests of certain groups. The bureaucrat is placed in a situation similar to the plight of Rousseau's citizen. The latter was to vote in accordance with the general will. If he found himself in the minority when the votes were counted, he knew that he had guessed incorrectly as to the *volonté générale*. The official, however, must endeavor to act in the public interest, but without the consolation of testing his judgment in a bureaucratic plebiscite. He must follow his star with but little light on the immediate pitfalls in his path.

The administrator has certain guiding criteria supplied by statutes, but inevitably a margin of discretion remains inherent in the administrative process. He can build up support for his policies and to some extent choose his adversaries. The choice may be of crucial importance. By supporting the groups demanding a strict interpretation of the law, he may bring about an ultimate effect quite different to the outcome resulting from coöperation with those who favor a liberal reading of the statute. He may even reach out for the opinions held by groups less well organized or aggressively directed.

The predicament of the bureaucrat now becomes clear. Special interests cannot be denied a voice in the councils of state since it is their concerns that provide the substance out of which the public welfare is formulated. On the other hand, a well-coördinated and responsible bureaucracy is essential if the purpose of the state is to be attained.[1] The solution of the liberal democratic state must lie in establishing a working relationship between the bureaucrats and special interests—a relationship that will enable the former to

---

[1] As Professor C. J. Friedrich has so cogently stated: "If a popular government is incapable of maintaining a bureaucratic hierarchy, it is bound to give way to a form of government which will accomplish that, whether it be the dictatorship of an individual or of a small group in the name of the nation, the people, or the proletariat." *Responsible Bureaucracy*, p. 28, Harvard University Press, 1932.

carry out the purpose of the state and the latter to realize their own ends.

Such a harmonious relationship is made all the more difficult in the United States by the diversity of conditions over the country and by the variety of activities undertaken by the government. Moreover, federal officials concern themselves with some problems over which they can exercise no coercive authority. The successful administration of many federal services depends upon the coöperation of state and local authorities with the national government. The ties between the community and the federal bureaucracy can best be described and evaluated in terms of the particular situations they are designed to meet. It is difficult to discuss these developments in general terms. Officials working in their own domains have used their ingenuity and found their own solutions.

Public administration in actual practice is a process whereby one individual acting in an official capacity and in accordance with his interpretation of his legal responsibility applies a statute to another individual who is in a legally subordinate position. The public as such is not concerned in this process.

To the officer executing the law, the public is simply an abstraction. Law is applied by one man to another. In the realm of discussion, the public is treated as a reality and words are directed to the populace. But this is a one-sided relationship. Officials receive many responses from individuals but the only reaction they receive from the public is that which they may choose to read into a collection of individual reactions.

Generally these responses may be arranged in more precise categories built around an occupational or economic interest. When this happens, the official finds it possible to negotiate with groups articulate and self-conscious because of a common concern.

Thus law is not administered in a vacuum, but in an environment composed of all those who have an interest in the application or the nonenforcement of the statute. The official is surrounded by a web of interests—and a web often dominated by an unpredictable spider. This ultimate determinator may be the courts, the legislature, an administrative superior, or a powerful economic interest. The administrator is one strand in a complicated mesh of forces, political, social, and economic. The public, viewed in the mass, is of relatively little importance in this context.

[25]

Our problem in this book is to consider the relation between federal administrative agencies and the groups with which they come into contact. As Charles Beard has written: "Whatever is done by way of better organization and fairer practices to improve public administration, its nature and quality are to a large extent determined by the social environment in which it is carried on."[1] Officials cannot escape environmental influences. Administrative functions must be organized to handle effectively the problems that arise from the conflict of economic forces. Officials do not function in bureaucratic glass houses protected from the hot air of politicians or the cool indifference of the public. Some would doubtless be content to live in such hothouses but there are too many self-righteous citizens ready to throw the first stone to make this practicable.

We cannot understand administrative problems unless we understand the conditions under which officials must work. Our administrative services must be properly adjusted to the social and economic structure of the community within which they are expected to operate. It has been said that "the evils of bureaucracy are largely the product of staff isolation and specialization of interest. The workers lose contact with the situations that make their problems, with other offices that are concerned with their own or related problems, and with the other contributors to the solution of their problem, to be found outside the government."[2] Administrative efficiency demands the elimination of all possible friction between the ruler and the ruled. The postulates of representative government dictate mutual understanding between citizen and official in carrying out the law. The democratic state fails of its purpose unless there is an accommodation of governmental institutions to the needs of the community.

Much thought has been expended upon securing well-qualified administrators and upon creating appropriate agencies to serve the public.[3] Personnel recruitment, administrative organization

---

[1] Charles Beard, *The American Leviathan*, p. 327, Macmillan, 1931.

[2] *Federal Relations to Education, Report of the National Advisory Committee on Education*, part I, p. 75.

[3] For a recent general treatise, see J. M. Pfiffner, *Public Administration*, Ronald Press, 1935; on the problem of improving the federal personnel, see L. D. White, *Government Career Service*, University of Chicago Press, 1933. See also Harvey

and integration, and legal competence are considerations of vital importance. These problems relate to the internal phases of public administration. The *external* aspects of the public service, however, are of equal significance. It is from this viewpoint that we approach the subject of public administration.

Walker, "An American Conception of Public Administration," *Public Administration*, January, 1933; L. D. White, "The Future of Public Administration," *Public Management*, January, 1933.

Chapter III

GENERAL CONTACTS OF RULER AND RULED

"If everybody minded their own business," the Duchess said, in a hoarse growl, "the world would go round a deal faster than it does."

"Which would not be an advantage," said Alice, who felt very glad to get an opportunity of showing off a little of her knowledge.

OFFICIALS cannot properly set themselves up as the sole expounders as to just what constitutes the public interest under the law, nor can any group speak with complete finality. Neither side has any exclusive right to interpret the public interest, and both may err in identifying their own aims with those of the public. With a concept so vague and protean as the "general welfare" for a guide, officials may well remain open-minded in their interpretation of the law. In most cases there is no reason why the process under which an administrative ruling is reached should not be entirely open. If the legislator is expected to function in the public forum, the administrator should be held to a similar obligation in the performance of his duties. His actions, being more specialized, are naturally restricted to the narrower "public" that is touched by his authority. This specialization of function tends to bring into clear focus the immediate interests with which individuals are concerned. Thus the administrator finds himself face to face with functional groups. These groups are usually organized into associations and become articulate forces in administration through their duly designated spokesmen. It is not an easy matter to delimit their field from that of public business. Mutually exclusive areas cannot and should not be fixed. What are the relations between these groups and the civil servants?

This question may be answered in part by considering some of the situations that have developed in the federal administration with respect to organized interests. There is discernible a tendency toward the systematizing of these relationships, toward according them legal recognition, and toward utilizing them in the routine of administration.

The confusion in administrative organization has its effect upon those dealing with the government. The illogical arrangement of bureaus and the bewildering array of subdivisions make it difficult for anyone unacquainted with the federal organization to do business easily and effectively with the proper officials. In the very complexity of the bureaucracy the spokesman for the special interest finds his opportunity. "Theoretically it still is true that an ordinary citizen may pack his bag, hop a train for Washington, and transact his own business with the Departments," a Washington correspondent writes. "As a practical matter, however, the foremost businessmen of the country seldom attempt to do so. The best minds have learned from bitter experience that it is much cheaper to retain a contact man in Washington at, say, $10,000 a year, plus office expenses."[1]

The growth of the federal government has been paralleled by the increased representation of organized groups at Washington.[2] National organizations of all kinds find it necessary to maintain a spokesman in the capital. The activities of the government are so varied that the uninitiated need guidance in dealing with the bureaucracy and so important that special interests must be kept informed of the many matters affecting their welfare.

One of the most active contact men in Washington has described his work in the following terms:

The duties of the Washington representative divide naturally into: (1) informational service in response to letters or telegrams; (2) regular or special service bulletins carrying information back to member organizations; (3) contacts with government officials for purpose of securing information; and (4) legislative activities.

The first three are relatively simple but involve a considerable amount of work. For example, the correspondence of a Washington representative is of such a character that almost every letter has to be made the subject of a special investigation before it can be answered. As a rule no two letters cover the same subject. It may require a half dozen telephone calls or a number of personal calls to get information which may be covered in a

[1] Lawrence Sullivan, "The Great American Bureaucracy," *Atlantic Monthly,* February, 1931, p. 142.

[2] This aspect of the subject is treated in the author's volume, *Group Representation before Congress,* Brookings Institution, 1929.

half-page letter. The representative must, of course, be familiar with sources of information. He must know and have a friendly relationship with individuals in the various departments who are authorities on particular subjects, otherwise he may experience much trouble in securing facts or informal interpretations of regulations.

The fourth duty is one popularly known as "lobbying."[1]

As a lobbyist, the contact man is chiefly concerned with Congress. The nature of this work has already been described and discussed by various students.[2] But the increasing importance of the administrative branch of government in the daily life of the individual is emphatically demonstrated by the special ambassadors that are paid to report on the activities of the federal authorities.

A good deal that has been written about the activities of such men is highly colored and exaggerated. The careers of some extraordinary manipulators have been cited as typical of the whole situation. The furor aroused by the investigation of William B. Shearer centered attention upon an adventurer who had been unwisely retained by large shipping interests to aid, supposedly, in the securing of certain merchant-marine legislation and to attend for dubious purposes[3] the Geneva conference on naval reduction. The late Wayne B. Wheeler was the subject of much

[1] From statement by Charles W. Holman, Secretary of National Cooperative Milk Producers' Federation.

[2] See especially E. B. Logan, "Lobbying," *Annals of American Academy*, Philadelphia, July, 1929; Peter Odegard, *Pressure Politics*, Columbia University Press, 1928; Hardwood Childs, *Labor and Capital in National Politics*, Ohio State University Press, 1930; John McConaughy, *Who Rules America?* Longmans, Green, 1934. See the following articles by E. Pendleton Herring, "Why We Need Lobbies," *Outlook*, Nov. 27, 1929; "What Makes a Lobbyist," *Outlook*, Apr. 9, 1930; "Legalized Lobbying," *Current History*, February, 1930; also the author's article on the "Lobby" in the *Encyclopedia of the Social Sciences*. "Lobbying and Lobbyists," Senate Report 43, 71st Congress, First Session, sums up the findings of *Hearings* before a Subcommittee of the Committee on the Judiciary, Senate, 71st Congress, First Session, 1929. The current lobby investigation is turning up much data on the public utilities.

[3] "Alleged Activities at the Geneva Conference," *Hearings* before a Senate Subcommittee of the Committee on Naval Affairs, 71st Congress, First Session, 1930. For the most recent revelations of the arms lobby, see U. S. Senate, *Hearings* before the Special Committee Investigating the Munitions Industry, 74th Congress, First Session, 1935.

publicity which painted him as a person of mysterious influence.[1] The very difficulty of estimating the probable significance of persons of this sort adds to their popular interest.

Senator Norris is responsible for bringing to the attention of Congress the following account of a contact man. An enterprising newspaper man by the name of Logan came to the capital as the Washington correspondent of a Philadelphia paper. His ability as a writer, however, enabled him to contribute to a growing number of publications. He wrote for a Wall Street journal, he contributed to a trade publication for newspapers, and he became one of the editorial writers for an economic magazine with a national circulation. In time he built up a large office force, maintaining two offices and surrounding himself with able assistants. He became active socially, entertained extensively, and enjoyed the friendship of members of the Cabinet, Congressmen, Senators, foreign ambassadors, and other people influential in national affairs. He was on terms of intimacy with the private secretary of the President of the United States and they frequently lunched together at what Norris designates as one of "the most exclusive and expensive hostelries" in Washington. Apparently Logan's new connections made him useful to important business interests for his name was added to the pay roll of several important corporations. Senator Norris states:

It was discovered upon investigation that Mr. Logan was getting $500 a month from the Standard Oil Company of New Jersey, $500 a month from the Standard Oil Company of Indiana, $700 a month from the Atlantic Refining Company, $400 a month from the Freeport Sulphur Company, and $500 a month from the General Electric Company.[2]

Mr. Logan's chief function appeared to be that of an adviser to these interests. He did not attempt to influence legislators directly, though apparently he was on friendly terms with many. He was more concerned with the creation of favorable public sentiment for his clients through arranging publicity. On some

[1] Justin Steuart, *Wayne B. Wheeler, Dry Boss*, Revell, 1928.

[2] *Congressional Record*, 66th Congress, Third Session, Jan. 22, 1921, vol. 60, part 2, pp. 1877–1878. Senator Norris stated that he gathered his information from hearings before senate committees and the Federal Trade Commission, although he fails to specify by direct citation.

occasions he was able to serve his employers through his close knowledge of what was happening in the government. Be this as it may, Senator Norris was not able to report instances where any vital secrets were thus discovered. The information Logan passed along to his employers seemed to be the kind of gossip that might be picked up by any shrewd person who understood the situation he was observing. In fact, the only surprising part about the Senator's recital is his report of the salaries Logan was credited with receiving.

But the Senator had further disclosures to make on this occasion. The Senate Committee on Agriculture, he relates, uncovered the existence of a mysterious being identified by the curious designation of Diamond T. This individual was a creature of the meat packers and in their correspondence he was never referred to by name, but rather by the figure T enclosed in a frame in the form of a diamond. Senator Norris implied from this that Diamond T was a very important person who made use of this cryptogram to hide his high position, and that he was secretly supplying the packers with advance information as to contemplated official action. The evidence produced to substantiate this is highly circumstantial and the instances cited are scarcely of grave import.

The Senator states that spokesmen for the packers on the witness stand denied all knowledge of Diamond T, though upon further questioning on a later occasion a witness attempted to identify this mystery man with Logan. Mr. Norris infers from this that the packers were in this way endeavoring to associate Diamond T with a person already known and thus prevent, if possible, any further investigation. These accounts of Senator Norris are repeated not so much for their own sake, but rather as indications of the attitude that is not infrequently taken toward those who act in the capacity of "contact men."

The story outlined above was placed in the *Congressional Record* nearly fifteen years ago, but similar tales still circulate about the capital. This matter came to the fore again in January, 1934, soon after President Roosevelt's ban on federal job holding by members of the Democratic National Committee. Senator Norris then demonstrated his continuing interest in the subject by suggesting the possibility of legislation compelling all lobbyists appearing before government departments to register and to file for public record copies of contracts with their clients relating to their compensation for services.[1]

The attitudes toward contact men vary all the way from those persons who regard them as a menace to those who look upon their work as entirely trivial. One Washington observer of long experience expresses the latter viewpoint very graphically. He writes:

As an influence upon legislation or administrative procedure they are, considering their number and the amount of money they spend, amazingly ineffective. Rather, they serve the Duluth Chamber of Commerce by picking up a telephone, asking for Branch 731 in the Agricultural Department and pleading: "Say, Phil, my boss out in Duluth's got a big idea. He wants the rainfall statistics in the Duluth industrial area since 1900. Will you have your girl copy 'em off and mail 'em to me tonight? I'll send 'em out by wire first thing in the morning. . . . Yeh, Phil, old man. . . . I'll be seeing you. . . . S' long."[2]

It is difficult to make any valid estimate of a group so varied and inchoate as these special-interest spokesmen. There is plenty of evidence that adventurers have bluffed their way around the federal departments. Some were rascals and others showed more zeal than balance. The newspaper notoriety received by "Big Bass Drum" Shearer in connection with his propaganda activities for a big navy was scarcely commensurate with his effectiveness, but his tribe continues.

Contact men are usually personable individuals with a good knowledge of the problems of the interest they represent and a good capacity for clearly expressing their thoughts. They cultivate a wide acquaintance and make it their business to understand the ramifications of the federal departments. There is nothing occult about their methods and little that is secret about their behavior. If they keep quiet on occasion, it is just as likely to be tact as strategy. Their value to their employer is due not so much to keeping their mouths shut as keeping their eyes open. The many services of the government cannot be utilized unless their existence is known and the proper agency approached. The growth of the

---

[1] Article by Raymond Clapper, *Washington Post*, Jan. 24, 1934, p. 2. See E. P. Herring's testimony on "Registration and Regulation of Lobbyists," *Hearings* before a Subcommittee of the Committee on the Judiciary on S. 2512, April, 1933, pp. 15 *ff.*

[2] Lawrence Sullivan, *op. cit.*, p. 143.

government has made it seem essential to many groups that they have an agent in the capital who knows how to run errands for them.

As men and women today confront the problems of their own occupations, they find that lines of interest extend out into an ever-widening community and reach into the federal administration at various points. That organizations are formed to represent and protect common interests is a natural consequence. Citizens within their own associations meet and consider their own particular problems. They learn to sort out the issues on questions which are near to them and which they can understand. Most so-called public questions are nothing more than the private problems of several groups in conflict. The conflict means that the government must act as arbiter. The substantive nature of the problem is not changed when the dispute itself is placed on the public stage. Considerations of national policy may render the problem more complex, but, if the parties directly concerned are accustomed to meeting their own common problems within their private association, the process of framing a compromise with a legal or official sanction is greatly facilitated.[1]

This mere fact of *organization* is important for several reasons. An active and strong association brings about a harmony of viewpoint among its members. The interest of the group is clarified and developed. Group opinion is made articulate. One Washington representative writes of his association:

Quite to the contrary from intimidating the government, our assistance and cooperation have been sought by the government. Our views and our opinions on this work were solicited and, by contacting with this Association as the national representative of the sand and gravel industry, they evidently feel that they can get a reliable opinion without going through the awkward procedure of consulting every sand and gravel producer in the country. Therefore, our Association maintained by the sand and gravel industry in Washington is an instrument of efficiency for the government.

[1] For a discussion of the relations between private organizations and the British government, see the author's article in the *Virginia Quarterly Review*, July, 1930. See W. A. Robson, *Justice and Administrative Law*, Chap. 4, Macmillan, London, 1928, for discussion of associations as judicial agencies. Lord Eustace Percy in *Democracy on Trial*, John Lane, London, 1931, presents an interesting discussion of the significance of private organizations in government. See also A. D. Lindsay, *The Essentials of Democracy*, pp. 80–81, University of Pennsylvania Press, 1929.

We save them time, expense, and the uncertainty of endeavoring to compromise between the many conflicting opinions which would be offered by the individuals of the industry scattered throughout the United States.[1]

A watch, perhaps on the whole salutary, is kept by private organizations on administrative officers.[2] Such associations are useful for watching the efficiency of a governmental department and for guarding against possible injustices arising in connection with a bureau possessing regulatory authority. For example, two companies engaged in manufacturing chemicals were directed to attach to their product a label containing an ingredient statement. The companies protested the order, pointing out that the product was shipped in bulk and was designed exclusively for purposes other than those enumerated in the statute requiring the content label. Correspondence with the bureau failed to bring results, and institution of legal proceedings was threatened. Not until a personal interview was had with the head of the bureau was the matter amicably settled. It is in the light of such experiences as these that the trade-association representative appears valuable.[3]

Congress, for example, passes the Lime Barrel Act, regulating the kind of container in which lump lime shall be shipped. The National Lime Association is naturally the body most interested in the operation of this law. Their viewpoint must be considered. Their opinion of its efficiency is of great importance. Their concern with its enforcement is genuine. There are innumerable

[1] V. P. Ahern of National Sand and Gravel Association in letter of June 26, 1930.

[2] For further examples, see E. Pendleton Herring, "Administrateurs et administrés aux Etats Unis," *Revue des Sciences Politiques,* July–September, 1933. For a discussion of the Veterans' Administration and the veterans, see the author's article in the *North American Review,* July, 1933. Many data in this chapter are drawn from an extensive correspondence with scores of federal agencies and national associations during the past three years.

[3] The appeal of statements such as the following is understandable: "In the ten years that we have maintained an office in Washington our Association has established valuable contacts with key men in departments and bureaus. Our facilities for transaction of business with the government and for handling problems arising from regulatory laws are exceptional, and members are urged to make use of them." *Annual Report of Executive Committee,* Manufacturing Chemists' Association, 1929, p. 408.

statutes of the same general character as this one dealing with lime barrels. It is to the ultimate interest of the public that lime be properly and safely shipped; but this concern is so distant that for all practical purposes it does not exist except in the rare event that lime barrels are brought to public notice through the occurrence of some grave maladjustment in the rules concerning them —some stubborn disagreement between the enforcers of the law and the "enforcees."

It is this situation that makes the organization of interests into associations significant; it is this that may make their headquarters at the capital of considerable usefulness on occasion. "The Washington Office is your 'service station' to which it is hoped that you will turn in time of need for any information or service connected with the complexities of our laws and regulation," the National Retail Dry Goods Association informs its members.

The Washington Office lays no claim to infallibility nor to the possession of any magic wand, but it will attempt to serve you to the best of the ability of its incumbents, and, by proper contacts and the confidence various officials repose in its representations, will secure for you sympathetic consideration of the problems you may have at present.[1]

These illustrations indicate in some measure the routine work of the associations. Giving expert opinions on technical questions, investigating administrative practices, recommending improvements, negotiating with officials, supplying data to their membership, and watching the execution of statutes too remote or specialized to interest the general public—in such matters the contact man and his Washington staff can perform work useful alike to the government and to his organization.

In much of the routine of administrative procedure cordial relations exist between the rulers and the ruled. Often it is to the direct advantage of the group concerned that the regulation applying to them be consistently applied. Often it is to the advantage of the bureau that those under its control observe and sometimes criticize the methods of administration. Both sides profit on occasion by this mutual surveillance. This close relationship brings about a common understanding that frequently

[1] *Report of Managing Director*, February, 1928, p. 19.

obviates the necessity of resort to the punitive provisions of the law. The government will prosecute readily enough, but many bureaus can often bring about compliance with the law by coöperation rather than by prosecution.

For example, the Bureau of Agricultural Economics, charged with the enforcement of the Standard Container Act, reports that, though the act has been on the statute books many years, they have yet to institute the first prosecution thereunder.[1] Yet the evil of short-measure packages which the act was designed to remedy has largely been eliminated. This has been due to the fact, the bureau reports, that "the package manufacturers have almost without exception coöperated cordially with the Bureau in avoiding violations of this Act." The mere existence of such a law exercises a restraining influence. Unless our governmental services have the support of the general public and the coöperation and counsel of qualified groups of citizens, progress toward an efficient and responsible bureaucracy will be slow indeed. A distrust of bureaucracy induces the very atmosphere that makes officialdom worthy of suspicion. Mutual understanding is essential.

The contacts of officials with citizens may often be perfunctory, but, when occupational, social, and economic interests are canalized through organization into strong pressure groups, the bureaucracy must respond quickly. It does not follow that governmental agencies are thus brought under the influence of the forces they are intended to supervise. As Professor Leonard White has pointed out: "The insistence of powerful social groups upon the practical realization of their legislative program is a constant spur to improved administrative methods."[2]

Civil servants not infrequently utilize outside group support in order to forward administrative projects before the legislature. Likewise, in presenting to the public new administrative policies, a favorable reception is more likely if it appears that the bureau is acting with outside support. Such relations between group spokesmen and civil servants facilitate the execution of the law

[1] *Official Proceedings*, International Apple Shippers' Association, 1927, p. 62.

[2] For a discussion of public administration and private organizations, see L. D. White, *Public Administration*, pp. 45 *ff.*, Macmillan, 1926. For a list, see Louis Brownlow, editor, *Organizations in the Field of Public Administration*, Public Administration Clearing House, Chicago, 1932. Later editions are available.

and innovations can be introduced with less discord. Furthermore, private interests, won over to a governmental policy and convinced of its helpfulness to them, may make this policy their own and through self-regulation may partially relieve the authorities of the burden of regulation.

The advantages of replacing compulsion from without by voluntary responsibility from within are obvious. Flexibility and experimentation in seeking the arrangement best suited to the needs of those concerned are further gains. Many organizations could extend this process: trade associations, chambers of commerce, labor unions, professional associations, and organizations with special purposes such as the American Standards Association, the National Safety Council, the American Arbitration Association, and the Better Business Bureau. Self-regulation by industry, however, has inherent weaknesses that limit its usefulness. Group organization is frequently very loose and often quite unrepresentative. Trade associations, for example, may be dominated by a few large manufacturers or in some cases may be rendered unrepresentative of an industry because several large producers refuse to coöperate with their smaller and more numerous competitors. Associations often pretend to speak for many more members than they actually represent. This is a very common abuse. Private organizations are only partially representative and largely unresponsible. They are bound to fight for their continuance as organizations and they may be controlled by leaders whose main object is to retain their power.

Since the associations themselves are very uneven as to influence and importance, it is difficult to secure a common basis for negotiation between them. How can their relative strength be evaluated? How can conflicting interest groups be persuaded to take a long view of their own ultimate advantage when more immediate ends beckon? How can recalcitrant minorities be controlled once the majority decide upon a line of action? No satisfactory answers have been found to such questions. Self-regulation has proved successful in promoting agreement upon technical matters: framing safety codes, calibrating screw threads, and standardizing manufacturing practices. On such problems businessmen have reached a basis of agreement. Endless friction and waste are thus avoided.

[38]

Through a study of all pertinent data and free interchange of views, a settlement can be reached that is more than a compromise. A *method* that has the sanction of utility is agreed upon. It is not a mere compromise of conflicting claims. This is always a danger where officials not sure of their ground are required by statute to intervene in complicated situations. It is often preferable to leave the formulation of rules to private interests, with officials standing by to keep the participants within the prescribed legal bounds and to impose governmental authority only when necessity demands. Maladjustments among economic groups are too disturbing to the rest of our complex society for such frictions to pass unnoticed. The government today must intervene if private interests fail to settle their quarrels.

Officials of the government go to trade associations, attend their annual conventions, and explain the provisions of the law, presenting the attitudes of their departments. Little room is left for misunderstanding. This personal contact is of great importance. It smooths over countless frictions, and, because it cannot be closely studied, its significance should not on that account be underrated. The stream of visitors consulting with administrators in the government offices and the avalanche of correspondence exchanged between officials and citizens are aspects of administering the nation's business which elude scholarly analysis, but which constitute in large measure the day-to-day process of government.

There is another side to the picture, however. A close and harmonious relationship between the bureaucrat and special interests, although conducive to democratic and efficient administration, carries also certain dangers. Officials in building up "public" support for their agency sometimes create a political machine of their own by identifying powerful vested interests with themselves. The bureau builds a place for itself in the community and makes demands of Congress in the name of the "public welfare." New fields of possible usefulness are outlined. Perspicacious, aggressive, well-meaning, confident, the officials, supported by the public benefiting from their services, bring forward plans for expansion. The more they have to do, the more important they become. Their very usefulness in meeting the ends of specific groups encourages their expansion into other fields and discourages the performance of these tasks by private agencies.

For example, the board of directors of the Hastings Potato Growers' Association of Hastings, Florida, requested the Division of Cooperative Marketing of the Bureau of Agricultural Economics to submit a report as to the fashion in which this association was performing its work. The task was undertaken and performed in an exhaustive manner. Records of the association were carefully examined. About 60 per cent of the active members of the potato growers' society were interviewed to "determine their attitudes toward the association and their opinions regarding its operation and management." A preliminary report was made to the directors; then further analyses of data followed; additional information regarding the marketing of these potatoes was obtained by interviewing representative potato dealers in three important markets. At length the final report was ready and the findings prepared for publication.[1]

This is but one of many similar studies undertaken by this governmental bureau. At the request of the National Pecan Growers' Association, a study was undertaken of the national economic factors that affect the pecan industry; in coöperation with the wholesale grocery associations, a study of the cotton bags and other containers in the trade was made. The North Pacific Nut Growers' Cooperative Association asked for a special report on filberts to be used in planning the marketing of the current crop. The almond and prune growers made their demands. The consuls in Tarragona, Barcelona, Naples, Messina, Palermo, and Constantinople were stirred into action. The agricultural commissioner canvassed the situation and arranged for reports on stocks and prices from Tientsin. A specialist in dried fruits was sent to Europe to make an exhaustive survey of the possibilities for prunes in Europe. His report provided "a valuable picture of the competitive position of the Jugoslav prune industry."

Certain bureaus relieve private associations of irksome tasks and others perform services of direct and tangible value. For years the National Canners' Association compiled statistics on the production of canned corn, peas, and tomatoes. There was no other agency to do it. Several years ago, t e association reports, the Census Bureau took over this work and extended it to cover some additional products. The Census Bureau was asked to

[1] *Report of the Chief of the Bureau of Agricultural Economics*, 1929, pp. 5–19.

undertake this service because of its experience in this field and because of its equipment. The association felt that the Census Bureau, commanding the confidence of the public and of the trade, was in a better position to handle the work. Consequently this association joined with others in requesting the government to make further surveys. Such bureaus, by relieving trade associations of responsibilities, extend their own activities into wider fields. The task is doubtless more efficiently and perhaps more economically performed in this fashion. But should the government thus come to the aid of particular groups? Is it to the public interest? Is this a proper governmental function?

The experience of the last two years has demonstrated the weaknesses of bureaus developed in response to the demands of organized minorities. During 1931, for example, headlines such as the following were frequently found in the *New York Times:* "National Council of Traveling Salesmen Urges That Appropriation for Study of Domestic Trade Conditions by Department of Commerce Be Retained"; "Salesmen's Group Urges Increased Budget for Domestic Commerce Division of Department of Commerce"; "Trade Association Leaders Start Campaign for Increase in Budget for Domestic Commerce Work in Department of Commerce."[1]

A year later a great drive for economy was under way and the press reported the protests of pressure groups against excessive expenditures. The bureaucracy, of course, is the ultimate victim of the fickleness of this support. Investigations must be dropped uncompleted, and experts must be discharged with consequent disruption to the morale and efficiency of the service.

What happens when a bureau becomes dependent upon the support of an interest group? The director of the Office of Education a few years ago described the effect of such help in connection with this bureau. He stated:

The Office has never been provided with an adequate staff, and additions frequently have been made upon demand of organized groups of educators. This system appears to me to have certain disadvantages which ought not to be overlooked. It encourages organized groups to become active in demanding service of the Office and the addition of specialists

[1] *New York Times,* Jan. 23, 1931, p. 35; Jan. 25, 1931, part 2, p. 19; Jan. 23, 1931, p. 43.

to render this service; to look upon these specialists once appointed as the peculiar agents and perhaps even propagandists of the interests of such groups.

It encourages other groups to organize and urge appointment of representatives of their interest to the office staff. It tends to develop a personnel in the Office of Education which reflects current organization in the school world rather than an organization designed to carry out the specific purposes for which the Office of Education exists.[1]

As government undertakes greater responsibilities, it affects more intimately a greater number of interests. Governmental devices must be invented to represent the views of those who are affected by the activities of officials. Democratic government demands that officials act with the consent and coöperation of the governed. Responsible bureaucracy is the only tolerable kind. There must be representation in administrative agencies as well as in legislative assemblies. The very intimacy of government's ties with the community emphasizes the need of official integrity, competence, and impartiality.[2] Yet, where a clear avenue of approach to the government is provided, the dangers of coercion and misrepresentation are much less likely to intrude.

British writers have clearly acknowledged the desirability of utilizing the voluntary association in government. "Wherever a department touches a social interest," Laski writes, "the associations which serve that interest ought to be related to the department for the purpose of consultative coöperation."[3] So forthright a view has not been taken in this country, but nevertheless organized interests are gradually making a place for themselves in the administrative process. Lay coöperation in federal administration is a development of increasing importance in the United States.

If officials are not to become aloof and arbitrary bureaucrats, ways must be devised for keeping them responsive to the groups with which they deal; but if these officials are to be guided by the dictates of the general welfare and not by the pressures of particular interests, coördination of effort within the service and agreement upon national objectives are essential.

[1] *United States Daily,* Oct. 16, 1929.
[2] For a stimulating analysis, see Felix Frankfurter, *The Public and Its Government,* Yale University Press, 1933, especially Chaps. 1 and 4.
[3] *Politics,* p. 115, Lippincott, 1931.

This study is based upon the following hypotheses: that the first duty of a democratic government is the preservation of democracy; that the burdens placed upon the government will continue to increase and that these responsibilities can be met only by a competent administrative service. The problem then is to retain the advantages of democracy without incurring the abuses of bureaucracy. We must find the means of ensuring public administration in the public interest.

These hypotheses we propose to investigate by examining past experience and recent developments in a number of important bureaus and commissions. The validity of these assumptions can be tested by the concrete situations that confront those engaged in the day-to-day task of running the government. The administrative situations selected for analysis fall under these three heads: (1) traditional tasks such as taxation and the conduct of foreign relations; (2) regulatory functions, especially those relating to public utilities, and (3) service activities for labor, business, and agriculture.

If the administrative service is to accord with the needs of a democracy, certain conditions must be met. Officials must make their purposes clear; they must be willing to explain their activities. They cannot be the final judges as to whether the intent of the legislature is being fulfilled. Special groups that are directly involved in the jurisdiction of certain bureaus must be brought into the administrative process. Specialists, whether in the government or not, should be given an opportunity to contribute their expert opinion. Special interests must be consulted. The federal services must be arranged so as to accomplish most effectively the major purpose for which they are intended. Only a limited number of groups can secure a federal department about which to focus their interests. The coördination of other interests can be brought about only through the creation of interdepartmental committees or *ad hoc* agencies. A close contact with the public and with the various groups that have a stake in the administrative process is essential. The bureaucracy must be responsive to groups, but it must also be responsible to those political leaders who are designated to speak for the public. It must seek to act always in the public interest. To explore the implications of these requirements is the purpose of the ensuing chapters.

Chapter IV

INTERNAL REVENUE AND THE TAXPAYER

"She ca'n't do sums a *bit!*" the Queens said together, with great emphasis.

"Can *you* do sums?" Alice said, turning suddenly on the White Queen, for she didn't like being found fault with so much.

The Queen gasped and shut her eyes. "I can do Addition," she said, "if you give me time—but I ca'n't do Substraction under *any* circumstances!"

UPON what standards of public interest can the tax administrator rely for guidance in carrying out his official duties? Congress enacts a statute prescribing a tax of a definite percentage upon a particular thing or a certain transaction. The administrative responsibility is set forth in so many words. What could be simpler? Yet when the official attempts to convert the legal word into lawful practice, difficulties arise on all sides. The public interest becomes much less clear.

Money to meet federal expenses must be collected quickly and efficiently. The taxpayer must be treated with impartiality and his point of view must be considered. Disputed cases must be closed within a reasonable period but all disputants must be heard.

Officials have for their guidance the principles developed in dealing with a multitude of past cases. But new circumstances always appear and often warrant a deviation from strict precedent; yet overriding established principles in order to meet the needs of one case may open up prior decisions for reconsideration. Reopening cases already settled upon an earlier basis is highly disruptive and the uncertainty caused for many may counterbalance the justice sought for one.

Two essentials of successful tax administration are certainty and promptitude. The citizen must feel that it is to his advantage to pay his taxes sooner rather than later. Moreover, if taxes become any less inevitable than death, tax administration will become demoralized. But equally demoralizing to the public is the feeling that officials are anything less than scrupulously honest and just in executing the law. Promptitude and certainty of collection must be accompanied by justice and accuracy in assessment. The officials in the Bureau of Internal Revenue have perhaps the most difficult and, at the same time, the most important administrative task in the entire federal government. The scope of their work is so colossal and its intricacy so minute that they cannot hope to perform their duties more than partially. The number of income-tax returns that can be investigated is limited by the capacity of the officials available for the work.

The effort has been made to select from a task utterly impossible with the force available (if we consider the undertaking as one requiring an examination of the records of each taxpayer) the number of returns that can be safely forwarded to the field offices without endangering the opportunity for orderly management of the job in the particular field division, and at the same time avoid additional record costs incident to mass return movements from the field to Washington and from Washington to the field. It must be appreciated that the Bureau does not claim that it makes all examinations which should be made.

Thus the assistant to the commissioner explains the practical administrative job with which his bureau is confronted.[1]

The Bureau of Internal Revenue has tried to investigate only those returns that seemed likely to produce additional revenue. Common-sense rules are applied. Is a sufficiently large sum involved? Are there patent inaccuracies in the return? Do the field agents know of circumstances that warrant further inquiry? Investigation must justify itself; for every dollar spent in the field in checking up on returns the government has recovered $20 in revenue. The bureau insists that, to the extent the tax dodger benefits, the honest taxpayer suffers. As a practical matter of administration, however, the catching of dodgers must pay ample returns in the revenue recovered.

What are the characteristics of tax administration? The citizen pays; the government collects. The relationship is clear but the complications are many.

The tax collector has before him the words of the statute and behind him a mass of experience and a wide range of general knowledge about taxation. The taxpayer is always in a better

[1] *Hearings* on the Treasury Department Appropriation Bill, 1936, p. 157.

position than the official for knowing the facts in his own case. As one official has stated: "No satisfactory solution of the whole difficulty can be reached until some combination of experience can be made by which each group will get the knowledge which it needs and furnish the knowledge in which it is proficient. It is unfortunate that the law should be so complicated to administer, but it is nevertheless true."[1]

The problem of administration is one of mutual understanding. The busy official, driven by the need of "getting things done," is more concerned with applying the general rule than with noting exceptions. Moreover, if the result means more rather than less revenue, he is content. The taxpayer is inclined to view his own case as exceptional where this may bring about a reduction in the assessment. His task is to prove to the official that the facts in his case warrant special consideration. There is always the danger that the facts selected for presentation to the administrator will disclose only that part of the situation advantageous to the taxpayer. To arrive at an agreement is difficult, even where both parties have an equal opportunity to examine the facts, but in this relationship of assessor and payer an *ex parte* presentation of evidence is inevitable.

A better understanding of just what the official is "up against" in carrying out his administrative duties can be obtained by reviewing the experience of the Bureau of Internal Revenue and by examining particularly the outside influences that have affected its work.

The important history of the bureau is very brief. Although the federal government sought revenue from internal taxation after the War for Independence, the War of 1812, and the Civil War, the internal-revenue service was not established until 1862 and did not become an agency of much significance until the income-tax amendment of 1913 opened up huge sources of taxable wealth. Officials had scarcely grappled with the problems of their new task before the need of money for war purposes added enormously to their burden. Within a period of about five years a large force of experts had to be recruited to a task of vast extent and great

---

[1] Address of Robert N. Miller, "Administration of Federal Income Taxes," before the tax conference at the Annual Convention of the American Mining Congress, Chicago, 1921.

technical complexity. From 1915 to 1920 the office staff in Washington jumped from 500 to 5000 and the field force from 4500 to 10,000. There are now 3500 in the capital and 8500 in the field. In the beginning, a number of very able lawyers, engineers, and accountants joined the staff as a war duty and a few have remained in the government service.

Today the Bureau of Internal Revenue is composed of the following units: the commissioner and miscellaneous unit, the accounts and collection unit, the alcohol-tax unit, the miscellaneous-tax unit, and the income-tax unit. Until 1927 the bureau was responsible for the enforcement of the National Prohibition Act. The task ensnared officials in the midst of warring interests and added greatly to their burdens. Under recent legislation the bureau is tied up with enforcing various tax provisions of the Agricultural Adjustment Act, the Cotton Act, and the Silver Purchase Act, together with other New Deal statutes.

The enormous variety of industries and special economic groups with which the bureau must deal directly is suggested by noting the products upon which the miscellaneous-tax unit levies a tax, namely, lubricating oils, brewer's wort, malt and grape products, matches, gasoline, tires, inner tubes, toilet preparations, articles made of fur, jewelry, automobiles, motorcycles, parts and accessories for automobiles and motorcycles, radio receiving sets, phonograph records, mechanical refrigerators, sporting goods, shells and cartridges, cameras and lenses, chewing gum, electrical energy, telegraph, telephone, radio and cable facilities, checks, drafts, or orders for the payment of money, leases of safe-deposit boxes, transportation of oil by pipe lines, admissions and dues, oleomargarine, adulterated and renovated butter, mixed flour, filled cheese, white phosphorous matches, playing cards, bonds of indebtedness, the issue, sale, and transfer of stock, deeds of conveyance, sales of produce for future delivery, passage tickets, foreign insurance policies, cotton futures, machine guns, mufflers, silencers and short-barreled rifles or shotguns, pistols and revolvers, tobacco, snuff, cigars and cigarettes, cigarette papers and tubes. Taxes are levied also on the purchase and sale of leaf tobacco by dealers, tobacco growers' coöperative associations, farmers, and farmers' agents. There is a tax on the processing of certain vegetable oils and mixtures or combinations thereof, on the production and refining of crude petroleum, and on gasoline produced or recovered from natural gas.

Such a list stresses the important fact that the bureau must not only deal with individual income taxpayers but also with functional groups and economic units. The official must do more than extract taxes from individuals; he must accommodate a number of intricate tax laws to very diverse groups of people and highly technical industries. He must adjust his administrative machinery in such a way as to make the laws work. During the past twenty years our tax officials have had to learn a great deal by hard experience.

The income-tax law was new in 1913 and by 1917 the government had embarked upon a policy of high taxation bringing in revenues of unprecedented magnitude. No one knew just how to proceed. The revenue legislation as finally framed in 1917 was a weak compromise between the House and Senate. Doubt was expressed as to whether the law could be carried into effect in view of the hasty and inconsistent fashion in which it was drawn.

Despite grave apprehension that the law could not be interpreted in a way that would admit of orderly and effective administration, and the expressed view of many citizens that immediate amendments of the law should be sought from Congress before attempting to administer it, the department proceeded with the analysis of the law in the confidence that the congressional intent and purpose could be interpreted and put into effect without further legislative action and without serious detriment to industry and business."[1]

In view of the great effect the law would have upon the economic life of the country, the administrators sought outside assistance in formulating the administrative rules. A committee of prominent business and professional men, designated as "excess-profits tax advisers," pooled their experience in assisting the commissioner. The group included men with experience and knowledge in manufacturing, finance, accountancy, agriculture, political economy, and sociology. With their training they combined an understanding of the administrative responsibility of the bureau as well as some knowledge of the industrial conditions in the sec-

[1] Commissioner of Internal Revenue Roper wrote to the Secretary of the Treasury in 1918. Senate Report 27, part 3, 69th Congress, First Session, p. 18.

tions from which they came. According to the report of the commissioner:

The appointment of the excess-profits tax advisors had the immediate effect of inspiring confidence in the purpose of the department to administer the law with due regard for established business practices and with proper consideration of the effect the large rates of tax would have upon business activities. The tide of general criticism that had arisen against the law was stemmed, and the bureau began to receive innumerable expressions of confidence and offers of coöperation and assistance from accountants, lawyers, bankers, and business men throughout the country."[1]

The commissioners sought advice and suggestions through "all known channels," and, after months of deliberations and extensive hearings, a course of procedure for executing the law was fixed upon and proper regulations were established. According to various officials at the bureau, this practice of consultation has continued down to the present time. Although official advisory committees are not regularly used, those who will be affected by administrative rules are given every opportunity to express their views.[2]

Letters are frequently received suggesting changes in the regulations, in order that the making of returns may be simplified or that existing rules may be clarified. A rule that seems clear to the official who issues it may be subject to several interpretations by those to whom it applies. The bureau sends out to associations the preliminary proofs of its regulations in order to secure criticism and recommendations. Formal hearings are also held, at which an Assistant Secretary of the Treasury and legal advisers of the bureau sit. Interested parties can here present their cases in more formal fashion. There is no statutory provision for such hearings, but the practice has been followed for a long time.

Once the rules have been promulgated, organizations are found useful for acquainting their members with the provisions and for aiding in their interpretation. When new rules are issued, they can be brought to the attention of the proper people through these associations. When the time comes for revising rules, trade associations offer suggestions for clarifying the law. If the language com-

[1] *Ibid.*

[2] For a very interesting account of group opinion in rule making in various departments, see J. P. Comer, *Legislative Functions of National Administrative Authorities*, 1927.

mon within a given industry is used in the regulations concerning the industry, a better understanding of the regulations necessarily follows. Revisions of the rules are made necessary by court decisions reversing the commissioner's rules and by new legislation adding to or subtracting from the bureau's jurisdiction. Economic interests keep administrative regulations under constant scrutiny. In administering the tax laws and drawing up the detailed rules relating to taxation of particular items, officials find it essential to consult those taxed in order to learn enough about the problems of their industries to frame practicable regulations. The bald provisions of the statute are quite meaningless unless they are adjusted to the conditions of the particular industry taxed.

Under the Internal Revenue Act of 1932 the law provides that the allowance for depletion in the case of coal mines shall be 5 per cent, in the case of metal mines 10 per cent, and in the case of sulphur mines 23 per cent of the *gross* income from the property during the taxable year. In the administration of this provision, questions arise as to what shall be the basis for determining gross income of a mining property. The raw material mined is often processed by the same company, and the income appears in terms of the amount received for the finished product. How is the value to be determined for the mineral in its raw state? The problem of making a fair allowance for depletion in relation to the gross income of a given mine presents problems not only of accounting, but of engineering as well. This provision in the act brings before the bureau representatives of the mining, oil, gas, and timber industries.

Regulation 45, relating to the valuation of inventories, brings the National Retail Dry Goods Association before the bureau. The tax on bank checks has occasioned contacts with the American Bankers' Association. In applying the tax on games and parts of games, exception must be made for playing cards and children's games. The question then has arisen as to what constitutes a "child's game." In deciding this subtle point, the Toy Manufacturers' Association was called into consultation. Considerable difficulty was encountered in deciding whether a jigsaw puzzle was a children's game or an adult game. The toy manufacturers supplied numerous samples; hearings and conferences were held in order to classify this product. It was finally decided that a puzzle of fifty pieces or less was a child's game. What is a pool table? The variations run from a toy pool table of very small size to the standard full-size table for adults. At some intermediate point the line had to be drawn in order to fix the tax on games.

In the final analysis such administrative decisions rest upon an arbitrary selection.[1] For example, in the Revenue Act of 1932 a tax of 10 per cent is levied upon all toilet preparations; but in carrying out the law the question arises as to the definition of a "toilet preparation." When does a toilet preparation become a medicine? A 5 per cent reduction is granted by Congress on toilet products having a medicinal use. Where does a product such as Listerine fall? As a mouthwash it is liable to a 5 per cent tax, but as a shaving lotion it is subject to the 10 per cent tax. It is advertised as suitable for both purposes. Which percentage should apply, or should the percentage be split? The interests concerned present their arguments, but the administrators must devise a rule to govern such cases.

The rules and regulations division of the income tax unit makes a practice of consulting the interests affected by its jurisdiction. Such contacts are particularly important where a new tax is concerned. It is only in this way that the law can be successfully applied. On the other hand, the officials in charge of administering the tobacco-stamp tax report that they have very little contact with the tobacco interests. This tax is one of the oldest internal-revenue measures of the government, and the routine is so well established that few administrative difficulties arise in the execution of this law.

The levying of taxes does not have for its only purpose the collection of revenue. Officials in the Bureau of Internal Revenue are charged with regulatory duties also. The tax collector in this role finds that he can wield discretionary power profoundly affecting the welfare of certain industries. Accordingly, pressure is exerted upon the official for rulings that will favor one business against its competitors.

One product that has been subjected to stringent regulation through taxation is oleomargarine. The dairy interests have been

---

[1] These illustrations were obtained through interviews with various officials in the bureau.

active in securing discriminatory legislation against this product. The Commissioner of Internal Revenue is empowered to make all needful regulations for carrying into effect the statutes relating to oleomargarine. A volume of over 100 pages of administrative rules has grown up around the statutes taxing this product.[1] The conflict between the dairy interests and the manufacturers of butter substitutes has continued from the legislative halls into the administrative offices.

An administrative rule may cost those affected thousands of dollars. For example, a provision pertaining to the retailing of oleomargarine fixed the conditions under which this product should be sold. It was provided originally that the retail dealers, in selling oleomargarine from bulk containers and tubs, were required to wrap it and stamp on the wrapper the word "oleomargarine." It was likewise provided that, where the butter substitute was taken in pound packages from the carton wrapper and sold in pound wrappers, these pound wrappers should be stamped. This work complicated the retail sale of the product and made it necessary for the manufacturer to provide stamps and pads. The organized margarine manufacturers succeeded in having this rule altered so that it would no longer be necessary to stamp the product when sold in packages already stamped with the word "oleomargarine." This slight change in an administrative rule resulted in an economy of over $100,000.

Another administrative rule provides that words with a connotation suggesting genuine butter should not be used in labeling oleomargarine. The words "cream," "milk," "butter," "Jersey," "Holstein," "Guernsey," "churn," "creamy," and the like are banned. The oleomargarine people protest that butter and milk are actually used in their product and that the churning process is employed. The administrative authorities are confronted with nice problems in determining where the line shall be drawn between the interests of the dairy people and those of the margarine manufacturers.

It is these details of administration that bring the organized groups before the administrative authorities in an effort to smooth the path of administrative action. Until these manufacturers retained a Washington representative, they worked under a decided disadvantage in their relations with the administrative

[1] See *Regulations No.* 9, 1925 edition, U. S. Bureau of Internal Revenue.

authorities. Through their representative they maintain a close scrutiny of all regulations affecting their product and call to the attention of the government those provisions which they regard as costly or unfair.

It is difficult for an administrator to envisage the effect that a simple rule may have. If such rules are to be practicable and effective, it is necessary to consult those who will be affected by these regulations. The exercise of discretion is of peculiar interest in the Bureau of Internal Revenue because of the immediate and tangible results that follow. In no other bureau is an administrative decision reduced so unmistakably to dollars and cents, and hence in no other bureau is the interest of "the administrated" so keen.

The official in the Bureau of Internal Revenue must reckon with the need of the federal government for revenue and with the desire of the taxpayer to disgorge no more than the law demands. The bureaucrat is playing upon the citizen's sensitive "pocket nerve." There is no lack of interest in the taxing activities of the federal government. The scrutiny is meticulous and out of the intensity of this interest arise administrative problems.

The Bureau of Internal Revenue is not a business designed to transfer funds from the taxpayer to the federal treasury by the simplest and quickest route. The standards determining its administration involve justice as well as speed. Tax liability cannot be determined with objective precision in each case. The great technical difficulties plus the financial interests at stake have placed officials in a difficult position.

In 1924 the administration of the Bureau of Internal Revenue was brought under the fire of the Senate. Senator Couzens introduced Senate Resolution 168 in March, 1924, calling for an investigation on the ground that the bureau was behind in its work, that taxpayers had been oppressed, that taxes rightfully owed had not been collected, and that the bureau was poorly organized and inefficiently managed. A select Senate committee held hearings during the winter of 1924 to 1925 and examined a large number of witnesses, including officials and former employees.

In the report as to its findings the committee divided by three to two along party lines.[1] The Democratic majority criticized the bureau on a number of counts. It held that the Commissioner of Internal Revenue had exceeded his authority in compromising

[1] Senate Report 27, 69th Congress, First Session, 1926.

cases by giving stockholders and creditors precedence over the government; also that too much power was concentrated in division heads and that protests from subordinate employees had been suppressed. The majority report noted a tendency on the part of officials to bargain with taxpayers. It was charged that unduly large deductions had been allowed to mining, oil, and manufacturing companies in estimating depletion and the amortization of war facilities. The methods of procedure, the formulas for computing taxes, and the failure to codify its rules had resulted in a lack of uniformity in the application of the law; secrecy of tax returns had resulted in unfair rulings, the committee held. The minority report on the other hand commended the bureau for the way in which it had met its severe duties.

It is impossible to pass upon the truth of these contradictory reports, and the Senate investigation is useful here chiefly because it provides documentary data as to the relations of tax officials and taxpayers. In what ways have these officials been affected by their "public"?

Commissioner of Internal Revenue Blair explained how his men were attracted away from the government service:

Here is a fellow that comes in and devotes his time to this work. He goes to school at night, and works like a dog and masters this income tax business. He is down at the bureau. The taxpayer comes in and sees him doing the work, and how he handles it, intelligently and quickly, and says: "There's a bright fellow; he will be worth a lot of money in our business." We are paying him $3000, and they will pay him $10,000.[1]

The commissioner described the turnover as "terrific." More than 30 per cent of the auditors and clerks in the income-tax unit left annually, and the turnover for those in more important positions was even higher. The bureau became little better than a training school for bright young men who wished to learn how to manipulate income-tax returns. Exployees resigned not only to capitalize upon their training and experience, but also to trade upon inside information.[2]

[1] *Hearings* before the Select Committee on Investigation of the Bureau of Internal Revenue, Senate, 68th Congress, Second Session, 1924–1925, p. 28.

[2] *Ibid.*, p. 24. The point is well illustrated in this interchange from the Senate testimony:

Senator King: Have you not observed that a large number of your employees have resigned after they had gotten hold of some information and learned, perhaps,

Abundant evidence was brought forward to show that this was a common practice. Officials resigned and came before the bureau a few days later to settle cases in the same units with which they had formerly been connected. Some former employees went into partnership and handled scores of cases.[1] They watched for refunds due to taxpayers and in some instances they undertook to collect such sums on a contingent basis. The Bureau of Internal Revenue cannot review the thousands of closed cases every time the Supreme Court hands down a decision that might possibly mean a tax refund under the changed interpretation of the law. Lawyers are on the alert for such possibilities and, if former employees of the bureau can find cases to reopen quicker than others who are less experienced in these matters, their services are worth using.

However, serious abuses arise where officials conspire with men on the outside.

This has happened [the commissioner said] and will continue to happen as long as you have an organization as big as this, and have men on the inside with small salaries. . . . They do go outside, and they solicit business, but as soon as we catch one of them soliciting business, we disbar him from practice before the Treasury Department. Yesterday a taxpayer came in and said, "I received a letter from a man who recently went out of the bureau." In ten minutes I had the letter in the hands of the Disbarment Committee . . . and told them to say that he was not admitted.[2]

---

that an illegal assessment had been made, which if called to the attention of the board would result in a refund being made; that they have resigned, slipped out and gone to the taxpayer, gotten the case from him, presented it, and were paid for it?

Commissioner Blair: I have no doubt that that has been done.

Senator King: I heard of a case the other day.

Commissioner Blair: We are trying very hard to prevent that.

Senator King: I learned of a case the other day of a man in Texas who was not acquainted with these things, and had been overcharged $200,000; it was apparent on its face and one of your employees immediately resigned and slipped down to Texas, got hold of this man, and received a percentage amounting to $80,000.

Senator Watson: Is there any way to prevent that?

Commissioner Blair: We are trying to prevent it, and we are in a measure preventing it. But I do not think we will ever get to the point where we will entirely prevent it. I think one answer to that is that Barnum was right.

[1] *Ibid.*, pp. 3323, 3329, 3478.
[2] *Ibid.*, p. 16.

In the period July 1, 1925, to June 30, 1931, 131 internal-revenue employees were discharged because of collusion with taxpayers. Sometimes for friendship, usually for money, they conspired with taxpayers to make returns that were not in accordance with the mandates of Congress. They accepted fees, solicited bribes, recommended certain accountants to taxpayers, or divulged confidential information.[1]

At the time of the Senate investigation the Committee on Enrollment and Disbarment was already making some effort to regulate all those who brought cases before the department. Such men were required to register and to state whether they were working on a contingent basis. Their fees were not limited, although if they seemed too high the bureau said as much. In 1924 the Secretary of the Treasury issued a regulation banning any former employee from appearing as attorney for claimants before the department until he had been out of the service for two years.[2] The department issues a list of those who have been disbarred from practice. In order to practice before the bureau, admission to the bar is not necessary and a representative for a taxpayer can qualify as an attorney, accountant, or agent. Some former employees have been able to avoid all these restrictions by advising taxpayers privately, preparing their claims and then filing the papers over the taxpayer's signature. The "expert" thus has no occasion to seek the sanction of the Enrollment and Disbarment Committee.[3]

Fighting graft within the department depends in large measure upon the taxpayer on the outside, but the latter often hesitates to report irregularities for fear of jeopardizing his case. As the solicitor of the bureau explained to the Senate committee:

It is only occasionally that a taxpayer will come in and say, "I think John Smith in the bureau can be reached," or that "he wants to be sweetened up a little." It is only in the most exceptional cases that that occurs, and they do not want their names used; they want to keep out of it.

We often get intimations [Commissioner Blair stated] but they are so indefinite that we can't act on them. But occasionally a taxpayer comes

[1] *Hearings*, Treasury Department Appropriations Bill, 1933, pp. 249–250.

[2] *New York Times*, Feb. 17, 1924, part 2, p. 6, col. 2.

[3] *Hearings* before the Select Committee on Investigation of the Bureau of Internal Revenue, Senate, 68th Congress, Second Session, 1924–1925, *op. cit.*, p. 205.

up and gives us something definite, and we catch the man every time when a taxpayer does that. We have to have help from outside people, and a great many of them do help us in that respect, because the fellow that is doing the grafting does not come to us; he goes to the taxpayer outside. We had a case of a woman who telephoned a taxpayer in New York, saying that there was an over-assessment going out, and saying that for a consideration she would get the returns and close them out. The taxpayer called immediately on the phone. We arranged to have one of our secret service men pose as the taxpayer. She came up, delivered the papers, and of course we got her.[1]

No clear evidence was offered the investigating committee, proving that some taxpayers had secured favored treatment through "political pull." Charges were made and hearsay testimony given, but nothing conclusive resulted. Those who were most eloquent in their accusations were discharged employees who had differed with their administrative superiors. It is impossible to separate the grain of truth from the chaff of disgruntlement. There can be no doubt that pressure is attempted and that favors are sought. The cases of fraud uncovered by the investigation are proof enough of this, but more subtle is the question of political influence.

Is it a common practice for officials or Congressmen to intervene with the Bureau of Internal Revenue on behalf of their friends? The investigation revealed one case where an Assistant Secretary of Commerce addressed a letter to the Commissioner of Internal Revenue stating that a friend of his had a case coming up before the bureau and urging sympathetic treatment. A pencil notation on the same letter indicated that Secretary Denby had telephoned concerning the case. A few months later the case was settled, but in a fashion that the investigating committee found open to criticism.[2] This incident seemed unusual.[3]

The Senators were very much concerned with discovering evidences of fraud and partisan favoritism. They deplored the tend-

[1] *Ibid.*, p. 29.
[2] *Ibid.*, p. 3493.
[3] It is highly probable that the following interchange more clearly reflects the relationship between politicians and internal revenue officials:
Senator Watson: What proportion of your time is taken up by Senators and Representatives coming up there and bringing their constituents to talk over tax

ency of employees to leave the federal service and they searched for instances where large taxpayers had been granted unduly large refunds. The Senate investigators assumed the tone of an inquisition. They subjected officials to rather severe quizzing and called upon them to defend their past decisions. It took some time for the effect of this investigation to wear off. The assistant to the commissioner testified a year later that the investigation had had an unfortunate effect upon departmental morale and that members of the income-tax unit hesitated to decide any doubtful case in favor of the taxpayer. As a result litigation increased.

Following the investigation the Revenue Act of 1928 provided (Section 710) that all refunds and credits in excess of $75,000 be reported to the Joint Committee on Internal Revenue Taxation. Congressional review of administrative action was thus instituted for these more important cases. The responsibility for granting refunds is no greater than the responsibility for collecting taxes, but the suspicious congressional attitude was an expression of our traditional distrust of bureaucracy and of the feeling that big business interests were influencing officials to give them special consideration.

When in 1928 and 1929 the federal government was refunding vast sums in taxes improperly assessed, there was much general

---

cases with you?

Commissioner Blair: Quite a good deal of my time is taken up that way. I have a long list of callers every day.

Senator Couzens: Does the fact that these Senators and Representatives come down there influence you in any way?

Commissioner Blair: No, I do not think any man ever influenced me, consciously, in any tax case.

Senator Couzens: What advantage is there in having a Representative or a Senator come down there with a constituent?

Commissioner Blair: Well, they feel they cannot refuse a constituent. A constituent always feels that they should accompany him.

Senator Couzens: But it does not help him any, as a matter of fact?

Commissioner Blair: No, it does not. As a rule, the Congressmen and Senators never argue a case. They introduce the man and say, "This is one of my constituents." They understand that I understand they are introducing a constituent from home, and they do not expect any favors.

Senator Watson: What he says is for home consumption?

Commissioner Blair: Yes. I always treat it so, at any rate."

Ibid., p. 25.

criticism and suspicion of the Treasury Department. Discussion was particularly aroused when the Commissioner of Internal Revenue decided that the United States Steel Corporation was entitled to a refund of $15,000,000. When it was noted that in the prior twelve years tax refunds had amounted to $975,000,000, many people were inclined to question the wisdom of permitting administrative officials to make decisions that involved turning such huge sums of money back to the pockets of individuals. The problem came down to the question of whether such refunds should be the result of administrative discretion or of a court decision. Should litigation be substituted for administration?

A bill was introduced in Congress during 1929 which would have required the Board of Tax Appeals to review every tax refund in excess of $10,000. The proposal was strongly criticized by the Secretary of the Treasury. "Responsibility must be placed somewhere under our taxation system," he said. "Obviously it should be placed in those high administrative officers whose positions were created for the purpose of the enforcement of the law. Nothing is gained by superimposing a semi-judicial review of such administrative action in all cases."[1]

Officials pointed out that a law that touched so many people, collected so much money, and dealt with such a variety of circumstances could not be executed without later adjustments. Cases were bound to occur where either the government collected too much or the citizen paid too little. "In neither case," Undersecretary of the Treasury Mills explained, "is there any occasion for criticism or for belief on the part of the public that it is confronted with anything abnormal, unexpected or alarming. Quite to the contrary! If you were to examine our revenue laws, you would realize at once the many constantly recurring situations which can be met only by refunds, and the many provisions which can be administered, solely by refunds."[2]

If large firms frequently attracted from the Bureau of Internal Revenue highly skillful tax experts, why was it that mistakes in taxation were made which necessitated huge refunds? It cannot be proved, but it is undoubtedly true that in some instances large

[1] *Bulletin of National Tax Association*, vol. 14, p. 166, March, 1929. An open letter from Mr. Mellon.
[2] *Ibid.*, p. 168.

corporations deliberately overpaid their taxes by very large sums. The government in making refunds paid 6 per cent interest on all taxes that had been illegally levied. This was a very good return on funds for which corporations had no immediate use. They could count on collecting interest for the several years of litigation and administrative review necessary before the case could be closed. While cases of this sort cannot be cited by name, officials state that several large refunds can be explained in no other way.

The problem has been to devise an administrative method for determining tax liability that will give the government its just due and at the same time satisfy the taxpayer. Since the assessment of the tax is left to the individual citizen, each return must be subjected to a close scrutiny. An auditor checks each return and, if he questions its accuracy, he either writes to the taxpayer directly or refers the matter to the field force.

If no agreement is reached by correspondence, the taxpayer may take up his case with a conference unit to which he submits a brief in advance. If no agreement is reached, the tax is fixed by the authority of the commissioner. The taxpayer then is sent a sixty-day letter which allows him this period for registering his case with the Board of Tax Appeals. While his case is pending, the technical staff makes a final effort to settle the dispute. Similarly in the field force the taxpayer's original protest goes to a reviewer. If he fails to reach a settlement, the case may go to one of the representatives of the technical staff in the field. The general counsel also has field officials to forestall the appeal of cases to Washington on purely legal points.

The basic aim of this procedure is to adjust tax disputes without litigation. The process has developed slowly and with administrative officials assuming an increasing responsibility. Although the situation today is far from perfect, it shows improvement. Prior to 1925 the Board of Tax Appeals was a part of the Bureau of Internal Revenue. This board of officials was called upon to review the administrative decisions made by their colleagues. They were expected to act impartially. Counsel for the taxpayers presented one side of the case; for the government's defense the board had only the written record of the case submitted to them by the bureau. They were put in the position of acting not only as judges but as advocates also, if the government's side was to be adequately considered. The arrangement proved unworkable. The Board of Tax Appeals is now an independent tribunal.[1]

In 1927 a Special Advisory Committee was set up to reduce the burden on the Board of Tax Appeals by withdrawing those cases involving some disputed question of fact. (The Technical Branch now carries on this function.) Later the Review Division was created to handle cases involving questions of law. Thus, within the last few years thousands of cases have been disposed of through this process of summary administrative justice, and the Board of Tax Appeals has been relieved of a large proportion of the cases on its docket. Nevertheless, a tremendous number of cases has remained for the board to adjudicate. This accumulation of litigation has placed a heavy burden upon the attorneys in the bureau. Many have had to handle 400 or 500 cases at a time. They could not properly prepare themselves and when they went before the board the government's side was not adequately represented. These attorneys have had to contest their cases often against the very ablest lawyers the taxpayers could find anywhere.

This administrative procedure is of interest because it is the most tangible evidence of the twofold character of tax administration. It stresses the importance (1) of getting the revenue in promptly and (2) of levying taxes fairly. An elaborate procedure is unavoidable if this second purpose is to be achieved. What is "red tape" to some taxpayers results in essential justice to others with disputed tax liabilities. It is the deliberation, the consideration, and the reconsideration with which bureaucracy moves that annoys the businessman who desires quick results. The merchant would lose money if he had to give his customers hearings and rehearings. If they do not like his wares, they are free to go elsewhere. Or the merchant may decide to take a loss in order to retain the good will of the purchaser. But such easy compromises are not possible for the officials in the Bureau of Internal Revenue. Their decisions are reviewable by the courts and their record may at any time be investigated by a congressional committee.

The problem is to build up a staff capable of surmounting these obstacles and winning the confidence of Congress and the public. The most serious difficulty has been in securing adequate com-

[1] G. M. Morris, "Work of the U. S. Board of Tax Appeals," *American Bar Association Journal*, April, 1933.

pensation for the experts and professional men needed to carry on the work of the bureau. In 1925 the assistant to the commissioners told the Senate investigating committee:

> We have never had a very large force of engineers, and it has been very difficult for us to get good engineers at the salaries that the Government will pay. We had a tremendous turnover of men that we did get. Very seldom did an engineer stay with us to exceed one year, especially if he was a good one. We paid those men $3000, $3600 and $4000. It was rarely that we could pay a man $5000, and usually, as soon as he got acquainted with the work and gained some knowledge of taxes, some taxpayer would come along and pay him three or four or five times as much as we could, and he was gone. . . . In the solicitor's office we are confronted with the same proposition. It is almost impossible to get lawyers. Mr. Gregg [the solicitor] is begging for lawyers, good lawyers, to come in and handle our work.[1]

Efforts were made to meet this situation. Under the Revenue Act of 1928 an unsuccessful attempt was made to provide for the appointment of a limited number of experts from outside the civil service. It was hoped that they might thus be paid a higher salary than that set by classified status. Finally the Personnel Classification Board and the bureau reached an agreement whereby a number of special attorneys were brought into the service. In 1930 the bureau requested Congress to provide directly for the employment of twenty-five extra lawyers in order to carry forward the policy of settling disputed cases administratively. There are now about 251 lawyers in the office of the Assistant General Counsel for the Bureau of Internal Revenue. The salary range begins at $2000 a year; nineteen receive $6500 or more, and sixty receive from $5600 to $6700. Most of the higher paid lawyers have been in the bureau for several years.

The change that has occurred lies not so much in the actual number of better paid positions as in the fact that lawyers, accountants, and engineers can now entertain the expectation of going ahead in the federal service and receiving more adequate compensation for their work. The turnover is no longer so high as to demoralize the staff. The government does not attempt to offer the same rewards as private business and it doubtless never will. Nor is it desirable that it should. The man primarily interested in personal gain does not belong in the governmental service. Public

[1] *Hearings, op. cit.*, pp. 3212–3213.

service must to some extent bring its own reward. The interest of the work, the sense of being part of the great machine of government, the security of the position: it is in factors such as these that compensation rests. These conditions of employment must be safeguarded if a strong service is to be built. Honest, able, and conscientious people are needed who are motivated by a sense of public duty rather than aggressive self-seeking. A search for such individuals is not chimerical. There are hundreds of them in the public service today and thousands more who might be recruited.[1]

The personnel of the Bureau of Internal Revenue has responded to good treatment. A spirit different from that disclosed by the Senate investigation ten years ago seems to prevail today. Morale is of tremendous importance in such a bureau. Successful administration depends upon the ready response of the employees when at certain times of the year the pressure of work grows very heavy. Before the closing date for income-tax returns (March 15) overtime is necessary, and the employees "take it very nicely."[2] There can be no doubt that the reallocation of positions and the salary increases of recent years have improved the atmosphere. Inaugurating a forty-four hour week did not result in decreased productivity.

In 1933 the turnover was very small indeed and largely confined to typists and comptometer operators. These clerks returned to their home states when they found their salaries inadequate or they transferred to other bureaus. Clearly the depressed condition of business had a direct effect upon stability of personnel in the federal employ.[3]

The experience of this bureau is encouraging. During the past two decades a large and generally competent corps of officials has been trained to perform a task of enormous complexity.

[1] For a classified list of positions and salaries, see Treasury Department Appropriation Bill, 1933, pp. 260 ff. For a thoughtful analysis of this general problem, see Marshall E. Dimock, "The Potential Incentives of Public Employment," *American Political Science Review*, August, 1933. See also the excellent article on the control of administrative authorities by the same author in the F. J. Goodnow memorial volume, *Essays on the Law and Practice of Governmental Administration*. Johns Hopkins Press, 1935; edited by C. G. Haines and M. E. Dimock.

[2] *Hearings, op. cit.*, 1933, p. 258.

[3] *Hearings*, Treasury Department Appropriation Bill, 1934, p. 176.

There was no chart to guide their course; they had to learn by trial and error. In 1914 the internal revenue taxes brought in $380,000,000. Three years later the figures were more than twice as large, and by 1920 a total of nearly five and one-half billion dollars was poured into the treasury by the bureau. The administrative organization was shifted and changed in an endeavor to discover the most effective arrangement. The bureau today has evolved methods of doing more work with fewer men and with a simpler organization than in the past.

Public interest dictates that such an agency be hedged about with every safeguard. What changes are desirable? The Field Audit Service, with thirty-eight field divisions for the collection of income and estate taxes, works under the direction of the deputy commissioner in charge of the income-tax unit. The Collection Service directed from Washington operates through sixty-four collection districts. There is little point in having the field work done by two separate agencies. It is not only unduly expensive, but it is also a nuisance for the taxpayer to have to deal with two sets of officials. Yet if a change were attempted, the opposition from politicians would be formidable.

District collectors of internal revenue are appointed by the President with the advice and consent of the Senate. These positions, together with the deputy collectorships, are an important feature of federal patronage. The negro politician who asked his Senator to have him appointed minister to Liberia or deputy collector of internal revenue in Ohio has many fellows. Their greed for jobs is undiscriminating and their qualifications for the various positions they covet are bad. The Collection Service remains the weakest spot in the bureau's organization.

The Joint Committee on Internal Revenue Taxation in 1927 recommended the consolidation of collectors' offices with those of the internal-revenue agents. These latter officials are a well-trained corps under civil service. About 80 per cent of those in the collectors' service are outside the merit system. The committee reported that the turnover in the collectors' force had exceeded 50 per cent in three years. Training new men added to the cost of administration, inasmuch as inexperienced employees were relatively useless during their first few months of learning the work. The best that the accounts and collection unit of the bureau can do is to send competent supervisors to inspect the books of the field officers and to make suggestions concerning proper methods of collection. The attempt to have the collectors select their deputies from approved lists of qualified men has met with little success, although such an arrangement has proved its value in the customs service.

The present system is particularly bad since it means that a highly centralized Washington office must deal with subordinate officials who are often local politicians and who are located in their own bailiwicks. With reliable officials in the field, discretion could be left in their hands and the central office thus relieved of unnecessary work. The collectors and their deputies constitute an army of about 4500 officials well entrenched by a time-honored political practice. They cannot be dislodged without a fight.

The office of the Commissioner of Internal Revenue is likewise a political appointment. There is no justification for this. There should be no "politics" in tax assessment and collection, and hence there is no reason for changing this official with every administration. Yet during the past seventy or more years the occupants of this position have served relatively short terms.

The problem of administration of internal revenue is peculiarly dependent upon the quality of the men doing the work. If assessments are arbitrary, the citizen must have final recourse to the courts. But if litigation is frequent the whole administration breaks down. Final decisions for practically all cases should be made in the first instance. This means that the matter is not disposed of in an open court with both sides presenting their cases before an impartial judge, but that the case is judged by a bureaucrat in the privacy of his own office. Such work calls for officials of intelligence and integrity who are able to hold the confidence of the taxpayers. Tax administration in the public interest can be secured in no other way.

Officials in the bureau need more freedom if they are to act in the public interest. The lack of authority to compromise tax cases at the present time means injustice for some businessmen. If a tax is owed and can be collected, the official has no choice but to collect without regard to the consequences to the individual. This policy makes for uniformity, but it is not always in the public interest to make arbitrary collections. There are cases where the lack of discretionary authority to arrange a compromise ruins a businessman, closes his factories, and throws his employees out of work.[1]

The administration of the tax laws in the public interest involves recruiting and training a corps of able and courageous officials. Their morale is of foremost importance. The spirit in which their work is done largely determines its success. Outside attractions have a disrupting influence when working conditions within the federal service discourage able employees. The only way to counteract external influences is to improve the caliber of the officials and this can be done only by increasing salaries and rewarding the able men through promotions. The higher the morale within the service, the greater the impartiality and efficiency of officials. The public interest in tax administration dictates accurate assessment and prompt collection with a minimum of disagreement as to what is due the government; and this goal cannot be reached unless official and taxpayer coöperate.

This "case history" of the Bureau of Internal Revenue serves to emphasize the need for developing a trained and intelligent personnel and for encouraging coöperative public relations, if the law is to be administered in the public interest. There is more to the problem than this, however. The bureau has had to evolve an administrative structure and a distribution of functions among tax officials appropriate to the responsibility of the bureau as set forth by Congress either expressly or implicitly in tax legislation. The establishment of the Board of Tax Appeals is the most arresting example of such a development. In 1924 the Secretary of the Treasury, Mr. Andrew Mellon, conferred with a group of lawyers, tax experts, and officials as to how the bureau could better meet its duties.

The administration of Federal taxes had about broken down. The departmental wheels of determination and enforcement were so clogged with swollen grist that the grind was unendurably slow, and the product unacceptable. About that time the tax game was the wildest and dizziest of the spectacles at the Washington carnival.[2]

The U. S. Board of Tax Appeals provided an independent agency, judicial in procedure and temper, for dealing with tax

[1] *Ibid.*, 1936, p. 172.

[2] Statement of E. J. Goodrich, member of the U. S. Board of Tax Appeals 1931–1935. *New York Times*, Apr. 7, 1935, part 4, p. 10.

disputes. It relieved officials in the Bureau of Internal Revenue of functions that they were not competent to perform simply because they could not occupy a neutral position with regard to tax assessment and collection. The board's success depended on its reputation for impartiality. Its handling of the "Couzens case" demonstrated that the board was not under the influence of the Treasury department.

> That case, the press declared, was a vigorous onslaught in the private vendetta between Mr. Mellon and Senator Couzens, the former using the Treasury as a means to hamstring the latter by whacking him with a tax deficiency of about $9,500,000 on the alleged profit arising from the sale of his Ford Motor stock. The main issue was the determination of value of the stock.
> The board's decision, based strictly on the evidence presented, and without regard to the supposed desires or the previous determinations of the Treasury, solidified its reputation for fearless independence.[1]

The suit for additional tax payment was decided in favor of Senator Couzens.

Congress in 1926 extended the board's jurisdiction and enlarged its membership. The Board of Tax Appeals marked a significant advance toward tax administration in the public interest. It eased the strain on the bureau officials where their burden was heaviest. It brought about a proper distribution of administrative functions. The impartiality and competence of officials acting in an administrative capacity can be increased through improving personnel conditions and through allotting to suitable agencies duties that are not compatible with the essential functions of the bureau.

In a larger sense, however, officials must always act within a context that is determined by prevailing political conditions. The presence of Andrew Mellon as Secretary of the Treasury, for example, created a different political climate in the Bureau of Internal Revenue from that existing at the present time. This was most strikingly illustrated in the spring of 1935 when Mellon himself was accused by tax officials of defrauding the government of several millions in back taxes. The chief counsel for the government in the Mellon tax case charged that technical

[1] *Ibid.*

constructions which "defied common sense" had twisted the law so as to reduce the taxes due on great corporate holdings.[1] The differences in interpretation of the same law were enough to bring a former Secretary of the Treasury before the very tribunal he had been instrumental in creating.

The meaning of the public interest at any given time is colored by the political leaders holding the key administrative posts. This point will be developed more fully in subsequent chapters. It is a fundamental conditioning factor in any consideration of administration, but it does not rule out the need for improving conditions within the limits thus set. The official cannot escape the political climate of his bureau but he can learn to weather the storm of politics and to cultivate his garden when under the sunny rays of public approbation.

[1] See press reports of hearings during March, April, and May, 1935.

Chapter V

THE STATE DEPARTMENT AND THE PUBLIC

"What do you know about this business?" the King said to Alice.
"Nothing," said Alice.
"Nothing *whatever?*" persisted the King.
"Nothing whatever," said Alice.
"That's very important," the King said, turning to the jury.

THE average voter knows little of foreign affairs yet the State Department must reckon with the domestic impact of diplomatic negotiations. The administration of foreign affairs, in so far as the permanent officials are concerned, becomes a pragmatic matter of finding the ways for achieving the ends set by the administration in power.[1] Interpretations of the national interest have varied greatly and have at times contained contradictory elements. The governmental machinery provided by the Constitution does not render the conduct of foreign relations an easy task. As Quincy Wright has stated: "Two things seem to be needed in an institution designed to conduct foreign relations with success—concentration, or the ability to act rapidly and finally in an emergency, and popular control giving assurance that permanent obligations will accord with the interests of the nation."[2]

[1] Our concern is not with the substantive merits of any foreign policy nor with our relations toward other nations. The attempt here is to treat the State Department simply as another administrative agency and to note some of the difficulties that confront its officials and that arise from the peculiar nature of their responsibilities. Able scholars have investigated the control of our foreign relations and the interpretation of national interest by the federal government. See, for example, studies such as: Charles Beard, *The Idea of National Interest*, Macmillan, 1934; B. H. Williams, *Economic Foreign Policy of the United States*, McGraw-Hill, 1929; J. M. Mathews, *The Conduct of American Foreign Relations*, Appleton-Century, 1922; E. S. Corwin, *The President's Control of Foreign Relations*, Princeton University Press, 1917; C. De Witt Poole, *The Conduct of Foreign Relations under Modern Democratic Conditions*, Yale University Press, 1924.

[2] *The Control of American Foreign Relations*, p. 362, Macmillan, 1922.

The Senate's right to pass upon treaties, the interest of the Committee on Foreign Affairs in international questions generally, and the congressional control of appropriations all contribute toward a lack of unity in the control of external relations. "Popular control" in practice often means narrow partisanship. Moreover, the President as well as various Cabinet officers may at times have something to say about matters coming before the State Department. The Secretary of State has to reckon with the politicians on the one hand and with his permanent departmental officers on the other. Private citizens acting directly or working through their political representatives may attempt to secure the support of the government for their ventures abroad.

The State Department is supposed to conduct the external affairs of the government in such a way as to safeguard or advance the national interest before foreign countries. It must negotiate with theoretically sovereign states in an actual world of economically interdependent states. It must talk in terms of the equal rights of states with nations that are anything but equal. The formula of "no entangling alliances" must be alternated with the shibboleth of "international coöperation." The amount of protection granted to our citizens abroad must be shaded to accord with the political complexion of the majority party in office. The conduct of foreign relations not only involves negotiation with other nations; it also means the conduct of domestic relations with the public, with groups of citizens specially interested in some particular question, and with other agencies of the government whose work involves foreign relations. In all these contacts the officials of the State Department try to maintain an impartial position. Their administrative responsibility is simply the execution of national policy, whatever it may be. They constitute the vehicle for the enunciation of our public interest before the world. Through the State Department must pass all official acts involving our relations with other nations.

The nature of this responsibility brings to the fore three factors of importance in this study. The first is the significance of securing a general public understanding of the department's policies. The second is the need for a coöperative and consultative contact with those private interests involved in foreign negotiations because of the possible political repercussions of such negotiations.

The third is the importance of coördinating through the State Department the activities of other agencies of the government that touch upon foreign affairs. These three aspects emphasize the fact that the State Department is, from the administrative viewpoint, a clearinghouse for all official contacts between this country and abroad. This may appear as too obvious to warrant elaboration. As a matter of fact, it has been the disregard of this fact that has led to difficulties in administration and to unjustified criticism of the department.

The officials of the State Department, in acting as the official contact agents of this government with other nations, are essentially concerned in a task of synthesis and coördination. Foreign policy comes from sources that are very diverse and basically hard to reconcile. The department is the instrument for applying these policies and also for elaborating and at times even initiating policy. Officials in the State Department and in the foreign service are "career" men. They have an *esprit de corps* and a unity of outlook that constitute a bureaucratic interest capable of offering resistance to the infringement of precedents or changes of policy.

On the part of Senators and political leaders in general there is an interest in foreign affairs that is predicated on the local popularity of certain issues rather than upon their international effects. The provincialism of such viewpoints is distasteful to officials alert to foreign reactions. Moreover, those in political control, whether in the legislative or administrative branch, are inclined to give less heed to departmental precedents than are the permanent officials. A new administration often profits politically by dramatically repudiating the policies of its predecessors. This often has a disturbing effect upon the officials who must carry on a continuing relationship with foreign governments and who therefore dislike violent changes in policy. Nevertheless, the domestic side of the administration of foreign affairs is exceedingly important. Painstaking negotiations may be swept into the discard if popular suspicion, rallied behind a slogan, condemns some contemplated action. The recent fate of the World Court shows the power of unreasoning adherence to the stereotype of "no entangling alliances." The administration of foreign policy sometimes touches very clearly the interests of particular classes. Racial, religious, and ethical considerations arouse politically significant groups to protest the action of the State Department. An arms embargo, a boycott, a ban on shipping or on a foreign loan must be considered, not only in terms of the relations between nations, but likewise with reference to its effect upon private interests and the party in power. Political leaders must constantly defend their policies, and administrators must explain their actions. The internal reaction to foreign negotiations cannot be disregarded.

Elements of national prestige become involved over which popular passion might be fanned into protest. It is necessary to win the consent of the public to the commitments made by the State Department. The officials, both political and permanent, are speaking in the name of this country. They cannot afford to be contradicted in too loud a voice. General acceptance or acquiescence is essential. The avowed attitude of the department that "public opinion is one of the most potent factors in the carrying out of a successful foreign policy in a democracy" is more than an abstract sentiment. Provisions are carefully made for keeping the public informed as to what takes place in the administration of international problems in order that a general understanding may be brought to the support of governmental policies. This is the more important when it is recalled that the Secretary of State cannot avail himself of the parliamentary interpellations or of addresses before Congress in order to elucidate his views. The policy of the administration may be set forth in messages of the President or volunteered by sympathetic congressional spokesmen in speeches before the House or Senate. On occasion the secretary or his assistants may testify before congressional committees or send written communications, but the great channel of communication to the ear of the public remains the press.

This important contact comes under the special province of the Division of Current Information, established for the sole purpose of keeping the public informed of what goes on within the State Department. This service is highly systematized and is especially equipped to supply the press, other governmental agencies, and the public generally with information regarded as important. Two officials devoting all their time to the work superintend this publicity service. One man is constantly on duty and may be called by correspondents seeking information at any hour of the day or night. These two men try to keep informed concerning all departmental activities in order either to answer queries directly or to place the questioner in communication with the appropriate official. All telegrams, all dispatches, and all instructions sent to representatives abroad and all communications coming into the State Department pass over the desks of these officials. They act as spokesmen for administrative policies and State Department activities and they are responsible for superintending all publicity that goes out from the department.

Six days a week the correspondents have press conferences with the Secretary of State or one of the assistant secretaries. At these conferences properly accredited representatives of the foreign press are also admitted. Everything that occurs at these meetings is reported verbatim and the statements thus recorded are typed and may be consulted later by the correspondents should they wish to refresh their memories as to what took place. A report of these conferences is prepared by the Division on Current Information and is sent to officials of the State Department and to representatives of this government abroad. It is intended thereby to keep all members acquainted with departmental news.

The information given out at these press conferences takes several forms. In the first place there is the material intended for direct quotation. This is written up in the form of press releases and subsequently published or mimeographed for distribution as government documents. Then there is data which may not be quoted as coming directly from the lips of the Secretary of State but which may be attributed to him. Using such introductory phrases as "It was learned in administrative circles today" or "It was learned from reliable sources that," the correspondents may proceed to give in their own words the information received from the secretary or other high officials. Of a similar character is the so-called "background material," which the secretary gives correspondents, not for direct quotation, but rather for their own use in understanding and properly interpreting current developments. When it is deemed advisable, the secretary may go further and relate highly confidential events to the newspapermen. This data they cannot in any way make public. Such revelations simply serve to prepare the way for situations that may arise in the future and that will require an intelligent understanding. The department will not give information where it might mean breaking a confidential relation with another government, endangering pending negotiations, stirring up national animosities, or going counter to some broad general policy of the department.

It is the view of the department that news is not made available to defend any particular stand or argue any specific case. Its policy is based upon the assumption that uncolored news can be presented to the press and that the public can thus in turn be intelligently and impartially informed. The result hoped for is the support of public opinion.

Assistant-secretary Castle has expressed the government viewpoint in this fashion:

There is no denying the fact that the attitude of the modern press is enormously important to the Government in all international relations. It gives us an index of public opinion; we must appreciate and understand public opinion and to a certain extent be guided by it. The press, furthermore, has a great influence in moulding public opinion, and we in the Government must, therefore, try to see that it leads in the right direction. This eliminates the statements which have from time to time been made by public men that no attempt is made by the Department of State to guide the press through coöperating with it. Of course, we try to guide the press aright because the press in its turn influences public thinking. Unless the public can be given facts and background to think about, unless thought can be guided into sane channels, the results may well be muddy, if not dangerous to international peace. This does not mean that we try to use the press as propaganda for the administration, for an individual, or for any specific theory. To do so would defeat the end we have in view because it would arouse immediate antagonism. We are not dictating as to the manner of thinking but rather giving substance for sound thinking.[1]

This attitude is in sharp contrast with the use made of the press by foreign governments.[2] The views of the French foreign office are found directly echoed in the news columns as well as in the editorial pages of certain French journals. It is a well-known fact, for example, that the Comité des Forges controls certain newspapers of Paris and that reports as to disarmament developments

[1] Press release 174, Jan. 28, 1933, p. 55.
[2] O. W. Riegel, *Mobilizing for Chaos, passim*, Yale University Press, 1934.

are not reported in an unbiased fashion by papers owned by great steel and iron interests. But while conscious propagandizing may not be so direct in this country, it is difficult to see how the expression of a definite news bias can ever be eliminated. Inescapably the State Department has its own viewpoint and unavoidably its releases tend to justify the actions of the department before the public. To this extent it is a propaganda agency of the government. Implicit in Mr. Castle's remarks are assumptions as to certain values. How else could words such as "sound," "proper," and "sane" be used?

The safeguards against a distortion of government news rest in alertness on the part of both newspapermen and leaders of the opposition party. The State Department is in a somewhat different position from that of other departments. Its officials may justify a refusal to give information on grounds of "state policy." As Secretary Castle has stated:

> We must, of course, be the judge of what is "secret"; and I can only repeat that we do nothing secret in the old diplomatic sense, but that we must consider as temporarily secret matters which might lead to misunderstandings both here and abroad, especially in these days when anything published in Washington may be published simultaneously in London and Berlin and Rome and Paris and Tokyo.[1]

This in the final analysis means that an extraordinary amount of trust must be reposed in the State Department. The integrity of our officials becomes the chief protection against public deception.

In view of the discretion that must be left to officials with regard to informing the general public of State Department activities, the private organizations concerned with international relations are particularly important. They bridge the gap between the ill-informed public with no immediate stake in foreign affairs and the selfishly interested groups working for some special ends.

Organizations such as the World Peace Foundation, the Foreign Policy Association, and The Carnegie Endowment for International Peace are too well known to warrant detailed description here. By stimulating an interest in foreign affairs and informing influential groups of citizens on current issues they develop a public better able to understand the problems confronting the State Department.

[1] *Ibid.*, p. 56.

In addition to the organizations primarily concerned with informing their members and the general public on international affairs, various peace societies and patriotic organizations occasionally send petitions to the State Department. Some of these organizations brew tempests in their teapots and draw up resolutions over their teacups. For example, a clash between the teacups and the wine cups occurred when the W.C.T.U. of Omaha, Nebraska, demanded that the State Department recall the consul at Bologne when he welcomed Gertrude Ederle with champagne after her channel swim.[1] One is inclined to criticize the consul for not selecting a good brandy instead! A constant bombardment of such trivialities greets State Department officials. More recently one group of indignant club women demanded that Einstein be barred, while others wanted the consul-general at Berlin removed for his treatment of the scientist.[2]

When Mr. Kellogg was concerned with the Geneva protocol, designed to outlaw the use of gas as a weapon of warfare, he was opposed by the organized chemical industry which feared government regulation.[3] According to the chemists gas was a much more humane instrument of warfare than quick-killing shells and bullets!

Organized groups communicate by letter or sometimes send delegations to the State Department. Newspaper correspondents are notified when a delegation is to appear before the Secretary of State and efforts are made to secure as much publicity as possible. After the interview news releases are presented to the correspondents present, as the chief purpose is to secure publicity for the cause of the organization.

Communications received from organized interests are given consideration by the officials and sometimes are the source of information or practical suggestions. It is impossible to make any estimate as to the effectiveness of the work of these groups, although at times their proposals may win acceptance. Their specific suggestions are soon lost in the grist of data used by the department in making reports and carrying forward policies. Communications from special-interest organizations are referred to

[1] *New York Times*, Sept. 4, 1926, p. 15.

[2] *Ibid.*, Dec. 7, 1932, p. 4.

[3] *Congressional Record*, Senate, Dec. 13, 1926, pp. 363–367.

the officials concerned with the problem presented or interested in the information supplied. The position of the State Department renders it immune to the influence of such pressure groups, and its contacts with these associations are of little significance in the administration of the department's work.

Since the depression pacifist groups have been less active, doubtless due to lack of funds. There have been occasions when these organizations have become a nuisance. Some of them show a lack of understanding of foreign affairs. Their protests are formally acknowledged by officials, but the department never enters into a dispute with them over any matter of policy. It is recognized that they often try to obtain publicity for their cause by seeking out public officials. The department tries to preserve a thoroughly neutral attitude.[1] One often senses an undercurrent of personal impatience among officials toward such organizations.

A typical example of the way a pressure group attempts to secure favorable action from the administrative authorities is furnished by the American Civil Liberties Union in the case of Count Karolyi.

The count was admitted to the United States in January, 1925, in order to visit his sick wife under the proviso that he would refrain from discussing Hungarian politics publicly while in this country. He was maliciously assailed by his unfriendly countrymen and the American Civil Liberties Union requested that the State Department allow Karolyi to answer the accusations of his enemies. A representative of the organization called upon Secretary of State Hughes and conferrred with other officials but no change was made in the departmental rulings. The union got Senator Hiram Johnson to bring the matter before the Senate Foreign Relations Committee, and Chairman Borah was persuaded to write to the department requesting an explanation. The newspapers carried the story in full. Upon the secretary's refusal to change his order, the union organized a protest luncheon meeting at a big New York hotel. Six hundred persons attended, speeches were made by prominent men, and resolutions were adopted condemning the department's "gag rule." A special committee of professional liberals took these resolutions to Washington. Mean-

[1] Interview with Mr. Walter A. Foote, Division of Current Information, State Department, June 8, 1933.

while the "Friends of the Magyar Republic" appealed to the President and editorial comment was widely evoked. People all over the country were aroused and much sympathy for the count was expressed. He finally withdrew to Canada and there gave vent to his bottled-up indignation. He stated: "I cannot understand why Washington should have treated me as it did, merely because Gladys Vanderbilt married Count Szechenyi!" (the Hungarian ambassador).[1]

The Secretary of State had acted under authority of a statute of Mar. 2, 1921, which retained certain of the wartime provisions relative to the admission of aliens. In defending his "gag rule" to the Senate committee, the secretary stated "that the information in the possession of the Department of State, which it would not be compatible with the public interest to make public, makes it advisable that this precaution should be taken."

This element of official secrecy, which is inherent by tradition, if not by necessity, in the administration of foreign affairs, befogs the public relations of these officials.

Officials are naturally annoyed by the efforts of propagandists to influence their actions. Very recently Secretary of State Cordell Hull rebuked high-tariff lobbyists for their campaign against the reciprocal-trade program. He reprimanded the lobbyists protesting the 50 per cent reduction on the manganese tariff in the Brazilian treaty and a few weeks later he was provoked into criticizing the Maine potato growers for their attack on the treaty agreement with Canada. Letters patterned after four or five set forms poured into the department.[2]

Where is the official to discover the national interest among the many special interests urging their views before the department? The public furnishes no guide; it rather adds to the department's burdens in that its general support and understanding must be sought. The duty of administering foreign affairs under a democracy entails the task of informing a mass of citizens who profess little interest in the problems explained. But the government must justify its actions. Under recent Republican administrations the State Department has tended to ally the national interest

---

[1] For the details of this incident, see "Foreign Dictators of American Rights," American Civil Liberties Union pamphlet, June, 1925.

[2] *Washington Post*, Apr. 17, 1935.

very closely with that of business. "When Mr. Hughes was Secretary of State he made the remark that one of the chief duties of the Department was to keep the highways of commerce open and in good repair," Assistant Secretary of State Castle told a trade convention in 1928. "A very large part of the work of the Department consists in making it possible and keeping it possible for you to carry on your foreign business. Mr. Hoover is your advance agent, Mr. Kellogg is your attorney, who enables you to take advantage of the opportunities that open before you."[1]

Professor Charles Beard in his two recent books has analyzed national interest in terms of the economic interests underlying our foreign policy. We are concerned with such questions in so far as the clash of these interests impinges upon the administrative process. The official finds that it is practically impossible for him to fulfill his duties without taking into account such "environmental" forces.

The policy of the State Department toward the flotation of foreign loans in this country admirably illustrates the dilemma of the administrator when dealing with economic forces.[2] Here we see the difficulties in the path of the administrator who must deal with men competing for economic advantage.

The rise of the United States as a creditor nation necessitated a policy on the part of the State Department to meet this development. For participation on the part of the government in the regulation of foreign loans, one must turn to China. At the request of the State Department in 1909 an American group composed of J. P. Morgan and Company, Kuhn, Loeb and Company, the First National Bank, and the National City Bank participated in the Hukiang Railway Loan agreement then being negotiated.[3]

[1] *Printers' Ink*, May 3, 1928, p. 88.

[2] The foreign-loan policy of the State Department has been the subject of many able articles, and the writer is not here attempting to add factual data to these careful studies. See, for example, John Foster Dulles, "Our Foreign Loan Policy," *Foreign Affairs*, October, 1926; Williams, *op. cit.*, part 1, "The Diplomacy of Investment"; *Survey of American Foreign Relations*, ed. Charles P. Howland, Chap. 3, Yale University Press, 1928; *Cumulative Digest of International Law and Relations*, Nov. 1, 1932, vol. 2, bulletins 32 and 33; D. Y. Thomas, "Foreign Investments and the State Department's Attitude," *Southwestern Political and Social Science Quarterly*, September and December, 1926; M. L. Ernst, "Controlling Foreign Loans," *Nation*, Feb. 10, 1932, pp. 168–169.

[3] *American Journal of International Law*, vol. 7, p. 340.

Under the Wilson administration the State Department took an unfavorable attitude toward this Chinese loan and the American banking group withdrew from the negotiations. The loan to Honduras in 1911 can be cited as another precedent of such negotiations made under the sanction of the State Department. Secretary Knox defended such a policy. Nevertheless, prior to 1914, American loans abroad were not sufficient to constitute a problem and the government seldom exercised any influence as to what loans should be made. It was not until the outbreak of the World War that the matter came up again. Secretary of State Bryan held that "in the judgment of this government loans by American bankers to any European nation which is at war are inconsistent with the true spirit of neutrality."[1]

Significant developments began in 1922. The Secretary of the Treasury reported later:

Early in the administration of President Harding it became apparent that one of the first problems to be dealt with was that of protecting the billions of dollars in loans made by the United States to foreign governments during the war. The cash advanced and credits granted represented money borrowed by the United States from its citizens. These sums must be repaid them, with interest. It was accordingly incumbent upon the government fully to inform itself regarding the finances of its foreign debtors and particularly to be advised regarding their further borrowings from the people of the United States.[2]

The inference seems clear from this statement that the government felt a definite responsibility concerning the financial dealings of its citizens with foreign nations.

Early in his administration President Harding called an informal conference at the White House between several members of the Cabinet and a group of investment bankers. At this meeting these bankers agreed to give the State Department an opportunity to interpose an objection before any foreign bond issue was offered to the American public. By Mar. 3, 1922, the Secretary of the Treasury could report:

It is now customary for American bankers intending to float foreign issues or to grant credits to foreign governments to consult the State

[1] A. D. Noyes, *The War Period of American Finance*, p. 111, Putnam, 1926.
[2] Extract from the *Report of the Secretary of the Treasury*, 1925, p. 53.

Department before final action is taken by them. Upon receipt of advice from the bankers the State Department confers with the Commerce and Treasury Departments and then notifies the bankers of the attitude of the Government, whether or not objection to the financing is interposed.

The State Department was careful to point out that these loans were not passed upon as business propositions and that the bankers were not to advertise their bonds as approved by the government.[1]

State Department officials did not wish to give the impression that they were sponsoring a particular loan when they told the bankers that this government had "no objection" to its flotation. They tried to act as impartial guardians of the "public interest," removed from any direct concern with the buyer or seller. In the case of some loans where the risk seemed especially great, the department admonished the seller to warn the buyer of the uncertainty of his investment. In these communications the State Department clearly stressed economic factors that might touch the validity of the loan. For example, in commenting upon the risks of the city of Frankfort loan, the department concluded thus:

These risks which obviously concern the investing public, should in the opinion of the Department be cleared up by you before any action is taken. If they can not be definitely eliminated, the Department believes that you should consider whether you do not owe a duty to your prospective clients fully to advise them of the situation.

While the foregoing consideration involves questions of business risk, and while the Department does not in any case pass upon the merits of foreign loans as business propositions, it is unwilling, in view of the uncertainties of the situation, to allow the matter to pass without calling the foregoing considerations to your attention. In reply to your inquiry, however, I beg to state that there appears to be no questions of Government policy involved which would justify the Department in offering objection to the loan in question.[2]

By admonitions of this sort officials tried to warn the investor without affronting the banker and without assuming any responsi-

[1] George W. Edwards, "Government Control of Foreign Investments," *American Economic Review*, December, 1928.
[2] Press release on German loans, Jan. 7, 1932.

bility for the transaction in which he was engaged. Elaborate pains were taken to devise a formula that indicated the attitude of the State Department without committing it to approving the loan. The usual form for acknowledging the advance notice of contemplated loans was as follows:

"In the light of the information before it, the Department of State offers no objection to the flotation of this issue in the American market."

For the unfavorable response in those infrequent cases where it was thought that public policy dictated rejection, the department, after reciting its reasons, used this triumph of negation for a time:

"You will therefore appreciate that this Department is not in a position to indicate that it perceives no objection to the financing to which you refer."

In 1929 the formula was simplified and the State Department signified that a proposed bond flotation was unobjectionable by stating that "the Department is not interested in the proposed financing." Noncommittal phrases were not enough to absolve officials of responsibility. Their contribution (like Alice's testimony before the King) although entirely negative was none the less significant.

Senator Glass called the administrative cautiousness of the department a "wretched subterfuge." "The State Department," he stated, "is morally responsible for every dollar that is lost by Americans in foreign bond issues and every indebtedness that will not be paid. It has no legal right to express its opinion regarding them, and when it does so it takes upon itself a moral responsibility for the issue."[1]

That this relationship between private bankers and the State Department resulted in frequent misunderstanding on the part of the investing public there can be little doubt. Even though the government abstained from passing directly upon the business merits of proposed loans, bond salesmen were not averse to suggesting that their wares had passed the scrutiny of the department. "There is little doubt that considerable amounts of otherwise unsaleable Latin American bonds have found a market in this country because of the rather innocuous visa to the effect that the

[1] *United States Daily*, Jan. 8, 1932.

'Department of State perceives no objection' to the proposed issue."[1]

The administration, as a result of its policy, found itself caught between two fires. On the one hand, it was sharply criticized for usurping too much power in passing upon these loans, while, on the other, the scrutiny was held to be inadequate for purposes of protecting the public. Senator Johnson, one of the most outspoken critics of the policy, summed up the situation thus:

> The attitude of the department, as I understand it, has been that it has nothing whatever to do with loans abroad, even to governments, unless political reasons intervene. Of course, to investors, the statement, accurate in letter, that the particular investment has been submitted to the State Department, and our Government had "no objection," was quite persuasive, and the ordinary American, laboring still under the delusion that he participated by virtue of his citizenship in the Republic, and that his Government would protect his interests as well as those of international bankers, fondly believed that if the State Department had no objection to his purchase of foreign securities his right had been safeguarded. How his credulity was imposed upon, and how illusory was his belief concerning the protecting arm of his Government, his present plight demonstrates.[2]

Was the policy of the State Department a realistic approval to its administrative responsibility? It refused to introduce the interest of the investor into its conception of administrative responsibility. Hence the purchaser of foreign bonds was left to look out for himself. It is only fair to note that the investor rushed in to buy bonds that the wiser bankers were willing to sell but not to hold as long-term investments. Whether it was the duty of the department in charge of foreign affairs to pass upon the worth of loans that private citizens were to buy was a question of policy that was highly debatable. It involved a matter that Congress had not legislated upon at the time. The problem was touched upon by President Roosevelt in one of his campaign speeches when he promised "that it will no longer be possible for international bankers or others to sell to the investing public of America foreign securities on the implied understanding that these securities have

[1] W. W. Cumberland, "Investment and National Policy in Latin America," *American Economic Review*, Supplement, vol. 32, no. 1, March, 1932.

[2] *Congressional Record*, Senate, Mar. 15, 1932, p. 6620.

been passed on or approved by the State Department or any other agency of the Federal Government."

The department characterized this as "an insinuation that the Department has thus assisted the bankers in the past." There is no doubt that the foreign-loan policy of the federal government, as it worked out in practice, aided the bankers and ignored the investors. Critics of the department differed with officials in their interpretation of the public interest. Was the protection of the investor the concern of officials primarily responsible for the conduct of foreign relations? How many interests were they to embrace in their view of the "public interest"? It would be mere rationalization to draw any distinct line between public versus private interests. The conduct of foreign relations involves the protection of citizens and their property abroad as well as bargaining for national advantages for the country generally.

In the case of these foreign loans, State Department officials decided that their responsibility did not extend to protecting the investors at home. They did not envisage these individuals as falling within their administrative purview. Their decision was consistent with the general policy of the administration. The party in office was guided by a concept of public interest that undertook to aid the businessman at home and abroad, but admitted no specific responsibility for protecting the purchaser of bonds. The State Department lacked the facilities and the resources for investigating the soundness of all foreign securities and for informing the public of its findings. But how was it decided that some loans were unobjectionable and that others could not be approved?

In the case of the Bolivian loans, for example, the procedure was very informal indeed. The chief of the finance and investment division of the Bureau of Foreign and Domestic Commerce stated:

The matter of these loans was frequently the subject of conversation between the economic adviser of the State Department, who handled them in the first instance for the State Department, and with persons in the Department of Commerce and in the Treasury Department, who were deputed to pass on them in the first instance for those departments. . . . As each loan came up—well, in many cases, I won't say in every case, but in many cases—the merits of the loan would be the subject of more or less discussion between the economic adviser and myself; not that it made a great deal of difference, except along the particular points that have been enunciated as a part of our foreign loan policy, but, sort of *entre nous*, speaking as man to man, we would exchange views as to whether we thought a certain government was overborrowing, or whether these loans looked good to us. I suppose we were amateur international bankers.[1]

In fact, State Department officials apparently thought in banking terms. They considered the probable effects of loans upon commodity prices, upon the indebtedness already incurred by nations, and upon the control of raw materials. When Brazil tried to borrow money abroad in order to buy up coffee in the world markets and thereby boost the price of coffee, this government disapproved of the flotation of Brazilian loans in this country as contrary to the public interest. Placing an embargo upon American capital, the State Department created an effective instrument of national policy highly useful in foreign negotiations. The State Department vetoed loans to governments in order to force a funding of their national debts to us. Loans were disapproved that were intended to support monopolies of raw materials. Embargoes were instituted against loans to Germany on the ground that further credit would interfere with reparation payments.

Thus the process of administering foreign relations necessitated an interference in banking operations. Bankers and diplomats by the very nature of their respective functions found themselves with problems of mutual concern. New York bankers were accused of exerting pressure on officials to hasten reparation agreements in order that issues of foreign bonds from the debtor countries might be put on sale. The State Department in its turn deflected bankers from floating lucrative loans by voicing disapproval. American investors thereupon purchased their bonds from foreign bankers. Official capital embargoes could not stem the flow of money abroad or check the speculator.

When in 1931 a rumor went the rounds that our international bankers were agitating for a cancellation of the war debts in order to protect the private bond issues they had floated, a senatorial investigation of our loan policy was brought about. It was shown in the course of the hearings that the State Department had not hesitated to sacrifice the money of American investors in

[1] Quoted from Senate hearings by Charles Beard, *op. cit.*, p. 509.

order to smooth our relations with Latin America. This inquiry resulted in an airing of the whole question.[1]

When the Roosevelt administration came into office, the case of the foreign bondholders was considered along with the general legislation relating to securities and stock exchanges. Title II of the Securities Bill authorized the creation of a Corporation of Foreign Security Holders.[2] This body was to protect the rights of foreign-bond holders and to negotiate for the resumption of interest payments by the defaulting foreign governments. This corporation would have made the welfare of the investors in foreign bonds a clear responsibility of the federal government. One authority states:

Had the Administration chosen to create the corporation in question, the effect would inevitably have been to associate the government closely with the collection of foreign bonds in default. While the act specifically denies the right of the proposed Corporation to represent the government of the United States, debtors as well as creditors very probably would have been led to believe that a real connection existed between the State Department and the Corporation. The Securities Act therefore embodied the same inconsistencies in policy that have heretofore prevailed. This fact was apparently recognized at the White House, for despite considerable pressure from various sources, the President did not issue the order putting this part of the act into operation.[3]

The Roosevelt administration was not willing to identify the interests of these investors with the public interest, but neither was it ready to repudiate all responsibility. The record of the past provided no consistent guiding precedents as to the proper governmental attitude toward the United States creditors of foreign governments. Officials in the State Department could hardly be expected to advise investors. President Roosevelt was opposed to armed intervention for the purpose of collecting bad debts and retrieving unwise investments. Could the government discover an appropriate administrative device for assisting the bond-

---

[1] For an interesting summary of this investigation, see M. R. Werner, *Privileged Characters*, pp. 453 *ff.*, McBride, 1935. For the testimony, see *Hearings* before Committee on Finance, U. S. Senate, 72d Congress, First Session, Senate Resolution 19, 1931, Government Printing Office, 1932.

[2] *Congressional Record*, May 8, 1933, p. 3045.

[3] Walter H. C. Laves, "Toward a Consistent Foreign Loan Policy," *The American Political Science Review*, December, 1934, pp. 1049–1050.

holder without involving the State Department? Previous experience had indicated that formulas were futile.

For some time State Department officials had been considering the possibilities of a privately organized council of foreign-bond holders.[1] President Roosevelt took up this scheme and in October, 1933, invited a group of persons to the White House in order to discuss the project. These persons were urged to undertake the "patriotic duty" of organizing an independent and disinterested Foreign Bondholders Protective Council. Officials assured the group of their interest and offered their "friendly aid" but declined to assume any responsibility. Upon this basis the council was organized and is now functioning.

The final solution has not been reached, but from the administrative viewpoint one thing is clear, namely, that a department concerned primarily in handling foreign affairs cannot be isolated from the effects of its policy upon internal interests.[2] In the administration of foreign affairs important domestic interests cannot be ignored. Organizations of foreign-bond holders sent their representatives to the State Department, but officials did not place much confidence in these spokesmen. A failure to give adequate attention to the investors' interests resulted in a political protest that aroused the department to the need of devising some means whereby this viewpoint might be introduced into the administrative process. A change in administration brought a new attitude of governmental responsibility toward the American foreign-bond holders and the unofficial bondholders' council relieved officials from the duty of directly protecting these investors. Thus officials charged with representing the public interest in foreign affairs were saved the embarrassment of negotiating with defaulting nations on behalf of a special group. It still remains to be seen whether the efforts of the Roosevelt administration to help the holder of defaulted foreign bonds will amount to anything. In its desertion of laissez faire the administration has hesitated to take the holders of foreign bonds under its official protection, but it has provided this special-interest group with a channel through which to approach foreign governments directly.

[1] See *Commercial and Financial Chronicle*, Apr. 16, 1932, p. 2825.

[2] For another view of this general problem, see Harold H. Sprout, "Pressure Groups and Foreign Policies," *Annals of the American Academy of Political and Social Science*, May, 1935, p. 114.

As we noted in the beginning of this chapter, the State Department is the administrative device for canalizing our relations with foreign nations and for conducting our external affairs so as to promote the national interest. Accordingly, it is very important that this department be able to coördinate all activities of the federal administration as they relate to foreign affairs. This chapter has illustrated the struggle of various interests to win recognition from the State Department. The State Department is not easily shaken. It is a career service. Its officers have a strong sense of tradition. Theirs is the federal department that has made the most systematic advance toward the goal of developing a trained corps of officials devoting their life's work to the government service. The first loyalty of such a corps is to the administration in power. The Secretary of State, as the President's minister of foreign affairs, is their responsible superior. As Professor White has pointed out:

The true function of a career group, so far as policy is concerned, is to aid the chief executive to prepare his legislative recommendations and to draft for his consideration the executive orders which may be necessary to put into effect the mandate of Congress. In so far as administrative policy is concerned, the proper duty of the career men is to study and to recommend.[1]

State Department officials have not been affected by the importunities of pressure groups nor have they quailed before the verbal thrusts of censorious Senators. Their task is to defend and clarify the policy of their department.

In the case of the foreign-loan policy they found themselves unable to achieve such clarity in the eyes of investors or of Congressmen. Their inventiveness was strained to the limit in seeking formulas with which to cloak the administration's policy. They found that it was virtually impossible to avoid at least the appearance of an entanglement with the investment bankers. Administration of foreign affairs in the public interest necessitates the development of contacts at home that will result in a general public understanding and support of departmental policy. It also demands that officials weigh in the scale of declared foreign policy the various domestic group interests that are affected by our international relations.

[1] Leonard D. White, *Government Career Service*, p. 23, University of Chicago Press, 1935.

Chapter VI

POLITICAL STORMS AND THE TARIFF COMMISSION

"Do you think it's going to rain?"

Tweedledum spread a large umbrella over himself and his brother, and looked up into it. "No, I don't think it is," he said: "at least—not under *here*. Nohow."

"But it may rain *outside?*"

"It may—if it chooses," said Tweedledee: "we've no objection. Contrariwise."

THE tariff has always been a political storm center. No issue in this country has been the occasion of more intense partisan conflict or has involved more strife among competing economic forces. It has sometimes brought about severe local disturbances and its rumblings over the nation have often drowned out the discussion of other important problems. Yet the tariff, the cause of so much turmoil among politicians and businessmen, has now for nearly two decades been the *raison d'être* of an independent administrative agency. The Tariff Commission has had a continuous existence since 1916, when it was set up hopefully as a device for protecting tariff fixing from partisan interference. Needless to say, the tariff remains a political issue. But what has been the fate of the commission?

What is the experience of an administrative agency when it addresses itself to a question touching powerful and persistent business interests and involving the convictions of political leaders? In the preceding chapter we discussed the difficulty of insulating an agency devoted to the conduct of foreign affairs from the domestic repercussions of its activities. Yet an essential of administration is a defined field of jurisdiction within which officials execute the law in accordance with their views of the public interest. How shall the limits of their responsibility be determined? What elements shall be included in their views of the public interest? The sphere of the State Department is distinguished by the nature of its major function—the conduct of foreign

[89]

affairs. The protection of the domestic investor, while admittedly of importance, is still not the direct concern of the diplomat. The Tariff Commission presents a different jurisdictional situation. It has been given a problem to consider rather than a clear function to perform. The purpose of this chapter is to depict the Tariff Commission in its political context and to show how its activities have been affected by the social forces and economic interests touching the commissioners. The tariff is a problem extending beyond the confines of any administrative commission. The commissioners have found that there are other voices more powerful than theirs in defining the public interest with regard to tariff questions.

The task of the Tariff Commission is peculiarly difficult because of the very nature of the tariff as a political issue. Granting that a tariff policy could be agreed upon by experts and brought to general public acceptance upon the basis of its intrinsically sound merits from a purely economic viewpoint, its political implications would give rise to acute difficulties. Even a tariff for revenue only would involve technical problems of rate fixing and classification of commodities, which would in turn incite importers and manufacturers to struggle for advantage within this relatively restricted field.

Although lip service has at times been popularly given to tariff slogans, no definite, clear, or generally satisfactory economic criterion for fixing schedules has been established in practice. The weighing of political-economic considerations, such as the encouragement of infant industries, protection against dumping, equalizing the cost of production, or evaluation upon a basis of domestic prices, has enormously broadened the possible basis for fixing a policy. Vague interpretations of the public welfare have served further to befog the issue by introducing such contradictory concepts as national self-sufficiency and the stimulation of foreign trade through tariff bargaining. One can trace a tendency toward greater or less protection through the manipulation of schedules, but it would be difficult to discover a consistent tariff policy as formulated and executed by Congress.

That our tariffs are not written by Congress, but rather by the industries concerned, serves to explain the legislative confusion, but scarcely exonerates the politicians unless the impossibility of following a declared tariff principle is admitted. However, even where Congress has been influenced by an enunciated policy in tariff revision, the actual fixing of rates has necessarily taken place not only at a level of technical *expertise* beyond the competence of most Congressmen, but also under conditions requiring an immediacy and intimacy of negotiation impossible for a legislative assembly.[1]

It was these technical difficulties in the framing of tariff legislation that were in large measure responsible for the creation of the Tariff Commission.

As far back as 1866 the need for expert advice was recognized when the office of Commissioner of Revenue was created. In 1882 a temporary commission was established to prepare for the general tariff revision then in prospect, and in 1888 indirect efforts were made by undertaking cost-of-production studies in the Department of Labor. Under the Tariff Act of 1909 President Taft was authorized to "employ such persons as may be required" to assist in administering the maximum and minimum provisions of the Tariff Act.

Organized agitation to create a Tariff Commission started in 1907 and 1908 through the adoption of resolutions by the Merchants' Association of New York and by the National Association of Manufacturers, urging that Congress institute a permanent nonpartisan agency to collect and report upon facts pertinent to the tariff question. The year following a convention was held in Indianapolis and was attended by representatives from various parts of the country and by spokesmen from 200 national and commercial organizations. A consensus of opinion was obtained from the discussions held at this convention and a committee was charged with the task of carrying forward the purposes of the convention as expressed in the resolutions. This committee set about effecting a permanent organization. The National Tariff Commission Association was the result. The president selected was a man reputed to have done "effective work in Washington in securing in the Payne-Aldrich Bill the provision for the Tariff Board." The other officers were men informed in tariff matters and enthusiasts for the cause. Systematic efforts were made to affiliate chambers of

[1] For a masterly analysis of the actual process of framing tariff legislation, see E. E. Schattschneider, *Politics. Pressures and the Tariff*, Prentice-Hall, 1935.

commerce and national commercial organizations with the association. Meetings were held, speeches made, resolutions passed, and publicity provoked.

A committee composed of six representatives of national associations of manufacturers and businessmen working through the National Tariff Commission Association asked President Taft for permission to examine the work of the Tariff Board. After examining this body, they reported very favorably, lauding the work accomplished and expressing the belief that there remained "no single doubt as to the expediency of maintaining it as a permanent function of the Government for the benefit of all the people." The report of this committee was used in the effort to establish a permanent Tariff Commission.[1]

President Taft's message to Congress in 1910 aided the cause:

> The request of the President for an appropriation for the continuance of the work of the Tariff Board and the public interest aroused by the efforts of the National Tariff Commission Association to impress upon Congress the necessity of continuing on a business basis to secure correct information to assist Congress in the preparation of any Tariff Bills, led to a general discussion of the pros and cons of the measure which was more than frequently permeated with heated arguments. It was at this time and during the months of April and May that it began to be apparent to the members of Congress of both parties that the business men of the country were earnestly endeavoring to obtain legislation, not only covering the appropriation asked for, but for the definite creation of a Tariff Commission as a government function.[2]

In June, 1910, the association brought to the capital hundreds of businessmen, manufacturers, and representatives of trade associations to urge upon Congress the passage of some satisfactory form of tariff-commission legislation. The political parties at length gave recognition to the movement. The Progressive Party in 1912[3] advocated the establishment of a nonpartisan scientific tariff commission with "plenary power to elicit information." The Republicans[4] condemned the Democratic party "for its failure

---

[1] *Congressional Record*, June 6, 1912, p. 7754.

[2] *Scientific Tariff Making*, a history of the movement to create a tariff commission, by Henry Tarleton Wills, secretary of the National Tariff Association, 1913.

[3] Kirk Porter, *National Party Platforms*, p. 346, Macmillan, 1924.

[4] Platform 1912, *ibid.*, p. 355.

either to provide funds for the continuance of the tariff board or to make some other provision for securing the information requisite for intelligent tariff legislation."

The findings of the tariff board established by the Republicans were disregarded by the Democratically controlled sixty-third Congress (1913–1915). But the varied and far-reaching economic changes brought about by the war convinced the Democrats by 1916[1] of the need for a nonpartisan tariff commission "to make impartial and thorough study of every economic fact that may throw light either upon our past or upon our future fiscal policy with regard to the imposition of taxes on imports or with regard to the changed and changing conditions under which our trade is carried on." Under the urging of President Wilson, Congress finally passed the act of Sept. 8, 1916, creating the present Tariff Commission.

This body from its inception has been an anomaly. Politically its creation was a concession to the clamor of business interests desirous of militating "sharp dealing" in tariff matters, but actually Congress had no intention of surrendering its powers over rate making. The purpose of this agency was simply that of collecting information so that Congress could frame schedules upon a factual basis, "rather than in accordance with the demands of selfish interests or upon information provided largely, if not exclusively, by them."[2] The commission was given wide powers for investigation but no authority for changing schedules. Nevertheless, great precautions were taken to insulate it from political influences. Although its duties might have been performed by one of several existing agencies, it was felt that the difficulties attendant upon considering tariff matters warranted special safeguards. Accordingly, a bipartisan board of six commissioners was created with their term of office fixed at twelve years.

During the early years of the commission no political difficulties obtruded. Professor Frank W. Taussig, an economist of established reputation, was made chairman, and much of the time during his incumbency was given to the problem of personnel. By 1919 a competent staff of experts had been developed. The exigencies of the war period limited the work of the commission somewhat, but

[1] Democratic Party platform, *ibid.*, p. 375.
[2] *Ibid.*

improvements relating to technical affairs of administration were suggested and a mass of trustworthy information on tariff problems was made available. The work of the commission in this limited field was found of genuine value.[1]

When in 1921 Congress again tackled tariff revision, chaotic postwar conditions made the problem of rate adjustment peculiarly complex, and House and Senate toiled and tugged for some twenty months in framing a bill. Schedules were greatly boosted while a critical press barked its protest. Congress, moreover, did not make full use of the commission's data and the old abuses in tariff making persisted. The feeling grew that there was a greater need of expert opinion.

Those distrustful of Congress and disgusted with the spectacle of logrolling loudly advocated a "scientific" method of tariff making. The blatantly protectionist complexion of the Tariff Act of 1922 caused some forebodings even among the Republican leaders and President Harding himself was desirous of having something moderate and conciliatory to which he might point in the new law. Granting authority to the Tariff Commission for the "adjustment" of schedules answered this purpose.

This new task was based upon a theory that tariff schedules could be determined by a formula and designated automatically by an impartial board of experts. The idea was supported actively by the Chamber of Commerce of the United States of America and was strongly urged by sympathetic Congressmen.

Political expediency combined with the demands of business interests to saddle upon the commission its novel responsibilities. The statute authorized that a thorough investigation be made of the cost of production of articles competing with American manufactures. The President, acting upon the recommendation of the commission, was to adjust the duty in order to equalize production costs for the benefit of the American producer. Determining costs, however, means selecting evidence, and hence value judgments must be made.[2] The exercise of discrimination is an unavoidable

[1] T. W. Page, *Making the Tariff in the United States*, p. 37, Brookings Institution, 1924; F. W. Taussig, *Tariff History of the United States*, pp. 481 ff., Putnam, 1931.

[2] Economists have so clearly demonstrated the limitations of the cost-of-production formula that it need not be discussed here. See especially F. W. Taussig, *Free Trade, the Tariff and Reciprocity*, Chap. 7, Macmillan, 1920, and T. W. Page, *op.*

part of the process. How determine cost? No figure automatically emerges.

As a result of the so-called "flexible provision" of the 1922 statute, the commission was placed in an entirely new situation. To the extent that it dared to exercise its powers, it would become liable to attacks from the same quarters that influenced congressional tariff making. Since the commissioners were called upon to use their own discretion, their private prejudices and their known views on tariff policy became of political importance. Tariff policy could not be determined by Congress while the actual rates were fixed by an independent agency. As Commissioner Page has stated: "The only means by which Congress can enforce the interpretation which it wishes to apply is by naming the duties through which its policy will be put into effect."[1]

The adjustments the commission recommended to the President were not to change the duty set by Congress beyond 50 per cent up or down and not to change the free list at all. By this device Congress avoided an unconstitutional delegation of powers, but it did not clarify the scope of the commission's actual power. The immediate impact of special interests was deflected from the legislators, but the pressures of economic and political forces were no less severe in other quarters.

President Harding soon intervened by urging the commission to investigate the tariff on sugar. This action encouraged other special interests to beg the President for an alteration of their schedules. The tariff was in the very thick of politics and dissension rent the commission. The President lent his support to the protectionist faction, but the discord continued into the next administration. President Coolidge felt that the Tariff Commission failed in its duty because of its inability to reach an agreement as to schedules. He was angered by the long complicated reports supporting majority and minority opinions that he was expected to plow through. He could not read such a mass of material. He

---

cit., Chap. 4. For a defense, see William S. Culbertson, "The Making of Tariffs," *Yale Review*, January, 1923. See text of authorized statement by Commissioner Brossard in *United States Daily*, Mar. 28, 1930, before the Inquirendo Club, Washington. Experience with flexible provisions of adjusting tariff law has "proved practicability of adjusting tariff rates by administrative action," index, p. 282.

[1] T. W. Page, *Making the Tariff in the United States*, p. 47.

felt that if the commission could not agree upon its findings it should be reconstituted. He resented this direct shifting of responsibility to the President. The commission was disrupted by deep personal animosities. The writer has it upon the authority of the President's secretary, who was directly in touch with the situation at the time, that a desire to restore harmony in the commission was the leading consideration in the President's mind.

Whatever the President's motivation may have been, his efforts were directed toward "restoring harmony" by removing those members who insisted upon the judicial character of the commission. He tried to break up the Lewis-Culbertson-Costigan trio, which was trying to lower tariffs and which objected to Presidential interference. These men were Wilson appointees. Coolidge offered Culbertson a place on the Federal Trade Commission (which was refused), and finally sent him off as minister to Rumania. Lewis, when the time drew near for his reappointment, was requested by Coolidge to leave an undated letter of resignation at the White House. When he refused, he forfeited the renewal of his appointment. Costigan continued his battle a few years longer, but finally resigned in 1928.

To charge an administrative agency with discretionary duties in interpreting so controversial a subject as the tariff was to invite trouble. By 1926 a senatorial investigation into the administration of the flexible provisions was under way.[1] The testimony before the investigating committee brought out the fact that interested groups tried to exert pressure, not only through the President, but also directly upon the commissioners. Commissioner Culbertson told the committee of having been invited to Senator Smoot's office; from there he was taken across the hall by the Senator and confronted with a room full of lobbyists, Congressmen, and politicians. The assemblage proceeded to urge as forcibly as possible that their interests be given favorable consideration. Mr. Culbertson stated:

I was conscious of the fact that this conference was indicative of a drive by the sugar interests to prevent, if possible, a report by the Tariff Com-

---

[1] This investigation is a storehouse of information on the administrative difficulties of the tariff commission. It has been indexed. See *Hearings* before the Select Committee on Investigation of the Tariff Commission, Senate, 69th Congress, First Session, 1926, index, part 11, 1928.

mission on sugar, and in my remarks, all of which I have not made note of here, I endeavored to give the sugar interests an assurance of fair treatment at the hands of the Tariff Commission, and at the same time to give them to understand that the Tariff Commission is a quasi-judicial body functioning under a principle laid down by Congress, and that the decision which we reach will be made fearlessly and in accordance with the facts warranted by the record regardless of any outside influence which may be brought to bear.

The conference concluded at 11 o'clock, when I told Senator Smoot that I had an appointment with the President which I was bound to keep.[1]

It was abundantly demonstrated that the commission had functioned in a far from judicial manner. Cost-of-production investigations were undertaken at the behest of commercial interests acting through the President and the Senate. On several products of trivial importance the tariff was lowered, while the reports on investigations of important products were delayed. Critics in Congress and in the press berated the commission for permitting politics to appear in tariff deliberations; yet little understanding was evinced of the impossibility of expecting any body of experts to deal objectively with a hot political issue. Responsibility was transferred from Congress to the administrative branch and shared by the chief executive and the Tariff Commission. The final work in fixing rates rested with the President, who was to act upon the findings of the commissioners. This relationship was uncertain and indefinite.[2] Disagreement among the commissioners as to the nature of their responsibility disrupted their work. Was the commission to be simply a fact-finding agency? Or was it to be a quasi-judicial tribunal for adjusting tariff rates in accordance with a definite statutory principle?

Costigan, Culbertson, and Lewis took the latter view, while Glassie, Marvin, and Burgess held to the more limited interpretation. It was really due to this difference in attitude as to the fundamental purpose of the commission that all the difficulty arose. The Costigan faction regarded the business antecedents of the others as disqualifying them for service upon the commission. Mr. Culbertson agreed with Mr. Costigan, not only that

[1] *Ibid.*, p. 712.
[2] For a thorough study of this relationship, see John Day Larkin, *The President and the Tariff*, Harvard University Press, 1936.

Mr. Glassie lacked the objectivity required for the proper performance of his duties, but that Mr. Burgess and Mr. Marvin, because of their prior connections, were still too closely identified with special interests.

Mr. Marvin held a different view as to the responsibilities of a commissioner. He explained his idea of the commission's duties to the Senate investigating committee thus:

All investigations, Senator, if they are as I understand them, are fact-finding investigations. And if the Commission has no power, as I do not conceive it has, to fix rates or modify rates or even recommend rates, I do not see how a financial interest could affect the ascertainment of facts as to the cost of production.[1]

This viewpoint was a far cry from actual tariff making by a scientific and impartial administrative tribunal, but it was more in accord with the realities of the political situation. Congress and Presidents Harding, Coolidge, and Hoover were not willing to leave the commission "undirected" in the task of setting schedules. The liberals on the commission held to an interpretation of their duties that was at odds with the political and economic environmental forces.

When the commission broke down under the impact of these forces, Congress took the view that with a higher type of man on the commission all would be well. Bad appointments were regarded as a major cause of the trouble.[2]

Certain commissioners, they argued, had been governed by political considerations and special interests. If outside interference had been the cause of the breakdown, could officials be found strong enough to resist these influences? Congress directly confronted the problem of determining the proper qualifications for members of the Tariff Commission. At the same time the Senate was aware of the general importance of establishing proper qualifications for membership on other federal administrative boards. Senator Borah raised the broad question as to what kind of man was needed on these bodies if administrative commissions were to prove acceptable:

[1] *Hearings* before the Select Committee on Investigation of the Tariff Commission, *op. cit.*, p. 112.

[2] *Congressional Record*, Jan. 13, 1931, p. 2046.

If we shall proceed to fill these commissions with men who have not expert knowledge, what shall we have done? We shall have created a body which is responsible to no constituency and yet is governed by the same influences by which Congress is governed. If we are to create commissions which are responsible to no constituency, certainly they ought to have an equipment, and that equipment ought to be peculiarly an expert knowledge with reference to the subject with which they are to deal. . . .

If we are to have commissions, I am in favor of letting those commissions do their work without the influence of the outside world, either from the Executive or the Legislative Department; and if they are equipped, as they should be, as experts, we can feel some comfort when a decision has been made that we have obtained the very best decision that can be reached in regard to the matter, that can be obtained through the commission form of government. . . .

In all the commissions which we are creating there is going to be, unless we change our program entirely, this exertion of outside influence from one department of the government on the other or both, and the only protection against that which I can conceive is an expert thoroughly devoted to his subject, a man who, as an expert, refuses to yield upon the facts and principles. Unless we are going to create that kind of commission, I repeat, we are creating tribunals to run our government which are not responsible to the constituency of the country and which at the same time are controlled by political influence.[1]

This view is apparently based upon the assumption that the expert in government, because of his technical training, can arrive at the correct decision simply by applying his intelligence to certain definite facts. But in selecting and interpreting facts, discretion must be exercised. Where the expert is charged with executing a declared policy, his judgments are directed by an objective criterion and his task is simply to bring the facts into accord with the principle. It is the task of the policy-determining agency to establish the principle under which the expert is to function. Impartiality is not guaranteed by expert opinion. There is no essential correlation between objectivity in dealing with conflicting interests and special competence. As Senator Reed pointed out:

Men become tariff experts because they are retained by particular interests to prosecute particular points of view; men become tariff experts because they are importers and have consequently to deal with the customs

[1] *Ibid.*, p. 1981.

authorities and customs laws of the United States. . . . It is a matter of bread and butter that they should be experts in those laws. If we were to put in the law a provision that the tariff commission should be composed of disinterested tariff experts, it is probable that the membership would never be filled. The ideal person would be a disinterested expert; but no expert is disinterested.[1]

Of course there are many tariff experts who have studied the subject with no commercial interest at stake. Nevertheless, Senator Reed stressed a significant factor. Any competent specialist develops a viewpoint with regard to his work and hence even the academician, although free from economic motivation, can scarcely be regarded as a totally disinterested expert. To be a student of the tariff is to form judgments concerning the subject.

The commission as originally conceived was to relieve Congress of the technical tasks that could better be handled by an expert body. But, as a result of the new duties imposed upon the commission by the flexible provisions in the 1922 act, the conception as to what was required of a member received a new emphasis. So strong were the political and economic influences bearing upon the activities of this expert board that a judicial mind came to be regarded as a more significant qualification than technical competence. By 1930 the need of ensuring the impartial character of this board was the consideration dominating the Senate debate over the nominees. Said Senator Robinson:

The task of the Commission is a very great and difficult one. It ought to be composed only of men who are impartial and just. . . . The effort ought to be to secure the services of men who are unbiased and impartial in character and whose record disclosed capacity and disposition to disregard extraneous influences and perform their duty within the letter and the spirit of the law.[2]

Senator Shortridge reflected the views of his colleagues when he expressed the desire for commissioners, first, of "unimpeachable character, who cannot and will not be improperly influenced by anyone or any set of men," and, secondly, "of intelligence, who can listen, who can hear, who can take evidence," and who can logically reach a decision.[3]

[1] *Ibid.*, p. 1982.
[2] *Ibid.*, p. 2050.
[3] *Ibid.*, pp. 2053 *ff.*

THE TARIFF COMMISSION

In accordance with these concepts, the Senate in 1931 considered the nominees to the reorganized commission. There was the frank recognition that, since the Tariff Commission operated in a context fraught with peril to objectivity, men should be appointed whose unquestioned integrity and disinterestedness would shield their activities from outside influences. Such characteristics were regarded as of more importance than special knowledge or understanding of tariff problems. This attitude was supported not only by those in the Senate but also by those who had direct experience upon the commission. Commissioner Culbertson testified thus:

My judgment is that the best commissioner in the long run is the trained impartial individual who, when appointed, knows nothing about the tariff at all. . . . After all, the Tariff Commission employs its experts, and what you want in a commissionship is not a so-called expert on the tariff, but you want a man of broad appreciation and intelligent judgment and judicial attitude, who can take the facts that are furnished him by the experts and reach a sound decision thereon.[1]

Accordingly, in drafting the act of 1930, special attention was given to securing a "higher type" of man to serve on the commission. How could able men be attracted to the work as a career? The opinion was expressed that if the office of Tariff Commissioner were "dignified" all would be well. Prestige, such as that accorded the members of the Interstate Commerce Commission, was needed. The law already provided for a bipartisan board with a six-year term and prohibited members from engaging in business while serving on the commission. These clauses were reënacted and the only statutory change relating to personnel was to increase the salary from $7500 to $11,000. From the debates in Congress, and from the provisions of the new statute, the intention of drawing men of ability to the commission clearly emerged. The choice of possible appointees was not restricted to those possessing certain technical qualifications. A broad view of the needs of the commission was taken. Yet these legal provisions have not been of much significance in actual practice. A higher salary was not enough to tap a higher level of talent or training.

[1] *Ibid.*, p. 537.

The President was authorized to select a new board. After canvassing various possibilities during the summer of 1930, President Hoover reappointed three members to the commission and designated Henry P. Fletcher to head the commission. The new chairman testified to a Senate committee that he had no views on the tariff prior to his appointment and that he had never read a book on the subject. Three of the new appointees after 1930 had served on the commission at the lower salary and it is highly doubtful whether the labor leader, the former professor of rural economics, and the ex-Congressmen since named to the new commission would have refused service because of "financial sacrifice." Nor can the present members of the commission be regarded as possessing qualifications of impartiality or expertness that sharply distinguish them from past commissions. It is impossible to say dogmatically that the members appointed since 1930 possess qualifications of impartiality or expertness that sharply distinguish them from past commissioners. They have not been subjected to the same stresses that burdened their predecessors.

"As regards the powers and duties of the Commission," Professor Taussig notes, "no changes of moment were made [in 1930]."

From 1930 to 1934 the commission worked quietly and without incurring any significant criticism. The commissioners administered the law smoothly, not because they were of a higher caliber than their predecessors or because of any substantial reforms in 1930. It was rather because the essentially political context of the commission had been made only too evident. The commissioners took a realistic view of their place in the political scheme of things. They were content to leave "policy" to political leadership.

One of the responsibilities that disrupted the commission in administering the flexible provision was selecting the commodities that were to be investigated with a view to altering the rate. Under the 1930 act the commission is required to make investigations not only on its own initiative but also upon the request of the President or upon the motion of either house of Congress. No matter how trivial the product, if Congress orders the investigation, the commission must comply. Special interests, therefore, have found it easier to approach some sympathetic Senator than to ask the commissioners directly for attention. During the first three years under the 1930 act, the commission undertook

105 investigations of which 61 were requested by the Senate, 9 by the President, and 35 by interested parties.[1]

The commission became less exhaustive in its investigations and more expeditious in its reports. Much less emphasis was placed upon finding manufacturing costs in foreign countries. Upon its own initiative, the commission turned again to making surveys upon general subjects not related directly to particular schedules. The onus of ordering investigations of particular commodities was left in large measure to Congress.

The President, likewise, had an indirect means of guiding the commission. Although, under the 1930 act, the chief executive was not empowered to fix schedules even within prescribed limits, he could reject the specific findings of the commissioners and refer their report back for further consideration. The commission as before reported upon tariff increases or decreases within a range of 50 per cent of the existing rate. But two authorities cannot exercise discretion upon the same subject without disagreement; the subordination of one to the other is the only alternative. Critics raised the cry that the commission was unduly acquiescent to the President in failing to press certain of its investigations, that the commission failed to complete investigations of important products because of Presidential opposition, and that it spent too much time studying things such as the production of ocean sponges, upholsterer's nails, and sperm oil. Senator Costigan stated that

. . . the tomato and cherry investigation resulted in 1931 in reports to the President favorable to lower duties; that the President thereupon returned the report to the Tariff Commission requesting it to make additional inquiries, and that nothing has been done by the Tariff Commission with these investigations in approximately a year and three months since the President, in April, 1931, so requested. It appeared further that the dried beans investigation which Senator Vanderberg of Michigan is said to have initiated through a Senate resolution was subsequently switched to a general inquiry under the commission's general powers. . . . We have here illustrations of external interference of the normal course of Tariff

[1] See "Work of the United States Tariff Commission since Its Reorganization, June 18, 1930, to March 15, 1932," U. S. Documents, Miscellaneous Series, 1932, p. 9; P. W. Bidwell, "First Year of the Flexible Tariff under the Reorganized Commission," *Annalist*, Sept. 11, 1931, p. 422.

Commission investigation, not intended when the commission was created.[1]

It can hardly be expected that the President, armed with his power of appointment and of "non-reappointment," will knuckle under to an administrative board. Frequent opposition on the part of the commission would discredit it politically and perhaps undermine its rather dubious position. It may exercise its duties of adjusting inequitable or irksome schedules and of relieving minor irritations. It can collect useful information and study significant commercial trends. But no commissioners, however well trained and impartial, can take the tariff out of politics. It must first cease to be a political issue in the minds of the public. Then the commission might function within a social and economic context where scientific norms could be applied. It is doubtful if there can be a blanket policy in regard to schedules. Particular shifts and changes will continue to be made to meet particular needs. Here is a question enmeshed in considerations of international affairs, of revenue policy, of national self-sufficiency, of the rivalries between classes and sections, of the conflict between political parties. Under such circumstances no formula devoid of value judgments can be devised for disposing of the problem. A principle is yet to be discovered that will clarify the duties of the commission and enable it to interpret, automatically, the concrete in terms of the general. Different duties must be levied to attain the various ends sought, and no coherent set of criteria is applicable. Unless a commission can be fortified by such principles, given a clear purpose, and left free from congressional interference, it cannot function without friction as a quasi-judicial administrative agency. Under present conditions the tariff question is beyond the competence of any administrative agency. The tariff is an instrument of national policy.

This was unmistakably recognized when the Reciprocal Tariff Act became law June 13, 1934. This act gives the President the authority to enter into reciprocal trade agreements with other nations without referring these treaties to the Senate for ratification. Thus the Tariff Commission has become little more than an adjunct to the chief executive in the administration of foreign

[1] *Congressional Record*, Senate, July 7, 1932, p. 14771.

affairs. The flexible tariff provisions of the 1930 law continue on articles not included in the new trade agreements. As a matter of fact, tariff bargaining has now become a major activity of the commission's staff.

The experience of the Tariff Commission demonstrates that an important political issue can neither be solved nor shelved by committing it to a special administrative agency. The tariff issue disrupted the commission. It had to be administered finally in accordance with its nature. The tariff involves our relations with other nations too profoundly to be settled by any set formulas. It is the concern of our political leaders. Tariff schedules must be coördinated with our foreign policy and reconciled with domestic industrial interests.

The administrative machinery set up under the Reciprocal Tariff Act, while cumbersome, is realistically conceived. It attempts to bring together all those elements in the federal administrative service that are concerned with foreign trade. It provides also for hearing all the private parties holding stakes in the tariff.

Broad questions as to our commercial relations with foreign nations are considered by an Executive Committee on Commercial Policy. The immediate responsibility for formulating and negotiating agreements rests with the Interdepartmental Committee on Foreign Trade Agreements. This committee brings together representatives from the Departments of State, Agriculture, and Treasury, the Tariff Commission, and the A.A.A.

The technical work of negotiating trade agreements is done by interdepartmental committees set up for each country. The various departments or agencies concerned contribute members to these committees. Officials describe the organization as follows:

The Department of Commerce makes the preliminary studies and recommendations for consideration by the country committees regarding the concessions that may be asked from foreign countries; the Tariff Commission makes similar studies and recommendations with respect to concessions that may be offered to foreign countries. The Department of Agriculture assumes principal responsibility with respect to preliminary studies and recommendations regarding concessions asked and offered on agricultural products. Representatives of the A.A.A. and N.R.A. are consulted to avoid conflicts between the tariff and domestic recovery programs. The recommendations of the country committees are submitted to the Committee on Foreign Trade Agreements for review.

On the basis of the recommendations thus formulated the Department of State initiates exploratory conversations with the governments of the countries with which trade agreements are contemplated. If it appears that there are definite possibilities of arriving at mutually advantageous trade agreements, public announcements are made that this Government intends to negotiate such agreements with the countries concerned and provision is made for receiving the views of all persons interested in the proposed agreements, as provided in Section 4 of the Trade Agreements Act.

The views of persons interested in trade agreements may be presented to the Committee for Reciprocity Information, an interdepartmental committee established by Executive Order especially for the purpose. This committee, of which Thomas Walker Page, Tariff Commissioner, is Chairman, prepares digests of briefs, oral views and correspondence for the use of the country committees referred to above. These digests make available to the country committees the criticisms, suggestions, and technical information received by the Committee for Reciprocity Information from producers, manufacturers, importers, exporters, and trade associations interested in the agreements.[1]

An Assistant Secretary of State supervises this entire organization and reports to the Secretary of State. The task of coördination is directly met by the trade-agreements section of the State Department. These details demonstrate how drastically our conception of tariff administration has changed. The tariff is back in politics. It is linked with the general policy of the administration. Responsibility is clearly placed in the chief executive. The Tariff Commission has found its place in the administrative hierarchy.

The farther the government extends its reach into the economic life of the country, the heavier become its administrative duties. We have noted the administrative problems created by heavy income taxes, by nuisance taxes, and by regulatory taxes. The more the government regulates, the more discretion must be granted officials if they are to make regulation effective. In the State Department officials found that the conduct of foreign affairs affected both bankers and investors. Did the public interest entail an administrative responsibility to both? The Roosevelt administration, in the creation of the Securities and Exchange Commission

[1] Mimeographed release.

and the encouragement of a foreign-bond holders council, has acknowledged such a responsibility. Likewise in tariff administration a conception of "public interest" prevails which is different from that of preceding administrations. The fixing of tariff schedules is now a matter of bargaining, not only with domestic industrial interests but with foreign nations as well. Today tariff bargaining may be classified along with the collection of taxes or the conduct of foreign relations, since in all these fields the ultimate responsibility rests with the President for directing administrative action so as to promote the general welfare. The political restrictions on the independence of the Tariff Commission have been discovered. Officials cannot be removed from the storms of politics by erecting an independent commission over them in umbrella fashion.

Chapter VII

THE PLACE AND POLICY OF THE FEDERAL TRADE COMMISSION

"Have you guessed the riddle yet?" the Hatter said, turning to
Alice again.

"No, I give it up," Alice replied. "What's the answer?"

"I haven't the slightest idea," said the Hatter.

"Nor I," said the March Hare.

THE Federal Power Commission, the Federal Communications
Commission, the Federal Trade Commission, and the
Interstate Commerce Commission are independent agencies.
They are not responsible for their acts to the chief executive.
They exercise functions that are judicial in character. They
have executive tasks to perform and some have legislative responsibilities also. The courts have found that these bodies have been
adequately provided by Congress with criteria for determining
what is in the public interest within their respective jurisdictions.[1]

[1] On this point, the Supreme Court in the recent Schechter case, stated: " By the
interstate commerce act, Congress has itself provided a code of laws regulating the
activities of the common carriers subject to the act, in order to assure the performance of their services upon just and reasonable terms, with adequate facilities
and without unjust discrimination. Congress from time to time has elaborated its
requirements, as needs have been disclosed. To facilitate the application of the
standards prescribed by the act, Congress has provided an expert body. That
administrative agency, in dealing with particular cases, is required to act upon
notice and hearing, and its orders must be supported by findings of fact which in
turn are sustained by evidence. *Interstate Commerce Commission v. Louisville &
Nashville Railroad Co.*, 227 U. S. 88; *Florida v. United States*, 282 U. S. 194; *United
States v. Baltimore & Ohio Railroad Co.*, 293 U. S. 454. When the commission is
authorized to issue, for the construction, extension or abandonment of lines, a
certificate of 'public convenience and necessity,' or to permit the acquisition of
one carrier of the control of another, if that is found to be 'in the public interest,'
we have pointed out that these provisions are not left without standards to guide
determination. The authority conferred has direct relation to the standards prescribed for the service of common carriers and can be exercised only for findings,
based upon evidence, with respect to particular conditions of transportation.
New York Central Securities Co. v. United States, 287 U. S. 12, 24, 25; *Texas & Pacific*

Congress and the courts, however, have not disposed of the ultimate problem by creating special agencies to consider special problems.

A larger question remains unanswered. How shall the work of these independent commissions be integrated with the rest of the executive branch? Shall we assume that the general welfare will be realized if each commission interprets to the best of its ability the statutes entrusted to its charge by Congress? Or should the activities of a given commission be joined with related federal activities in the same field and the work of all administrative agencies be integrated through the White House? Here are riddles that remain unanswered.

The establishment of independent bodies to carry out special tasks in the public interest has in a sense defeated the very aim that was sought. We have one board to consider monetary policy, another to handle certain aspects of transportation policy, another dealing with phases of the communications problem, and another concerned with water power. To other boards we have delegated tariff questions and the regulation of unfair trade practices. These commissions strive to act independently, yet their jurisdiction is incomplete. Their powers, for example, extend to only a part of the general field of transportation or of business regulation. How can the public interest be discovered from such a partial view of their problem? These bodies cannot remain entirely independent of other agencies doing related work. The question arises as to how independent they should be. We have already discovered that the Tariff Commission cannot function without the close coöperation of the State Department. In order to evaluate the usefulness of the independent commission as an administrative device, we must examine the actual experience of these bodies and note the difficulties that have befallen them in the course of their careers.

If the government under presidential leadership passes laws for social security and for the economic development of the nation, it cannot achieve its goal without reference to the independent administrative agencies already charged with the supervision of

---

Railway Co. v. Gulf, Colorado & Santa Fe Railway Co., 270 U. S. 266, 273; *Chesapeake & Ohio Railway Co. v. United States*, 283 U. S. 35, 42."

important closely related problems. On the other hand, persistent political interference, whether expressed through changes in personnel or "influence" upon policy, breaks down continuity of precedent and objectivity of judgment. There is no point in creating a special independent commission unless full confidence is reposed in its discretion and unless freedom of action is permitted. From the experience of such a body, the legislature can secure reliable recommendations for statutory amendment and amplification. Before this is feasible, however, there must be agreement, either as to ultimate purpose or, at least, as to general orientation. An example may clarify these points.

The Federal Trade Commission arose out of an attempt by the political leaders of 1914 to dispose of a troublesome problem. Dissatisfaction with the Sherman Act was general, and the 1912 platforms of all three major parties dealt with 'the question of trusts and combinations. The control of monopolies challenged attention as a campaign issue. When the Federal Trade Commission came into existence, there was apparently a general belief that the "right" policy meant the protection of the little businessman against the trusts. But the problem has since been recognized as much less simple than this. Witness the efforts of late to get away from "the hindrance of cutthroat competition" which industry claims has been imposed by the antitrust law.[1] An agreed-upon policy concerning government regulation of industry has not yet been developed with the clarity or objectivity essential in establishing a basis for the free exercise of discretion by an independent commission. Vacillations as to fundamental policy have disrupted the career of the Federal Trade Commission. Its administrative tribulations raise the question as to whether an independent commission is an administrative device properly suited to meet present demands for the regulation and guidance of industry and commerce.

Following the trust-busting era, a demand that the antitrust laws be made more specific arose from both the friends and foes of

[1] Senator D. I. Walsh introduced bills in January, 1932, and in May, 1933, providing for advance approval by the Federal Trade Commission of contracts to curtail production. Safeguards as to fair price and fair wages were included. *Congressional Record*, May 1, 1933, p. 2602. There is of course our experience under the N.R.A.

big business.[1] President Wilson attempted to meet these divergent demands for remedial legislation by supporting two bills. One (later the Clayton Act) set out specifically to condemn certain practices as unlawful and "in restraint of trade." The other bill established an interstate trade commission to investigate corporate policy and organization and forestall malpractices by "pitiless publicity." This body was to take over and carry further the investigatory function of the existing Bureau of Corporations. Before the measure was enacted, an important provision (Section 5) was added, authorizing the commission to prevent the use of unfair methods of competition in interstate commerce and prescribing a procedure by complaint, hearing, and orders to "cease and desist." According to former Commissioner Abram F. Myers,

Section 5 was added in the Senate as a sort of complement to the Clayton Act which was undergoing the legislative process at the same time. It was thought that this catch-all provision would embrace all monopolistic practices not specifically enumerated in the Clayton Act, including minor abuses not worthy of the attention of the courts in the first instance.[2]

The legislative debates show very convincingly that this general language was adopted with deliberate purpose: Congress was stating a broad ethical and economic principle. Apparently Congress expected the commission to deal with the prevention of monopoly rather than the punishment of fraudulent practices,[3] but the intention of Congress with regard to the actual responsibili-

[1] G. C. Henderson, *The Federal Trade Commission*, p. 17, Yale University Press, 1924. "Business men, trade associations, and commercial and industrial interests to whom the uncertainty of the law had become exasperating . . . took the view . . . that after nearly a quarter of a century of experience with the anti-trust law, it should be possible for the statesmen in Washington to make up their minds just what conduct they wished to forbid, and to describe it in language which the citizen could understand."

[2] Abram F. Myers, address at the Institute of Public Affairs, University of Virginia, July 9, 1932.

[3] "It is not conceived that Congress, which laid down no definition whatever, intended to either limit or extend the matters which constituted unfair methods of competition prior to the passage of the Clayton Act, but that its object was the creation of a board of commissioners." *Kinney-Rome Co. v. Federal Trade Commission*, 275 Fed. 665. See also George Rublee, "The Original Plan and Early History of the Federal Trade Commission," *Proceedings of the Academy of Political Science*, January, 1926, vol. 11, no. 4, p. 114.

ties of the commissioners remained vague. It was clear that the President and the legislature wanted a stricter control of commercial practices, but what share of this task was to be borne by the commission? Was the commission to emphasize its investigatory functions? Was it to attempt a broad interpretation of unfair methods of competition? Was it to coöperate with those business interests desirous of learning the limits of lawful combination? In 1916 Woodrow Wilson said to a group of businessmen: "It is hard to describe the functions of that Commission; all I can say is that it has transformed the Government of the United States from being an antagonist of business into being a friend of business."[1]

Since the possibilities for variety in interpretation were so great, the scope for pressure upon the commissioners was equally wide. By leaving their powers vague, Congress left an opportunity for building up a law merchant through administrative rulings. At the same time the chance was given for partisan influence to affect mightily government relations with business.

The trade commissioners in examining a complaint have to consider two questions: First, does the matter fall within their jurisdiction, *i.e.*, is it interstate and is it an unfair method of competition? Secondly, does it appear to the commission that prosecuting the offender "would be to the interest of the public"? The commission, however, has not been able to interpret freely these vague criteria. The "public interest" presumably is the standard for all legal acts by responsible officials, but the phrase was added to the law here in order to give the commissioners discretion in choosing cases for prosecution. The courts, however, have made this standard of public interest a jurisdictional requirement and have not hesitated to override the judgment of the commissioners as to the admission of complaints.[2] The commission

[1] Address before Grain Dealer's Association, Baltimore, Sept. 25, 1916.

[2] In the Shade Shop Case the Federal Trade Commission took jurisdiction over a petty dispute between two little shopkeepers. Justice Brandeis, in overruling the commission, stated, "In determining whether a proposed proceeding will be in the public interest the Commission exercises a broad discretion. But the mere fact that it is to the interest of the community that private rights shall be respected is not enough to support a finding of public interest. To justify filing a complaint the public interest must be specific and substantial." *Federal Trade Commission v. Klesner*, 280 U. S. 19. When the commission ruled that using false and misleading trade names constituted an unfair method of competition on the part of the Winsted

has not enjoyed greater freedom of administration as a result of this statutory phrase.

While the question of fairness in trade relationships is at bottom an ethical one, the task of the commission is not to punish the wicked but rather to decide what business practices should be eliminated in order to free competitive forces. The problems of trade methods it must consider are those discussed by businessmen themselves in their trade associations and in their conventions. The commission's question is: does an unfair practice restrict the play of competition to *an extent* detrimental to the public interest? But what is to be understood by the "public interest," what is meant by "competition," and what constitutes an "unfair method?"

The administrative experience of the Federal Trade Commission centers largely around the efforts made to answer these questions. Learned treatises have followed the lines of judicial interpretation with great care.[1] The purpose here is to touch other threads in the web of interests surrounding the commission. A

Hosiery Company, Justice Brandeis stated that, "As a substantial part of the public was still misled by the use of the labels the Winsted Company employed, the public had an interest in stopping the practice as wrongful." *Federal Trade Commission v. Winsted Hosiery Company*, 258 U. S. 483. It remains for the courts to decide when a complaint sufficiently affects the specific and substantial interests of the public. *Ostermoor and Company, Inc., v. Federal Trade Commission*, 16 Fed. (2d) 962. Is the public misled into dreaming of impossible resiliency by looking at a trade-mark showing the hugely swelling contents of an unfinished Ostermoor mattress? Is the public interest concerned in the accuracy with which a particular breed of hogs is advertised? *L. B. Silver & Co. v. Federal Trade Commission*, 289 Fed. 985. For an excellent analysis of the "public interest" in the Federal Trade Commission Act, see H. R. Seager and C. A. Gulick, Jr., *Trust and Corporation Problems*, pp. 538 ff. Harper, 1929.

[1] The recent study by Carl McFarland, *Judicial Review of the Interstate Commerce Commission and of the Federal Trade Commission*, Harvard University Press, 1933, conclusively demonstrated the hampering effect of judicial review upon the initiative and independence of the commission. While this study admirably discloses the control by the courts, the political and economic factors that influence the commission lie beyond the author's purpose. McFarland concedes that "to attribute the lack of success entirely to unsympathetic treatment at the hands of the judges would be error—causes are rarely so simple. Personnel and amplifying legislation, among other things, are of first importance." Page 99. See also T. C. Blaisdell, *The Federal Trade Commission*, p. 76, Columbia University Press, 1932, for an excellent broad treatment.

picture of its administrative problems is not to be found in one factor but rather in the pattern made by the interweaving of many elements. Some of these may appear inconsequential; others are of unmistakable significance. All have contributed to making a difficult task still more difficult.

For years the commission was housed in a temporary wartime emergency structure excessively hot in summer, often extremely uncomfortable in winter. For years the work of the commission was in arrears, and cases were brought to court long after evidence was fresh.[1] Its rulings have been presented in meager and unconvincing form and its organization and procedure have been justly criticized.[2] The turnover in the staff has been exceptionally high. During the first ten years six members withdrew to one that stayed. Of the 418 employees in 1920, 348 entered and 297 employees left the commission. Of the 450 employees in 1930, 116 entered and 46 left the service during the year. The tenure of the commissioners was brief on the average during the early years.[3] Of the original appointees none served for more than about half of their allotted time. Since 1920, however, the actual tenure has increased and during the last decade has remained comparatively stable. Of the recent appointees, Charles E. Hunt has served from 1924 to 1932, Edgar A. McCulloch from 1927 to 1933, G. S. Ferguson from 1927 to date, and Charles H. March from 1929 to date. The term of Victor Murdock was over six years, that of Huston Thompson seven years and eight months, that of J. F. Nugent six years and eight months, and that of W. E. Humphrey, eight years and seven months. While brevity of tenure has been regarded as an explanation for the weak policy of the commission, of more importance is the influence exerted by the commissioners who remained for some years. Continuity in policy was not so much disrupted by frequent changes in commissioners as by the fundamental differences of opinion held by those who served longest on this body. Factionalism was aggravated by shifts in personnel, but it was the dissension within the commission itself that created difficulties.

[1] *Annual Report*, 1924, p. 14.
[2] See Henderson, *op. cit.*, p. 334, and McFarland, *op. cit.*, p. 178.
[3] *Annual Report*, 1925, p. 4.

THE FEDERAL TRADE COMMISSION

It seems apparent that from the beginning the commission was in a precarious position, for not only were its legal powers vague and its resources inadequate, but its relations with Congress were uncertain. The parties coming within its jurisdiction were often very powerful. The more important the business, the wider its ramifications, and the more numerous its allies and subsidiaries, the closer it came within the commission's responsibility. To review the firms with which this agency has had official contacts, especially in its early years, is to go down the roster of big business in this country. Making political enemies was soon found to be an incident in the routine of administration. The discharging of official duties meant interfering with business and often "big business."

Blaisdell, after reviewing the commission's experiences with the oil, aluminum, steel, and meat-packing industries, concludes that the attempts to restore competitive conditions have been of slight effectiveness.[1] The studies published and the recommendations made by the commission have been in the main disregarded. Certainly the commission has played an insignificant part in curbing the trusts. Its chief function today, as Abram Myers has said, with some exaggeration, is in "preventing false and misleading advertising in reference to hair restorers, anti-fat remedies, etc.— a somewhat inglorious end to a noble experiment."

The commission can hardly be taken to task for going after easy game when the inadequate response from Congress is considered. The federal legislature has done nothing to support the commission in developing its indefinite initial criteria into a body of administrative law for the regulation of business. The basic reasons for this may lie in traditional attitudes of respect for the courts, suspicion of bureaucracy, and distrust of official intervention, even when it is intended to free competitive forces.

But more immediate factors in the environment of the commission indicate that "politics" in the sense of partisan and economic influences have determined the course of administrative development. The commission has suffered a fate that has been shared to some extent by the Federal Power Commission. Both agencies are called upon to deal with great corporations, and

[1] T. C. Blaisdell, *The Federal Trade Commission*, p. 255.

consequently they have been dragged around the political arena behind the chariots, sometimes of the people's champions and sometimes of the defenders of honest business and the foes of socialism. The Trade Commission has been a focal point of attack for those who are dissatisfied with the prevailing governmental policy toward business. The "masses" versus the "moneyed interests" is a perennially good issue for a politician to talk about, but it is not a problem for a bureaucrat to deal with. Only with strong political support can the Federal Trade Commission consistently administer its statutory responsibilities. Congress, instead of striving to strengthen the independence of the commission, has actually hampered its development. A former commissioner[1] testifies that

. . . Senators who would not think of seeking to influence a court in the decision of a case pending before it, have no compunction about stalking the halls of the commission and offering *ex parte* arguments and representations concerning cases pending before it. This attitude toward the commission also is reflected in the efforts of individual legislators to control its acts; and it is not uncommon for the commission to be under fire in the Senate for exercising its powers too gingerly and in the House for daring to use them at all.

The commission has indeed been the victim of many oratorical outbursts in Congress and of protests from interests outside. Democrats and Republicans, both liberal and conservative, have at different times criticized in scathing language the work of the commission. "I have been overwhelmed for several years with complaints from businessmen concerning the Federal Trade Commission for its inefficiency, incompetence, and inability to discharge the public business," declared the conservative Penrose of Pennsylvania in 1919. "I have hardly heard an epithet of condemnation in the English language that has not been visited upon every individual member of the Federal Trade Commission."[2] In 1926 Senator King, in order to express his disapproval, introduced a bill to abolish the commission. He denounced its policy in a two-hour speech—"a Federal Trade Commission," he said, "that is blind to trusts and combinations and monopolies and unfair methods of competition in commerce and misinterprets

[1] Abram Myers in *Anti-trust Law Symposium*, p. 133.
[2] *Congressional Record*, Aug. 22, 1919, p. 7311.

the law is not only a useless appendage but is a real menace."[1]
In 1919 the commission, pursuing a policy of rather strict control,
was described as a hindrance to business; in 1926 under a less
stringent regime it was denounced as an enemy of the people.

This administrative agency is expected to interpret under a
vague mandate from Congress an issue concerning which there
is no stable consensus of opinion. Congress has set no clear goal
for the commission. Political vicissitudes have prevented its
shifting personnel from evolving one for themselves. A scrutiny
of the *Congressional Record* and of the hearings before the Appropriations Committee reveals little appreciation of the problems
of the commission as an administrative agency. When Congressmen discuss its affairs, their interest is obviously dictated by the
situation in their own locality. The commission has not been able
to keep a systematic record of the activities of whole industries.
Its investigatory work has been dictated often, it would seem,
by the political caprice of Congress. Instances of this can be found
in the way that Congress has exercised its right of directing the
commission to undertake investigations. The great majority of
these inquiries have not been initiated by the commission, but
were ordered by Senate resolutions.

Sporadic investigations have served as sensational crusades
against "predatory interests" and for a time have silenced the
clamor of disgruntled minorities. In 1923, for example, the high
price of calcium arsenate, a poison used to destroy the boll weevil,
prompted the Senate to order an investigation by the commission.
Inquiry revealed that the raise in price was not due to machinations
in restraint of trade but rather to a sudden increase in demand.
Making big business the scapegoat for the plight of the depressed
cotton planter, however, seems to have an unmistakable appeal
to certain southern politicians. In 1927, the House ordered the
commission to investigate the alleged fixing of the price of cotton-
seed. No violation of the antitrust laws was found. The Senate
forthwith directed that a further inquiry be made respecting the
control of cotton gins by big mill operators in order to find some
explanation for the low prices paid the southern farmer. Congressmen have found that some of the activities of the commission
caused "trouble" while others were useful in winning votes.

[1] *Ibid.*, Feb. 9, 1926, p. 3630.

Whether viewed in its relations with Congress, with the courts, or with business, the Federal Trade Commission has generally been confronted with grave difficulties in attempting to enforce its statutory responsibilities. The political or economic elements that pressed for the accomplishment of the purposes of 1914 have grown weaker. The story becomes clear if we consider chronologically those experiments that bear upon this discussion.

During its first years the commission proceeded cautiously. The first three annual reports show a number of investigations under way, but more than a third of the applications for complaints against unfair methods of competition were disposed of informally. Many communications were received from businessmen commending the purpose of the Federal Trade Commission Act, although the commission "made no attempt to define in general terms what methods of competition were unfair."[1] During 1918 and 1919 the commission was much occupied with war work. In its brief existence before the war, problems of organization and preliminary study of its legal powers scarcely left time for the development of policy.

The first undertaking of major importance was the food inquiry authorized by President Wilson in 1917. This investigation took much time and money and resulted in a number of reports, the most notable of which dealt with the meat-packing industry. What happened to the trade commission when it interfered with the meat packers provides a concrete illustration of the political and administrative problems involved in attempting to regulate a powerful industry. Lobbyists for the industry fought bitterly to prevent an investigation and they strove to render its results ineffective. "The packers have tried to employ men who had influence with members of Congress or the Government agencies. They have not stopped at anything in their propaganda," Senator Harris stated.[2]

In August, 1919, in response to Senate Resolution 177 (initiated by Senator Norris), the commission sent to Congress the unpublished report prepared for the President. The document was ordered to be printed as a public document in September and a storm of indignation arose soon afterward. The evidence offered

[1] *Annual Report*, 1916, p. 6.
[2] *Congressional Record*, Oct. 22, 1919, p. 7310.

by the commission indicated unlawful combination and restraint of trade by the five largest meat packers—Swift & Company, Armour and Company, Morris & Co., Wilson & Co., Inc., and the Cudahy Packing Company.[1] The commission recommended changes in the organization of the meat-packing industry and public owner- ship of some branches. The sweeping character of this investigation and the bold changes suggested caused a political backfire almost fatal to the commission. Five federal officials aroused the enmity of five great meat-packers and the battle was on. The advertising expenditure of Swift & Company alone by 1919 had risen to nearly six times the total appropriation of the commission.[2]

The response in Congress was divided. Said Senator Smoot: "I think the report of the Trade Commission is not only sensational but the conclusions in many respects are absolutely false."[3] Many bills and resolutions were introduced and the debates were long and heated. The case for the packers was presented at length. On Oct. 20 Senator Watson introduced a resolution that was apparently intended to punish the commission for its boldness in attacking big business and recommending government ownership of the stockyards. Watson demanded a thorough investigation of the Federal Trade Commission on the ground that certain employees were believed to be engaged in socialist propaganda and in furthering the growth of socialistic organizations. "If the Senator can discredit the Commission in this investigation," one of his colleagues remarked, "he has accomplished more for the packers than they could for themselves with all their millions spent in lobbying and propaganda."[4] The federal employees suspected were exonerated after a private investigation but later they were dropped from the commission. It was charged that the desire to placate Senator Watson (of the Appropriations Com- mittee) accounted for the discharge of these civil servants.[5]

Meanwhile the Attorney General, on the basis of the commis- sion's evidence, had announced that a criminal suit would be brought against the packers. The packers thereupon entered into

[1] *Annual Report*, 1919, p. 38.
[2] T. C. Blaisdell, *op. cit.*, p. 190.
[3] *Congressional Record*, Oct. 3, 1918, pp. 11041–51.
[4] *Ibid.*, Dec. 3, 1919. p. 67.
[5] G. T. Odell, "The Commission Yields to Pressure," *Nation*, Jan. 12, 1921.

negotiations for a consent decree. The Department of Justice differed from the Federal Trade Commission as to what the packers should be allowed to do. The courts accepted the department's interpretation and peremptorily forbade the spokesmen for the commission to present their case.[1] Here the officials were at odds as to the government's view. Moreover, no sooner was the consent decree approved by the courts than efforts were started to modify it. The wholesale grocers were opposed to any modification of the decree that would permit the packers to deal in products unrelated to meat. But the packers had well-organized systems for distributing food products. Why should they not be allowed to compete with the wholesale grocers or with the chain stores? What *kind of competition* was in the public interest? The relative nature of its criteria was demonstrated for the commission.

Many were the interpretations that might have been placed upon the phrase "unfair methods of competition," but, as events continued to prove, its meaning was to be determined, not by the commission alone, but by a combination of economic and political elements, among which this regulatory body was at times scarcely *prima inter pares*. The questions falling under its jurisdiction touched conflicting economic groups and involved likewise other branches of the government. Congress, the chief executive, the courts, and various administrative departments were at times concerned with the situation. There was no inherent consistency or unity on the part of the government.

The packers were desirous of getting from under the jurisdiction of the Federal Trade Commission. They seemed to feel that they would receive more sympathetic treatment from the officials in the Department of Agriculture.[2] Before the responsibility for regulating the meat-packing industry passed to the Department of Agriculture, the political strength and legal resourcefulness of big business was clearly demonstrated. The commission received its baptism of fire when it engaged the five titans of the stockyards. The Packers and Stockyards Act of 1921 transferred the supervision of the meat-packing industry to the Secretary of Agriculture. This move was strongly opposed by national organizations of

[1] *Annual Report*, 1921, p. 46.
[2] See *Hearings* before the Commission on Agriculture and Forestry, Senate, 65th Cong., Third Session, S. 5305, p. 17.

women, farmers, and workers, among which the National League of Women Voters, the National Grange, and the railroad brotherhoods voiced protest.

The reaction of organized groups and of their spokesmen in Congress to the meat-packing investigation showed the difficulty of protecting the impartiality of an independent commission. Assuming this body to be unbiased in its findings, nevertheless the very character of the inquiry aroused the enmity of certain interests and attracted the support of others. Samuel Gompers testified before the conference committee: "The Federal Trade Commission has proved its value in the many investigations it has made. It has been found that its findings cannot be influenced and that its work is in the interest of all the people instead of a few."[1] Some groups thus supported the work of the commission and identified its aims with their own. The gratuitous loyalties that closed in about the commission tended to obscure its disinterested character. Farmers, workers, and housewives were ready to proclaim the commission their champion.

Then in 1920 an event occurred that precluded any such possibility. Here, at the very beginning of the commission's development, the Supreme Court intervened and in the Gratz Case (233 U. S. 421) asserted its authority to define the scope of the commission's powers. The vague terms of the statute were not to be freely interpreted by the commission. The development of a law of business practices by administrative rulings was thus checked at the start by judicial decision and held within the precedents of common law.[2] Very early in its career the commission learned of the pitfalls in its way. If the commissioners trod upon the toes of important industrialists, they aroused protests from important politicians. Disagreement with the Department of Justice added to the commissioners' difficulties in making their rulings effective, and the growing restrictions of judicial review further limited their authority.

The commissioners were slow to admit this development if we can accept their annual reports as any indication of their attitude. In 1922 the commissioners reported as the notable feature of the year—"the development of the law of unfair competition as

[1] *Congressional Record*, Aug. 9, 1921, p. 4786.
[2] McFarland, *op. cit.*, pp. 45–47.

exemplified by those decisions in the courts which further established and defined the powers of the Commission."[1] Repeated efforts were made to widen the concept of unfair methods of competition by intróducing new principles regulating business practices. The commission condemned "tying contracts" whereby a manufacturer, because of his control over the supply, bound dealers to observe certain conditions. The commission likewise regarded the policy of "resale price maintenance" as an unfair trade practice. The Beech-Nut Packing Company refused to sell its products to merchants who offered these articles to the public at a different price from that fixed by the company. The commission decided that price discrimination based on trade status was an unfair competitive device. Thus a manufacturer was not allowed to charge a wholesaler one price and a coöperative purchasing agency or retailer another price. Exclusive dealer arrangements were likewise proceeded against by the commission as fostering monopoly, lessening competition, and constituting an unfair trade practice.

The point of significance for this discussion is the fact that the Federal Trade Commissioners prior to 1925 made positive efforts to extend their powers and build up new criteria with regard to business behavior.

Henderson, writing in 1924, saw "no reason why the Federal Trade Commission should not realize fully the promise of the legislation of 1914," provided a few changes in procedure were made.[2] In other words, he found no fundamental obstacle to the development of the commission's power in the adverse decisions that had been handed down by the courts.

If between 1920 and 1923 the courts circumscribed the powers of the commission, it was likewise during that same period that the commissioners were most aggressive in seeking to extend their authority. While a "liberal" majority dominated the commission, adverse court decisions did not discourage efforts toward clarification and expansion of the concept of unfair methods of competition. When the composition of this board changed, its policy changed. McFarland concludes that "the restraining hand of the judiciary was an important factor in turning the attention of the

[1] *Annual Report*, 1922, p. 2.
[2] Henderson, *op. cit.*, p. 342.

commission to activities other than trade regulation through orders enforceable only in the courts." The commission, however, cannot be regarded as a passive body easily turned about by the courts. The commission, dominated by Murdock, Nugent, and Thompson, differed basically from the commission of Humphrey, Hunt, and Van Fleet. The judiciary cannot be held entirely responsible for the commission's quiescent attitude after 1925.

The explanation is rather to be found in political changes and in the personal views of the new appointees to the commission after 1925. It was the politicians as well as the judges that turned "the attention of the Commission to activities other than trade regulation." There is no inevitable causal relationship between the court decisions and the policy of the commission. The courts were concerned for two years or more in passing upon cases undertaken by the commission before this date. Once these cases were disposed of, no major disagreements as to statutory interpretation occurred between the courts and the commission. This is not attributable to the court's defining the commission's sphere clearly, but rather to a shift in personnel which brought a majority of the commission who were of a like mind with the courts. Moreover, under the changed procedure of the commission, many questions of unfair methods after 1925 never reached the courts. The commission's new relations with business meant that the possibility of judicial review was side-stepped.

Evidence to substantiate this case can be found by comparing the commission proceedings of 1924 and 1925. In 1924 Commissioner Van Fleet was the dissenting voice. The grounds for his disagreement with the majority indicate a more restricted view of the commission's interstate jurisdiction in regulating unfair methods of competition. He was more critical of the evidence relied upon in condemning industries and he was less ready to interfere with private business "in the public interest."

By 1925 Thompson and Nugent had become the dissenting minority. Their conception of the commission's function was in sharp contrast with that of Van Fleet. They disagreed with his narrow interpretation of the commission's authority. To them the commission's function was essentially "prophylactic"—not merely corrective but also preventive of business abuses. To dismiss the charges against a businessman guilty of an unfair trade practice upon promise of reform, but not to make public the facts of the case and the findings of the commission, was to fail in deterring others. "The making of wrong a personal matter," Thompson stated, "causes a shrinking by the offender and may be a hardship on him, but the rights of the consuming public to be put upon notice, and of the competitor to be protected from unfair business practices, far outweighs the damage done to the reputation of the one committing the wrong."[1] Thompson was inclined to emphasize the interest of the consumer; Van Fleet, that of the entrepreneur. The welfare of both are implicit in the welfare of the public. But at what point shall one special interest be regarded as closer to the public interest?

The phrases and words supposed to serve as criteria in making judgments have entirely different meanings for these dissenting commissioners. What constitutes deception? What is a monopoly? When is the public interest affected? Underlying the answers given these questions were fundamentally different philosophies of economics and politics. It is the attitude of the individual commissioner toward business, rather than the relations of the courts to the commission, that explains, in chief measure, the significance of the Federal Trade Commission as a regulatory agency. Here is an outstanding case where conflicting political and economic influences have disrupted the course of administrative development. Here, as in the case of the Tariff Commission, conflict as to what was in the public interest was absolved by presidential intervention. New officials in whom the chief executive had confidence were appointed.

[1] *Dissent in Federal Trade Commission v. Mack, Miller Candle Company.*

Chapter VIII

PERSONALITIES, POLITICS, AND THE FEDERAL TRADE COMMISSION

"When *I* use a word," Humpty Dumpty said, in rather a scornful tone, "it means just what I choose it to mean—neither more nor less."

"The question is," said Alice, "whether you *can* make words mean so many different things."

"The question is," said Humpty Dumpty, "which is to be master—that's all."

PRESIDENT COOLIDGE'S appointment of William E. Humphrey to the Federal Trade Commission in 1925 served not only to establish a Republican majority on that body, but also to inaugurate a "new era" in its activities. Humphrey entered upon his duties Feb. 25, and on Mar. 17 sweeping changes in policy and procedure were announced. No longer was the bureau to be used as a "publicity bureau to spread socialistic propaganda." The opposition from the "vocal and beatific fringe, the pink edges that border both of the old parties" would not deter the new commission from its determination to "help business to help itself." Humphrey, in his effort to stress the fact that a new course was being pursued, emphatically condemned the commission of his predecessors.

Under the old policy of litigation it became an instrument of oppression and disturbance and injury instead of a help to business. It harassed and annoyed business instead of assisting it. Business soon regarded the commission with distrust and fear and suspicion—as an enemy. There was no coöperation between the commission and business. Business wanted the commission abolished and the commission regarded business as generally dishonest.[1]

In explaining the change that occurred on the commission, the power of Humphrey's personality and the influence of his speeches and writings must be considered. It is not that these declarations

[1] Address by W. E. Humphrey at Institute of Statesmanship, Winter Park, Florida, Jan. 6, 1931.

[125]

are particularly cogent or marked by profundity of thought; it is rather that they reflect in bald and obvious form the prevailing views of the conservative leaders in his party and in business at the time.[1] The shifting of political fortunes had brought a combination of groups into control whose leaders expressed theories very different from the Wilsonian disciples of the New Freedom. Big business had become more than respectable. Calvin Coolidge declaimed: "We justify the greater and greater accumulations of capital because we believe that therefrom flows the support of all science, art, learning, and the charities which minister to the humanities of life, all carrying their beneficent effects to the people as a whole."[2]

Business was commended by the President for correcting its own abuses through its responsible organizations with a minimum of interference on the part of the government. As the exponent of this philosophy, W. E. Humphrey joined the commission. "He dominated it from that day on," said Senator Norris, "and the majority have followed him."[3] The effect of Humphrey's appointment was more far-reaching than any decision of the Supreme Court. It gave a radically altered policy and viewpoint to the commission.

[1] The following creed was recited by Commissioner Humphrey before the annual meeting of the U. S. Chamber of Commerce, May 20, 1925:

"I express the faith of the majority of the Commission as it is composed today when I say:

We do not believe that success is a crime.

We do not believe that failure is a virtue.

We do not believe that wealth is presumptively wrong.

We do not believe that poverty is presumptively right.

We do not believe that industry, economy, honesty, and brains should be penalized.

We do not believe that incompetency, extravagance, idleness, and inefficiency should be glorified.

We do not believe that big business and crooked business are synonymous.

True, we will give closer scrutiny to big business than to small business because of its greater power for good or evil.

We believe that 90 per cent of American business is honest.

We believe that 90 per cent of American business is anxious to obey the law.

We want to help this 90 per cent of honest business.

We want to control or destroy the 10 per cent that is crooked.

In this endeavor we want your help. We hope to deserve it."

[2] *Boston Herald*, Nov. 28, 1920.

[3] *Congressional Record*, Mar. 20, 1926, p. 5963.

The new commissioner, together with his conservative colleagues, wished to stop certain investigations being made for the Senate. As already noted in the case of the meat packers, the power to conduct investigations under Section 6 of the Federal Trade Commission Act had been the cause of grave disagreement and virulent political criticism of the commissioners for their interference with business. The attack centered upon the economic division of the commission which, under the able Dr. Francis Walker, conducted these investigations. Members of the commission as well as certain Congressmen were desirous of curtailing this work, but they hesitated to do so directly for fear of the political reaction in the Senate.

Commissioner Van Fleet and Representative W. R. Wood, Republican chairman of the House sub-committee in charge of the Independent Offices Appropriations, had previously contrived a rider to the appropriation bill (approved Mar. 3, 1925, Ch. 468, 43 Stat. 1203), designed to narrow the commission's investigatory authority. This rider provided that: "no part of this sum shall be expended for investigations requested by either house of Congress, except those requested by concurrent resolution of Congress, but this limitation shall not apply to investigations and reports in connection with alleged violations of the antitrust law by any corporation." Under the authority of this rider the majority members ordered the chief economist to drop all investigations *except those of antitrust-law violations*. Dr. Walker refused to be put in the position of deciding which investigations involved infractions of the law. The next move was to refer the whole question to the Comptroller General.

This official side-stepped the issue by holding that the commission itself had to decide whether a particular investigation involved a violation of the antitrust laws. Meanwhile, Senator Norris began to inquire why the commission was not carrying forward an investigation in which he was deeply interested. The Van Fleet-Hunt-Humphrey triumvirate thereupon asked the Attorney General for his opinion as to the legality of the Senate's requests.[1] His ruling held that all the cases proposed for investigations by the Senate were alleged violations of the antitrust laws

---

[1] The annual report of the Federal Trade Commission for 1925, pp. 112–127, contains the text of the opinions, resolutions, etc., referred to.

and thereby made it the duty of the reluctant commission to proceed.

Balked in their first efforts at narrowing their own scope of jurisdiction, the conservative commissioners found another opportunity in 1928. Abram F. Myers, who as a lawyer in the Attorney General's office had written the opinion concerning the Senate investigations, was now a member of the commission. He proposed that the power to undertake economic studies under Section 6 of the act be broadly exercised. The violent reaction to this suggestion from conservatives in the House and on the commission showed the forces desirous of limiting the commission's significance as an independent regulatory body. Representative Wood tried vainly to cut off the appropriations for economic studies and to discredit the work of this division. His committee on appropriations condemned "economic investigations" and called the attention of Congress to this "mis-directed energy of the Commission."[1] Said Chairman Wood: "I am not able to grasp the necessity of the economist [Dr. Walker] or any good that he does except to promulgate a lot of wild-eyed theories and idealisms."[2]

By 1929 there was little sympathy with the Wilsonian conception of "pitiless publicity." Those dominating the commission had a very different attitude as to the relations of government and business and they coöperated with those in Congress who held similar views. The commission could not remain "independent" of the new political climate surrounding it and even its experts were eventually affected by the storm in which their superiors were principals. There was no magic haven to which the nonpolitical expert could withdraw when his directing officers disagreed upon fundamental matters of policy. The House refused to support Representative Wood's attack on the economic division. Although its sustenance was thus not dried up at the source, its effectiveness was considerably withered by the glare of unsympathetic commissioners.[3]

[1] House Report 293, 70th Congress, First Session, p. 9.

[2] For a dramatic debate of this whole question, see *Hearings* before the Subcommittee of the House Committee on Appropriations, Independent Offices Appropriations Bill, 1929, 70th Congress, First Session, pp. 515–605.

[3] The investigative work of the commission has been encouraged of late. The Seventy-fourth Congress granted $150,000 for an inquiry into the profits of the middlemen handling farm products.

The advent of Humphrey to the commission meant not only the discouragement of embarrassing investigations but also a more lenient regulatory policy. This was made manifest in changed rules of procedure.[1] There was adopted the practice of granting an informal hearing to a business concern before action was brought through a formal complaint. Thus opportunity was given for persuading the commission not to prosecute. Another innovation was the settlement of cases by stipulation. By pledging to discontinue objectionable practices, business concerns were thus saved the publicity of formal complaint and public prosecution. The commission carefully refrained from mentioning by names the companies involved. The procedure was widely used and applied even in cases of fraud and deliberate misrepresentation. The minority members, Nugent and Thompson, vigorously objected to this innovation, holding that pitiless publicity of wrongdoing was a weapon that the commission had no right to relinquish. The new policy was likewise denounced by progressives in the Senate.[2] The coming of Humphrey to the commission meant that private negotiation with concerns accused of unfair methods was substituted for the former policy of prosecution. The new commission definitely wanted to keep out of court. "In carrying out this new policy of coöperation, in no instance has any concern been unjustly driven into bankruptcy," Humphrey stated. "The credit of no honest business has been destroyed, nor the reputation of any innocent person blackened—results that frequently happened and were inevitable under the old policy."[3]

Another change under the new policy was the trade-practice conference. Although, as already noted, trade-practice submittals were started in 1919, they had not been emphasized or developed. Their purpose was to clarify for businessmen the meaning of unfair competitive methods. The commission simply invited representatives from a particular industry to meet and discuss "frankly and fully" those practices regarded as unfair or uncertain. Their conclusions were accepted by the commission as of informative value, but were accorded no legal significance. This was

[1] *Annual Report,* 1927, pp. 1-4.
[2] *Congressional Record,* Mar. 20, 1926, pp. 5944 *ff.*
[3] Speech at Winter Park, *op. cit.*

the first concession made by the commissioners to the industrialists who desired advice and coöperation from the government in self-regulation of business. Until 1926 two or three submittals were the average yearly, but during the next three years the average increased rapidly. The high point was reached in the winter of 1929 to 1930 when fifty-seven conferences met. This was twice the number held the year before and nearly half the total of 125 held between 1925 and 1930.

When the new procedural policy went into effect in 1926, Humphrey, Hunt, and Van Fleet were the ruling majority. In August, 1926, Van Fleet was replaced by Abram Myers. The latter had always favored the development of a law merchant and he looked upon the trade-practice conference as a means of broadening the legal conception as to what constituted unfair methods of competition. There was even the hope that, if the consensus of business opinion supported by the commission condemned certain practices, the courts might be brought around to a broader interpretation of unfair methods of competition. It might be possible thus to counteract the limitations of the Gratz Case in the face of a "new common law" built up by administrative precedents. Thus the commission might possibly reopen the path obstructed in the past by adverse judicial decisions.

If the commission could be persuaded to sponsor such rules, the definition of unfair methods of competition might be broadened and practices condemned that were not banned by the common law. By 1928 the trade-practice-conference agreements had been expanded to include not only the Group I rules, *i.e.*, those banning practices clearly unlawful under the statute, but also the Group II rules, *i.e.*, those eliminating methods not illegal but unfair and unethical in the opinion of the industry. The commission accepted these rules as "expressions of the trade."

Self-regulation of business was the current slogan for leaders in business and government. The 1926 meeting of the Chamber of Commerce of the United States of America was devoted to the topic. A trade-practice-conference division was created in 1926 to facilitate this aspect of the commission's work. A special director now superintended the preparation for and conduct of these conferences. He was, likewise, supposed to watch for violations of the rules agreed upon, but he was unable to do so because of inadequate facilities and the ever-increasing pressure of his work. By the end of 1929 the commission could not keep up with the applications for conferences. This same year, with enthusiasm for the trade-practice procedure at its height, the commission condemned as illegal the *secret* violation by industrialists of trade-practice agreements to which they were parties. If a businessman wished to denounce a trade-practice agreement, he should do so openly. A clandestine violation the commission decided to treat as a fraudulent practice. Could the commission punish for this offense? Would the agreements entered into by businessmen be enforced by the courts? The commission's acceptance of the secret-violation rule as an unfair method of competition under the law could be used to put the whole procedure to the test.

Myers, as an appointee of Hoover, believed that industry should remain as independent of government regulation as possible, but he thought also that the commission should assist in the formulation of trade practices by expressing an opinion with regard to business rules of conduct. Commissioner McCulloch likewise thought that the commission should "open the trail by deciding whether or not a given practice is lawful or unlawful so as to give the court an opportunity to adjudicate the question."[1]

Then suddenly the commission rescinded the secret-violation rule and in the spring of 1930 announced that it had decided to reconsider the rules which it had already accepted and which had been in use for months and years by over eighty industries. The commission offered no explanation other than the statement of the chairman that "some of the rules are, to say the least, questionable."[2]

The reaction from industry was one of consternation and strenuous objection. Why this sudden change of front? In May, 1930, a congress of industries was organized in Washington to negotiate with the commission. To the protest issued by this conference, the commissioners replied that, unless the industries by October, 1930, filed briefs showing why their rules should not be revised, the commissioner's revisions would stand. Few con-

[1] Memorandum as of May 29, 1929, p. 1. Quoted in *Public Regulation of Competitive Practices*, p. 241, National Industrial Conference Board.

[2] See statement of Senator G. P. Nye in *Hearings* before Subcommittee on the Judiciary, Senate, 72d Congress, First Session, (S. 2626, etc.), 1932, pp. 294–295.

cessions were actually made and the trade-practice-conference procedure was generally discredited among businessmen. This change in policy so restricted its scope and rendered so uncertain its validity that industrialists could see little point in attempting further coöperation with the commission in formulating codes of ethics. Various theories were put forward by businessmen in explaining the commission's change. Said one such apologist: "Recent criticism alleging lack of authority to function in this manner and misrepresentation of the purpose and effect of the trade-practice conference have undoubtedly been the cause for the varying views which the Commission has expressed."[1] Another explained:

It may be that the apparently vacillating and weak policy of the Commission is really based upon its fear that it may lead an industry into conflict with the Department of Justice, and that to prevent such an unfortunate contingency it uses extreme care and caution, thereby giving the impression that it "draws the teeth" of the trade-practice rules and weakens them unnecessarily.[2]

In fact, on May 1, 1930, John Lord O'Brian, assistant to the Attorney General in charge of the antitrust work, reassured the American Trade Association executives that the Department of Justice had "no hostility to the Federal trade-practice conferences," nor to the "proper activities and healthy growth of trade associations," but he indicated that there had been some "unhealthy" price fixing through so-called codes of ethics.[3] He protested informally to the Commission.

Although any explanation of the commissioners' motivation in making this "about-face" is necessarily speculation, the Department of Justice undoubtedly influenced them. The commission's reversal of viewpoint can be also correlated with certain changes in personnel. Commissioner Myers resigned in 1929 to become general counsel for an association of motion-picture exhibitors. He had successfully conducted the Motion Picture Conference and these interests were desirous of his further services. He was succeeded by Commissioner Charles March, who joined with Humphrey and Hunt and thereby created a conservative majority. The change in

[1] *Hearings, op. cit.*, pp. 152–153.
[2] *Ibid.*, p. 52.
[3] *Ibid.*, p. 306. For text of speech.

policy followed. The secret-violation rule was rescinded and a year later the general revision of rules was ordered.[1]

Conflicting personalities and widely divergent viewpoints among the commissioners must be put down as a basic cause of weakness in the Federal Trade Commission. These differences that handicapped accomplishment reflected in turn a change in national policy. "Politics" entered the commission directly through its members and further influenced its deliberations through the President and Congress.

Great faith has been placed in expert and independent administrative tribunals as the agencies best suited for exercising control over public affairs which, because of their technical character or peculiar complexity, lie beyond the competence of Congress. The theory has been accepted that such commissions suitably empowered by an act of Congress can then be left free to execute the law. The chief concern was that of securing experts who would function impartially. It was assumed that these officials would grow in wisdom and experience and build up a body of precedents that would in time (the courts being amenable) develop into a system of administrative justice.

These commissions establish their integrity and develop their prestige to the extent that their decisions are supported by the courts and their officers are freed from political interference. This means that once their field is indicated by Congress, the commissioners are left to interpret the statute in accordance with their views of public policy. It also means that when amendatory legislation is added it comes at the initiative and in accordance with the views of the commissioners. The Interstate Commerce Commission is the outstanding case of the development of administrative law under these favorable conditions. Henderson in 1924 wrote of the Federal Trade Commission: "I conceive it to be, potentially, an expert tribunal, of steady tenure and scrupulous judicial poise, firm in the public interest but impartial as between the private economic groups affected by its action."[2]

Any administrative agency should, of course, remain free from petty favoritism in dealing with private parties. But whether such

[1] A former member of the commission, Nelson B. Gaskill in his recent book *The Regulation of Competition*, 1935, throws new light upon the commission's change of policy at this time. See also J. T. Clark, *Federal Trust Policy*, Johns Hopkins University Press, 1931, pp. 236*ff.*

[2] *Op. cit.*, p. 341.

a commission can give substance and form to the "public interest" and remain detached from the conflict of special interests before it, is another question. Basically the function of the commission is to *favor* one interest as against another, the standard of judgment being the abstract concept of public welfare in the minds of the administrators. The application of such a criterion causes no particular difficulty in the Patent Office or the Steam-boat Inspection Service. The standards applied by these bureaucrats are not the subject of political controversy. The Federal Trade Commissioners, however, function in a very different context. Under the Republican party of Coolidge and Hoover, governmental policy *was* business policy. The official laissez faire attitude in so far as the *regulation* of industry was concerned inevitably meant the recession of the Federal Trade Commission from the supervision of big business. No group of bureaucrats was to sweep back the rising tides of economic enterprise and private initiative. The public interest in any given situation can only be interpreted in terms of certain group interests. The selection of the groups whose welfare is to be identified with the general welfare depends upon the policy to which a particular administration is committed.

The Federal Trade Commission was created under one conception as to how the general welfare was to be attained, but after 1925 its political and economic background had changed radically. The public interest was now identified with another combination of economic and social forces holding to a viewpoint antithetical to the recent past. What is possible for an administrative commission under these circumstances?

It seems to me [said Senator Norris] that if the Commission is to function, if it is to continue to perform the work that the law designed it to perform, its personnel must be of men who believe in that kind of a law. For the purpose of the discussion we must assume that that kind of a law is right. I am not quarreling with any man who disagrees with me in that assumption, but he must agree, even though he does not agree in the law, that if we have a law at all, and if we are honest about it, it is based on the assumption that the law is good and that that kind of a commission can do some good for our people.[1]

The Federal Trade Commission kept within the letter of the law, but, as we have seen, the statutes can be variously adminis-

[1] *Congressional Record*, Mar. 20, 1926, p. 5962.

tered. Special interests recognized this and fought for their interpretation of the law. The commission as a form of organization
has proved adequate in protecting administrators from coercion
by special interests. The commissioners abruptly altered their
course despite the violent protest from trade associations. They
investigated powerful corporations in spite of the efforts of the
congressional critics to discredit their work. If no remedial legislation has followed their reports, it is the politicians, not the administrators, who must be held accountable. The character of
their responsibilities and the great resources of the interests they
are called upon to regulate have rendered their task difficult but
by no means insuperable. Special interests have on the whole
responded hopefully when the commission has attempted coöperative undertakings. With regard to investigations, the commission
has found that some concerns willingly assist while others debate
every step, create difficulties, and prolong negotiations unduly.[1]

It cannot be said that the commission consciously succumbed to
certain economic groups, even though their pressure has been
great at times. The commission has clearly responded, however, to
the indirect influence of these forces as they have acted through
their political representatives. It was to this that Senator Norris
objected. At the time of Humphrey's appointment, he stated:
"It seems to me that we are justified in saying that there has been
an attempt going on at the head of the government to fill the
commission, as well as other commissions, with men who have no
sympathy for the law that is provided for the commission itself."[2]

Humphrey's views were well-known and his appointment
could well be taken as an expression of policy by the chief executive. Although the commissioner was harshly criticized in both
House and Senate, no reflections were cast upon his honesty,
ability, or sincerity of purpose. He was known as a staunch
defender of business and of laissez faire. Members of Congress
who differed with these views condemned his appointment. The
issue raised is really a very fundamental one. Can we question the
President's right to appoint any one he chooses to serve on administrative bodies if his appointees meet the statutory requirements

[1] *Hearings* of Independent Offices, Appropriation Bill, House Appropriation
Committee, 1931, p. 134.
[2] *Congressional Record*, Mar. 20, 1926, p. 5963.

and are known as men of honesty and ability? Is the President to be restricted in his selection to men whose views coincide with the theories of those already serving on a given commission? We are confronted with contradictory concepts of administration. If an integrated and responsible bureaucracy is sought, then Presidential control and leadership is necessary. Such a system cannot be reconciled with the concept of administration by *ad hoc* regulatory agencies working independently in fields that are the storm centers of politics.

Could President Coolidge be accused of bad faith in appointing commissioners who differed in viewpoint from the political leaders of 1914? He could not dodge his responsibility when the time came to make appointments. There was no guarantee that his appointee's view of standing "firm in the public interest" would be acceptable to a later President. Yet, if the officials on such boards are not in sympathy with the administration, the President's program is threatened when it falls within the ambit of their authority. To the extent that the interposition by the chief executive is admitted, the concept of administration by independent, judicious, and expert tribunals is vitiated. The economic and political theories of Humphrey were anathema to the new administration.

President F. D. Roosevelt, in requesting Humphrey to resign, said: "I do not feel that your mind and my mind go along together on either the policies or the administering of the Federal Trade Commission, and, frankly, I think it is best for the people of this country that I should have a full confidence." In other words, the President felt that the public interest demanded unity of direction in the regulation of industry. He did not regard the commission as unrelated to executive policies.

The court, in considering the removal of Humphrey, stated: "Whether the power of the President to remove an officer shall prevail over the authority [of Congress] to condition the power by fixing a definite term and precluding a removal except for cause will depend upon the character of the office."[1] Commissioner

---

[1] *Rathbun v. United States*, 79 L. ed. (Adv. 908) or New York Times, May 28, 1935, p. 1. See James Hart, *Tenure of Office under the Constitution*, Johns Hopkins Press, 1930, for a brilliant discussion of the necessity for judicious, scientific, and independent commissions.

Humphrey was held to occupy a position essentially judicial in character. A distinction was made between such an officer and "officers appointed to aid the President in the performance of his constitutional duties." The court acted within the narrow and necessary confines of legalism. The judges looked at the office and not the man. The former was deemed judicial in character. That the latter was not judicial in character was not the business of the court. By nature Humphrey was a fighter and a partisan. He brought a definite philosophy to his task. He differed from the President as to how business should be regulated. The President regarded the regulation of trade practices as part of his task of promoting business recovery. But he suffered a double defeat before the Supreme Court. In the Schechter poultry case, decided at the same time, the President was told that he could not constitutionally approve codes of "fair competition" for industry. The delegation of congressional power was too broad under the N.R.A. and the procedure too sweeping. The court declared that what are unfair methods of competition must be decided "in particular instances, upon evidence in the light of particular competitive conditions and of what is found to be a specific and substantial public interest."[1]

The courts have consistently discouraged the efforts of the Federal Trade Commission to develop a law merchant. Business regulation has meant the prevention of those abuses which the courts are willing to regard as unfair. Judicial precedents rather than present needs are thus made the determining factors. The judges reserve the privilege of deciding when business practices affect the public interest and thereby come under the jurisdiction of the Federal Trade Commission. The commissioners have had their sphere defined by a series of court decisions. Humphrey championed these restrictions. President Roosevelt was unwilling to accept such limitations on the power of the federal government to control business practices. The Supreme Court upheld the Humphrey philosophy.

The President cannot constitutionally prescribe fair methods of competition nor can he bring an independent commission into line by removing antagonistic members. The issue is a basic one. Can the federal government take an active and responsible

[1] *Schechter Poultry Corporation v. United States*, 295 U.S. 495.

part in fixing the conditions of business enterprise when the chief executive lacks the power to unite all federal agencies in the achievement of this goal? The Supreme Court has decreed that constitutional limitations bar the way. The Constitution cannot, of course, anticipate all the demands made upon government by an industrial society. Even rubber cannot be stretched beyond a certain point. But the action of the Supreme Court caused the cynical to remark that the depression was perfectly constitutional but that efforts toward recovery proved contrary to our fundamental law. If the federal government is to be held responsible for business recovery, constitutional objections must be met. Administrative agencies must have adequate authority and unified direction. Independent and hence isolated commissions restricted to the performance of police duties are not suited to a positive and constructive leadership in industrial relations.

For the present, the control of business remains too controversial and too vital a political issue to be entirely relegated to any commission independent of close control by the policy-formulating agencies of the government. Administrators cannot be given the responsibilities of statesmen without incurring likewise the tribulations of politicians. The administrative machinery must be suited to the nature of the burden it is to bear. The Supreme Court was consistent in its decisions upholding Humphrey and condemning the N.R.A. Whether the nation will alter the Constitution and give the authority needed by administrative agencies to control industry under Presidential direction depends upon the view of governmental responsibility that is ultimately taken. The Supreme Court found a legal limitation upon the President in his relations to administrative commissions. Can a coherent and responsible view of the public welfare ever be achieved by various independent agencies working in their limited jurisdictions? The Supreme Court chose to regard the quasi-judicial functions of the Federal Trade Commission as being of determinant importance. But our independent commissions have also legislative and executive responsibilities that call for the formulation of policy. What is the President to do when the work of "independent" commissions and their province of administration impinges upon his task of executive leadership? The story of the Federal Power Commission casts some light upon this question.

Chapter IX

THE FEDERAL POWER COMMISSION

"Here! You may nurse it a bit, if you like!" said the Duchess to Alice, flinging the baby at her as she spoke.

THE Federal Power Commission took its place in the federal administration as the product of a bitter and protracted legislative struggle between the conservationists and the water-power interests. Congress had long been their battleground. Here the legislators were torn between satisfying the cry for strict regulation and the demand for free and rapid development of power resources. The first general water-power legislation, put through Congress in 1910, defeated its own purpose by making too many concessions to both the grabbers and the conservationists. The enactment of the Water Power Act of June 10, 1920 (41 Stat. 1063), established the Federal Power Commission and marked a victory for the forces striving to extend federal control. Congress placed in the arms of administrative officials a bothersome problem that it was unable to handle itself. The political turmoil that marked the inception of the act has likewise characterized its subsequent administration.

"Just one more commission!" exclaimed a critical Congressman when the measure was brought up. "Just one more arm of Congress which will be stronger than Congress itself. The bill is bureaucratic, written by bureau chiefs, and endorsed by three Secretaries. It gives no western states any hand in the control of water power within their confines and no share in any of the returns."[1]

An infringement of states rights was seen by Representatives and Senators from the far West and the South where quick water-power development was desired. Westerners objected to strengthening federal jurisdiction because of the power that the government

---

[1] Quoted by Jerome G. Kerwin, *Federal Water Power Legislation*, Columbia University Press, 1926. This study is invaluable for the events leading up to the creation of the commission.

already held through its control of the public domain in their states. Opposition to conservation was voiced by the eastern and Middle Western investors in private water-power enterprises. The electrical industry presented a united opposition for years, although after 1911 a faction friendly to conservation appeared.

In the years just before the World War the conservationists built up a well-organized and ably directed lobby. They saw their opportunities and they took advantage of them. They used the prestige of presidential support, and they found allies in the Forest Service, in the Interior Department, in the War Department, and among the House Committees. They regarded themselves as the guardians of the people's rights and they successfully identified their cause with the public welfare.

That regulation of the water-power industry was necessary, Congress conceded. An *ad hoc* regulatory body was its contribution to a problem demanding leadership of the first order. The proper control of water power meant both the conservation of natural resources and the development of the electrical wealth in the streams and rivers. The creation of the Federal Power Commission did not reconcile this paradox—it merely shifted the scene of conflict. Relieving Congress of this burden and placing it before a body of qualified administrators might in time have brought a solution, but the commission established was woefully inadequate in the light of its responsibilities.

This body was composed of the Secretary of the Interior, the Secretary of War, and the Secretary of Agriculture, all serving ex officio. The statute provided for a full-time executive secretary at a salary of $5000. The work of the commission was to be performed by the engineering, technical, and clerical personnel of the three departments represented by their secretaries. The duties of the board were to collect data on the utilization of water-power resources and the power industry and to issue licenses for developing water power on navigable streams or waters on the public lands of the United States.

Reassured by the existence of this agency, the conservationists lost some of the drive toward a definite goal that had fired their zeal and justified their agitation. Their scrutiny relaxed. Postwar problems absorbed the attention of the public. But the power interests were very vitally concerned in what the government proposed to do. The promoters and developers of the industry, the hydroelectric engineers in their employ, the bond brokers, the real estate agents—all turned their attention to the Federal Power Commission and focused it upon the solitary executive secretary who bore the brunt of the labor and responsibility.

How were the officials now to execute the Water Power Act in the public interest? The terms of the statute were broad. The law as finally enacted has aptly been called a kind of hybrid. It reflected the long struggle between the private operators and those favoring government ownership. The statute provided for the licensing or leasing of federal power sites for a period not to exceed fifty years and for possible recovery by the federal government or transfer to a state or municipality upon compensation equal to the net investment.

On its face, the statute indicated that the purpose of Congress was to provide for the improvement of navigation and the development of water power through the instrumentality of private and governmental agencies that the commission was to license. The valuable privilege of generating electrical power from the streams under the jurisdiction of the federal government was to be granted under conditions that would promote the fundamental conservation purposes of the act and at the same time protect the consumers of the generated power against exorbitant charges. The act contained one provision for guiding the commission as to the policy to be pursued in the allotment of water-power facilities. Section 7 stated that the commission should give preference to applications by states and municipalities if their plans were as well adapted as those of private applicants for conserving and utilizing in the public interest the navigation and water resources of a region. As between private firms, the commission should consider the relative ability of the applicants to carry out plans best adapted to utilize water-power resources in the public interest. What actual conditions should the applicant meet? What plans could best carry out the public interest? Despite the detailed provisions of the act, its purposes were open to broad differences in interpretation.

Nevertheless, the bill was hailed hopefully as marking "the end of the period of discussion and controversy which for more than a decade had been waged both in Congress and outside over a national policy with respect to water power under Federal

Control."[1] Certainly the measure was an improvement over the entirely unsuitable acts of 1901 and 1910, passed when there was little understanding of the significance of electric power for industry and transportation. The new commission regarded the flood of applications for licenses as "abundant evidence both of the extent to which former legislation stood in the way of power development and of the generally satisfactory character of the present legislation."

The act made available privileges that industrialists were eager to secure, but the law hedged these prizes about with certain provisions that were regarded as irksome. The power companies sought a liberal interpretation from the commission. Chief Accountant King has stated,

> While the rules and regulations of the commission were being considered, it was repeatedly asserted by representatives of the power interests that they had a part in the preparation and passage of the Federal Water Power Act, that they knew what was meant by certain passages and provisions of the act, and that Congress never intended that the act should be construed and administered as proposed by the Commission's staff.[2]

According to King's observations, the power interests even pressed the commission to recognize in its rules and regulations acts prohibited by the statute itself. They wished to render inoperative the statutory provisions relating to net investments, they objected to any regulation calling for the establishment of a depreciation reserve,[3] and they denied the authority of the commission to regulate accounting practices.[4] This controversy extended over a period of almost two years.

From the very beginning of its activities the commission had sought the advice and coöperation of those coming within its jurisdiction. Soon after the staff was organized in 1920, a draft of regulations relating to forms of applications, permits, licenses, etc., was drawn up by the commission and mailed to applicants, to officers of the National Electric Light Association, and to other interested persons for examination and criticism. Some written

[1] Federal Power Commission, *First Annual Report*, 1920, p. 5.
[2] *Hearings* before Senate Committee on Interstate Commerce, Senate Resolution 80 and S. 3619, 71st Congress, Second Session, 1930, p. 36.
[3] Federal Power Commission, *Second Annual Report*, p. 226.
[4] *Ibid.*, p. 244.

replies were received, and in August, 1920, a series of conferences was held between representatives of the commission and bankers, engineers, and representatives of the National Electric Light Association. The Water Conservation Committee of the Engineering Council of America was consulted as well as government officials concerned with public health, Indian rights, forest preservation, etc.

The regulations as amended by these conferences were approved by the commission and promulgated in September. These first regulations included matters covered in considerable degree by earlier departmental rules, but new and more complex problems remained. Intricate questions of finance and proper methods of accounting had to be considered. Preliminary drafts of rules were prepared and submitted to government officials and interested parties. Further conferences were held with the Engineering Council and with representatives of the N.E.L.A. to decide upon rules governing technical matters in order that the regulations might be suited to the actual conditions of electrical development. After extensive hearings, the regulations were adopted and promulgated in February, 1921. Certain groups, notably the Empire State Gas and Electric Association, objected to some of the rulings relating to depreciation and amortization, but the commission overruled the objections.[1]

On Mar. 4, a new administration came into power and new Cabinet officers appeared on the commission. Upon the urging of the Water Power Committee of the N.E.L.A., the matter was reopened and further hearings were held. A group of bankers from Lee Higginson & Co., the Guaranty Trust Company, Harris, Forbes & Company, and the Electric Bond and Share Company were invited to attend and present their views. This conciliatory attitude on the part of the Federal Power Commission was deliberate. Its first annual report carried this significant statement:

The coöperation which has been effected between the Commission and other agencies, such as the American Engineering Council, the National Electric Light Association and the National Association of Public Utility Commissioners is the expression of a definite policy on the part of the Commission. It is charged under the provisions of the law with the protection

[1] *Ibid.*, pp. 226, 244.

of the public interest in the great national water power resources, and this is its first duty. It is also its duty to encourage by every legitimate means the development of these resources for public use and enjoyment and in the interest of the country's economic progress. It believes that this development can best be hastened through united action; and it stands ready to coöperate with every agency, public or private, that is willing to approach mutual problems in a spirit of coöperation.[1]

In November, 1921, the National Electric Light Association reopened the whole matter of requirements for accounting systems, and at its request further hearings were granted. At this time both the law itself governing the commission and the commission's policy were attacked. As a result the commission asked its chief counsel to draw up an exhaustive opinion interpreting the whole Water Power Act and also requested the N.E.L.A. and the National Association of Public Utility Commissioners to submit briefs. The chief counsel's final opinion was reviewed and approved by the solicitors of the War, Interior, and Agricultural Departments, and then definitely adopted by the commission itself, thereby settling the matter. Since the regulations already adopted were in accordance with the powers and duties of the Commission as thus interpreted, no changes further were made.[2] But the commission's policy of harmony and coöperation in regulation had received a rude blow.

This experience of the commission is significant as an outstanding case where outside interests were permitted to exercise great influence in the formulation of regulations. Many of the problems were technical and the rulings of the commission had to be adjusted to actual conditions if they were to prove workable. The task in law making here lay beyond the competence of a legislative assembly. Organized groups in the industry clearly acted as a check upon the administrative discretion of the power commission. The "public interest" lay at some undefined point between preventing selfish exploitation of the nation's power resources and encouraging companies to engage in the generation of electricity.

The executive secretary was doubtless speaking in good faith when he wrote that in rule making the commission and its staff "represent the public as other governmental agencies represent

[1] Federal Power Commission, *First Annual Report*, pp. 19–20.
[2] Federal Power Commission, *Annual Report*, 1922, p. 3.

the public in performing the duties with which they are charged by law."[1] Administrative inefficiency resulted from the commission's lack of control over its work. The distribution of water-power regulation among three departments plus this special commission made it impossible to determine clearly the cost of administration or to fix responsibility.

Since the law provided that the work of the commission should be performed through the technical, clerical, and other personnel of the departments that were represented on the commission, the Comptroller General ruled that assistance could not be sought elsewhere and that it was optional with the department secretaries as to what extent they would undertake the work of the commission. The Bureau of the Budget turned down the request of the commission for increased appropriations, and appeals, of course, could not be taken to the congressional committees on appropriations.[2]

The staff was confronted with the physical impossibility of keeping its work current. The commissioners wrote to the Director of the Budget in 1926 recommending amendments to the Federal Water Power Act so as to secure direct appropriations for all its activities, direct employment of personnel, and authority to use receipts from government dams to build a fund from which Congress might appropriate for the work of the commission. These proposals were rejected although nearly six years' experience had demonstrated the need for reform.

It seems obvious that a strong administrative commission is essential if powerful economic forces are to be controlled. Yet, the Federal Power Commission as first established was entirely inadequate to the task confronting it.

Practically all the work devolved upon the executive secretary and, since his recommendations were almost always accepted by his superiors, one-man control resulted.[3] A commission of Cabinet officers meant a shifting group of political leaders unfamiliar with the problems of the commission. The development of an intelligent policy was hardly to be expected by men who were able to give so

[1] Quoted from private letter of Merrill to Comer. J. P. Comer, *Legislative Functions of National Administrative Authorities*, p. 243.
[2] *Hearings, op. cit.*, pp. 259–260. Testimony of Merrill.
[3] *Ibid.*, p. 9.

little time to the problem. Nor could a consistent policy be carried out by a commission with an impermanent personnel. Before the commission had been in existence ten years, the commission changed five times, twice with a clean sweep, there having been five different Secretaries of War, five different Secretaries of the Interior, and four different Secretaries of Agriculture. A rapid turnover in personnel is unfortunate in any administrative body, but the condition was here aggravated by the fact that the commissioners were ex officio. They were therefore less likely to take a direct interest in the peculiar responsibilities of this regulatory body. Even when this occurred, their short tenure and the pressure of other duties made almost impossible any consistent interpretation of the public interest in water-power development.

The permanent group of subordinate officials who might have provided some degree of continuity and consistency was lacking. Many of the administrative tasks were "farmed out" to the departments. Each department regarded jealously its contributions to the power commission. With no guidance in policy, disagreement among experts in subordinate positions occurred. After trying for nearly nine years to regulate effectively water-power development, Secretary Merrill finally joined forces with the industry and became permanent chairman of the American section of the World Power Conference. His new salary was twice that received in governmental employ. He was discouraged with his losing struggle and with bucking the politicians. The service hereby lost an active, able, and experienced official. With the knowledge acquired during eleven years in the Forest Service, of which seven years were spent as chief engineer in charge of water-power work, Merrill collaborated with congressional committees in formulating water-power legislation and in supplying data and advice. He organized the Federal Power Commission and, while sympathetically inclined to the power companies, he did not fail to stress the inadequacy of the commission's facilities as tested in actual practice.

Defects in organization can be put down as a partial explanation of the commission's weakness. Congress had saddled a heavy burden upon an administrative body incapable of carrying the load.

The officials charged with the direct responsibility of enforcing the Federal Water Power Act of 1920 were well aware of the faults of organization and personnel of the power commission. The various Cabinet officers who served as ex officio commissioners prior to 1930 were dissatisfied with the conditions of administration. These commissioners attempted to secure amendatory legislation in 1921, in 1926, and again in 1928. They bluntly stated that the public interest could not be protected under their limited authority.[1]

Their problems cannot be appreciated without considering the attitude of the power interests toward the commission. There cannot be the slightest doubt that great pressure was exerted upon the Federal Power Commission and that the commission was forced to give way to this administrative lobbying. Abundant proof of this was uncovered by the Senate investigation in 1930.

The question turned largely upon how closely the federal authorities were to scrutinize the accounts of the power companies. The commission had the task of auditing and preserving the records of the original cost of water-power projects for two purposes: (1) in order to aid the commission and state regulatory bodies in passing upon the rates charged by these companies for the electricity generated; (2) in order to fix the "net investment" that the government would have to pay if it were to take over the property at some future date.[2]

The personnel definitely assigned to the work of the commission was wholly inadequate to make these cost determinations and valuations, the result being that much of this work was delegated to the field agencies of the three departments, namely, the Corps of Engineers of the War Department; the Forest Service of the Department of Agriculture; and the Geological Survey of the Department of the Interior. In the opinion of Executive Secretary Merrill and Chief Accountant King, the field agencies of the

---

[1] Federal Power Commission, *Annual Report*, 1928, p. 2.

[2] The basis for determining "net investment" is the actual legitimate original cost of projects constructed new under license, or the "fair value" as of the date of license of projects already constructed when license is issued. Under certain specific provisions of the act the actual cost of projects constructed new under license was to be determined by the application of certain rules and principles laid down in the act itself, namely, the accounting rules of the Interstate Commerce Commission applicable to steam railroads. The act prescribed no rule or method to be followed in determining the fair value of projects already constructed when license was issued.

departments were not equipped for this work.[1] A generous valuation was obviously to any company's advantage and many were charged with questionable practices and with padding their accounts. If these abuses were to be checked, experienced valuation engineers and accountants were needed. Since ordinary bookkeepers were not qualified, the commission was forced to rely upon such specialists as the department chose to employ. Over a seven-year period one valuation engineer and one to four accountants were appointed. King found that the power companies failed to comply with requests for information, to answer correspondence, to file statements, or to produce records. They were lax in keeping their accounts according to the commission's rules and some even used obstructive tactics.[2]

Out of this disagreement as to how thoroughly the books of the power companies should be supervised arose the chief defection within the commission. When Merrill was secretary he supported Chief Accountant King's pleas for more assistance. After his resignation from the commission in 1929, his successor, F. E. Bonner, pursued a very different line.

Here is a very clear illustration of how a difference of personal viewpoint may occasion a complete reversal in administrative policy. Had the commission been composed of active and alert administrators, the personal views of their executive secretary would have been a matter of little consequence, but the peculiar structure of the commission placed great discretion in the hands of this civil servant.

On Mar. 4, 1929, three new Cabinet members had become the ex officio commissioners. On July 1, 1929, Bonner undertook his duties and in the next three months a new chief engineer, a new solicitor, and a new chief counsel came to the commission. Of the eight chief officers only the chief accountant remained as a link to the old commission.

In marked contrast with his predecessor, the new secretary was entirely complacent in his acceptance of the limitations of the commission's activities. He saw no need for a special staff of accountants and even expressed the suspicion that "the work was

[1] See *Annual Reports* from about 1923 to 1928 inclusive, where statements to this effect are made and repeated from year to year.

[2] *Hearings, op. cit.*, p. 37.

purposely allowed to fall behind in order to provide bases for demands on Congress for increased appropriations."[1] He charged that the auditing department had been much too strict and that the widespread publicity accorded their findings had amounted to persecution of the power industry.[2] Much more was brought out in the Senate investigation to show Bonner's exceedingly conciliatory attitude toward the power interests. It was at his request, for example, that Russell, the new solicitor of the commission, before taking office, conferred with a representative of the Electric Bond and Share Company. At this conference Russell was told how he ought to run the solicitor's office, and was especially advised against following the advice of Mr. King, chief accountant, who was alleged to have treated the power companies unfairly in accounting matters. Bonner said that he had insisted on this conference in order that Russell might have the power companies' side of the case as well as King's.[3]

The solicitor testified that, when he protested to Bonner about the illegality of certain plans, the latter replied, "I think it is your duty as the solicitor, when I find unworkable provisions of this water power act that cannot be complied with, to find me a way around it."[4]

Without going into the validity of the charges and countercharges which were evoked by the Senate investigation and which furnished the press with sensational stories, the fact can be clearly established from the annual reports that a reversal of policy took place under Bonner. He recognized no inadequacies in the commission's authority. "During the nine years that have passed since the enactment of the law its administration has suggested no need for altering the present scope of its regulatory provisions," he reported. He greatly minimized the importance of federal regulation of electrical power, according to the view that "its transportation lacks the complicated interstate relations affecting large groups of states, as in the case of railroad transportation."[5] His desire to hasten water-power developments was manifest.

[1] *Ibid.*, p. 92.
[2] *Ibid.*, pp. 105–107.
[3] *Ibid.*, p. 13.
[4] *Ibid.*, p. 21.
[5] Federal Power Commission, *Annual Report*, 1929, p. 6.

In his last report he stated: "Through efforts made during the past year the docket has been practically cleared of applications for large projects contemplating early construction operations."[1]

In evaluating the part of Mr. Bonner, it is exceedingly difficult to get at the truth. The investigation conducted by a Senate committee revealed many facts which, according to their selection and arrangement, can be made into a case more or less derogatory to Bonner's administration. The judgment of his attitude by the press and by those in important governmental positions is of more significance than the truth or falsity of the accusations themselves, for these opinions were determining factors in subsequent events.

President Hoover in a message to Congress Dec. 7, 1929, urged a reorganization of the commission and an extension of its authority. Several bills were introduced to accomplish these ends. The complexities involved in bringing within the scope of the commission's authority certain aspects of interstate power transactions apparently discouraged Congress from undertaking such legislation,[2] but the Senate investigation held during the spring of 1930 abundantly demonstrated the breakdown of power regulation. Something had to be done.

Congress wiped the slate clean and directed the President to appoint a fresh commission. On June 23, 1930, an amendatory act was approved by President Hoover's establishing a board of five full-time commissioners. A great deal of indignation was expended upon the iniquities of the power trust and the shortcomings of Executive Secretary Bonner. Righteous wrath characterized most of the discussions. The basic problems were not considered. Congressional energy was expended in denunciation of the "power interests" and in tinkering with the details of the administrative board. Should there be three members or five? More fundamental questions were left unanswered: Should conservation be stressed or rapid development of water power? Should the authorities actively coöperate or strictly and severely regulate? Should the federal government play an active or a passive role?

Congress made no positive statement as to what it understood to be the public interest in water-power development. Wide

[1] *Ibid.*, 1930, p. 7.
[2] *Ibid.*, p. 15.

discretion for interpreting the act accordingly remained in the hands of the commissioners. Immediately upon taking up their duties the new commissioners discharged the solicitor, the chief accountant, and the executive secretary. Commissioner George Otis Smith explained: "Our reason for treating the three men alike is to stop immediately the internal strife which has made the staff anything but a working body."[1]

The Senate was not satisfied with this explanation: was not Bonner the discordant element and had he not already indicated his intention of resigning? In the Senate the commission's removals were compared with decimation of the Roman legionaries, in which every tenth man was counted off for slaughter regardless of his guilt or innocence in order that discipline might be restored in the ranks. Political capital was made of the fact that Russell and King were dismissed in the midst of trying a much disputed case, and that Bonner shortly after leaving the power commission was given a job in the Department of the Interior.

The Senate attempted to recall the name of Commissioner Smith which they had already ratified, arguing that confirmation did not become final until the conclusion of the two-day period allowed by the Senate rules for the presentation of a motion to reconsider. By a vote of 44 to 37 the Senate sought an opportunity of retiring from office the appointee just confirmed.

President Hoover on Jan. 10, 1931, informed the Senate: "I cannot admit the power in the Senate to encroach upon the Executive functions by removal of a duly appointed executive officer under the guise of reconsideration of his nomination." At the same time, in a statement to the press, Hoover protested against the attempt made in the Senate to symbolize him as the defender of the "power trust." The problem of power control was much discussed as a possible campaign issue and the opportunity to turn this situation to political account was not neglected by the President's opponents.

Senators displayed an eagerness to criticize, but the entire episode of recalling appointees was doomed to futility. The chief executive was under fire from the Senate and his appointees were made the target of political sniping. From the liberal camp in Congress and without much criticism arose. The records of the

[1] *Congressional Record*, Jan. 5, 1931, p. 1390.

new appointees were severely scrutinized. McNinch's standing as a Democrat was attacked and his appointment was alleged to have been in recognition of his aid to Hoover in the 1928 campaign. Garsaud's record was combed for evidence of subservience to the public utilities in Louisiana. George Otis Smith's past was reviewed and his writings on power development examined. The charges were not conclusively proved, but many critics were willing to condemn the new commissioners on circumstantial evidence. The commissioners apparently tried to "live down" the fact that they had newly emerged from the hotbed of politics. Despite the efforts of the new commissioners they could not entirely divorce themselves from the recent past. Placed in this difficult position, they responded courageously by endeavoring to investigate power problems and submit positive recommendations to Congress.

Many informal conferences were held with representatives of applicants and licensees and studies were launched to gather facts upon which judgments might be made. Far from agreeing with Bonner that electrical transmission was a local problem that might be left chiefly to the states, the new commissioners took the view that electrical-power development transcended state or even regional lines and was national in scope.[1]

The commission reported that the public interest required "the early vesting of authority in the Federal government to control, so far as it may be determined to be within its jurisdiction, the regulation both of electricity in interstate commerce and the holding company in the power industry."[2] Specific amendments to the Federal Water Power Act were suggested, to wit: that the prudent investment test be adopted to strengthen the commission's authority in fixing the proper cost basis, and that its regulatory authority be clarified, particularly with regard to the troublesome question of state versus federal jurisdiction. While these recommendations are in themselves not important to this discussion, if taken as reflecting the more positive nature of the reorganized commission, they are highly significant.

The fact remains that representing the public interest is a matter of individual judgment. No objective standard is possible. The

[1] Federal Power Commission, *Annual Report*, 1931, p. 7.
[2] *Ibid.*, 1932, p. 5.

policy of the commission from 1920 to March, 1933, was that of the Harding, Coolidge, and Hoover administrations. The commission, for example, in its annual report for 1931[1] stated that "excursions into management in the name of regulation, should be avoided. Results can be asked and required by the regulatory bodies, but the choice of means and the discovery of methods can better be left to private initiative." At that time the "public interest" dictated that the commission should do no more than supervise the development of power by private enterprise.

"That is a complete misconstruction of the intent of Congress as embodied in the Federal Water Power Act of 1920," the present vice-chairman of the commission recently declared.[2] "That act clearly contemplated not only the formulation of a national power program after a thorough survey of the nation's power resources, but specifically provided that the commission should submit recommendations to Congress whenever it deemed that any project should be developed by the federal government itself." Here the lapse of a few years has brought diametrically opposed interpretations of the statute.

The Roosevelt administration has provided strong political support for the aspirations of the commission. The changes in personnel, particularly the resignation of Chairman George Otis Smith and the appointment of Basil Manly, have brought the commission into full accord with the New Deal. Now the commission is stronger than it has ever been. It is engaged in the development of a national power policy.

Congress instructed the commission to build up a factual foundation for future action. The Norris-Rankin resolution passed by the Seventy-third Congress directed the commission to discover the rates charged for electricity in this country. The Electric Rate Survey was authorized in order to provide a factual basis to aid in standardizing rates. The National Power Survey was to disclose our needs for electrical power and the most efficient and economic sources for filling these requirements. Agreement between the administrators and the chief executive on basic policy has resulted in clarifying and strengthening the position

---

[1] Federal Power Commission, *Annual Report*, 1931, p. 10.

[2] Address of Basil Manly before City Club of Boston, Mar. 9, 1934. Also printed in *Congressional Record*, Mar. 26, 1934.

of the commission. Through the chief executive, the commission is linked with the other agencies of the government concerned with the development of power and the conservation of natural resources. The Federal Power Commission deals with a portion of the great mass of problems involving rivers, forests, and public lands. Its work has become to some extent coördinated with other agencies facing similar problems. A device for coördination was provided in President Roosevelt's appointment on July 9, 1934, of a National Power Policy Committee. Here representatives were brought together from the various federal agencies concerned with power development. The committee has served as an advisory body to the President for developing a unified national power policy.

In establishing the National Power Policy Committee on July 16, 1934, the President described its purpose in these words:

· Its duty will be to develop a plan for the closer coöperation of the several factors in our electrical power supply—both public and private—whereby national policy in power matters may be unified and electricity be made more broadly available at cheaper rates to industry, to domestic and, particularly, to agricultural consumers.

Several agencies of the government, such as the Federal Power and Trade Commissions, have in process surveys and reports useful in this connection. The Mississippi Valley Committee of Public Works is making studies of the feasibility of power in connection with water storage, flood control and navigation projects. The War Department and Bureau of Reclamation have under construction great hydro-electric plants. Representatives of these agencies have been asked to serve on the committee. It is not to be merely a fact-finding body, but rather one for the development and unification of national power policy.[1]

The Federal Power Commission is thus regarded as but one among several agencies that must work together in a common purpose. The Roosevelt administration has undertaken to create cheap electricity and to develop national water-power resources. To achieve this broad and inclusive goal it is necessary that

[1] Taken from the President's letter authorizing creation of the committee. The members of this committee are: Secretary of Interior Ickes, Chairman; Dr. Elwood Mead, Reclamation Bureau; Frank R. McNinch, Chairman of Federal Power Commission; Morris L. Cook, Water Resources Committee, P.W.A.; Major-general Edward M. Markham, Chief of Engineers; Robert E. Healy, Federal Securities Commission; T. W. Norcross, Forest Service; David E. Lilienthal, T.V.A.

officials plan and coöperate. Thus the power commission is guided in its administrative tasks by a policy created in part by another agency. So far no evidence of disagreement has appeared. This is a crucial time.

What is to be the place of the Federal Power Commission? At present we cannot entertain the concept of administration by an entirely independent commission. The President's economic philosophy, his political theories, and his legislative program touch upon the general jurisdiction of the Federal Power Commission. His task as chief executive is to fortify the commission so that it can meet its statutory responsibility. It now has the political support that is essential if any accomplishment is to result. It is now protected from the influences of economic and sectional groups by the strength of the President's interest and guidance. If the commission during this administration lays down a definite policy after a careful survey of our power resources and national needs, its chances of realizing its objectives and of retaining its leadership will be vastly enhanced. The White House is occupied by transients; our commissions are better able to ensure continuity in policy. No sensible commissioners will bluntly defy the President, but no wise President will ignore the views of a commission that has gained public confidence and esteem through the clarity and thoroughness of its understanding of the nation's power interests. In the past unfavorable political conditions made accomplishment almost impossible. Now the situation is changed and the commission need only take advantage of the opportunities of the present. Once a definite, constructive policy is established, the Federal Power Commission need have little fear of political storms that may arise in the future.

The case of the power commission throws much light on the fundamental question of this book. What conception of the public interest determines our federal administrative organization and activity? Prior to the Roosevelt administration neither the Federal Power Commission nor any other administrative agency assumed that water-power development was the clear responsibility of the federal government. The New Deal brought a change of viewpoint. With the sweeping terms of the holding-company legislation we are not concerned. From the standpoint of administration, the striking development is the attempt on the part of officials to formulate under general presidential supervision "what is in the public interest."

Expert commissions such as the Interstate Commerce Commission, the Federal Power Commission, and others have long had the duty not only of carrying out the laws laid down by Congress but also of suggesting amendatory legislation. A further development along the same line, particularly during Mr. Hoover's time, was the use of *ad hoc* commissions. These bodies were to make specific recommendations for legislative action. During the Roosevelt administration the chief executive and the bureaucracy have attempted to write the laws that they later expect to execute. Administrators have been invited not only to shoulder heavier responsibilities but likewise to inform Congress how this should be done. This tendency has gone very far in water-power legislation. The Power Policy Committee strongly recommended outlawing holding companies. The President in a message to Congress on Mar. 12, 1935, denounced the propaganda used by these companies in opposing such legislation. He clearly endeavored to arouse the investors against holding-company propaganda by a counterblast from the White House. "I have watched the use of the investors' money to make the investor believe that the efforts of Government to protect him are designed to defraud him," the President stated.

In the past the politically powerful groups with which the commission came into contact were chiefly identified with the private control and operation of power utilities. A change is now taking place among the social and political forces surrounding the commission. The creation of the Tennessee Valley Authority and the great federal projects on the Columbia River and at Boulder Dam will probably build up in time great vested interests supporting government ownership of power plants. In this way the political influence of those favoring governmental ownership can counteract the influence of those standing for private operation and vice versa. The pressure on the commission in the future will probably not be as one-sided as it has been in the past. A balance can thus be struck among the representatives of special interests. As advisers and co-workers in the technical field and as frank exponents of their own interests on controversial matters, they can then lay before the administrator their opinions, their desires, and their needs. Free coöperation with these various interests is compatible with the general welfare when the official is instructed in accordance with an accepted and responsible declaration of public policy. He cannot make his way against adverse economic and social pressures unless his administrative purpose is clear and his authority is commensurate with his goal. Establishing these conditions is a duty of political leadership which, if neglected, leaves the administrator as the residuary legatee of those political pressures to which the legislator is the rightful heir.

Chapter X

THE FEDERAL RADIO COMMISSION AND THOSE WHO SHARE THE AIR

"I passed by his garden, and marked, with one eye,
How the Owl and the Panther were sharing a pie:
The Panther took pie-crust, and gravy, and meat,
While the Owl had the dish as its share of the treat."

THE record of the Federal Radio Commission exemplifies in striking form the problem of administration in the public interest that underlies all our federal regulatory bodies. Congress has ordained that regulation is necessary to the national welfare and has set general statutory standards, but the terms in which this control is to be applied depend largely upon the way the law is interpreted by officials. If they are to act freely, certain conditions are essential. The Federal Power Commission demonstrated the necessity of an organization and staff adequate to carry the burden imposed by the statute. The story of the Federal Trade Commission shows how regulation can be weakened by unfavorable treatment at the hands of the courts and by dependence upon the Department of Justice for the prosecution of cases.

Of basic significance in all cases is the prevailing political climate. Commissioners have not interpreted the public interest in a positive and constructive fashion when the dominant political philosophy directed a minimum of interference with business enterprise. Now more aggressive regulation of business has become a national policy. Commissioners have thus gone forward on the political band wagon. Administrative activity has been coördinated in certain fields. The Federal Power Commission is linked with a Power Policy Committee. The Interstate Commerce Commission will probably extend its jurisdiction over all forms of commercial transportation crossing state lines.

The Federal Radio Commission has been absorbed by the Federal Communications Commission. Congress has given this new commission authority "to regulate interstate and foreign commerce in communications by wire and radio, so as to make available, so far as possible, to all of the people of the United States a rapid, efficient, nation-wide and world-wide wire and communications service with adequate facilities at reasonable rates."[1] The new commission has proceeded in a conservative fashion. The commissioners have stated that "if any changes are made, they will be evolutionary rather than revolutionary."

The first important act of the commission was its recommendation to Congress in January, 1935, that "no fixed percentages of radio broadcast facilities be allocated by statute to particular types or kinds of non-profit radio programs."[2] This was a victory for the commercial stations, although the commission reported that most of the interests concerned with radio were satisfied with the present system and desired no remedial legislation. The new commission has undertaken to discipline stations advertising products that are in disfavor with the Federal Trade Commission or under the ban of the Post Office Department. The most positive step on the part of the Federal Communications Commission was its order of June, 1935, that outlawed interlocking directorates. The application of ten leaders in the communications field to serve as officers or directors in more than one company in the communications industry was denied. Officials of the American Telephone and Telegraph Company, the International Telephone and Telegraph Company, the Western Union Telegraph Company, and the Radio Corporation of America were affected. Whether this decision will be upheld by the courts remains to be seen.

It is too soon to pass upon the work of the Federal Communications Commission, but the difficulties of its task can be appreciated by reviewing the experience of the Federal Radio Commission. Legislation to regulate broadcasting was enacted through the active aid and urging of the radio industry. The need for state "interference" in this field was evident to broadcasters long before Congress could be persuaded to act.

[1] The Federal Communications Commission was authorized by Public Act 416, 73d Congress, approved June 19, 1934.
[2] *Report of the Federal Communications Commission to Congress* pursuant to section 307(c) of the Communications Act of 1934, Jan. 22, 1935.

The initiator and guiding spirit of this movement for government regulation was the "rugged individualist," Herbert Hoover. Ardent advocate of self-government in industry, Secretary of Commerce Hoover strove to limit the sphere of coercive political authority and to utilize the resources of the state for the benefit of business. In radio, however, he saw an exceptional case. The first license to broadcast was issued by the secretary in 1921, but within a year over 500 stations were on the air. The necessity for regulation was inherent in the situation. With the number of wave lengths fixed by nature and by technical limitations, chaos was the alternative to regulation of competing broadcasters. In February, 1922, Secretary Hoover called the first American Radio Conference and brought together representatives of all branches of the radio industry. Extensive government control was advocated, suggestions for legislation were made, and a bill was introduced. Congress took no action and the Secretary of Commerce continued to license stations.

The conferences on the other hand became an annual fixture and the radio regulations promulgated by the Department of Commerce were based largely upon suggestions made at these meetings. Hoover became very popular with the radio interests and succeeded in ironing out various difficulties that arose, but his right to regulate the industry through exercising discretion in the issuance of licenses was uncertain.[1] In 1926 an adverse court decision followed by an opinion of the Attorney General reduced the secretary's powers to the ministerial function of granting permits to broadcast at request.[2] A mad scramble to get on the air ensued and a broadcast of bedlam resulted. The demand for government regulation was now imperative since the very existence of the industry was threatened.

The explanation of this paradoxical desire on the part of the radio industry to be regulated is, of course, obvious. But the question immediately arose in Congress as to whether radio should be regulated through one of the existing administrative agencies or by a special independent board.

[1] J. H. Morecraft, "What the Hoover Conference Did," *Radio Broadcast*, December, 1924.

[2] *United States v. Zenith Radio Corporation* (1926), 12 Fed. (2d) 616, 617. Opinion Attorney General, 132, July 8, 1926.

The uncertain answer to this question affected the early years of radio regulation in the United States. President Coolidge favored control by the Department of Commerce and opposed "government by commission" but the Senate frowned upon one-man control. The opinion was widely held that certain members of Congress wished to prevent Secretary Hoover from gaining the political prestige of disentangling the radio snarl.[1]

Where should the licensing authority be placed? The legislative battle hinged on this point. "Over on the House side," Senator Watson stated, "they were in favor of casting all this on the Department of Commerce, and when it came over to this side we said 'Commission or no legislation.' And then there was a sort of compromise arrangement, the idea being that the commission should operate for a year, and then should go back to the Department of Commerce."[2]

Thus the commission, established under the White Act of February, 1927, was the result of a political deal. Its "expectancy" of life was brief. Aligned against it, moreover, were the commercial radio interests that desired regulation by the Secretary of Commerce.

This hostility appeared clearly when the question of continuing the existence of the commission was considered. Whether or not to scrap the commission was an open question for several years. Some politicians appeared willing to kill the commission on one occasion by catching the bill to extend its life in a legislative jam with other radio legislation and thus block its passage. "No one seems to be particularly worried," declared the spokesman for the Radio Manufacturers' Association, "because they realize that should the control of broadcasting pass to the Department of Commerce, it will be in able hands, as it was previous to the creation of the Commission."[3] The general attorney of the Radio Corporation of America urged upon the Senate Committee the desirability of relying largely upon the Department of Commerce[4]

---

[1] "Politics in Radio Control," *Literary Digest*, May 22, 1926.

[2] *Hearings* before the Committee on Interstate Commerce, Senate, 70th Congress, Second Session, on S. 4937, a bill continuing the powers and authority of the Federal Radio Commission, p. 143.

[3] *New York Times*, Jan. 22, 1929, p. 32, col. 2.

[4] *Hearings, op. cit.*, p. 71 *ff.*

and the commission form of control was criticized by the National Association of Broadcasters.[1]

Business interests were definitely mistrustful. Manton Davis of the Radio Corporation of America predicted that the commission would fall into ever-increasing arrears in its work and eventually become swamped. The commission form of organization was thought to encourage disagreement and delay. The early accomplishments of the commission were belittled and a dark future was predicted. Commissioner Caldwell, who was closely associated with commercial radio by his work as an editor of the McGraw-Hill radio journals, took the view that "radio was handled best and the complaints were fewest when radio was under the supervision of the Department of Commerce, under Secretary Hoover."[2]

Joined to this unfriendly attitude on the part of businessmen were the additional handicaps of limited financial resources, an inadequate staff, and impermanent power and existence. Congress practically kept the commission on probation by renewing its licensing powers for short intervals only and by keeping the commissioners uncertain of their jobs. From 1927 to 1930 reappointments were made for one year and the possibility that the board would be abolished was held constantly before its members.[3]

To the threat of the business interests which weakened the commission in its early period must be added the disrupting influence of sectionalism. The White Act divided the country into five zones and provided that one commissioner be appointed from each zone. This geographical distribution of positions was but a reflection of the underlying sectional jealousies which regarded commissioners as champions of regional interests and which led to demands for equal allotment of the spoils of air space.

The White Act provided that the commission distribute broadcasting facilities among "the different states and communities as

[1] *New York Times*, Apr. 7, 1929, xi, p. 20, col. 1.

[2] *Hearings, op. cit.*, p. 145.

[3] Laurence F. Schmeckebier, *The Federal Radio Commission*, pp. 21–40, service monograph, Brookings Institution. For a general discussion, see J. G. Kerwin, *The Control of Radio*, University of Chicago Press, 1934. The January, 1935, issue of the *Annals of the American Academy* deals with many aspects of radio today.

to give fair, efficient, and equitable radio service to each of the same." The commission found, however, that the radio industry was less highly developed in the South and Southwest than in other parts of the country. The commission proceeded cautiously in granting licenses to applicants from these "backward sections," taking the view that if programs could be received the state from which they came was of little consequence. But Southerners felt that they were not getting their just share. The issue became one of local pride and of states rights. Were "damn yankees" to inflict their tastes and tunes upon the southland?

The commission tried to avoid forcing stations off the air simply because their zone was over the quota. Individuals promoting radio in the South became impatient. Irritation arose over the commission's delay in granting increased facilities for two Tennessee stations. The commission quarreled with the owner of a powerful southern station who thereupon undertook to arouse popular protest. Commissioner Sykes of Mississippi was criticized for not exerting himself more on behalf of the South. This dissatisfaction arose during the first year of the commission's work and was given a hearing in a general investigation of the board's activities. Little confidence was felt in the commission at the time. The struggle was along sectional lines and Congress knew no scruples in dictating to this new and untried administrative body.

After a long debate, the Davis Amendment was enacted Mar. 28, 1928 (44. Stat. L., 373). It provided for *equal* allocation of licenses, bands of frequency, wave lengths, periods of time for operation, and station power to each of five zones; and for *fair* and *equitable* allocation to states *within each zone*, according to population.

The amendment placed the commission in a difficult position. Difference of opinion arose among the members as to whether the immediate reallocation of broadcasting facilities was prescribed or whether the equitable distribution was to be approached by gradual steps in future applications. The amendment proved administratively unsound and President Hoover in 1929 recommended that even the appointment of commissioners by zones be abolished. Sectionalism must be reckoned with as one explanation of the commission's difficulties. Class interests are another.

Dissatisfied with the attitude taken by the radio commissioners in limiting the facilities of its Chicago station, the American

Federation of Labor appealed directly to Congress in 1930. None too tactfully the labor spokesman expressed the opinion that those with the best radio frequencies were "so influential that I doubt that Congress will dare to meet the situation."[1]

Nevertheless, an amendment was introduced by Senator Glenn directing the radio commission to assign one cleared channel to labor with unlimited time and power equal to the maximum power assigned any broadcasting station. The measure passed the Senate without a dissenting voice but was defeated in the House. In 1932 similar attempts were made in both House and Senate, and the Federal Radio Commissioners were called before the Senate Committee on Interstate Commerce to explain their policy toward labor. After considerable questioning and discussion, a compromise was finally reached. The labor organizations agreed to abandon their legislative activities for a clear channel and to accept an increase of power from 1500 watts to 5 kilowatts, with full time for their station on the old frequency.

Here was a clear case of legislative interference in the administrative policy of a quasi-judicial and supposedly independent agency instigated because of the demands of a special group. But labor was not alone! Certain educators, convinced that the commission was giving too much air space to business, took their case to Congress. Senator Fess in January, 1931, introduced a measure calling for the allocation of 15 per cent of broadcasting facilities to educational purposes. The National Committee on Education by Radio lent its support to the measure, but Congress failed to act favorably either in 1931 or in 1932 when the bill again appeared.

The commission declared that "radio is not education itself, or the means of its dissemination, but at best education is only one use to which radio may be put."[2] In its first five years the commission granted licenses to ninety-five educational institutions. By 1932 only forty-four of these stations were in operation; the licenses of twenty-three were relinquished voluntarily to commercial enterprises, eighteen were abandoned voluntarily, and ten were discontinued for cause. The commission concluded that

[1] *United States Daily*, Jan. 23, 1930, index, p. 3231.
[2] Docket 984, University of Wisconsin and the Department of Agriculture and Markets.

educational programs could be "safely left to the voluntary gift of the use of facilities by commercial stations."[1]

Although the commissioners were open to assault from organized groups working through their Congressmen and urging legislative direction of administrative discretion, only on one occasion (the passage of the Davis Amendment) did Congress enact legislation for instructing the commission. This does not mean, however, that the regulation of broadcasting remained free from congressional interference, but rather that statutory direction was unnecessary. Laurence F. Schmeckebier writes that "probably no quasi-judicial body was ever subject to so much congressional pressure as the Federal Radio Commission" and that "much of this came at a time when a majority of the Commission had not been confirmed."[2]

Members of Congress were frequently requested by their constituents to urge the Federal Radio Commission to grant licenses in their home communities. Congressmen did not scruple to communicate with the commission in order to "explain" their local situation.[3] Without full knowledge of the facts and without responsibility for the results of their actions, these Congressmen used their official positions for nonofficial purposes. Of course, representatives have the clear duty of acting as spokesmen for their states or districts, but these activities are better confined to Congress than directed toward improperly influencing a quasi-judicial commission.

The threat of disruₚtion in the administrative routine was great. Public responsiveness to the appeals of broadcasting for support was remarkable, in some cases thousands of letters being sent into the station and passed on to the commission. One hundred and seventy thousand official affidavits of listeners were executed in one instance and submitted as evidence. The pecuniary value of licenses is large and broadcasters have shown their readi-

---

[1] Committee reports of the fifty-fifth annual meeting, American Bar Association, Washington, D. C., October, 1932, p. 139.

[2] *Ibid.*, p. 55.

[3] Private interests tried to get at the commission through Congress. For a list of bills affecting the Federal Radio Commission, see the *American Bar Association Report*, 1932, p. 147. See also, *Hearings* before the Interstate Commerce Committee, Senate, 71st Congress, Second Session, 1929–1930, on S. 6, a bill to create a commission on communications, p. 32.

ness to hold on to their privileges by resorting to political pressure. Local pride and local desires and tastes for certain kinds of programs combined with the financial investments of local station owners in demanding broadcasting privileges from the commission.

Under the threat of interference by Congress and the pressure of special interests, the commission undertook to administer its enormously difficult task within the wide provisions of the statute.

What criteria did the commission follow in determining the public interest, convenience, and necessity? Breadth and flexibility, it declared, were essential to any such standard. Under this genial vagueness the commission functioned, though not without criticism from the American Bar Association for the resultant uncertainty of its discipline. No clear line guided its policy.

It is the task of the commissioners to read some meaning into the general mandate that they hold from Congress. Whatever competence as experts they may possess is of little more than incidental significance in determining policy. *Expertise* can apply only to scientific problems and, while it ensures a grasp of technical limitations and possibilities, it does not contribute to a positive elucidation of the public welfare. Here even the expert must rely upon his fallible judgment and his integrity. The commissioners, however, have attempted to designate certain elements as part of the substantive content of public interest. How is this concept fulfilled in actual practice? To answer this question is to summarize the working policies of the commission.[1]

Priority was one general principle governing the commission. The station having the longest record of continuous service had a superior right, other conditions being equal. But a "fair and equitable" distribution of facilities geographically may outweigh priority since the limited broadcasting facilities must serve many communities. Did the applicant have a firm financial standing? Was his equipment modern and efficiently handled? Adequate apparatus is necessary for clear transmission and for the elimination of interference. It is in the public interest that a station stay upon the frequency assigned. Had the applicant obeyed the rules

---

[1] The quotations on the commission's views are from the decision on the application of Great Lakes Broadcasting Company, No. 4900. See *Annual Report of the Federal Radio Commission*, 1928, pp. 32 ff.

of the commission—as, for example, with respect to indicating the use of phonograph records and announcing its call letters properly? Had the station followed the statutory provisions relating to the banning of obscene, indecent, or profane language or to nondiscrimination between political candidates? "In so far as a program consists of discussion of public questions," the commission stated, "public interest requires ample play for the free and fair competition of opposing views, and the commission believes that the principle applies not only to addresses by political candidates but to all discussions of issues of importance to the public."

Stations controlled by a particular group for the dissemination of propaganda were not favorably regarded by the commission. "As a general rule," the commission stated, "postulated on the laws of nature as well as on the standard of public interest, convenience or necessity, particular doctrines, creeds, and beliefs must find their way into the market of ideas by the existing public service stations, and if they are of sufficient importance to the listening public the microphone will undoubtedly be available."

This laissez faire attitude and trust in the benignity of the laws of nature in providing a hearing for all ideas takes for granted a great breadth of social vision and liberality on the part of the commercial interests in control of the so-called "public service stations." To believe that ideas critical of the existing social and economic order will *naturally* win a hearing if they are of *sufficient importance* to the listening public is to ignore the fact that actually programs are drawn up and determined by private interests. It is true that a fairly liberal policy has been pursued by the big broadcasters. But the stubborn fact remains that such a hearing is at the sufferance of commercial interests. The commission declared that "broadcasting stations are licensed to serve the public and not for the purpose of furthering the private or selfish interests of individuals or groups of individuals. The standard of public interest, convenience or necessity means nothing if it does not mean this." Yet the commission frankly admitted that advertising was an exception because it furnished the economic support that made broadcasting possible. As an exception contrary to the general policy of the commission with respect to special interests, it might be supposed that advertisers would be expected to submit to a strict supervision. But this is not the case.

Commercial advertising stations were encouraged and other stations discouraged. "While the commission is of the opinion that a broadcasting station engaged in general public service has, ordinarily, a claim to preference over a propaganda station, it will apply this principle as to existing stations by giving preferential facilities to the former and assigning less desirable positions to the latter to the extent that engineering principles permit." It is hardly to be expected that such stations could succeed when given poor facilities and unpopular hours. But the commission went on record as discriminating against special interests other than those of advertisers wherever opportunity offered. To the critics who objected to the present wordy advertising methods and who advocated limiting advertisers to a statement of sponsorship, the commission had a response. Such a limitation, they argued, would favor a few national advertisers and would discriminate against other national advertisers and virtually all local and retail advertising.

By this reasoning the radio commission was reduced to the position of regulating the radio so as not to interfere with the local retailers and certain national advertisers. In other words, not only were the interests of advertisers as a class given preference, but the commission further refused to discriminate against descriptive advertising or to encourage sponsored programs.

Without reference to the merits of the case, the point seems clear that the Federal Radio Commission interpreted the concept of public interest so as to favor in actual practice one particular group. While talking in terms of the public interest, convenience, and necessity, the commission actually furthered the ends of the commercial broadcasters. They formed the substantive content of public interest as interpreted by the Federal Radio Commission. How will the Federal Communications Commission interpret the "public interest"?

This phrase is an empty concept that must have meaning read into it. The Federal Radio Commission professed to take a relatively negative part, while at the same time expressing its "great confidence in the sound judgment of the listening public as to what types of programs are in its own best interest." The populace actually is given little choice when confronted on one hand with the programs of the favored commercial stations and on the other with those of the special-interest stations, which are handicapped by unpopular and inconvenient time schedules and low power.

The fact that many listeners respond favorably to crooners, black-face comedians, astrologers, demagogues, and mountebanks, whether political, religious, or theatrical does not necessarily mean that the radio industry is being regulated according to the public interest, convenience, or necessity. The tastes of many potential listeners are not considered in this policy.

One can scarcely agree with President Hoover that "there is no proper line of conflict between the broadcaster and the listener," or that "their interests are mutual, for without one the other could not exist."[1] The conflicts in taste and opinion between the listener and broadcaster are sharp and frequent and the only weapon of the radio auditor is turning the dial to another station or writing a letter of protest.

It might readily be conceded to the public interest that the extravagant and often false claims of advertisers warrant exposure. But it is obvious that any scheme for such debunking over the radio is impossible under present conditions. It may be argued that the radio commission has no powers of censorship and hence cannot be held responsible for the character of programs. In granting renewals of licenses to stations accused by the National Food Products Association of insidious cigarette advertising on the air, the commission disclaimed its power to refuse licenses to organizations with whose ideas it disagreed.[2] Yet in other cases it did not hesitate to rule stations off the air because of the character of their programs. The commission actually exercised a very great power over what was broadcasted since in considering the renewal of licenses the past performance of a station was reviewed.

The radio commission moreover, laid down certain criteria as to the kind of program that it regarded with approval. It definitely took the view that "the tastes, needs, and desires of all substantial groups among the listening public should be met in some fair proportion, by a well-rounded program, in which entertainment, consisting of music of both classical and lighter grades, religion, education, and instruction, important public events, discussions of public questions, weather, market reports, and

[1] *Proceedings of the Fourth National Radio Conference*, p. 7. Washington, 1925.
[2] Charles Beard, *The American Leviathan*, p. 443, Macmillan, 1931.

news and matters of interest to all members of the family find a place."

With so comprehensive a view one could scarcely take exception, but the commission has acted upon the assumption that commercial agencies are best able to supply such a service and hence should be favored above all others. "By and large," the commission states, "propaganda stations do not have the financial resources nor do they have the standing and popularity with the public necessary to obtain the best results in programs of general interest."[1]

This broad policy, although attempting neutrality, actually has the contrary effect. The commission has tried to keep clear of commitments. But public welfare in this field cannot be interpreted in a negative fashion. Unless the government enunciates a clear policy of its own, its regulation will amount to little more than throwing its weight to one side or the other when a dispute arises. And unless it is to support confusion and establish vacillation, it must support one side with some degree of consistency. This is what the Federal Radio Commission has done. It has thrown the weight of its authority in support of the advertisers.

The domination of broadcasting by large commercial enterprises means that plenty of money is available to employ leading actors, musicians, and entertainers. Broadcasters received over $77,000,000 during 1931 for the rental of their facilities. Here the determinants of policy are necessarily pecuniary in the final analysis. In accordance with its so-called editorial policy, a well-managed station lets the politicians talk and occasionally gives the professors a chance. Such donations are decorations on the station's record when the time comes to seek a license renewal from the Federal Radio Commission. But underlying all considerations is the necessity of eliminating any element that might lessen the usefulness of the station as a device for attracting the buying public.

Leaving the interpretation of the public welfare to this purely economic determinism means surrendering into commercial channels enormous potentialities for political leadership, popular education, and the control of public opinion.

"Radio is too great a thing to be used purely for entertainment," the counsel for the American Federation of Labor told a Senate

[1] Great Lakes case, *op. cit.*

committee. "This marvelous power that can help the people is just being prostituted."[1]

This is the view of protesting minorities, but from the great mass of listeners very little discontent is heard. The fact of the matter seems to be that the radio is best operated by a unified organization with great financial resources and connections all over the nation. Chain broadcasting and the employment of the best artists is thus made possible. The National Broadcasting Company and the Columbia Broadcasting System have won widespread public approval and support. But the public interest is not to be determined in terms solely of what interests the public. There are many factors in radio regulation which may affect the public but which lie beyond the competence of the public to judge. Pandering to the vacillating tastes of the populace may mean a degrading of the possibilities of the radio. As to whether this has occurred is a matter of individual judgment. But leaving control in the hands of commercial broadcasters means risking the effect of an economic determinism with profit making as the basic consideration. This is what public interest, convenience, and necessity are reduced to as now interpreted by the Federal Radio Commission. The writer is not concerned with the ethical values or economic policy implicit in such a stand, but is concerned simply with disclosing the substantive content of public interest as practiced in radio regulation. The point is rather to emphasize the fact that the commission, while discriminating against special interests as such, not only makes an exception for the benefit of certain advertisers but even identifies their interest with the general welfare. This policy is the result of the commission's worship of conventionality and its cautious, uncertain, and nugatory attitude.

In a weak political position and surrounded by many minority interests making impossible demands, the commissioners have apparently hesitated in embarking upon a clear and definite policy of regulation. They have faced a peculiarly difficult task from a technical viewpoint and they have found in their environment rival social and economic forces threatening to disrupt their work. Whether consciously or not the fact seems clear that the

[1] *United States Daily*, Jan. 23, 1930, index, p. 3231.

policy followed by this regulatory body has favored primarily the big commercial radio interests. This is the more significant when it is noted that this industry is to an unusual degree concentrated and closely organized.

The Columbia Broadcasting System, one of the two great national radio organizations, owns five stations, manages one, and has financial interests in another, besides providing program service to ninety-five stations on its network. The National Broadcasting Company, controlled by the Radio Corporation of America, owns five stations, operates or leases two others, and has a financial interest in five more. It provides program service to seventy-six stations grouped into four chains.

The Radio Corporation of America with its numerous subsidiaries forms the greatest aggregate of private capital engaged in broadcasting. Ownership of over 3800 patents of great importance for electrical transmission explains in part the widespread control of this company. It manufactures radio equipment and pools the patents of General Electric Company, Westinghouse Electric & Manufacturing Co., and the American Telephone and Telegraph Company. Through the Radio-Keith-Orpheum Corp. it manages many artists. The Radio Corporation of America has developed the industry and now virtually controls it.

The cry of monopoly has been raised against the Radio Corporation of America, and in 1931 the courts decided that the Clayton Act had been violated. No licenses can be issued (according to the 1927 Radio Act) to parties adjudged guilty of unlawful monopoly. The renewal of over 1200 licenses held by the Radio Corporation of America was thus endangered. The radio commissioners, however, finally decided that, inasmuch as the monopolistic malpractices had related to radio apparatus and not to actual broadcasting, they lacked authority for denying the renewals. The decision was three to two and the distinction was nice. It did not serve to allay the criticism that the commission was under the control of big business.

The record of the Federal Radio Commission shows clearly the great influence that outside economic influences play in the determination of public policy when the responsibility of defining this policy is placed under an administrative tribunal politically weak and manned by businessmen and politicians.

THE FEDERAL RADIO COMMISSION

These commissioners enunciated no consistent, clear, and positive criteria as to what is in the public interest, convenience, or necessity. They applied first one standard and then another, guided by the expediency of the moment and by the assumption that what was good for the radio business was good for the radio public. Special group interests met great obstacles in their struggle to secure recognition at the hands of the commission. The Davis Amendment has been a failure and the radio commission increased rather than reduced the over-quota condition of the over-quota states. The radio commissioners were accused of showing favoritism toward the Radio Corporation of America, of exercising illegal censorship in denying improved channels to labor, and of permitting broadcasters to censor programs of a controversial character.

The radio creates a peculiar problem that can be resolved satisfactorily only within its own inherent limitations. There is no gainsaying the fact that there are many more interests demanding their place on the air than there are wave lengths in the ether. It is likewise evident that broadcasting is an expensive and highly technical process that is best conducted by those possessing large financial resources.

There is a public demand for lively, brisk entertainment on the air. The aesthetic standards here are comparable to the general tastes of the movie-going public. In other words, the great mass of the listening public wishes to be amused, not introduced "to the better things in art, music or literature." This may be regarded by some as a situation to be deplored, but it is a fact that must be acknowledged to be of basic importance.

The control of the air up to the present time has been in accordance with these aforementioned factors. The broadcasters with the most efficient equipment, the highest technical competence, and the large popular following have been favored. Despite the general complacency of the public, strong minority interests now demand consideration. Something must be done. What are the alternatives?

1. Government ownership and operation. The British Broadcasting Corporation is pointed to as a satisfactory administrative device, but, even were it politically feasible to think of complete socialization of the radio, this move would bring grave difficulties

in its train. It would mean establishing a governmental authority to select what the public is to hear, and censorship would necessarily be entailed. The British Broadcasting Company, although remarkably successful in meeting its heavy responsibilities, nevertheless encounters much criticism. Professor Dimock writes: "The principal criticisms of the British Broadcasting Company arise from minorities who contend that they are not given a fair opportunity to use the facilities of broadcasting. This is the point at which unified control pinches tightly."[1] Listeners object to the uplift character of its programs from the artistic side and to the pontifical "specious anonymous mugwumpery" in its treatment of political broadcasting. Whatever the injustice of these attacks may be, the authoritarianism of the British system is inescapable.

2. Another solution offered is to allot by statute a fixed percentage of radio facilities for nonprofit programs. Obviously this would mean a reduction in the amount of advertising on the air. But how would the time thus freed be filled? Two courses are open: (a) to license nonprofit stations; (b) to require the commercial stations to give a certain ratio of time to nonprofit programs. Judged in the light of experience, both courses leave much to be desired. Very few nonprofit stations have resources comparable to commercial stations. Their popularity in most cases contrasts most unfavorably with those established upon a more solid economic basis. Moreover, there are not enough wave lengths to meet the demands of the special interests desiring channels. Nor could the problem be solved by dividing the air between "educational" and commercial stations. As one of the radio commissioners has explained,

The Commission has never cancelled a single license of an educational institution. The reduction in the number of educational stations since 1927 has occurred by virtue of the voluntary assignment or surrender by educational stations of their licenses, because either they were unable for financial reasons to maintain them, or because they did not have sufficient program material to continue operation.

As a matter of fact, it appears that commercial stations have been very generous in offering time to educational institutions.

[1] Marshall E. Dimock, *British Public Utilities and National Development*, p. 293, University of Chicago Press, 1934.

Unless a nonprofit broadcasting system is to be endowed (and this seems very unlikely), such stations are impracticable. The problem is not solved by giving unequal competitors the right to compete.

Is there any middle course between government ownership and the domination of the radio by business? An interesting proposal has been made by the two most important noncommercial radio organizations, the National Committee on Education by Radio and the National Advisory Council on Radio in Education. The council grew out of the American Association for Adult Education and represents a number of very influential people. The National Committee represents the National Education Association, the American Council on Education, the National Catholic Welfare Association, the National Council of State Superintendents, the Jesuit Educational Association, the National Association of State Universities, etc. Both the National Committee and the Advisory Council have proposed the creation of a government-owned chain. This chain might be operated by a "National Radio Institute." This institute would be financed by the states and directed by government officials working in coöperation with professional, educational, and civic groups. It would serve to coördinate the efforts of all those interested in the educational and cultural possibilities of broadcasting and would provide an official focal point for their activities.[1]

It is argued that only by bringing under federal management a small fixed percentage of the available wave lengths can the virtual monopoly of the air by commercial broadcasters be avoided; only in this way can nonprofit broadcasts be relieved of their sole dependence on the business interests controlling the radio industry. These organizations believe that a federal broadcasting chain would go far toward meeting the problems of radio regulation today.

It is true that great broadcasting facilities already exist as part of our system of national defense. Financing an official broadcasting system would raise some perplexing questions. A federal radio chain would have to be guarded from the abuses of partisan politics and the spoils system. Here the British system suggests a form of organization. The British Broadcasting Corporation

[1] See the mimeographed digest of *Hearings* before the Broadcast Division of the Federal Communications Commission, Nov. 7-12, pp. 28, 31.

is an autonomous administrative unit free to use wide discretion as to what is best for the public to hear. It is the utter dependence of our present system upon the advertiser that constitutes its chief weakness. The public interest cannot be consistently interpreted as the advertisers' interest and yet the present economic basis of the radio world makes this consequence almost inevitable. Whereas at the present time what goes on the air is determined by advertisers and commercial broadcasters, under the proposed scheme the standards of judgment would be broadened.

The experience of the Federal Radio Commission raises the question as to whether federal officials can regulate this great industry entirely from the outside. Direct governmental participation suggests a way of counterbalancing the domination of the air by commercial broadcasters. The regulatory commission type of control can scarcely be regarded as the final form. Undertaking control in a new and rapidly developing field has engendered difficulties of peculiar complexity. The need for governmental "interference" at the very start was recognized by the radio industry itself. Regulation was essential to the growth and success of broadcasting. But the most effective way of administering this control has yet to be discovered. A few powerful firms have been largely responsible for the remarkable development of radio as an art and industry. Thus far the government has taken a relatively negative part. The listening public has seemed content to regard the radio as an entertaining toy. Advertisers and commercial broadcasters have exerted every effort to sell their goods and amuse the public. Federal regulation has meant the maintenance of the *status quo*.

If officials are to interpret the public interest along constructive lines and in concrete terms, they must have the statutory authority, financial support, and administrative facilities commensurate with their task. In addition to this they must have political backing sufficient to counteract the pressure from those groups immediately affected by the results of official action.

Actual government participation in greater or less degree may in time become one means of safeguarding the whole regulatory process. Officials not only could secure a standard whereby private performance may be measured, but they would have an opportunity for expressing the public interest in a positive fashion.

They can construct and exemplify. They can add at the points where private enterprise is weak and abstain where the need has already been met.

The great increase under the Roosevelt administration in the number of government-owned corporations is eloquent evidence of this development.[1] These organizations, if they continue, will increasingly identify a powerful economic and political class with government participation in industry. Moreover, the great federal credit agencies have already made many business firms dependent for their existence upon the government. The Reconstruction Finance Corporation, for example, actually controls many private corporations to the extent of selecting officials, passing upon the promotion of employees, and supervising new business undertakings. Unless administrators have strong political allies, they cannot hope to attain their ambitious goals. The record of our regulatory bodies shows that the effectiveness of their work has depended in large measure upon the attitude taken by those groups of citizens immediately under their jurisdiction.

Where the President has not enunciated a clear national policy and rallied politicians and people behind his proposals, federal regulatory bodies have found little support in Congress. Past experience has demonstrated the difficulties of attempting to regulate industry under such conditions. More recent developments may place administrators in stronger positions. It remains a matter of individual opinion as to what is really "in the public interest." Reaching a personal judgment may be assisted, however, by facing frankly the administrative implications that follow from the two views of the general welfare considered in this study.

[1] A partial list of federal proprietary corporations includes the following organizations: War Finance Corporation, Inland Waterways Corporation, Textile Foundation, Inc., Reconstruction Finance Corporation, Federal Deposit Insurance Corporation, Federal Farm Mortgage Corporation, Federal Savings and Loan Insurance Corporation, Federal Prison Industries Corporation, United States Shipping Board Merchant Fleet Corporation, Home Owners Loan Corporation, Commodity Credit Corporation, Public Works Emergency Housing Corporation, Electric Home and Farm Authority, Inc., Export-Import Bank of Washington, Second Export-Import Bank of Washington, Federal Subsistence Homesteads Corporation, Federal Surplus Relief Corporation, Tennessee Valley Associated Coöperatives, etc. See also John Thurston, "Government Proprietary Corporations," *Virginia Law Review*, March, 1935.

Either the federal administration must be sufficiently strengthened to attempt its own positive interpretation of the public interest in accordance with the general policy indicated by Congress, or it will continue to be dominated by the private interests that are able to influence officials and threaten Congressmen.

Time and again our commissions have been run by officials who are merely the pale reflection of the very interests they are supposed to regulate. In such cases administration in the public interest merely means placing an official cloak over private selfishness. On the other hand, recruiting impartial officials and giving them power to act means risking the abuses associated with bureaucracy.

Some readers at this point may insist that the Interstate Commerce Commission has not been gored by either horn of this dilemma. This commission has a reputation for impartiality and efficiency and the cry of bureaucracy is seldom raised against it. The commission is generally regarded as the most successful regulatory agency in the federal government. In the next chapter we shall attempt to analyze its record in terms of the political and economic pressures touching its officials.

Chapter XI

THE INTERSTATE COMMERCE COMMISSION AND SPECIAL INTERESTS

"She never was really well brought up," the Red Queen went on: "but it's amazing how good-tempered she is! Pat her on the head, and see how pleased she'll be!"

A CONFLICT of interests is implicit in most administrative problems. The adjustment of these forces must take place within a predicated legal framework. An effort will be made here to examine the Interstate Commerce Commission in terms of the group pressures that are exerted upon it in its regulatory capacity. The purpose is to discuss the nature of the relations that arise between a regulatory body and the interests touched by its authority and to call attention to the possibilities and problems inherent in such a contact.

A survey of the relations of this federal agency with the non-governmental groups concerned with transportation presents an immensely confused and complicated picture. In its economic aspects, transportation is so closely entwined in the very texture of our commercial, industrial, and social life that grouping of interests takes place at every level of integration. Regional interest groups range from those based on the immediate community to those following the lines of great natural divisions of the country. Other groupings differentiate themselves according to the type of transport industry. The users in turn form a common-interest group. Cleavages appear within this latter category as between big and little shippers, and direct or indirect users. In any given transportation industry the groups of financial interests, investors, bondholders, insurance companies, and others confront the occupational groups of trainmen, warehousemen, and managers.

This attempt at classifying the complex of interests involved perhaps assumes more significance if considered in connection with a specific case showing the conglomeration of parties with which the government is faced and the enormous administrative difficulty of bringing about any adjustment among the various groups. The coördination-of-motor-transport case before the Interstate Commerce Commission is an example.[1] The number and variety of interests testifying reflect the many aspects of economic and social life touched by this problem: bus lines, transfer companies, freight depots, furniture corporations, storage companies, merchant truckmen, team and truck owners, expressmen's leagues, truck drivers' and chauffeurs' unions, motor carriers' associations, warehouse distributors, motor-truck clubs, coöperative livestock shippers, automobile dealers, gas companies, public utilities, wholesalers, and manufacturers. Steel, shade cloth, candy, rubber, biscuits, milling, brewing, printing, and publishing—all felt that their interests were involved. Many appeared as organizations, others singly.

The great corporate enterprises made statements: Remington Arms, International Harvester, Woolworth, The Great Atlantic & Pacific Tea Company, and even the Hearst papers. National and regional associations sent their spokesmen to the commission: the Association of Railway Executives, the American Short Line Railway Association, the Western Traffic Executives Committee, the Southwestern Passenger Association, the New England Railroad Committee, the National Industrial Traffic League, the National Poultry and Refrigerators Express Association, the National League of Commission Merchants, the Chain Store Traffic League of New York, the American Newspaper Publishers' Association, the Eastern Confectioners' Traffic Bureau, and the Motorized Circuses of the United States. To this list must be added the half dozen or more great brotherhoods of railway employees.

Such a list gives some slight idea of the reaction from the business community elicited by the consideration of an important phase of our economic life. The Interstate Commerce Commission, in the course of discharging its weighty administrative duties, works in this intricate web of interests and can take no action

[1] Interstate Commerce Commission, Docket 23400. *The Coördination of Motor Transport.* Listed in this report are to be found not only the interests represented but also the lawyers speaking on their behalf. The list is an excellent place to find the array of legal talent employed by transportation groups.

without affecting a vast structure of interrelated forces, whose adjustment may easily be upset by ill-considered action and whose opportunities for conflict are well-nigh limitless.

It is possible to conceive of a purely economic solution of the transportation question in terms of service and operation, using the canons of efficiency as sole determinants. But the tangle of political and social interests is at once too significant to be ignored and too intricate to be summarily dealt with. Nor can it be assumed that the federal government stands over against the welter of transport and sectional groups as a single-minded and completely disinterested arbiter. The idea that the federal administration has a unified interest in the transportation field is illusory, since there are groupings of interests forming complexes within the government itself. As the owner of the Alaska Railway and of barge lines, it presents a face quite different from that shown as a distributor of the mails. But in addition to its proprietary and its functional interests, the government has also a strong financial interest as a collector of revenue, *e.g.*, from the taxation of gasoline and steamship tickets. It has also a distinct interest as the employer of innumerable agents in connection with its transportation activities. All of these relations may be classified under the business administration of the government respecting transportation, as contrasted with its regulatory responsibilities.

Such a pluralism of interest within the government itself accentuates the need for a national transportation policy at the same time that it renders understandable the difficulty of any unified direction. The federal government in the past has failed to provide the necessary leadership, and, in the words of a recent authoritative study, "instead of being welded into a coördinated system, our various transport agencies are working more or less at cross purposes. Instead of a unified program of regulation designed to promote common objectives, we have a series of unrelated and often antagonistic policies carried out by a variety of government agencies."[1]

The Interstate Commerce Commission is charged with the duty of interpreting the public interest in specific cases. How can the work of such a body be related to the broad consideration of de-

[1] H. G. Moulton and associates, *The American Transportation Problem*, p. 881, Brookings Institution, 1933.

veloping the whole transportation system along constructive lines of national welfare? Theoretically the conception of the public interest stands over and above both the forces identified with transportation interests and those relating to the internal business administration of government, but an examination of the external relations of the government to the transport interests fails to reveal any well-defined norm as to what constitutes the public interest. However intangible the idea of the public interest may be as a general guide for administrative action, its influence is always imminent and may add the weight of the imponderable to a judgment arrived at upon wholly different grounds. When a widespread strike or similar emergency threatens a complete dislocation of transport facilities, the public itself is directly concerned in the problem of resolving such a conflict and in restoring normal relations. In such emergencies the force of public opinion demands a rapid adjustment, but the actual handling of the problem must be delegated to an appropriate agency.

While Congress holds wide powers in respect to the regulation of commerce among the states, it is nevertheless bound by inherent limitations. By reason of its very composition, it cannot come directly to grips with the transportation groups it seeks to control. Congress can do little more than indicate general policies and establish certain norms, in the hope that through such means a procedure of regulation will result which will operate in the public interest. Viewed economically, it may be to the public interest that the cheapest and most efficient transportation system be established. But such standards may be balanced by Congress with considerations of national defense, the development of certain industries or particular regions, or the protection of certain classes. The powers and duties devolved upon special administrative agencies further indicate the direction regarded by Congress as tending toward the general welfare. Through its appropriating and investigating powers Congress is enabled to control and check the operation of administrative bodies, thus guiding them toward its conception of the public interest. The fact remains that the form and composition of a legislative assembly render it an awkward instrument for the direct execution and continuous scrutiny of the policies that it has prescribed. Judicial review has similar limitations. The Court's interpretation as to what constitutes the public interest is affected by its concern with enforcing the traditional sanctions of private property rights.

The Interstate Commerce Commission, then, stands against this background of public opinion, congressional authority, and judicial review. It is charged with the positive task of administering legislative mandates in the public interest, subject always to possible check by the Supreme Court. These limits are evident and recognized, but yet allow a broad field for discretion. Heavy responsibilities devolve upon an independent administrative tribunal because of the complexity and technicality of the problems that must be met. The plane upon which the norms as to what constitutes the public interest are applied is far removed from that of public opinion or that of the representative assembly. The milieu is distinctly one of special interests, and the regulatory body lives in an environment of conflicts. It must function here, not in accordance with thin, vague concepts, but in terms of concrete situations where the real content of the public interest must be extricated from a maze of technical detail. Despite its broad legal powers, the Interstate Commerce Commission becomes in practice dependent upon the assistance of outside interests in meeting its responsibilities of regulation and it could do but little without such assistance. How, then, can the public interest survive and receive fulfillment?

Harmonious resolution cannot take place through bureaucratic autocracy imposing the "national interest," nor yet through the exercise of compulsion over government officials by outside groups. The public interest has to be made effective in the process of composing the struggles of competing forces. As Laski has put it, "the state of our time must make its authority valid not by the sanctions it can enforce, but by the sense it creates in each of us that its activities are a genuine response to our experience."[1] It is essentially in the administration of technical detail that the force of this statement appears most clearly.

An important aspect of the Interstate Commerce Commission's work is, for example, concerned neither with legal coercion of private interests nor with political coercion of this regulatory body by organized groups, but simply with the problem of bringing about harmony between carriers and shippers so that an agree-

[1] *The Dangers of Obedience*, p. 90, Harper, 1930.

ment is reached and litigation before the commission forestalled. Thus, despite the fact that one of its most important functions is the fixing of rates, the commission coöperates with private organizations in avoiding the expense and delay of formal hearings. Each of the three groups concerned in every controversy—the carriers, the shippers, and the Interstate Commerce Commission—has set up agencies to aid in this process of informal settlement.[1] The commission has established a bureau of informal cases and a bureau of traffic charged with the task of reducing the amount of formal rate litigation. The railroads, as a part of the nine major regional freight associations, have appointed standing rates committees. In conference with the National Industrial Traffic League, a procedure has been devised to give every shipper an opportunity to present his side of the case to the carrier before any change can be made in rates that affect him. The shippers have established in local and national trade associations and in local chambers of commerce bureaus or committees concerned with adjusting rate controversies through conference and coöperation.

The commission's bureau of traffic helps in the settlement of controversies between shipper and carrier concerning rates and between carriers over division of joint rates. The bureau receives complaints, either orally or in writing, and then seeks to bring the matter to the attention of all those who are affected. After each has had full opportunity to present his views, an informal opinion is handed down in writing by the officials of the bureau. Such expressions are not binding upon the commission, nor do they prevent any of the parties from disputing such findings or resorting to litigation.

When matters are handled by conference rather than by correspondence, due notice is given by the bureau to all interested in the problem, and an opportunity is afforded such parties to present their views at a meeting usually held in the capital. It is the function of the bureau to bring out all the facts by discussion or direct questioning, with a view to effecting an agreement among the parties themselves, rather than to pass judgment upon the merits of the controversy. The director of the bureau

[1] For a description of the procedure, see *Informal Settlement of Railroad Rate Controversies*, issued by the transportation and communication department of the Chamber of Commerce of the United States, Washington, 1930.

reports that frequently the solutions obtained by these informal hearings prove more satisfactory than anything that could be done by the commission as a result of formal proceedings.[1] This is because the commission, in deciding a formal case, must act in strict conformity with a statutory authorization which necessarily limits its freedom of action and which may lead to a decision less pleasing to both parties than a compromise adjustment involving no direct order.

The bureau of informal cases of the Interstate Commerce Commission is designed to serve as an intermediary in settling through correspondence controversies between railroad companies and complainants. The informal complaints section assists in the process of adjusting differences, and its advice is in no way binding upon the parties, who may proceed to a formal hearing if they wish to do so.[2] Similarly, disputes concerning the reasonableness of tariffs may reach a voluntary settlement with the assistance of the special dockets section. More difficult cases and those for which there is no ready precedent may receive adjustment with the help of the board of reference. In these ways the commissioners are relieved of the problem of holding formal hearings on thousands of cases that would otherwise come up for action in the course of the year.

This coöperation among officials, carriers, and shippers in the adjustment of freight rates is symptomatic of the general attitude of the commission toward the groups that it regulates, and it extends to other important branches of the commission's work. The director of the bureau of service reports that his bureau follows a definite policy of seeking the greatest possible measure of coöperation between shippers and carriers,[3] and in respect to this policy the commission coöperates with the railroads through the special agency of the car-service division of the American Railway Association.

The railroads have agreed to follow the directions issued by this body, created by their national association, and to accept

[1] *Thirty-fourth Annual Report of the I.C.C.*, p. 42, 1920.

[2] For a detailed account of the functions of the bureau of informal cases, see the *Report of the I.C.C.*, 1916.

[3] See article by William P. Bartel, director of the bureau of service, on the work of his bureau, *United States Daily*, Mar. 14, 1930.

it as their statutory agent in all matters relating to car service. It functions as the collective voice of the railroads and supplements the work of the commission in directing and controlling transportation in an efficient manner. The commission has assisted this development and encouraged its extension into the field where the car-service division has organized regional advisory boards, composed exclusively of purchasers of transportation.[1] Fourteen districts have set up such boards, and the aggregate membership is about 15,000. Within each district the board strives to overcome difficulties of car service and to anticipate car requirements by meeting regularly with representatives of the railroads. Committees dealing with specific commodities keep in constant touch with railway officials, and apparently this form of coöperation has proved quite successful. The report of the Committee on Recent Economic Changes attributes the credit for better railway service in part to their activity, other factors not in themselves being sufficient to account for the improvement in service, particularly with regard to anticipation of needs in relation to seasonal or unusual movements.[2] Equally significant of this important development in relieving the commission of much complex rule-making is a statement made by Chairman McManamy of the Interstate Commerce Commission, in addressing the American Railway Association:

[1] For discussion of the relations of the bureau of service to the car-service division of the American Railway Association, see *Annual Reports of the I.C.C.*, 1920. In its report for 1924, pp. 62–63, the commission states that the boards were organized: "(1) to form a common meeting ground between shippers, local railroads, and the carriers as a whole, as represented by the car-service division, for the better mutual understanding of local and general transportation requirements, and to analyze transportation needs in each territory, and to assist in anticipating car requirements; (2) to study production, markets, distribution, and trade channels of the commodities local to each district with a view to effecting improvements in trade practices when related to transportation, and promoting a more even distribution of commodities where practicable; (3) to promote car and operating efficiency in connection with maximum loading and in the proper handling of cars by shippers and railroads; (4) to secure a proper understanding by the railroads of the transportation needs of shippers, that their regulations may fit shippers' requirements, and to secure understanding by the shippers and their coöperation in carrying out necessary rules governing car handling and car distribution."

[2] *Recent Economic Changes in the United States, Report of the Committee on Recent Economic Changes of the President's Conference on Unemployment*, vol. 1, pp. 301–302.

THE INTERSTATE COMMERCE COMMISSION

One of the first duties of this Association was to provide . . . rules from which have grown our present rules of interchange and other rules established by this body, which, if just and reasonable, as required by the Interstate Commerce Commission, are the law. Paragraphs 10 and 11 of section 1 of the act make it the duty of each carrier to establish, observe and enforce just and reasonable rules, regulations and practices with respect to car service. This organization, having undertaken the task of establishing such rules for all carriers, is therefore a law-making body, and it is but fair to say that there have been few instances in which the Commission has found it necessary to modify or change the rules of interchange which you have established.[1]

The necessity for this coöperation of the interests concerned arises from a situation in which government officials are confronted with tasks of huge proportions and handicapped by lack of resources. It is impossible for them to rely solely on their own expert knowledge, however profound, and in the administration of the law they must obtain necessary information by sympathetic contacts with those in possession of it. Government experts must supplement their knowledge with the expertness of the interests regulated.

This is clearly shown in the attempt to deal with the problem of safety on the railroads. The Senate committee on interstate commerce discovered in 1890 that "out of every 105 men directly engaged in the handling of trains one was killed, and out of every twelve men so employed one was injured." The chief cause of the excessive number of fatalities was the type of coupler and hand brake used. Working conditions called for federal interposition and led to the passage of the Safety Appliance Act of 1893. "It is no secret," states the present director of the bureau of safety, "that the passage of this legislation was vigorously opposed by the railroads." The roads had already adopted a standard type of automatic coupler and set up standards of equipment following the recommendations of the Master Car Builders' Association, and they felt that they were proceeding as rapidly as their finances would permit in installing air brakes. They resented the employment of legal pressure to accomplish measures already under way.

In effect, the statute had to be based on the work done by the Master Car Builders' Association, and the law sought to protect

---

[1] *Railway Age*, vol. 88, pp. 1548d 114 *ff*. June 24, 1930.

workmen by these standards. An interesting feature of the act left the standard height of drawbars to be determined and certified to the commission by the American Railway Association within ninety days after the passage of the act, after which the duty was to revert, in case of failure to set up standards, to the officials of the commission.[1] The association lost no time in presenting its standards to the proper authorities, but the execution of the act as a whole was delayed, and, in fact, it did not become fully effective until Aug. 1, 1900. The standards of the Master Car Builders' Association received general recognition and were put into operation in due course, the commission itself being concerned chiefly with fixing the time at which rules were to become effective.

In prescribing these time limits, the commission had to adjust the conflicting claims of the carriers and the brotherhoods. Delay, litigation, experiment, and the passage of supplementary acts set a slow pace for the development of a complete code of safety laws. The carriers repeatedly begged for extensions of time under the law for installing safety devices,[2] while the brotherhoods did not regard the enforcement of the law as sufficiently drastic and were critical of the Interstate Commerce Commission's endorsement of the Master Car Builders' Association with respect to standards. The director of the bureau of safety states that the brotherhoods sent a representative to Washington as soon as the law became effective, who "took it upon himself to speak for the employees and sought to dictate the manner in which the law should be administered."[3] It was impossible, of course, for a group of officials to sit at their desks in Washington and prescribe the type of safety appliances that should be installed. Many such contrivances were in the experimental stage. The Safety Appliance Act thus created a situation that made it necessary for the commission to establish direct contact with the American Railway Association in order to administer the law effectually and by the most practical and least expensive methods.

[1] The constitutionality of this delegation of authority to the American Railway Association and the Interstate Commerce Commission was expressly upheld in *St. Louis and Iron Mountain Railway Co. v. Taylor*, 210 U. S. 281 (1908).

[2] See, for example, *Extension of Time to Comply with Safety Appliance Acts*, 36 I.C.C. 370 (1915); *Safety Appliances*, 44 I.C.C. 303 (1917); *Safety Appliances*, 58 I.C.C. 655 (1920).

[3] *Railway Age*, vol. 88, pp. 1454*d* 115 *ff*. (June 20, 1930).

THE INTERSTATE COMMERCE COMMISSION

In the beginning there was, says Commissioner McManamy,

. . . some friction, and occasionally the discussions developed more heat than light. With experience came understanding and knowledge of each other's motives, until at the present time the laws relating to the operation of railroads are being administered with a degree of coöperation and effectiveness which equals, if it does not surpass, that between different departments of the same railroad.[1]

Coöperation in the safety problem was largely a question of testing the mechanical qualities of devices in practical experiments on a number of railways. When Congress by joint resolution of June 30, 1906, called upon the Interstate Commerce Commission to investigate and report on the use of block-signal systems and automatic controls, the commission naturally turned to experts outside the government. Four engineers of national reputation were appointed to serve on the block-signal and train-control board, and a member of the commission's staff acted as secretary. Over a period of five years the board examined plans and specifications and carried on its tests, recommending in its final report that the block system of control be required on all passenger lines, but that investigation be continued on the use of automatic train control. This was carried on by the bureau of safety, and during the war period another committee was appointed to investigate.

Section 26 of the Act of 1920 gave the commission authority to order the installation of train controls upon proper investigation, and the commission reported that in the administration of this section it invited the coöperation of the American Railway Association. A joint committee of twenty members on automatic train control was organized, consisting of an equal number of representatives from the operating, engineering, and mechanical divisions and signal section of the American Railway Association. This committee worked in close and continuous coöperation with the chief of the bureau of safety of the Interstate Commerce Commission and members of his staff, who took part in the proceedings although they were not members of the committee. The work of investigation and experimentation proceeded steadily. The commission ordered use of automatic train control in some cases

[1] *Ibid.*, pp. 1548d 114 *ff.* (June 24, 1930).

and in others the railways did the installation of their own accord, until the point has now been reached where it is possible to travel from Boston to Omaha on trains automatically controlled for every mile of the distance. Developments are still under way, and the continuing coöperation of carrier and regulatory authority remains the chief safeguard in dealing with the perennial problem of safety in travel.[1]

The American Railway Association has definitely coördinated its work with that of the Interstate Commerce Commission on all matters relating to automatic train control, signals, and allied safety concerns.[2] Such relations promote the ends of both parties. The commission can fix workable standards of safety only if it has a knowledge of actual railroad experience and conditions. Since the railroads must submit to control, they desire that the regulations be framed intelligently. It sometimes happens that no one is in a position to prescribe precise specifications for safety devices. This was the situation with regard to power brakes. Accordingly, the committee on safety appliances of the American Railroad Association conducted elaborate experiments for four and one half years and spent hundreds of thousands of dollars in order to test various kinds of brakes. It was upon the basis of this private investigation that the Interstate Commerce Commission was able to promulgate its regulations. In the whole problem of safety regulation this contact between regulator and regulated has continued as the inevitable concomitant of administrative rule making in a highly technical field.

This reliance of the ruler upon the aid of the governed appears again and again in the work of the Interstate Commerce Com-

---

[1] *Automatic Train Control*, American Railway Association, Bulletin 1, November, 1930.

[2] Similar coöperative work was done by the American Railway Association and the bureau of safety in adopting a uniform application of safety appliances to an improved design of boxcars. The jointly formulated regulations were reported by the commission to have "resulted in a uniform and material improvement in the condition of air-brake equipment" (*Forty-first Annual Report of the I.C.C.*, p. 33, Dec. 1, 1927). In the past the association has established standards for various parts of brake equipment, including pressure-retaining valves, brake beams, brake shoes, strength requirements and total leverage of foundation, brake gear, air hose, hose couplings, hose-coupling packing rings, and gauges for checking couplings and packing rings.

mission. A body of government experts speedily reaches the end of its resources if left to cope single-handed with the problem of regulating so complex and extensive a system as that of transportation, where new developments are forever appearing. Thus even the statute that placed the transportation of explosives and other dangerous articles within the purview of the commission specifically authorized that body to avail itself of the services of the bureau of explosives of the American Railway Association in the task of formulating proper regulations.[1] In much the same way the railroads, acting through a committee of the mechanical division of the American Railway Association, are legally authorized to pass upon the specifications of tank cars. If upon investigation this body finds them satisfactory, their use is permitted; in case of rejection the matter may be brought before the commission for final action, at which due weight will be given to the committee's expert opinions.

The administration of the boiler-inspection act and the locomotive-inspection service further illustrate this willingness to base regulations on the experience and opinions of the parties affected. The director of this service points out that the requirements covering the construction, inspection, and repair of locomotives and tenders under the law are those established as "standard" by the American Railway Association, locomotive builders, and other authorities both prior to and subsequent to the enactment of the law. But this fact does not make the work of the Interstate Commerce Commission any the less necessary, nor does it entail the surrender of an essential function into private hands. The guidance of the state introduces the element of authority per se, since the voluntary character of the American Railway Association makes uniformity of observance difficult to achieve. It was because of the failure of the railroads to observe their own rules and standards that government action became necessary. Mr. McManamy, of the Interstate Commerce Commission, made this point in addressing the association:

[1] "This bureau will make inspections and conduct investigations and will confer with manufacturers and shippers with a view to determining what regulations will within reasonable limits afford the highest degree of safety. . . . The commission will give due weight to the expert opinions thus obtained. Report of these investigations should be made to the commission, with recommendations." Regulations for the Transportation of Explosives, revised Oct. 1, 1930, p. 4.

Agreements may be reached with respect to proper rules, and they may be approved by a majority of your voting membership. However, a dissatisfied minority or an indifferent membership of the majority may, under the national system of railroad operation, render unsatisfactory or even unworkable the best system of rules and regulations that it is possible to devise. The authority, therefore, to see that the regulations which are established are just and reasonable, and that they are applied and observed with fairness and with justness, was lodged with the Interstate Commerce Commission. That, I think, is where it must rest if the rules are to be given their full force and effect.[1]

A legal sanction of this type is therefore necessary, but it remains without practical effect unless it is vitalized through the coöperation of the interests to be regulated and is backed by the experience they possess. On the technical plane, determining the public interest becomes a purely pragmatic affair of discovering what can be done within certain limits. This thesis is submitted: that the greater the degree of detailed and technical control the government seeks to exert over industrial and commercial groups, the greater must be their degree of consent and active participation in the very process of regulation, if regulation is to be effective or successful. The only alternative would be an identification of interests brought about by some form of government ownership and operation. The Interstate Commerce Commission cannot exercise its great powers in a legal vacuum, issuing orders from afar, but must meet specific situations as they arise and must settle them in accord with what is technically possible under the circumstances. A workable agreement demands the coöperation of those with special competence, and the administrative process finally becomes effective by drawing upon experts wherever available and by securing the practical assistance of the direct participators.

The Interstate Commerce Commission, through its regulatory responsibilities, is actually engaged in the task of railroad management and direction. The government cannot help to run the railroads without keeping in the closest contact with those interests especially concerned in railroad matters. The relationship works both ways. As the Supreme Court said in *Smyth v. Ames* (169 U. S. 466, 544), "A railroad is a public highway, and none the

[1] *Railway Age*, vol. 88, pp. 1548d 114 *ff*. (June 24, 1930).

THE INTERSTATE COMMERCE COMMISSION

less so because constructed and maintained through the agency of a corporation deriving its existence and powers from the State. Such a corporation was created for public purposes. It performs a function of the State."

Since the railroads are performing functions for which the government would otherwise stand responsible, their control must be in accord with the public interest. Their control becomes a question of national policy, yet their regulation must not be disrupted by political tampering. The Interstate Commerce Commission was devised as a means for ensuring public control that at the same time would be unbiased and competent. To act competently it must have the coöperation of the carriers and shippers. Can the commission remain objective in the execution of its duties?

Chapter XII

POLITICAL PRESSURES AND THE INTERSTATE COMMERCE COMMISSION

"Let the jury consider their verdict," the King said, for about
the twentieth time that day.
"No, no!" said the Queen. "Sentence first—verdict afterwards."

IN THE juristic sphere the Interstate Commerce Commission is charged with enforcing and interpreting certain statutes, hearing and weighing evidence, and rendering formal judgment when the facts have been ascertained. But the recognized judicial character of this work does not render the commission immune from efforts to influence its judgments. The struggles of contending economic groups and political influences give rise to actions intolerable in a court of law and to repeated efforts to obtain favorable decisions through the use of propaganda. The commission performs its duties in surroundings far from neutral, and it must cope with pressures too powerful to be exorcised by simple exhortation or condemnation. The problem is one of canalizing influences that cannot be eliminated to the end that they may increase rather than decrease the efficiency of the administrative process and that the public interest may not be submerged in the undertow of sectional and political cross currents.

In any consideration of these pressures upon the commission, its relations with Congress stand out as of foremost importance. Congress forms a natural expansion chamber for the energies of the many interests concerned. Congress cannot be condemned in general fashion for "political ratemaking," since questions of national policy are wrapped up in the very texture of the transportation problem and freight rates may be a matter that the legislative body must consider under certain conditions. The right of Congress to direct the commission along a general and agreed-upon line of policy can scarcely be challenged. But the question of propriety can certainly be raised when Congressmen seek indirectly to influence the commission's decision in particular cases. The delimitation of the proper spheres of competence is a nice question.

Under our geographical system of representation, sectional interests find so direct a channel for expression that no member of Congress can altogether avoid the responsibility of considering the demands of the great shippers in his region in a fight for favorable rates. The aim of the Interstate Commerce Commission may be a calm and judicial adjustment among the conflicting transport interests, but the Congressman has the job of obtaining full consideration for the views of his constituents, and time and again he may find himself impelled to inquire into the stand taken by the commission. Conflict thus arises from the very nature of the component elements, and quite different springs of action become evident.[1] The one thinks in terms of sectional or group demands as a spur to action, the other in terms of discovering a fair adjustment of rates on legal or economic grounds.

This difference in point of view appears again and again. A survey of the legislative proposals relating to the Interstate Commerce Commission during the past ten years shows clearly a tendency on the part of Congressmen to seek to influence the commission in favor of special classes or regions.[2] The character of these legislative proposals warrants the assumption that selfish interests seek to procure favors through the houses of Congress, and that but few of these would prove compatible with the permanent statutory basis of the Interstate Commerce Commission's

[1] The following interchange between a Senator and a commissioner over the suspension of rates for wheat shipments to the Pacific coast illustrates the point:

Senator Wheeler: But the real reason why it was done, the fundamental reason why it was done, was because of the fact of the protest of the farmers of the Northwest . . . and the Interstate Commerce Commission took the view of the farmers.

Mr. Woodlock: Quite true, and the farmers were right.

Senator Wheeler: And they did it because of the fact that they wanted to help the farmer.

Mr. Woodlock: The farmer was right.

Senator Wheeler: Of course he was right.

Mr. Woodlock: The rate was right.

Nomination of Thomas F. Woodlock. *Hearings* before Committee on Interstate Commerce, 69th Congress, First Session, 1926, p. 64.

[2] For a list of these proposals, see the author's "Special Interests and the Interstate Commerce Commission," *American Political Science Review*, December, 1933, pp. 900-901.

authority. Fortunately, the commission itself has been the source of most of its amendatory acts. As Professor Sharfman notes, "Few of the significant legislative enactments of the past four decades have emerged without the imprint of its potent influence."[1]

In certain cases, however, a disposition on the part of Congress to intervene in matters already entrusted to the commission has appeared. As the result of pressure by groups of commercial travelers, Congress directed the Interstate Commerce Commission to issue interchangeable mileage books at just and reasonable rates—an order later voided by the Supreme Court.[2] Of much greater importance was the Hoch-Smith Resolution which directed the commission to consider the conditions prevailing in different industries in adjusting freight rates and which specifically put forward the case of agriculture. This measure was clearly passed in response to the clamors of the farmers. In the words of Representative Tincher of Kansas: "This bill will authorize and practically direct the reduction of freight rates on agricultural products," though Representative Shallenberger of Nebraska stated that it was "simply a gesture to placate the farmer."[3] This meddling added nothing to the commission's powers, and its instructions were not sufficiently explicit to be effective strategy for the farm interests. As a basis for the reconstitution of rate principles, the measure imposed a task so enormous and confused that, as one commissioner said, "it could not be performed in 100 years by 100 Solomons." But the passage of this resolution complicated the work of the commission and paved the way for similar attempts to influence rates for the benefit of particular groups and classes.

Pressure upon the commission is not attempted solely through legislation. Threats to investigate and petitions and memorials from unions, business organizations, and farm and livestock associations add their weight to the tug of war. Members arise in fiery denunciation of the commission, read letters of criticism, and reprint editorials and magazine articles in the *Congressional Record;* these attacks range all the way from threats against the

[1] *The Interstate Commerce Commission*, vol. I, p. 200.
[2] 42 Stat. 827, amending Section 22 of the Interstate Commerce Act, paragraphs 2 and 3. *Cf.* Sharfman, *op. cit.*, p. 227.
[3] *A Legislative History of the Hoch-Smith Resolution*, by Examiner Warren H. Wagner of the Interstate Commerce Commission, 1925.

continued existence of the commission to indictments of particular decisions.[1]

The sectional jealousies prompting interference with the commission emerge with unmistakable clearness in connection with appointments of commissioners. The line-up of economic forces is to some extent coincident with regional divisions, and a long dispute such as the lake-cargo coal-rates controversy reverberated in the Senate hearings in the nomination of Cyrus Woods and the reappointment of John J. Esch as commissioners. The smoldering struggle between the coal producers of Pennsylvania and the southern mine operators has been fully studied[2] and concerns us here only in so far as it served to bring to the surface the close connection between these industries and senatorial defense of regional interests. Senator Reed of Pennsylvania stated his position thus unequivocally: "I claim that one-eleventh of the population of the United States live in Pennsylvania, and that we are entitled reasonably once in 40 years to one-eleventh of the Interstate Commerce Commission."[3] He further stated: "We can talk all we please about abstract justice, about the Commission deciding always on the fairness of the facts laid before them; but, as a matter of practical humanity, we know that they speak for the regions from which they come, if only because they understand their needs better."[4]

This conception of the Interstate Commerce Commission as a representative rather than regulatory body naturally arouses jealousies and recrimination. The defenders of other sections will not sit silent when Senator Reed demands the appointment of a Pennsylvanian. Senator Swanson wants to know why his section has not been given consideration, and he attributes the omission to "political considerations, personal considerations and pressure, or because these nominations are made by some outside interests."[5]

[1] For a list of such threats, *American Political Science Review, op. cit.*, pp. 903–906.

[2] Each side fought for freight rates that would enable it to dispose of its products to advantage in the lake-cargo coal trade. See Harvey C. Mansfield, *The Lake Cargo Coal Controversy*, Columbia University Press, 1932.

[3] Nomination of Cyrus Woods. *Hearings* before Committee on Interstate Commerce, Senate, 69th Congress, Second Session, January, 1927, p. 133.

[4] *Ibid.*, p. 68.

[5] *Congressional Record*, 69th Congress, First Session, Dec. 21, 1925, Senate, pp. 1252–1258, for debate on representative character of Interstate Commerce Commission.

Senator Neely of West Virginia is up in arms over a statement in the *Washington Star* that "two or three" members of the Interstate Commerce Commission would resign in a body if the Senate rejected Commissioner Esch's confirmation; he stigmatizes it as "a most extraordinary and reprehensible attempt . . . to intimidate the Senate." But he is equally on his guard against the attitude of his senatorial colleagues. He calls their attention to the stupendous blunder of bowing to the clamor for sectional representation on the commission, since this would make it "necessary for the senators representing that particular section that is in jeopardy to engage in an elaborate and in a most reprehensible scheme of horse-trading with other members of the Senate to obtain confirmation of their friends to protect their particular interests."

The injection of this principle of representation of interests into the make-up of the Interstate Commerce Commission would inevitably destroy its judicial character. To carry out the recurring proposal to make the commission representative of regions would mean enlarging it to unwieldy size. Yet the pull of economic and sectional interests plays a much larger part in conflicts over appointments than partisan politics. Failing to secure the representation on the commission at which he aimed, Senator Reed, for example, would declare political warfare and abolish the commission if that were within his power. Another indication of the attitude maintained by some Senators is the ill-founded intimation that Commissioners Esch and Aitchison refused to heed the clamors of the Pennsylvania coal operators until the eve of the expiration of their terms of office. Similarly, Commissioner Woodlock's opinions of the farmers were viewed by some as rendering him ineligible for appointment. Said Senator Wheeler:

This man has simply been a propagandist for the big interests in New York City, whose views are absolutely opposed in every single way, not only to our views upon railroad matters, but our views upon farm problems, and the farmers' problems are the problems of the Interstate Commerce Commission.[1]

It is true that some of the commissioners have been closely connected with particular interests. F. I. Cox was once president of

[1] *Nomination of Woodlock. Hearings* before Committee on Interstate Commerce, Senate, 69th Congress, First Session, January, 1926, pp. 62–63.

an organization of commercial traveling men; Edgar Clark was head of the brotherhood of railway conductors; Mark W. Potter was for years a leader in the fight of the farmers against the railroads in the western intermountain territory. Some professional link with transportation and a knowledge of its problems constitute a natural qualification for office, but the idea of direct special-interest representation is not to be regarded with equanimity.

The commission form of organization was designed primarily to avoid the pressure of political, class, and sectional interests. The commission was to be treated as a court. The scope of its huge administrative responsibilities has exposed the commission to unforeseen pressures.[1] For example, when the Bureau of the Budget passes upon the requests of the commission, it may exert a great influence upon its activities. The independence of the commission to carry out various tasks may be greatly limited by a lack of funds. The very interests that the Interstate Commerce Commission is supposed to regulate have on occasion fought the commission's battles for higher appropriations from Congress.

Pressure upon the Interstate Commerce Commission has been exerted by the Comptroller General. It has not been directed toward decisions, but rather toward the internal organization of the commission. For example, General Lord insisted that the Bureau of Inquiry be joined with the office of the Chief Counsel. From the viewpoint of the commission this would have been unfortunate. The men selected to fill these offices were intended to perform certain particular functions, and combining the two divisions would have created a new situation demanding a different type of man at the head. The fight was taken to the "Hill" before the commission was able to get its way.

When there is a change in administration, bringing a new party into power, pressure is turned toward the White House and the new President is urged to intervene with the Interstate Commerce Commission on behalf of certain interests. The Pennsylvania coal interests got busy on Franklin D. Roosevelt soon after he came into office. Recently members of the Interstate Commerce Commission received letters from the governors of many states urging them to take a favorable stand in a pending case. The let-

---

[1] For another analysis, see Lewis C. Sorrell, "Political Rate Making," *The Traffic World*, Oct. 26, 1929, pp. 1049 ff.

ters were very similar in form. In a few instances the postmark differed greatly from the date on the letter, suggesting that they had been either antedated or held for mailing. Other signs likewise indicated that a systematic effort was being made to influence the commission.

During Hoover's administration the President composed a form letter which he sent in reply to all those urging him to intervene with the Interstate Commerce Commission. He stated that it was as improper for him to intercede with the Interstate Commerce Commission regarding a pending case as to interfere with the deliberations of the Supreme Court. Vice-president Curtis was not so punctilious. One morning he telephoned a bureau director on the commission and demanded that a certain action be taken at once. He threatened to introduce in the Senate that very afternoon a resolution calling for an investigation if his wishes were not acceded to. His demand was ignored and the resolution was introduced. It died in committee.

The safety of the Interstate Commerce Commission is to be found in the fact that, although a few politicians attempt to bring pressure to bear, the majority in Congress or on the committees retain too much respect for the objectivity of the commission to disrupt its work. But the petty-minded continue to seek favors. A Congressman not so long ago requested that the Interstate Commerce Commission hold hearings in a small and out-of-the-way town in a Middle Western state. To ride to the end of the branch line in order to reach this place would have been a nuisance to all concerned and of value only to the politician who sought the prestige of bringing the Interstate Commerce Commission hearings to the home town. When the Congressman pointedly stressed the fact that he was a member of the subcommittee of the House Appropriations Committee that passed upon the grants for the Interstate Commerce Commission, he made no great impression. One of the commissioners explained that if the appropriation was decreased the work of the Interstate Commerce Commission would be appropriately curtailed—that the scope of the commission's work rested with Congress. Against the Interstate Commerce Commissioners, standing firmly in an attitude of judicial detachment, the individual politician has no chance.

THE INTERSTATE COMMERCE COMMISSION

To maintain this position, the support of Congress is necessary. Political sniping there has been, but no concerted drive has been made against the independence of the Interstate Commerce Commission. Its great strength lies in the general recognition that the railroads must be socially controlled and that this control must be left to an impartial expert body. The coördinator stated in his last report:

It may be taken as settled that there is no substantial body of opinion in this country in favor of permitting competition to reign in the transportation field free and without restraint. The strength of this opinion, such as there is, diminishes with the degree of intimate knowledge and use of the agencies of transportation. The great bulk of well-informed opinion favors public regulation.[1]

The most significant thing about the special interests surrounding the Interstate Commerce Commission is the support they give this regulatory body. To find a propaganda campaign on the part of the railroads comparable to the present battle being waged by the electric-power companies, one must go back about twenty years. The outstanding example of the propaganda method of pressure is to be found in the campaign waged by the railroads in connection with the rate-advance cases in 1914. So great were the efforts to influence the commission's judgment on this matter that they received lengthy comment in the commission's official report. Senator La Follette introduced a great mass of evidence into the *Congressional Record* to substantiate his charge that the railroads were attempting to sway the commission.

There appears to have been a set purpose to convince us [the Commission reported], that the people were of one mind respecting the very important questions involved in the case, and that in order to satisfy every public requirement, there remained nothing for the Commission to do but to register this consensus of opinion by immediately entering an order permitting the carriers to make their proposed charges effective. The letters and telegrams received disclosed an unmistakable purpose to hurry the Commission to a conclusion before the record had been closed and before there could be an opportunity to hear, much less to consider, the

[1] *Report of the Federal Coördinator of Transportation*, 1934, House Document 89, pp. 13–14.

testimony that the protestants and others desired to offer in protection of what they conceived to be their interests as shippers.[1]

Rural as well as metropolitan papers were made vehicles of railroad propaganda, and reputable journals joined in the clamor for immediate approval of the proposed rates. The manufacturers and distributors of railroad supplies, through their organization, the Railway Business Association, maintained a publicity bureau from which circulars were issued, appeals made to businessmen's clubs, chambers of commerce, and similar organizations. Trade and financial journals and magazines presented the case for the railroads. Senator La Follette stated:

Through this means and through many others great pressure has been brought to bear on the business public, so that in turn business men have written scores upon scores and hundreds upon hundreds of letters, and business organizations have sent hundreds upon hundreds of resolutions and communications to the Interstate Commerce Commission, to the President, to members of the cabinet, and to members of Congress, urging them to use their influence with the Interstate Commerce Commission. For what? To secure a prompt and favorable decision for the railroads in this case.[2]

Nor was this all. The stockholders and bondholders were enlisted to plead with the commission, and railway employees, threatened with reduced wages or loss of employment, addressed petitions to it. The total number of letters received by the body, either

---

[1] The Five Per Cent Case, 31 I.C.C. 351, pp. 425 ff.

[2] *Congressional Record*, 63 Congress, Second Session, May 12, 1914, pp. 8859 et seq. On pp. 8866–9224, the Senate had printed about four hundred pages of exhibits, including bulletins, pamphlets, and addresses issued by the railroad publicity bureau or made by railroad officials; newspaper stories and magazine articles; copies of editorials sent to the Interstate Commerce Commission to suggest the public reaction; communications from individuals sent to the President, Cabinet officers, and Congressmen and forwarded to the commission; letters showing the agitation on the part of bankers and businessmen for a rate increase; and resolutions from boards of trade, chambers of commerce, and manufacturers' associations. For an account of the agitation of the railroads before Congress in connection with the Elkins Act of 1903, see W. Z. Ripley, *Railroads, Rates and Regulations*, pp. 496–498, Longmans Green, 1912, which shows a similar publicity campaign directed in this case to influence legislation.

directly or from the mail pouches of Senators and Representatives, aggregated several thousand.

Concerning these letters the commission reported:

Those that have been examined disclose that the writers were without any real understanding either of the many intricate questions involved in the investigation or of the facts disclosed in the record; and they show little appreciation of the statutory standards by which we must be controlled when considering the rates and practices of carriers.

Such propaganda efforts by the railroads served to create a false impression of the powers and duties of the commission. Apparently, many of the writers had been persuaded that it was up to the commission to "restore confidence" in the business world, and that this aim gave it a sufficient warrant for action. But the commission has no authority to increase freight rates in order to "stimulate" business, and it must act in accordance with the standards fixed by statute. Clearly the dissemination of a false idea of the commission's functions serves to weaken its position as an independent tribunal charged by law with definite duties.

At present the shortsightedness of attempts to influence the commission's action by propaganda has been generally recognized by most of the carriers. *Railway Age* takes the view that "the policy of pressure is equally dangerous to the railways and to those who use and pay for their services. To criticize and appeal from the commission's decisions is one thing. To resort to political coercion to influence its decisions and policies is an entirely different thing."[1] Critics, however, must be boldly confronted and confounded. The *Railway Age* states:

Various organizations of the railways, most of them branches of the Association of Railway Executives, are engaged constantly in preparing data and arguments which completely refute the calumnies constantly being circulated by those who desire to destroy private ownership and management of railways. The trouble is that not enough is being done through the organization of most of the individual railways to get the facts about the railway situation presented to the people in their territories. . . . There are railways in every part of the country which, through special departments established and maintained for that purpose, are

[1] *Railway Age*, Jan. 12, 1929, p. 136.

doing effective work to nullify the effects of anti-railroad propaganda being carried on. This ought to be true, however, not merely of only part but of all the railways. Not a single false or misleading statement regarding railway management or railway regulation should be allowed to be published anywhere without an answer to it being promptly sent to the paper in which it appears, with a request for publication of the answer.[1]

The railroads themselves have, on occasion, been frank to admit that they consider counterpropaganda necessary for the protection of their interests.

The right of the railroads to present their side of a controversy in a bid for public support cannot be challenged, but how far can this general opinion be brought to bear on the commission without possible infringement of its judicial independence? To what extent can the railroads legitimately conduct a publicity campaign? An effort is made to influence public opinion, and then to direct the force of this opinion upon the commission. Where does political pressure begin? Judging by pronouncements in the *Railway Age*, by the attitude of the Railway Business Association, and by the policy of the American Railway Association, the carriers are well aware of the dangers of partisan interference and find the threat of congressional participation particularly distasteful. Theirs has been a losing fight against governmental regulation, but its arrival despite their efforts does not alter the fact that they vastly prefer regulation by an expert board rather than by a political assembly swayed by winds of expediency.

On the whole, the force of both the organized carriers and the organized shippers has been exerted to counteract legislative interference in rate making and to combat undue influence by sectional interests. Having national memberships, these groups can afford to take a large view of the transportation problem; the Railway Business Association, for example, has strenuously opposed the idea of regional representation upon the commission. It has gone on record as advocating the selection of commissioners without regard to section, interest, or occupation. Working in coöperation with the National Industrial Traffic League, it has tried to arouse businessmen and local, state, and national bodies to discountenance attempts to put pressure upon the commission.

[1] *Ibid.*, Dec. 3, 1921, p. 1075.

For example, in the campaign against the Pullman surcharge, the association reported:

Especially do we count upon our members and friends to take the subject up with their salesmen, well situated to discuss the economics of the proposal with commercial travelers, whose organization sponsors it. . . . Our association has been the most active body in the country in pleading for protection to the Commission against attacks upon its independence.[1]

Efforts to influence the commission have not, however, disappeared. In the Fifteen Per Cent Case, it was brought to the attention of the commission that certain large traffic areas were not protesting against the proposed rate increase, and it was argued that the commission should take their views into consideration. To this the commissioners answered:

These facts are not without significance in so far as they indicate an existing state of the public mind. They are quite without significance as a basis for determining the propriety and reasonableness of the proposed rates. The statute does not authorize us to arrive at a decision with respect to the reasonableness of rates on the basis of preponderating views.[2]

The attitude of the commissioners to propaganda tactics by the railroads is further illustrated in a warning issued by Commissioner B. H. Meyer which is very much to the point. In a letter addressed to Paul Shoup, president of the Western Pacific Railroad, Ralph Budd, president of the Great Northern, and H. M. Adams of the Western Pacific, he said:

In connection with the applications . . . many resolutions and communications of various sorts are being received by us, it appears obvious that a great deal of propaganda work is being done both for and against this project . . . It is assumed that you gentlemen know that cases are determined by us on the record and not by consideration of resolutions, communications, newspaper articles, and the like. Of course, we recognize that some of this material may be spontaneous, but experience indicates that a very considerable portion of it is the result of solicitation by opposing interests. When a hearing is held on these applications there will

[1] "General Executive Committee Report of Railway Business Association," *Railway Age*, Nov. 24, 1928, pp. 1021–1022.

[2] The Fifteen Per Cent Case, 45 I.C.C. 303, p. 316.

be an opportunity for an expression by witnesses who have something to adduce in the way of testimony relating to this project, but propaganda of the sort apparently now in vogue is not helpful and should not be tolerated.[1]

The maintenance of a correct relationship is definitely a responsibility of the spokesmen of the various interests who appear before the commission. One of these men, a general counsel for the Southern Traffic League, says:

I think that in reality it is upon the traffic men and the commerce lawyers that the responsibility and duty rest in aiding the Commission to correct the situation. . . . We have encouraged the Commission to be too tolerant in its entertainment of attempted influence of sectionalism and partisan attitudes. We have been too lax in failing to support the Commission in its obvious wish that testimony, briefs, arguments, letters, telegrams, and other forms of appeal shall not be presented when they are remote from issues contemplated by law, and which can only be described as clamorous appeal for class or sectional recognition. We have by our own course of conduct accentuated the looseness of the Commission's system of pleading and practice with the tendency to convert what ought to be law suits into something like town hall meetings and, I regret to say, at times political gatherings.[2]

The Association of Practitioners before the Interstate Commerce Commission was organized in 1930 with the declared purposes of promoting the proper administration of the laws under which that body operates, upholding the honor of practice before the commission, and encouraging cordial relations. At its first meeting, a comprehensive code of ethics covering every aspect of its work before the commission was adopted, based largely upon suggestions made by Commissioner Aitchison and the standards of the American Bar Association.[3] This code recognized the need for stopping such abuses as those described above.

---

[1] *United States Daily*, June 29, 1929.

[2] Charles E. Cotterill, in address to traffic clubs as reported in *Railway Age*, May 3, 1930, p. 1070.

[3] Canons of Ethics and Rules of Procedure of the Professional Ethics and Grievances Committee. The following excerpts are particularly pertinent:

"4. Attempts to Exert Political Influence on the Commission.

"It is unethical for a practitioner to attempt to sway the judgment of the Commission by propaganda, or by enlisting the influence or intercession of members

Much may be expected from extraofficial efforts on lines like these to build up an environment around the commission which will protect its deliberative character and facilitate its administrative operations. As we have seen, it is through outside expert assistance that the solution of many technical problems has been reached. Regulations framed in this direct relation to existing conditions carry their own validity and exert an intrinsic force parallel to that of the law. Outright coercion is apt to defeat its own ends and indicates as a rule that defective methods are being employed. But the importance of adjusting conflicting interests extends far beyond the technical field, and the application of the law may be enfeebled if pressures from outside interests are not properly directed and controlled.

The force of enlightened self-interest may be turned to protecting the commission from the influence of the narrower selfishness that appeals through Congress for special legislation or attempts to influence the appointment of commissioners. National associations of carriers and of shippers are built upon a base sufficiently broad to counterbalance the forces of sectionalism and partisanship. They serve to bring order into the multifarious private agencies concerned with transportation and to create general categories according to functions and occupations. Internal disputes between individuals within these associations can first be disposed of, and a unified presentation can be made by the association on matters of major importance engaging the attention of the commission.

The potentialities for autonomy and responsibility on the part of these organizations seem great, and still remain to be fully explored. In the end such organizations can but recognize that an impartial and completely uninfluenced commission is to their ultimate advantage. Their recurrent concern with the same

---

of Congress or other public officers, or by threats of political or personal reprisal.

"5. Attempts to Exert Personal Influence on the Commission.

"Marked attention and unusual hospitality on the part of a practitioner to a commissioner, examiner, or other representative of the Commission, uncalled for and unwarranted by the personal relations of the parties, subject both to misconstruction of motive and should be avoided. A self-respecting independence in the discharge of duty, without denial or diminution of the courtesy and respect due the official station, is the only proper foundation for cordial personal and official relations between the Commission and practitioners."

problems suggests that a shortsighted policy on their part would work to their disadvantage in the end. A dependence upon expediency would appear impolitic in the long run. Already leaders of the American Railway Association are coming to realize that publicity campaigns are of questionable value when instigated to arouse favorable opinion on part of the public with regard to cases pending before the commission. Such tactics are regarded with suspicion by the public and with disapproval by the commission.

Indirect pressure upon the commission through political channels, though attempted time and again, has not proved effective. The sectional jealousies and the class and occupational conflicts brought to light in these efforts have occasioned much strife and few victories. Carriers and shippers alike recognize the danger and futility of this strategy. This attitude is well summarized thus:

> If powerful political and industrial influence, coupled with the selfish desires of those dominating the business of certain localities or regions, are to dominate the Interstate Commerce Commission, which has heretofore been independent of these influences and uncontrolled by such desires, then the hope for a "scientific and non-partisan development of administrative law" has perished and the future findings of this Commission will be thought of by fair-minded men with contempt.[1]

That those practicing before the commission are developing a code of ethical standards is a most healthy sign. In the final analysis, it is in the hands of those directly affected by the commission's work that the best hope for the future lies. The public, as such, can take no positive part, and Congress time and again has done little more than reflect the economic conflict of sections. The existence of reputable and responsible national organizations representing the economic forces concerned with transportation problems may make for an environment discouraging to sectionalism and individual selfishness. Such organizations can transcend the issues offered by the disputants in any one particular case and retain a broader viewpoint. They stand in a better position to see that a commission protected from political rate making and guarded from coercion by economic interests works to their ultimate advantage.

[1] Testimony of Mr. Belcher, *Hearings* before Committee on Interstate Commerce, Senate, 69th Congress, Second Session, January, 1927, p. 79.

THE INTERSTATE COMMERCE COMMISSION

The Interstate Commerce Commission cannot be insulated from its economic contacts and its political context, but the powerful currents of interest with which it is surrounded can perhaps be utilized for discovering the *public* interest. The pressures from the outside may be of utmost significance in exhibiting the strength of important elements deserving attention at the hands of officials. The conception of the public welfare is derived in any given case from the substance presented by certain special interests. The administrative problem lies in the adjustment of these interests, not in terms of some abstract ideal, but rather in terms of the parties at conflict and in relation to the law.

Legal norms, however, must be supplemented by economic standards and by technical considerations. This is implicit in any "just and reasonable" settlement. Hence the public interest cannot be given concrete expression except through the compromise of special claims and demands finally effected. Special interests cannot then be banished from the picture, for they are the parts that make the whole. Properly organized, such interests serve, not only as responsible and articulate agencies of group opinion, but also as sources of technical competence. The experience of the Interstate Commerce Commission in its relations to carrier and shipper associations suggests that the "pressures" of such groups can be directed to useful ends and that the influence of partisanship and sectionalism can be subdued by a salutary functionalism.

In the field of railroad transportation carriers and shippers alike have recognized that the Interstate Commerce Commission merits their support. This attitude has been a matter of gradual growth. The commission in the beginning placed chief emphasis upon guarding the safety of the traveling public and protecting the shippers from excessive rates.

The early years of Federal regulation were marked by a long series of court contests and meager progress in the fight against discrimination [Commissioner Eastman has stated]. Increasing public resentment culminated in a great strengthening of the Commission's powers in 1906 and 1910. Thereafter, the thought that the companies as well as the public were in need of protection gained momentum. This resulted, after the brief period of Federal operation during the World War, in the Transportation Act, 1920, which undertook to provide comprehensive means of protection against all important abuses, in the interest of the owners of the railroads as well as of those who use them.[1]

Under the sheltering arm of the Interstate Commerce Commission, the railroads and the shippers have both found protection from the harsh impact of laissez faire. They have exerted themselves in their turn to protect the commission from assaults upon its independence. The basic external economic pressures upon this commission have strengthened its hand in dealing with narrow partisans and in discouraging political rate making. The railroads have come to identify a high degree of regulation in the public interest with their own best interests. What will happen to the commission if and when it tries to harmonize the conflicts between motor-bus, water-carrier, and railroad interests is a question to ponder.

[1] *Report of the Federal Coordinator, op. cit.*, p. 10.

Chapter XIII

SHIELDING REGULATORY COMMISSIONS FROM POLITICS

"I haven't tried it yet," the Knight said, gravely; "so I can't tell for certain . . . but I'm *afraid* it would be a little hard."

THE great question under a democracy is how to establish an effective regulation of industry in the public interest when important business groups must be brought under such control. Men of foresight may point the way toward broad social objectives, but can these views carry enough weight to bring over to their side the mass of men who take a firm stand on immediate self-interest? Can we pull ourselves above the play of special interests when the general welfare demands such a difficult move? It does seem "a *little* hard."

Democracy ensures the freedom of a people to adjust their government to meet those conditions that harmonize with the majority's conception of how to promote the public welfare. Until recent years the federal government has not taken a positive role in this search for the "good life." It was assumed that the economic system, if not interfered with too much, would provide enough for all. Most men believed that the public interest was promoted by the natural working of the competitive capitalistic order. Today so many men have lost faith in this system that the government is forced to take the lead in interpreting the public welfare. Many voters seek economic security through political channels. They demand protections from destitution. They are not concerned with the difficulties engendered by their demands. They have little concern in improving the faulty means through which the government must struggle to reach their ends. They may, for example, blindly support the "Constitution of the Founding Fathers" while insisting upon a degree of federal protection that is quite beyond the purview of this very document.

At present the federal government cannot interpret all aspects of the public interest. It is debatable as to whether even the social objectives of the Roosevelt administration can be implemented with appropriate agencies. Constitutional limitations bar the way in some directions. If, as a matter of national policy, an organic conception of the public welfare is to be developed by the federal government, powerful and efficient administrative machinery is essential. This administrative structure must be able to offer resistance to those groups bent solely upon their own self-interest. Sectional differences will have to be discounted and economic influences counterbalanced before a federally ordained conception of the general welfare is possible. All the groups vitally affected should be considered in the administrative process. It becomes a governmental responsibility to provide a place for such interests and to seek their coöperation. The bureaucracy must reflect a balanced view of the public interest.

But it is one thing to describe what should be done and quite another thing to carry the process into execution. We know that the process is fraught with difficulty, and whether it is worth attempting is still an open question. Only within the depression years has the federal government been frankly regarded as a general pack mule for carrying the burdens that the industrial machine could no longer support. Federal officials "interfered" in the past, but today more is demanded. It is not enough to discourage unfair trade practices and to outlaw monopoly. Industrial regulation has been attempted in more positive form.

The National Industrial Recovery Act was intended as a constructive effort toward recovery. The act was to restore prosperity by adjusting the relations between production and consumption. In its actual application chief emphasis was placed upon the raising of prices and wages. The administration of the act became a process of bargaining, with employers and employees doing most of the talking. Government officials were faced with problems so new and so complex that they often felt like babes in a dense industrial wood. They had great difficulty in coping with industrialists on an equal footing and they were often unable to answer immediate concrete questions by relating these problems to clear ultimate objectives. What theory was to guide officials in interpreting the act? "The theories were as numerous as the expectations of persons concerning the use which would be made of the powers. The powers were so great that there was no means of prognosticating in what particular directions they would be used."[1] An efficient administrative machinery for directing the business life of the nation could not possibly be built up in a few short months or even years. The fatal decision of the Supreme Court showed the constitutional limits of federal authority. It forestalled a complete revelation of the practical limitations to democratic control of industry.

Our experience with regulatory agencies shows the immense difficulty of imposing, through democratic machinery, a close control on industry. Government regulation has done little more than outlaw practices that are frowned upon by the majority of businessmen. It has brought order into fields where the industrialists themselves recognized the need for control. The self-interest of politically effective groups has been identified with such departures from laissez faire. Under a democratic government the problem is how to transcend the selfishness of economic groups that are politically powerful. All our commissions must regulate powerful economic groups in accordance with the public interest. This means that the demands of one group should be denied and those of another granted without regard to their respective political strength. But if regulation is to be effective, politically important sections or groups must support this process. Highly significant is the opportunity offered the conservative investor for holding bonds in "mixed" public-utility undertakings composed of public and private capital.

Government regulation of industry in the past has been effective only where the interests regulated have recognized the necessity of such control. With the struggles that take place on the plane of policy formulation, we are not here concerned. But administration as well as legislation involves a conflict of forces. The course of administrative action is not charted by dead reckoning with the statute books as the only point of reference. In order to counteract hostility to a strict interpretation of the policy set by Congress, this objective must be aggressively supported by executive and legislative leaders. There must be a national leadership that rallies the public behind a general program and that stirs up opposition to selfish demands.

[1] L. S. Lyon and others, *The National Recovery Administration*, p. 25, Brookings Institution, 1935.

The pressures of sectional and economic interests have not been escaped by placing the administration of certain controversial issues under the jurisdiction of "independent commissions." This administrative device has not eliminated political interference. "Good men," however able or well intentioned, cannot successfully cope with questions that involve unsettled national policies. The United States Tariff Commission has demonstrated the difficulties that arise in such a situation.

In the cases considered thus far, the administrative problem has been the adjustment of conflicting special interests in accordance with the bureaucrat's interpretation of the law. Congress has done little more than declare that certain economic activities must be regulated in accordance with the "public interest, convenience or necessity." This has meant that in practice officials have swung the weight of governmental authority to the side of one of the several contending interests before them. Even in the conduct of foreign relations or the collection of taxes, officials find themselves aiding one economic group and obstructing others. In the protection of American interests abroad, in tax collection, and in tariff negotiations, the administrative officer has a public function of major importance to perform. A similar responsibility rests upon the officials regulating interstate commerce, communications, unfair methods of competition, or federal water-power development. None of these tasks can be directly correlated with the interests of any one class. Administrators have tried to maintain an impartial attitude. Independent commissions have been established to settle with judicial detachment the conflicts between powerful economic groups. In actual practice officials have been forced to identify the interests of certain groups with the national interest.

The lack of coördination within the administration narrows the official's view of the general welfare to his own sphere of experience. Under these conditions general standards for administration in the public interest are impossible. Criteria must be developed for each administrative situation. For example, where the governmental responsibility is limited to policing the arrant offenders within a certain industry for the benefit of the non-offenders, the welfare of this industry constitutes a standard of reference. This is an unduly narrow basis for administration in the public interest.

Where a regulatory body, charged with controlling a powerful industry, finds itself in surroundings dominated by these interests, the problem cannot be met by the ordinary devices for securing objectivity of judgment. Security of tenure and wide legal authority for administrators do not meet the difficulty since the first need is for standards by which to ascertain the public interest. If we assume that the welfare of all is the inevitable product of our industrial system, then officials need do no more than assist that segment of business activity falling under their jurisdiction. If, on the other hand, the federal government is to take the lead, coördination within the administration is essential. There must be generally accepted standards for promoting the public interest. Whatever the present political temper may be, a long-time view points to the federal government's assuming an ever-increasing responsibility for the general welfare. Yet the administrative agencies established to meet these responsibilities create fresh problems because of their diversity and uneven development.

Professor Arthur MacMahon writes:

The abandonment of *laissez-faire* is indicated most forcefully in the multiplication of *ad hoc* regulatory boards. Far from representing sound legislation and perfected administration, they are significant as confessions of a need and as the crude beginnings of control. A society intent on exploitation and schooled to leave adjustments to initiative and competition has become uncomfortable and been forced to act without knowing what it wished to do. The first steps have taken the form of a congeries of unrelated statutes nearly devoid of policy, by which undigested problems have been devolved upon amorphous agencies that administer a kind of compulsory arbitration among conflicting interests.[1]

Before the Wilson administration the only independent commissions of any importance were the Civil Service Commission and the Interstate Commerce Commission. Their novel functions could not be readily brought into any of the then existing categories of the administrative hierarchy. The strength of the spoils system emphasized the logic of making the Civil Service Commission an independent agency, and its responsibilities for the personnel in

[1] *Encyclopedia of the Social Sciences*, vol. 7, p. 20. For an illuminating discussion of government by administrative rules *vs.* statutes, see James Hart, *Ordinance Making Powers of the President*, Johns Hopkins Press, 1925, pp. 264 ff. *Tenure of Office* by the same author has several very valuable chapters on administrative commissions.

all departments made inappropriate its union with any one. When the Interstate Commerce Commission was established in 1887, there was no department to which it clearly belonged. The present development of independent regulatory commissions dates back about twenty years.

The departmental organization as it emerged in 1913 was ill-adapted to the task of controlling rival economic classes. Government regulation had to be impartial if it was to be effective or even tolerable. Yet the necessary detachment was not to be expected from departments set up for the special benefits of certain groups.

Congress dominated by political forces was not in a position to give these problems the expert or detached consideration they required. Political support, for example, could be marshaled to "crush the power trust" but the painstaking effort of thinking through a suitable program of developing and regulating electric power was quite another matter. The unloading of such responsibilities upon special commissions offered a way out. Their impartiality was not to be jeopardized by identification with any one of the special-interest departments.

The first independent commission established was the Board of Mediation and Conciliation (Newlands Act, July 15, 1913), empowered to bring about agreement between employer and employee when industrial disputes affecting interstate commerce threatened the public interest. Although the Secretary of Labor urged that the task came within the scope of the Division of Conciliation in his department, organizations of both workers and employers prevented Congress from subordinating the board to the department.

The next creation was the Federal Reserve Board. An effort was made to put it in the Treasury Department, but in the terms of the statute (act of December 23, 1913) was expressed the intention of establishing an independent body selected with due regard for rival interests. The law specifically provided that the membership of the board be recruited from various sections and commercial and industrial sectors. The act was later amended in order to provide for the representation of agriculture.

When the tariff and trade commissions were established, Congress deliberately placed them outside the existing administrative structure. Yet the Federal Trade Commission took over the functions of the Bureau of Corporations in the commerce department and the United States Tariff Commission absorbed the investigatory work once done by bureaus in the Department of Commerce and the Department of Labor.

The executive departments established to serve business, labor, and agriculture have not only been too closely allied to one class, but they have also been too narrow in their scope to handle properly certain problems. Evidence of this is found in the failure of commissions manned by ex officio cabinet officers and designed by Congress to regulate fields in which several departments had stakes. The Federal Power Commission in its early days and the Federal Oil Conservation Board more recently illustrate this approach. The breakdown of the former agency as an ex officio board clearly showed the disadvantages of this form and stressed emphatically the superiority of the independent commission. The public servant is required to execute the law, presumably embodying the purpose of the community, in an environment of interest groups concerned with their own fulfillment. Inescapably the administrator's attitude is colored in greater or less degree by this context. If the public purpose of the state is to be achieved, the bureaucrat must be released from an environment that makes objective judgment difficult if not impossible. The existing independent commissions are *forms* well adapted to impartiality and *expertise*, but they lack coördination with the rest of the federal hierarchy.

Congress has accepted the independent commission as well suited to meeting the demands of warring groups. This confidence is illustrated in the striking degree of discretion permitted these agencies. Congress has been content to allow them to follow their own bent with only such vague standards as "fair," "just," or "reasonable" to point the way. In giving these abstractions concrete application, officials do little more than apply their own private judgment of social values. Reconciling the theory of a rule of law with this situation becomes very difficult. This is very clear in the case of the Federal Trade Commission and the Federal Radio Commission.

We assume that the purpose of the state is the development of a unified rule of law and the subordination of those group purposes contrary to the broader aims of the state. These *ad hoc* commissions are expected to bring order and justice into important spheres of economic activity. Operating independently of one another and of the rest of the administrative hierarchy, they vary in their strength and strategy in controlling economic activity.

Under the democratic process a statute represents the compromise of conflicting interests of the time and circumstances surrounding its enactment. There is no certainty that this same balance of forces will be observed in the execution of the law. A bill that is the product of one combination of political and economic factors becomes a very different law when interpreted against an administrative background radically different from its legislative context. This task of interpretation is in fact a continuation of the legislative process. The full implications of this should be faced. Independent commissions are called upon to give substance to a vague congressional mandate by establishing rules and regulations. They are subjected to the same pressures that assailed the legislators. Through their rule-making authority officials can determine policy to a very considerable extent. Yet they are independent of the chief executive. These officials at the same time perform judicial functions. They determine the extent to which private rights are affected by the very rules that they have drawn.

The Special Committee on Administrative Law of the American Bar Association recommended in a recent report that the executive and legislative duties of independent commissions "should be transferred to the several executive departments of the federal government (or to one or more new executive departments if it is found necessary to create them), responsible to the President."[1]

Such a transfer has been carefully considered by Joseph B. Eastman, Federal Coördinator of Transportation, and his arguments are so cogent that they warrant full quotation. Concerning the Interstate Commerce Commission he states:

There is much misunderstanding about the Commission's work. Among those not well informed, an impression is common that it can readily be classified under three heads—legislative, administrative, and judicial. No such classification can be made. There is a mixture of functions. The prescribing of rates for the future is legislative; the awarding of reparation

[1] *Report of the Special Committee on Administrative Law of the American Bar Association*, 1934, p. 201.

for rates found unreasonable in the past is judicial; in both instances quasi-judicial procedure is necessary, as it is in all the Commission's work where controversies exist and public hearings are required. The prescription of safety devices may seem to be purely administrative; yet such cases are often sharply litigated and must be decided upon facts developed of record in a public hearing. The same is true of such matters as approval of security issues and the granting of certificates of public convenience and necessity. The accounting and statistical departments play a vital part in rate regulation. As stated in the Report of the Transportation Conference of 1933–34, "Such commissions are legislative, in the sense that they do work similar to that of the legislatures; they are judicial in the sense that they decide particular controversies, and employ procedures that resemble those of the courts, and they are executive, in that they undertake to see that the laws they administer are enforced.[1]

Mr. Eastman admits, however, that certain administrative functions might be transferred from the Interstate Commerce Commission to a Department of Transportation and that other agencies might be thus grouped together, as, for example, the Merchant Fleet Corporation in the Department of Commerce, the Bureau of Public Roads in the Department of Agriculture, the Alaska Road Commission and the Alaska Railroad in the Department of the Interior, and the Inland Waterways Corporation in the Department of War. As a matter of political expediency, it appears unwise to place all these functions in a separate department at the present time. The Coördinator states:

Transportation is essentially a technical subject and should be dealt with accordingly. It is vital that it be kept out of politics, so far as possible. A Cabinet member, concerned with general affairs of State as well as with transportation, would have difficulty in mastering the subject. Necessarily, also, he is in politics and has no greater permanence than the administration of which he is a part. There would thus be frequent shifts in the personnel of a Secretary of Transportation, militating against any continuity of policy and development of wisdom from experience. Moreover, the situation here differs from that found in countries, like Great Britain, having a parliamentary system. There, the executive and legislative branches of the Government are normally in harmony. Here, the President and Congress are often in discord. In these circumstances, a non-political officer would have an advantage over a Cabinet member in dealing with the two branches of the Government. It is also the fact that there is a degree of permanence below the top in the personnel of the

[1] *Report of the Coördinator*, 1934, p. 28.

[219]

British executive departments, owing to well-established traditions in the civil service, which we do not enjoy in the United States.[1]

These are practical considerations of great weight. Changes in the administrative structure will lead to failure if they are not adjusted to the rest of the governmental system. The creation of permanent undersecretaries in the various departments would partially meet this need for administrative stability and expert direction.

If officials are to cope with their duties, they must have the means of developing standards of public interest. A Department of Transportation may be inadvisable today. Nevertheless the idea deserves consideration. The problem is not simply the control of railroads but the development of a national system of transportation. Regulation has been very restricted in its outlook. The Interstate Commerce Commission started out as a body to regulate freight rates. It has broadened its jurisdiction to a control of all important phases of the railroad industry. The problem, however, has continually been thought of in terms of balancing the interests of the railroad owners and the railroad users. The interest of the railway employees has been considered chiefly in terms of providing such conditions of work as to ensure the safety of the passengers. At present we are groping toward a national transportation policy. It is from this higher plane that the public interest can be effectively surveyed by an administrative body. If officials are to discharge their duties in the public interest, they must be thus advantageously situated. Their duties in the past have been confined to ferreting out those who have committed certain illegal acts.

Enlarging the jurisdiction of regulatory commissions provides a *possible* way of slowly reorganizing the bureaucratic structure. The process arouses less virulent opposition. There is less unanimity in the "publics" concerned with these agencies. One group tends to counteract the influence of another. Accordingly, the chief executive can move with a freer hand in making changes. The President can exercise his powers to best advantage in a situation where a counterbalance of forces exist. When President Roosevelt made Commissioner Eastman Coördinator of Transportation, he established a focal point about which a national

[1] *Ibid.*, pp. 28–29.

transportation policy might evolve. It now seems only a matter of time before Eastman's recommendations are acted upon by Congress and the Interstate Commerce Commission is empowered to extend its authority over all forms of interstate commercial transportation. The new Federal Communications Commission has served to bring together in one body control of electrical communications. We have noted the efforts to develop a federal policy in regard to electric power. These steps all lead toward a greater degree of coördination. They mean that federal officials will be confronted with interests in conflict along a broader front.

Officials should gain in perspective through this widening of their viewpoint. Reorganization in these terms means the development of public policy in transportation, in communications, and in power development. The attention of the official is no longer concentrated upon the railroads, the broadcasters, or the electric-power companies. The problems of regulation are posed in broader terms; more interests must be considered. Great boards dealing with broad national problems like transportation, communications, and the development of natural power resources must arrange a division of labor before officials can face their duties. Thus a distinction between those doing executive work and those performing judicial duties might well be made in time. As in the Bureau of Internal Revenue, a separate board might be established to perform the judicial functions. "The Board of Tax Appeals has demonstrated that when this is done, it is possible to maintain a high order of judicial integrity and independence, a freedom from political considerations, and generally, the demeanor of the traditional court of justice," the A.B.A. Committee on Administrative Law states.[1]

While administrative officials cannot be insulated from their environment, they can be placed in a position to offer more or less resistance to temptation or coercion from the outside. We have noted how persistently the forces with which internal-revenue officials worked affected the routine of administration. In this case an improvement of personnel conditions was one means of counteracting the disruptive influence of outside employment opportunities. The creation of the Board of Tax Appeals relieved officials of much pressure from aggrieved taxpayers.

[1] *Report of the American Bar Association, op. cit.*, p. 212.

PUBLIC ADMINISTRATION

In other chapters we have noted how changes in policy, shifts in the directing personnel, and reforms in administrative organization have strengthened the position of officials. Enlarging the scope of a commission's responsibility may bring about a division of functions and broaden the basis for judgment, but it leaves unanswered a very important problem.

There is a fundamental divergence between administration by expert and independent commissions and administration by a responsible chief executive. Yet commissions should function in general harmony with the policy of the administration in power. If differences arise, either the President or the commission must back down in order to avoid disruption. Two conflicting and equally authoritative views of the public interest cannot continue within the federal administration. If a commission is to do effective work, it must have the support of the chief executive. The pressures of private groups can be met; political interference cannot. Judicial impartiality cannot be expected of officials burdened with executive and legislative duties. They cannot defend policies and remain objective at the same time. Congress has unloaded unsettled national problems upon independent commissions. It has expected the commissioners to recommend legislation and to frame regulations. Yet they were to be independent of the chief executive and of all private interests. Their record discloses how this theory was crushed by the hard impact of actual conditions.

When President F. D. Roosevelt embarked upon his plans for national recovery, he gathered into his hands every strand of authority that might lead toward his objectives. At the level of the Presidential office a greater degree of integration was introduced into the federal administrative organization than has ever been witnessed in peace-time experience. And the reach of the President did not falter before the independent commissions. The problems of these bodies were regarded as Presidential responsibilities as well. The tasks of the Federal Trade Commission, the United States Tariff Commission, or the Interstate Commerce Commission could not be separated from the rehabilitation of trade and industry. Yet how could they be made part in a national recovery program and still remain independent administrative agencies?

The President got around this difficulty in his characteristically adroit fashion. Placing his keymen in the departments was a simple matter, but bringing the independent organization within his control required more ingenuity. The judicial calm of the Interstate Commerce Commission was left undisturbed, but the most able and aggressive commissioner was created Federal Coördinator of Transportation. The United States Tariff Commission was reduced to a harmless condition through the passage of the Reciprocal Tariff act. The Federal Radio Commission was abolished outright and a New Deal commission took its place. The President secured the resignation of Hoover's chairman of the Federal Power Commission and added two appointees of his own.

Only in the case of the Federal Trade Commission did he meet opposition—and when William E. Humphrey demurred the President demanded his withdrawal in no uncertain terms. The Supreme Court denied the President's right to remove Humphrey on the ground that the commissioner was engaged in judicial work. The stubborn fact remains that none of our independent commissions has solely judicial responsibilities. While it is doubtful that Congress will institute outright a system of administrative courts, the necessary segregation of judicial duties from executive and legislative functions may evolve slowly. The decision of the Supreme Court in the Humphrey case, however, indicates that any basic integration of independent commissions with the White House or the executive departments must come through congressional authorization rather than through Presidential initiative.[1]

The Supreme Court emphasized the intention of Congress to keep the Federal Trade Commission "free from political domination or control" and "separate and apart from any existing department—not subject to the orders of the President." Yet in denying the President the right to remove commissioners appointed by his predecessors, the court foisted upon the succeeding administration officials who represented policies that had been repudiated. The decision of the Supreme Court is a clear reading of the statute, but it raises a question for Congress to ponder. The independent

[1] For a full account of the documents in the Humphrey case see *Hearings* before Committee on Interstate Commerce, Senate, 73d Congress, Second Session, On the Confirmation of George C. Mathews, Jan. 18, 1934. On the problem of administrative responsibility see C. J. Friedrich, Chap. 3, "Responsible Government Service under the American Constitution," in *Problems of the American Public Service*, McGraw-Hill, 1935.

commission is a protection against narrow partisan favoritism. It serves a useful purpose, politicians being as they are. But in guarding against political meddling, administrative integration and direction should not be sacrificed.

The President has certainly no right to intervene on behalf of any private party who may come before a commission, but this does not mean that he has no concern with its general interpretation of the law. Can some way be found for admitting his influence upon policy without causing interference with the commission's judicial activities? How can the chief executive, for example, be given a means of exerting his influence in national transportation problems without disrupting the work of the Interstate Commerce Commission?

The new position of Federal Coördinator of Transportation offers a way of avoiding such an impasse. This position, if made permanent, might become a focal point through which to study and direct the development of an integrated transportation system. The coördinator would maintain close relations with the President, the Interstate Commerce Commission, and all the carriers. He would report annually to the public on transportation problems and carry on frequent inquiries.[1] As envisaged by Mr. Eastman, the coördinator "would be designated from the membership of the commission by the President, but could be relieved from the duties of the office at any time, if in the judgment of the President the public interest should so require, and another member designated." Thus through this officer the policy of the chief executive in transportation questions might become explicit. Here at least is one administrative experiment that seems to answer the need of present conditions. It provides no final solution, but it suggests

---

[1] For a full description of this position, see the *Report of the Coördinator, op. cit.,* pp. 30–31. "'The officer of the government should lend his aid to the promotion of leadership in the industry, to organization for common ends, and to the initiation of general studies of various phases of operation, service, charges, and management, where such studies are needed. He should have full power to procure information and require studies, and should also be authorized to utilize the services of men loaned by the industry for specific purposes, but not to require such services. To secure such help, he should depend upon his ability to convince the industry of its value. He should, in short, be primarily a means of concentrating and bringing to focus the best thought of the industry rather than a means of supplying or imposing thought from without.'"

a workable means of approaching the ideal of administration in the public interest. It provides one way for reconciling administration by special commissions with guidance by an independent chief executive.

All the regulatory bodies considered thus far have been independent commissions. They have not been placed under any department. They have been given a special status in order that they may secure a maximum degree of detachment. The price of this independence has been a loss of coördination with other administrative bodies and occasional conflict with the chief executive. What has happened when the task of regulation has been placed in a subordinate bureau in one of the great executive departments? The experience of the Food and Drug Administration in the Department of Agriculture is revealing.

Chapter XIV

PROTECTING THE CONSUMER

"I suppose I ought to eat or drink something or other; but the
great question is, 'What?'"

The great question certainly was, "What?" Alice looked all round
her at the flowers and the blades of grass, but she could not see anything that looked like the right thing to eat or drink under the
circumstances.

THE experience of the officials enforcing the Federal Pure
Food and Drug Act for nearly three decades presents a
significant case history in governmental regulation of industry.
This becomes clear if the execution of the law is reviewed in relation to the social forces and economic influences touching the
administrators themselves. What is the bureaucratic environment
within which these government officials carry on their work?

In the Food and Drug Administration we find a personnel of
about 500 scientists and specialists: chemists, bacteriologists,
physicians, veterinarians, entomologists, plant pathologists, mi-
croscopists, pharmacologists, and the like. About one-half of this
force man the executive supervisory offices and technical control
laboratories in Washington. The rest are scattered over the
country in the various branch stations. Sixty-one inspectors are
designated to watch for infractions of the law. These officials
are responsible for enforcing not only the Pure Food and Drug
Act, but also five other acts regulating insecticides, caustic poisons,
naval stores, and importations of milk and tea. They unquestionably
have plenty to do. An idea of the enormity of the task is shown by
the fact that the total value of the year's output of canned goods
alone amounted to about $745,000,000 in 1932, while drug products
exceeded $400,000,000. With an appropriation of about $1,250,000,
a small corps of officials is charged with regulating a vast number
of products in a great variety of industries.

These bureaucratic specialists confront a highly specialized
"public" composed of the manufacturers, the producers, the ship-

pers, and the distributors engaged in the colossal work of supplying the nation with nourishment through the arteries of interstate commerce. Officials come into daily contact with dairymen, patent-medicine men, canners, fruit growers and shippers, retail grocers, and wholesalers. The variety of interests is kaleidoscopic and their number is legion.

Under the best of conditions one cannot expect very much when three score inspectors are given the job of watching the interstate commerce in foods and drugs for over 100,000,000 people. The task is rendered all the more difficult by the fact that those who are subject to regulation are prone to take an active interest in the administration of the law while those for whose protection the law was passed are apt to remain indifferent.

The Pure Food and Drug Act of 1906 was sponsored by wide public demand and passed upon a wave of popular enthusiasm. Such regulatory legislation directly touching many industries great and small can be enacted only when the clamor of an aroused people silences the protests of special interests. The passage of the law marked the successful culmination of a campaign of intensive agitation to demonstrate the great need for federal control of the interstate commerce in foods and drugs. Dr. Harvey Wiley as chief of the Bureau of Chemistry had awakened people to the dangers of certain preservatives commonly used in prepared foods by his experiments upon the "poison squad." This group of volunteers during 1902 to 1906 agreed to follow a prescribed diet of adulterated foods so that the resultant ill effects could be studied and given publicity. The muckrakers likewise exposed the current abuses in the food and drug industry and identified those Congressmen who for selfish reasons opposed remedial legislation. Attempts had been made vainly for many years to secure a federal law but it was not until the public was fully aroused and informed that a law was enacted.[1]

The conditions under which the law was to be administered proved very different from those which led to its enactment. Once the law was on the books, popular interest flagged, but the concern of the multitudinous economic and social elements coming within its jurisdiction was all the greater now that the threat of regulation

[1] Thomas Bailey, "Congressional Opposition to Pure Food Legislation, 1879–1906," *American Journal of Sociology*, July, 1930, p. 52.

had become a reality. It was these forces that dominated the milieu within which the administrators of the new law were to function. Producers and dealers hastened to express their cordial acceptance of the principle of the act and offered their hearty support in its execution.[1]

The officials thought it a part of wisdom to make haste slowly, recognizing their "double duty of securing justice for the manufacturer and the consumer alike."[2]

But how was this duty to the consumer to be ascertained? The problem was in part the purely technical one of determining what ingredients were deleterious and what products misbranded. The task here was to train a personnel of inspectors and chemists competent to ascertain the facts. But the determination of matters of fact was found to be inevitably linked with policy.

What agency was to interpret the act? The chief of the Bureau of Chemistry, Dr. Wiley, was inclined to hold the producers to a very strict account. He objected to the use of saccharin as a sweetening for canned goods, to the branding of rectified spirits as whisky, and to calling canned sprats and other small fishes "sardines." He was criticized for "crankiness" and incurred the enmity of canners and manufacturers who did not wish bureaucratic interference with those common trade practices that were not entirely within the strict letter of the law.

Protests began to reach the Secretary of Agriculture soon after the act became effective in January, 1907. Accordingly in April the Board of Food and Drug Inspection was established to conduct hearings upon alleged violations and to consider all questions as to the meaning of the law. The Bureau of Chemistry was limited to performing whatever analytical work was necessary for the information of the board. But the scientific findings of Dr. Wiley's bureau with regard to the definition and legality of certain food products and preservatives were challenged by a number of important manufacturers.

They protested to the Secretary of Agriculture and they went to President Theodore Roosevelt. The new law had not been in operation a year before business interests had effected a further change in the machinery of administration. At the request of the

[1] Department of Agriculture, *Annual Report*, 1907, p. 72.
[2] *Ibid.*, 1908, p. 81.

manufacturers, the President directed the Secretary of Agriculture to select a committee of scientists from the universities to pass judgment upon the dispute "as to whether sulphur dioxide, saccharin, and benzoate of soda are harmful when used in foods, and to consider and report to the Secretary of Agriculture upon the wholesomeness or deleterious character of such other foods or such articles used in foods as might be referred to them by the Secretary."[1]

This Referee Board of Consulting Scientific Experts advised the secretary upon technical matters for the next eight years and proved less severe in its findings than the Bureau of Chemistry. The enforcement of the pure-food law was placed in the hands of the Department of Agriculture because Dr. Wiley was in this department. But when the protection of the consumer ran counter to that of the fruit grower and the canner, the Secretary of Agriculture was inclined to look upon the bureau somewhat askance. The Department of Agriculture had been established to aid the farmer rather than to protect the consumer of food products.

Dr. Wiley resigned in 1912. His work was really done when the pure-food law was passed. He was a great crusader, but administrative work was not to his liking. The Bureau of Chemistry passed from the attention of the press. The actual task of applying the statute held little of dramatic interest for the public.

The administration of the Pure Food and Drug Act from 1907 to 1930 functioned in an environment where the officials heard much from the producers and little from the consumers. It was recognized at the very beginning that if industry actively opposed the act the difficulties of enforcement would be "practically insuperable."[2] Every effort was made to "avoid working hardship upon any one." At the same time the officials took the view that much of the "moral effect of the law depended upon a rigorous enforcement of its provisions."[3] Experience soon showed that many violations of the act were the result of ignorance rather than willful

---

[1] Gustavus A. Weber, *The Food, Drug and Insecticide Administration*, p. 18, Brookings Institution, 1928. Harvey W. Wiley in *The History of a Crime against the Food Law*, p. 63, Bobbs-Merrill, 1930, gives a list of the Bureau of Chemistry findings suppressed by the Secretary of Agriculture.

[2] Department of Agriculture, *Annual Report*, 1907, p. 72.

[3] *Ibid.*, 1908, p. 82.

intent.[1] Honest producers saw that it was to their own advantage that gross frauds and adulterated foods be removed from the market. The bureau encountered few serious obstacles in removing obvious abuses during its early years. There was plenty to do without insisting upon a rigid interpretation of the act.

A few years of vigorous enforcement, however, served to clean up the blatant infringements of the law. More subtle and hence more dangerous forms of adulteration and misbranding began to appear. Borderline cases were more frequent. Finer distinctions had to be drawn. The officials found that violations of the law were more likely to be those of the clever adulterator who anticipated the ordinary means of detection by so preparing his products that not infrequently the most detailed and painstaking chemical analysis combined with factory inspection was necessary before the irregularity became apparent.[2] Thus the task of enforcement became progressively more technical.

Moreover, the law itself was restricted in its scope. It authorized the federal authorities to seize food and drug products in interstate commerce containing putrid, filthy, or decomposed animal or vegetable matter or ingredients harmful to public health. Foods or drugs so grossly adulterated or misbranded with false or fraudulent claims as to constitute a serious imposition on the public or a demoralizing influence on legitimate trade practices were likewise to be seized. The law failed, however, to provide penalties onerous enough to serve as an effective deterrent, with the result that fines were treated by some firms as little more than a tribute levied upon illegal practices.

While officials were able to correct obvious and notorious cases by seizing and condemning the product, they soon found they were placed at a disadvantage in securing convictions in the courts against the producers. This was true particularly of prosecutions for the misbranding of drugs, where the government had to convince a jury that the manufacturer was guilty not only of making false claims for his product but also of willfully trying to deceive the public. Proving that a producer had evil intentions was a difficult task and prolonged litigation.

[1] *Ibid.*, 1915, p. 191.
[2] *Ibid.*, 1917, p. 212.

After ten years of experience, the shortcomings of the law had become so apparent that the Secretary of Agriculture in 1917 recommended amendatory legislation. His proposals were not acted upon and the matter was not pressed further.[1]

At the same time it was further reported that

. . . the act has been one of the influences which has helped to draw competitors together into associations like the guilds of the Middle Ages, associations shorn of the special privileges which the ancient guilds often enjoyed.[2]

While the bureaucrats were discovering the limits to what they could do under the law, the interests regulated were drawn together under the impact of federal regulation. Competitors saw the mutual advantage of presenting a united front to the bureaucracy.

The officials were faced with the necessity of accommodating themselves to the restrictions upon their authority and the limitations upon their funds and personnel. The facilities of the Food and Drug Administration were not sufficient for the complete coverage of the entire food- and drug-manufacturing industries. A "project plan" of administration was accordingly adopted whereby certain products were selected and the resources of the bureau concentrated upon policing them.

A desire to increase their powers and expand their staffs and appropriations is popularly supposed to be an inherent characteristic of bureaucrats. This does not appear to be true of the officials in charge of food and drug administration. On some occasions they

[1] In 1917 the chief of the Bureau of Chemistry stated in his annual report: "While the accomplishments of the Food and Drugs Act have been considerable, It must be admitted that it has its serious limitations. Especially conspicuous ones are the lack of legal standards for foods, of authority to inspect warehouses, and of any restriction whatever upon the use of many of the most virulent poisons in drugs; the limitations placed upon the term 'drug' by definition which render it difficult to control injurious cosmetics, fraudulent mechanical devices used for therapeutic purposes, as well as fraudulent remedies for obesity and leanness; the limitation of dangerous adulterants to those that are needed so that the interstate shipment of a food that naturally contains a virulent poison is unrestricted. Furthermore, the law fails to take cognizance of fraudulent statements covering foods or drugs which are not in or upon the food or drug package." Quoted in *Annual Report of Chief of Food and Drug Administration*, 1933, p. 1; the *Annual Report* of 1912, p. 361, also pointed out the need for remedial legislation.

[2] Department of Agriculture, *Annual Report*, 1917, p. 211.

called public attention to the limitations of the law and pointed out the inadequacy of their resources for handling the increasing volume of commerce. But during the decade of 1920 to 1930 the administrators of the Pure Food and Drug Act largely reconciled themselves to protecting the public as best they could with the forces at their disposal.

Interpreted from the viewpoint of self-interest, this policy appears as logically consistent as the usual view that expansion is always sought by bureaucrats. The project plan added to the discretionary powers of the officials since they were free to choose the concerns against which they would proceed. Their critics accused them of ignoring powerful offenders and going after the "little fellow." The bureaucrats, since they were unable to police all manufacturers, could always point to their necessity of choice.

Harassed administrators had an ever-ready alibi if accused of laxness or ineffectiveness. Time and again the enormity of their task was contrasted with the limited statutory authority and the inadequate staff for enforcement. It was not necessarily to their advantage as bureaucrats to seek greater and greater responsibilities. They settled down to do what they could with the means at hand. They had to content themselves with their restricted powers since conditions were unfavorable to any further increase.

Experience proved that the proper enforcement of the law was not simply a matter of changing a statute or securing more inspectors. Problems were encountered that could not be solved by force. More than 18,000 regulatory actions have been instituted for violation of the act, but many cases occur where the strict letter of the law has little significance.

Limitations upon the bureaucrat are not simply the result of inadequate facilities for enforcement or restricted authority. Technical and scientific considerations affect the exercise of administrative discretion and social, economic, and political factors enter into the routine of law enforcement. The circumstances surrounding particular cases very materially limit the activity of the bureaucrat. These elements must be weighed before an understanding of bureaucratic problems is achieved.

The tendency was for the official to become more familiar with conditions within particular industries and to consider the internal problems with which manufacturers were confronted.

PROTECTING THE CONSUMER

In the early days of pure-food regulation there were few trained food or drug analysts and almost no experienced inspectors. Obviously to such inexperienced men little discretionary power could be granted.

The administration was highly centralized and scientific research played an important part. Personal contacts were not of much significance; the chemist in the laboratory discovered violations of the law by examining samples. As precedents were built up and inspectors were trained, it was possible by 1913 to reorganize the regulatory service so as to place a larger measure of responsibility upon the field force and at the same time divorce the scientific from the regulatory work. As far as possible all work of a regulatory character was relegated to the field and the headquarters staff in Washington took over the planning and supervising of law enforcement.

This movement was taken a step further when in 1927 the Food, Drug and Insecticide Administration was established. The prime purpose was to set up a law-enforcement agency separated from all research work having no regulatory significance.[1]

During the past twenty-five years a group of trained food and drug inspectors have developed. They are distributed widely over the country and exercise wide discretionary powers. Their work brings them daily into contact with dealers and producers. Their duty is to protect the public but they find little guidance in their daily work as to what constitutes the interests of the consumer.

This environment has had its effect upon the policy of the administration. When the present Director of Regulatory Work had been in charge a year, he explained thus the viewpoint of his bureau:

In enforcing the six statutes entrusted to it, the administration has attempted to adopt a constructive attitude. Observations through more than 20 years of law enforcement have demonstrated convincingly that only an insignificant proportion of the members of the industries concerned deliberately violate the law. Most of them earnestly desire to comply with all reasonable regulations, not only on ethical grounds but also because it is the part of good business. Recognizing this, the department has chosen to regard the six laws as corrective rather than punitive, and has adopted an advisory-before-the-act attitude by offering con-

[1] *Annual Report of Food, Drug and Insecticide Administration,* 1928, p. 1.

structive suggestions which should enable manufacturers to keep their products in compliance with the law.[1]

The officials found that cultivating friendly relations with those they were supposed to regulate made their work of law enforcement easier and pleasanter. They decided to "educate" their public. They adopted the practice of addressing gatherings of canners, druggists, etc. Manufacturers and distributors of food products invited them to attend trade-association conventions. Regulators and regulated dined and talked together. Cordiality and coöperation were made the keynotes.

Justice, of course, requires the consideration of the social and economic effects of regulation. Consumer protection is but one aspect of the public welfare. The canning of blueberries illustrates the point. This is an important industry in Maine and in certain parts of the state supplies a livelihood for large numbers of people. Some years ago it was found that the canned berries were heavily infested with worms. Seizures were made and shipment stopped. The canners did not know how to improve their pack. If the government had been content with merely punitive action, not only the worms would have been eliminated, but perhaps the blueberry industry also. Government experts were sent to study the problem. They devised a simple and effective piece of machinery that eliminated the unfit fruit from the berries delivered to the canneries. Coöperation on the part of the packers and officials has now resulted in a high-quality product in Maine.

The annual reports of the Food and Drug Administration multiply examples of law enforcement by friendly suggestion. Twenty years ago the methods used by the manufacturers of catsup and tomato sauce were so crude that the final product would not keep. The pure-food bureau decided that the remedy lay in improving the process rather than condemning the product. Officials conducted classes where canners were instructed in eliminating bad materials so that their product might pass government inspection. Some years ago certain packers in Alaska and the Pacific North-

[1] See *United States Daily*, index, p. 962, May 24, 1930, for the director's explanation of his administrative policy. *Consumers' Research General Bulletin*, July, 1933, contains a list of references to its publications on the enforcement of the pure-food laws.

west persisted in canning salmon that was quite unfit for human consumption. Repeated seizures were made and upheld by the courts time and again. Little improvement occurred, however, until the bureau, as a supplement to its legal activities, sent inspectors into the canneries. These experts showed just what types of fish were unfit for canning. This policy of demonstration did more than the courts had accomplished in improving the product and correcting the situation.

How the enforcement of the Pure Food and Drug Act renders assistance to industry as well as protection to the consumer is illustrated further in the action taken upon frozen oranges. Disastrous freezes worked havoc in the orchards of Florida and California. The effect of frost is not apparent upon the uncut fruit, but by the time it has reached the market the frozen fruit is dry and pithy. Reputable fruit growers realized the value of public confidence in the quality of citrus fruits and appealed to the administration to supervise shipments closely so that seizures of fruit after reaching the market would not be necessary. The industry coöperated with the authorities in order to protect its own prestige.

Many other cases could be cited as illustrative of the fact that administrators in regulating industry must consider the social and economic effects of their action. Businessmen can be made to see that there is often no conflict between their self-interest and the welfare of consumers. Coöperation as an administrative policy is conducive to more effective execution of the law in many cases. This is very clear where technical complexities arise. Punitive action is of little avail here.

The purity of anesthetic ether offered a peculiarly perplexing problem. It was charged that the bureau had been remiss in punishing the manufacturers of ether when their product was found not to be in conformity with the standard of purity as prescribed by the United States Pharmacopoeia. Bad ether, when found by the drug inspectors, was returned to the manufacturers upon the payment of court costs. The statute merely provided for libel proceedings against the goods itself. The manufacturers could not be prosecuted for shipping a deleterious product since investigation disclosed that the ether was in perfect condition at the time of shipment. The presence of aldehydes and peroxides was discovered in this same ether when it was examined after storage for a period.

The output of every important manufacturer of anesthetic ether in the country was affected by the seizures made in 1925 and 1926. As a result of these seizures, the manufacturers, dealing as a group with the bureau, confessed that they knew neither the cause nor the remedy for the deterioration of ether. Little was to be gained by continuing prosecutions; the cause of the trouble must first be found. The bureau agreed to delay legal action while the ether people sought some scientific solution. In the meantime the manufacturers promised to withdraw from the market all ether found to be faulty, to examine from time to time samples from ether that they had shipped, and, when evidence of deterioration appeared, to recall outstanding stocks. The bureau, likewise, continued its inspection service and condemned stocks when faulty. By 1929 so much progress had been made in the preservation of ether that the bureau terminated the period of grace.

In one outstanding instance the government has frankly recognized its limitations in technical regulation and has delegated the task directly to the trade organizations. What variations from the *declared* strength should be permitted in pharmaceutical products? This was not a question that could be answered adequately in a government laboratory. The conditions of large-scale production had to be taken into consideration. In the commercial manufacture of pills, for instance, the component parts are placed in a container and mixed. This mass is then divided into minute pellets. The difficulty arises from the fact that, mix as they will, the manufacturers cannot be sure that in each pill the same precise proportions of the compound exist as in every other pill. Unavoidably, from the very nature of the process, a small amount of variation creeps in.

From time to time, by analyzing various samples given by pharmaceutical manufacturers the Food and Drug Administration Bureau was able to attain a fairly extensive notion of the degree of accuracy prevailing under good commercial practice. It was felt, however, that first-hand knowledge of all factors embraced in large-scale production was essential if the law was to be enforced in a reasonable and intelligent fashion. The bureau's view in this matter was presented to the American Drug Manufacturers'

Association and the American Pharmaceutical Manufacturers' Association. These organizations offered to coöperate through the Combined Pharmaceutical Contact Committee. By experimentation and agreement among the representatives of the drug manufacturers and of the government, tolerances are fixed and the methods of assay approved by this committee are promulgated by the bureau for the information and guidance of enforcement officials.

The bureaucrat, it appears, is restricted in many directions. The determination of what is technically possible must sometimes be left to outsiders. Scientific and legal demands cannot always be easily reconciled. The social and economic results of administrative action often point to coöperation as a more desirable course than coercion. Those with whom the bureaucrat comes into closest and most frequent contact are those he is called upon to regulate. A mutuality of interest is stimulated by the search for solutions to technical problems and by the frequent cases where both regulators and regulated can coöperate in achieving a common goal. The official handicapped by a faulty law and inadequate resources can only make the best of his situation. Often he must carry out the law in spite of hostile political and economic forces. The reaction from these forces inevitably influences the viewpoint of the administrator. The tendency in the execution of the Pure Food and Drug Act has been away from emphasizing the punitive provisions of the law. The policy of the bureau has been to obtain "a maximum of compliance with a minimum of resistance." Officials seek to accomplish this end by stressing the service features rather than the penal clauses of the law. Of course, the result is an easier discharge of administrative duties, with substantial advantages to manufacturers, shippers, and dealers. Since the bureau is surrounded by potentially hostile forces and is poorly armed with legal power, this conciliatory policy is easily understandable.

Coöperative activity has arisen, moreover, from a necessity inherent in the very nature of its work. The technical character of its problems has often meant that a priori legal rulings lacked the ultimate sanction of practicability. The public interest is not satisfied by mere punishment for wrongdoing. It calls for the solution of those specific difficulties in trade practices or manufacturing technique that serve to bring the statutory purpose to

[237]

fruition. A danger lurks in the possibility that administrators, having worked with canners and manufacturing druggists in mutual accord, will tend to overemphasize this coöperative work and hesitate to prosecute their erstwhile co-workers.

Enforcing a law that necessarily touches upon the operations of many businesses, large and small, in its day-to-day administration naturally causes protests. Businessmen seeking protection from bureaucratic interference go to their representatives with tales of woe or appeals to political officials higher up. In the past on more than one occasion the Secretary of Agriculture has over-ruled his subordinates in the Food and Drug Administration when their interpretation of the law brought strong protests from the food or drug interests.

A recent example of this was the corn-sugar case. The refiners of corn products objected to the restrictions on corn sugar. The pure-food officials had ruled that, when corn sugar (dextrose) was used as a substitute for sugar in jams, preserves, and jellies, the manufacturer must state this fact on the label. The corn-sugar lobby decided to go over the heads of the bureaucrats. They tried to get a law passed tolerating the use of corn sugar without a declaration on the label. They failed. They then sought a departmental ruling from the Secretary of Agriculture. In December, 1930, the Secretary of Agriculture decided that the previous policy of the pure-food bureau had been too severe and that henceforth dextrose might be substituted for cane sugar without its use being mentioned. This reversal in policy not only made the consumer unwittingly eat a sugar substitute, but it made the secretary's subordinates eat their own words.

The director of regulatory work in charge of food and drug administration under the Secretary of Agriculture had already declared: "I am opposed, as a matter of principle, to the sale of corn sugar, either as such or as an ingredient in food, to you, to me, or to anyone else, without knowledge of what it is. That is the principle on which the whole food and drug act is constructed and around which it revolves." But he and his fellow scientists had to back down.[1] Officials are loath to discuss political intervention,

[1] See *Hearings* before the Committee on Agriculture, House, 72d Congress, Second Session, on H. R. 9760; "Big Business Served in Corn Sugar Hearing," *Consumers' Research Non-confidential Bulletin*, 2.32, May, 1932; for data on the canners'

but they admit that they must reckon with it. On more than one occasion Congressmen or Senators have asked sharply why their constitutents were being proceeded against by the bureau. If the reasons given are regarded as unsatisfactory, the administration wins an opponent in Congress; and if bureaucrats are to escape criticism, unfavorable publicity, or a cut in their appropriations, they must be discreet in their relations with the legislative body. Law enforcement is always exposed to pressure from the outside, both political and economic, and the character of the jurisdiction of the Food and Drug Administration accentuates this tendency.

In this corn-sugar case the canners, the beekeepers, the spokesmen for consumers and the officials of the Food and Drug Administration protested against permitting the unstated substitution of dextrose for beet or cane sugar in prepared foods. They took their case to President Hoover, but to no avail. Secretary Arthur M. Hyde supported the case of the corn-products refiners. Consumers' Research characterized this action as "the major capitulation of the Department of Agriculture to commercial influence within the past decade."

This episode merely emphasizes the anomalous position of the bureaucrats. Considerations of political expedience must be added to all the other restrictions that handicap their activities. As one critic has pointed out,

. . . the Department of Agriculture, since it functions both as defender of the consumer in a sense in some of its branches and as the friend of the agricultural producer and more especially of the manufacturer using the agricultural producer's raw materials, is often in the impossible position of trying to do an economic service to both producer and consumer at the same time.[1]

The policy of the officials has been consistently to stress that "the enforcement of the laws within the jurisdiction of the Food and Drug Administration, though primarily intended to protect consumers, also benefits producers. This is particularly true of the

---

opposition to the corn-sugar label dispute, see *United States Daily*, Aug. 1, 1930, index, p. 1727, and July 26, 1930, index, p. 1668.

[1] F. J. Schlink, in the *American Federationist*, April, 1931.

farmers." But unfortunately the interests of the producers cannot always be so easily identified with those of the consumer. When punitive action threatens, however, those who fear strict regulation attempt political pressure upon officials.

The bureaucrats in the Food and Drug Administration are in a strategically weak position. Theirs is a subordinate bureau in the Department of Agriculture and hence under the control of a politician—the Secretary of Agriculture. These officials are called upon to regulate powerful industries, but they are vulnerable always to attacks from special interests working through political channels. Their decisions may be overruled by their administrative superiors. The possible reaction from the political and economic forces on the outside inevitably influences the work of the bureau and the viewpoint of the administrators.

During most of their administrative experience the bureaucrats have been exposed to pressure from the producers, but they have heard little from the consumers. Officials realized that, if they were to strike a balance between the interests of the consumer and of the producer, they must understand the viewpoint of each side. But how can the consumer interest be discovered? Just because all of us consume, it does not follow that the consuming activity can be extracted from each and then reassembled into a concrete entity. It takes more than a large appetite to represent intelligently the public interest in pure-food regulation. The officials have undertaken deliberate campaigns to awaken the public to their interest as consumers. Consumer support was needed when the officials were called upon to defend their standards for foods and drugs in court. Housewives, for example, were brought in to testify that these official standards were reasonable and generally accepted among consumers. There was, however, no organized consumer opinion.

By 1930 a change had occurred. The report of that year states:

A gratifying feature of the food and drug enforcement activities during the year has been the evidence of renewed public interest in the measures taken by the Government to insure a wholesome, pure and honest foods and drugs supply, a development decidedly encouraging.

A Senate investigation brought about by the agitation of a speculator, alleged to have had a corner on the supply of Spanish ergot, called public attention to the bureau.[1] The propaganda of a small group of critics speaking for the consumer made articulate this neglected viewpoint. The Food and Drug Administration inaugurated a series of radio broadcasts to explain its work, established a special information service, and undertook a "Read-the-label" campaign among housewives. The officials soon had increased appropriations from Congress for extending their activities. During 1931 to 1932 the number of criminal prosecutions instituted by the administration more than doubled.

Officials in this country do not occupy a sphere apart. They are unprotected by a strong bureaucratic tradition and politicians do not hesitate to interfere in the administrative process. In the Food and Drug Administration there is a rather unusual degree of stability in the personnel. The chiefs of about a dozen of the field stations have been in the service more than twenty-five years. Five of the division heads in the Washington office today were among the original group who undertook the work in 1906. The chief and his assistant have had over a quarter of a century of experience in enforcing the pure-food law. These officials have been able to develop an *esprit de corps*. Their pride in their work and their solidarity enables them to offer a stubborn resistance to the many pressures that arise from the routine of administration. Sometimes their congressional critics have been erstwhile offenders against the provisions of the pure-food laws. On occasion they may be engaged in activities the bureau is supposed to regulate. One Senator who has been most unfriendly toward the bureau is a large fruit grower. The position of the officials would be greatly strengthened if they were not left unaided in their interpretation of the law. Efforts are being made to introduce into the administrative process the viewpoints of both producers and consumers.[2]

[1] Administration of Federal Food and Drugs Act; *Hearings* before the Committee on Agriculture and Forestry, Senate, 71st Congress, Second Session, on Administration on Federal Food and Drugs Act, Feb. 12 to June 30, 1930.

[2] One of the most interesting phases of the 1935 Food and Drug Bill is the advisory committee for aiding the Secretary of Agriculture in fixing standards and definitions for foods:

"The committee is to consist of seven members.

"Three representing the public and two representing the food industries are to be appointed by the President without regard to political affiliation. Those repre-

Unless a balance of interests between the producer and the consumer is effected, the public interest cannot be clarified. Even though the individual consumer remains elusive, introducing a *consumer interest* into administration is not impossible. Officials have been able to gather some support from women's clubs and home-economic associations. A potentially strong consumer interest lies in labor unions and in various professional associations, as, for example, societies of engineers, architects, physicians, teachers, etc. Hotels, hospitals, universities, and other institutions that employ purchasing agents and buy in large quantities could marshal strong powers of persuasion, singly or through their respective national associations. If these special interests are brought to realize their stakes in the objective execution of the pure food and drug laws, the dominating influence of producers might be offset. The battle for a new act to regulate the interstate commerce in food, drugs, and cosmetics has aroused many groups to the seriousness of the need.[1] If and when the Pure Food and

---

senting the public can have no financial interest in the manufacture and sale of food, drugs, or cosmetics. No other qualifications are imposed on the selection of representatives of the public, since the President should be given the greatest possible freedom of choice to insure the most competent public representation. It is expected that State and municipal food officials will be among those available for such appointments. The Secretary of Agriculture is to designate the other two members from the Food and Drug Administration. When the Secretary determines that for the purposes of the act a definition and standard of identity is required, he will notify the committee, which will proceed with the formulation of an appropriate regulation. With the approval of at least four members the proposed regulation will be referred to the Secretary, who will give due notice of public hearing at which all interested parties will have an opportunity to present their views. Subsequent to the hearing the Secretary may finally formulate the regulation and, with the approval of not less than four members of the committee, promulgate it to become effective in not less than 90 days." Report 361, Senate, 74th Congress, First Session, p. 11.

[1] For a discussion of the struggle in the 73d Congress, see the author's article on "Food, Drugs and Poison," *Current History*, April, 1934. The following list of members of the Legislative Committee on the Revision of the Food and Drugs Act indicates some of the organizations representing the consumer interest: American Association of University Women, American Dietetic Association, American Home Economics Association, American Nurses Association, Girls' Friendly Society of the U.S.A., Medical Women's National Association, National Board of the Y.W.C.A., National Congress of Parents and Teachers, National Council of Jewish Women, National League of Women Voters, National Women's Trade

Drug Act is revised, officials will be in a much stronger position to protect the consumer. Little will be gained, however, unless appropriate means are provided for integrating their activities on the consumers' behalf with the related responsibilities of other federal agencies.

Union League, Women's Homeopathic Medical Fraternity, General Federation of Women's Clubs, W.C.T.U.

For an extended discussion of the problem, see C. C. Regier and others, "The Protection of the Consumer of Food and Drugs," *Law and Contemporary Problems*, December, 1933. See also "The Ultimate Consumer," edited by J. B. Brainerd, *Annals of the American Academy of Political and Social Science*, May, 1934.

Chapter XV

BRINGING THE CONSUMER INTEREST INTO ADMINISTRATION

"The Dormouse is asleep again," said the Hatter, and he poured
a little hot tea on its nose.

The Dormouse shook its head impatiently and said, without
opening its eyes, "Of course, of course. . . . "

T HE protection of the consumer is becoming a responsibility
of the state. The federal government cannot attempt a
positive interpretation of the public welfare without taking the
consumer into consideration. For most people this is a latent
interest and one that they are willing to sacrifice to their more
immediate interests as producers. This makes it all the more
necessary that some responsible agency guard this weaker side.
Attempts to this end have been made within the federal administration though in no case very effectively. The interest of the
consumer cannot be advanced without affecting that of the
producer. Officials are thus expected to offset the demands of one
interest group by acting as the champions of another. Will the
dormant consumers appreciate these well-meant efforts?

Since Roosevelt's recovery program was designed primarily
to restore purchasing power, it was essential to guard the consumer. If prices rose in proportion to the increase in wages, the
gains would cancel each other. It was the logic of the New Deal
economics and not the urging of consumers that brought their
spokesmen into the administration. Since these officials had no
direct way of ascertaining consumer interest, they were ground
between the upper millstone of the employer and the lower millstone of labor. The Consumers' Advisory Board under the N.R.A.
had a very difficult time. One official stated:

In most of the code hearings organized consumer interests have not been
directly represented. In most of the earlier codes where they were repre-

sented, their opinions, where offered, were given little serious attention, and their standards data ignored.[1]

Employers through their trade associations were accustomed to working together and they used their organizations for reaching agreements and making demands. The Labor Advisory Board had the backing of the unions. The spokesmen for the consumers had no group to which they could appeal for support. One official described the situation thus:

If the Administrator of the N.R.A. could have appealed to a broad array of well-digested facts bearing upon the issues involved in the drafting of codes, this lack of balance between the powers of employers, wage-workers and consumers as pressure groups might not have been of major consequence. On disputed points a decisive appeal could have been made to established facts to guide the Administration steadily toward the goal of the N.R.A. But, most unhappily, when the N.R.A. came upon the scene there was a pitiably small foundation of fact about the conduct of American industry upon which it could rely. And this unhappy state of affairs, coupled with the fact that many issues in code writing inevitably had to be decided on the basis of conjecture, tended to convert code writing into a contest between pressure groups. For such a contest which, for better or for worse, was conducted at terrific speed, consumers were obviously ill-equipped.[2]

The officials speaking for the consumer could appeal to the logic of economics or the lessons of history; they could not rely upon the demands of organized groups or the force of experience in the application of codes. The process was all too new. Moreover, the chief administrator did not back the Consumers' Advisory Board very strongly. In bald outline, the N.R.A. was a way of inducing employers to raise wages by relieving them of some of the legal bans on monopolistic practices. Price fixing was permitted. This would enable the employer to pay higher wages and thus restore purchasing power. The consumers' needs had to be recon-

[1] Statement by R. A. Brady, special adviser on standards, Consumers' Advisory Board, made before Group 111 of the Code Authority Conference, Mar. 7, 1934, Washington Hotel, Washington, D.C.

[2] Statement of Dexter M. Keezer, executive director of the N.R.A., Consumers' Advisory Board, and director of the Consumers' Division of the National Emergency Council, at the Institute of Public Affairs, University of Virginia, July 12, 1934.

ciled with the producers' goal of higher prices and the workers'
demand for higher wages and shorter hours.

The Consumers' Advisory Board felt that the pressure of these
two groups deflected the N.R.A. from its true purpose. The board
found that the N.I.R.A., as actually administered, was unduly re-
strictive. It reported that some of the codes were "anti-consumer
both in intent and effect." Ideally the codes should have set rules
of fair trade practice for the industrialist, established minimum
hour and wage rules for labor, and created quality standards for the
consumer. The interest of neither labor nor the consumer was
adequately represented on the code authorities. The Consumers'
Advisory Board stated, "we are not prepared to recommend a
simple formula for the designation of labor or consumer members
on each of these bodies. It may be well for a time to experiment
with different methods of representing these interests, both direct
and indirect. Our only insistence is that they be represented."[1]

It is not this principle but rather its application that is the
perplexing problem. Various recent experiments have served to
show the difficulties of bringing the consumer interest into administration. The Consumers' Counsel in the A.A.A. occupied a
very difficult position. Paying farmers to restrict production was in
essence a tax on consumers. This was justified on the ground that a
better price for farm products would redound to the benefit of all
through a more equitable distribution of income. The Consumers'
Counsel expressed the view that the consumer was obligated to
pay the farmer higher prices for food since the farmer needed a high
return if he was to purchase the products of the factories. This meant
securing a balance between the agricultural and industrial producers. The Consumers' Counsel was to see that the taxes levied
upon the processors of agricultural products were not pyramided
upon the shoulders of the ultimate consumer. An official in this
office stated:

The weaknesses of the Consumers' Counsel goes back to the fact that it
is a part of an administrative agency concerned primarily with an agricultural production control program. The fact that the activities of the
Consumers' Counsel have not received more vigorous criticism has always
been a source of wonder to me. The only explanation of the mildness of this
criticism has been the public attitude of the Secretary of Agriculture and

[1] N.R.A. release 9508.

the officials of the Agricultural Adjustment Administration, who, in both their official statements and their actions, have indicated a genuine concern for the problems of the consumer and a frank recognition that pushing a restriction program too far would harm not only the consumer but also the producers of agricultural commodities.[1]

The crux of the problem lies in this statement. In most instances the consumer must rely upon officials who are not primarily concerned with his welfare. Those few officials who deal directly with consumer matters are in subordinate positions. Their superior officers are charged with promoting industry or agriculture. The consumers' welfare is not the primary responsibility of the department. Officials in the Food and Drug Administration are frank to admit that their bureau has been treated as the stepchild of the Department of Agriculture. A recent episode showed that the present Secretary of Agriculture was ready to support the Bureau of Home Economics on behalf of the consumer, but that to do so meant fighting powerful groups from the great agricultural states.

In November, 1933, the Bureau of Home Economics issued Circular 296 on *Diets at Four Levels of Nutritive Content and Cost.* This study recommended diets in which the average use of wheat flour was discouraged and fruits and vegetables were stressed as highly important foods. A number of bakers and millers interpreted the pamphlet as an "insidious campaign against bread consumption,"[2] and accordingly brought strong pressure on the Secretary of Agriculture to have it suppressed. The Millers' National Federation and the National Food Bureau sent a delegation to see the secretary. A conference of Senators from the wheat states was called and the entire Kansas delegation in the House of Representatives joined the protest. The fight was taken to the Appropriations Committee of the House. A resolution was introduced to the effect that no federal appropriations should be used to pay an official who advocated the reduced consumption of any wholesome agricultural commodity. A defender of this resolution stated:

It serves notice on the bureaucrats, male and female, in the Department of Agriculture that if they do not quit meddling with the food aptitudes and

[1] Address of T. C. Blaisdell, assistant director, Consumers' Counsel, A.A.A., before American Statistical Association, Dec. 29, 1934.

[2] *Baker's Weekly,* Feb. 9, 1935.

[247]

appetites of the American people, their salary checks will stop coming. It hits the would-be autocrats of the breakfast table, the dinner table, and the supper table in the only place where they are vulnerable. It threatens their meal ticket.[1]

This agitation was directed by the so-called National Food Bureau, an agency supported by forty millers and one baker. The pages of the *Northwestern Miller* carried detailed news of each move that was made during the early months of 1935. Here is a fully documented account of pressure upon administrative officials. Congress did not yield to the demands of this minority group. The bulletin on diets reached many thousands of people, but officials in the Department of Agriculture had to pay heavily in time and trouble. For nearly two years they had to defend their position through conferences, letters, and speeches. The issue attracted much attention among the millers and bakers; it meant little to the bread eaters and breadwinners of the country. Such episodes are enough to induce a cautious attitude on the part of officials. The Bureau of Home Economics has been the favorite butt of senatorial sarcasm on various occasions. These officials would be very unwise to provoke further congressional disapproval. They have no specific statutory responsibility for guarding the health or wealth of consumers.

The Bureau of Home Economics was created to assist the Secretary of Agriculture in investigating "the relative utility and economy of agricultural products for food, clothing and other uses in the home." The bureau grew out of the department's effort to help the farmer and his family. The farmer was looked upon as a producer. Only in very recent years has the idea arisen that the government has a responsibility toward the consumer as such.

The Consumers' Division of the National Emergency Council attempted none too successfully to serve as a rallying point for this interest. In practice the division was independent of its parent body. It was nontechnical and no scientists were placed upon its staff. Its function was the collection of data of importance to the consumer. It also attempted to organize groups of consumers and to arouse them to some understanding of their interests. At

[1] *Congressional Record*, Mar. 15, 1935, p. 3869.

that time there were about 150 county consumers' councils and of these only about fifty were really active. They were intended to deal with local problems and they received little leadership from headquarters. *Consumers' Notes*, a mimeographed publication, was prepared in Washington and distributed among the councils.

Their activity depended upon the leadership of interested individuals in their locality. Sometimes their strength came from a woman's club, an energetic minister, or a consumers' league. The St. Louis council demonstrated what could be done. This body complained that the retail coal setup was wrecking the community. As a result of this protest the N.R.A. investigated the situation and completely revised the price-fixing agreements there. Consumers' councils in states reflected the local prejudices of the region. The people who ran the councils were often enthusiasts lacking in discrimination and technical knowledge. No consistent consumer opinion resulted from this uneven development. It was difficult to find leaders in many counties. Officials hesitated when they thought of the force that might be created by such councils.

What would be the nature of the pressures which they would develop? To what extent would they genuinely represent the consumer interest? What should their character be? Should they be groups chosen from various existing organizations such as labor unions, women's clubs, consumers' coöperatives, farmer organizations and organizations of industrialists? Or should they be chosen from a group of intellectuals who have some theoretical conception of what the consumer interest is?[1]

Faced with these questions officials proceeded very slowly. The Consumers' Division of the National Emergency Council found that its most effective work could be done by serving as a clearing-house for information.

Various administrative agencies deal with matters that relate to the consumer. The Bureau of Agricultural Economics under the Warehousing Act has authority to fix standards for canned goods. The Food and Drug Administration must determine standards of purity in order to protect the consumer from adulterated food products. These two agencies overlap in their jurisdiction and no administrative device exists for heading off such conflicts.

[1] Blaisdell, *op. cit.*

In the Department of Commerce voluntary agreements are entered into by certain industries working through organizations such as the American Standards Association. There is no guarantee that the standards agreed upon through this coöperation will be in accord with the government specifications set by the Bureau of Standards for the purchase of government supplies. The Bureau of Home Economics in the Department of Agriculture is concerned with rating various types of household equipment. Standards and grades for these same articles are set by the Bureau of Standards and yet there is no contact between the two agencies doing the same work. The Navy Department fixes its own standards for gas and oil although these materials are also graded by the Bureau of Standards.

The Consumers' Division of the National Emergency Council tried to promote coördination. The director called meetings of all those who were likely to be interested in a problem touching the consumer that had arisen in one of these agencies. He did not attempt to tell the bureau what to do nor were any resolutions agreed upon at the meeting. The problem was simply presented to all those who were interested and they were invited to contribute whatever data they deemed pertinent. Thus the facts upon which action may be based were quickly made available. The bureau originally concerned made its own decision, but the data placed at its disposal through the efforts of the Consumers' Division enabled it to see the problem in its broad aspects and in its relation to other federal activities.

The experience of the Consumers' Division demonstrated the possibilities that lie in coördination through the collection and correlation of data. Under existing conditions in the federal administration coördination must be treated as an advisory and not an executive function. The loyalties of departments and the vested interests of officials make it impossible effectively to buck departmental lines. Coördination cannot be imposed from outside. It must arise from the fact that a group of men are engaged in a common undertaking.

In trying to protect the consumer, however, it is very difficult to establish a common basis. Who is the consumer and what are his interests? Administrators in defining the consumer are like the blind men who differed so greatly in their description of an elephant. The one who grasped the tail compared the animal to a snake while the one who touched the elephant's leg insisted that the pachyderm resembled a tree. No official has succeeded in defining the true welfare of the consumer. The effort to awaken a widespread consumer consciousness has thus far failed. There are as yet no clear points of reference whereby coördinate action on behalf of the consumer may be directed.

Consumers' Research, Inc., has taken the lead in advocating the establishment of a Department of the Consumer with a secretary in the President's Cabinet. Under this department would be placed the testing activities of the Bureau of Mines relating to oil, gasoline, coal, and coke; the Bureau of Standards; the Office of Education; and the Bureaus of Chemistry, Entomology, and Home Economics. Instead of a Bureau of Dairy *Industry*, there would be a bureau for the study of dairy, meat, and poultry products. The Food and Drug Administration would presumably be included in this new department.

Its duties would be to encourage and advance research in the sciences, economics, and technologies related to consumers' goods and services, to coördinate all governmental activities affecting consumers' interests, to deflect and to guide them ever in the direction of advantage of consumers at large, and to keep a watchful eye and issue ceaseless publicity on other governmental departments, such as the tariff commission, food and drug, and public health administrations and other agencies whose operations closely affect or in any way directly or remotely threaten or invade consumers' protection and interests.

While admitting the inherent weakness of any such agency operating under the very aegis of the government which it would be its duty to criticize and to orient, we see little hope for establishing a consumer-conscious governmental and industrial system in America unless and until a beginning is made to set up specific, publicly recognized services within the government itself.[1]

This suggestion by the director of Consumers' Research, Inc., recognizes the need for getting the officials concerned with consumer problems from under the control of administrative superiors

<hr/>

[1] F. J. Schlink, "What Can the Consumer Expect from the New Deal?" *Executive Purchaser*, March, 1934; see also "What Government Does and Might Do for the Consumer," *Annals of the American Academy of Political and Social Science*, May, 1934, p. 125. The entire issue is concerned with the "Ultimate Consumer."

who are primarily responsible to producer groups. An administrative setup independent of the Departments of Commerce, Labor, or Agriculture seems essential. That the federal government could take a much more effective part in developing consumer consciousness is well within the realms of political possibility. To advocate the creation of a new Cabinet post as the first objective, however, is to overestimate the political strength of consumer-conscious citizens. The administrative agencies at present concerned with consumer problems did not appear because consumers were strong enough to demand them. They were the product of administrative policy and of economic stringency.

Administrative organization must of necessity reflect the political strength of various groups, but, if the federal government is to aspire to a general responsibility for the country's welfare, it must find a place for the consumer viewpoint. Whether a Department of the Consumer is established depends upon the power of the consumers to organize and fight their own political battles. Such a development seems highly improbable at the present time. The ultimate fate of the consumer depends on the degree of self-consciousness that he attains.

It is to be expected that under a democratic government various groups will urge the government to curb rival interests and will seek to forward their own aims through political channels. As a matter of theory, one might argue that the administration should be organized in accordance with the major functions of the state and that such functions should not be serving any one class, however large and influential, but rather serving the whole nation. Performing services to groups would be incidental to this major function, and the breadth of the department's responsibility would in itself subordinate such service bureaus. Thus one might envisage a rearrangement of bureaus under a Department of Conservation and Development of Natural Resources, or a Department of Public Health and Social Welfare. It would be rather hard to imagine such departments, however, displacing the departments that now serve the needs of agriculture or business.

The consumer interest is a very recent arrival in the federal administration. The government has not heretofore recognized any sharp line of distinction between the welfare of the producer and that of the consumer. The consumer was supposed to be

[252]

able to take care of himself. That businessmen would exploit the ignorance and vanity of their customers was not considered a matter for the federal government. The abuses of advertising have now arisen as a problem for government regulation. Government regulation of business has meant that agreements in restraint of trade were outlawed and certain grossly unfair trade practices banned. It was assumed that once business was freed of these abuses it would proceed in the public interest. The positive welfare of the consumer did not have to be considered as a thing apart. Now the consumer has become a factor to be reckoned with: his interests are vague; he is inarticulate and politically weak. Yet protecting the consumer often runs counter to the immediate interests of producers who are powerful politically and very outspoken in their protests against regulation.

The task of balancing these interests must rest in large part with the administrator. Standards of consumer welfare cannot be fixed in detail by legislation. This is too clumsy and inflexible. If a practicable solution is to be obtained, the task must be done by administrative officials. The exercise of a great amount of administrative discretion is inevitable in this process. What the consumer wants is then regulated in some measure by what the government thinks is good for him to have. A great amount of discretion must be placed in the hands of officials simply because the interest of the consumer is such a remarkably elusive conception.

What are the standards for ascertaining the interest of the consumer? If we assume that this interest can be promoted (1) by eliminating misrepresentation, and (2) by outlawing poor quality products, the problem of administration is not entirely solved. Misrepresentation is a very vague conception and it ranges all the way from subtle misleading suggestion to downright falsehood. Appeals are directed to fear, to sex, to beauty, to emulation, and to reason. Shall one appeal be outlawed and another sanctioned? Utility is not the only thing the consumer seeks. Less rational factors undoubtedly motivate many purchasers. Many of those who presume to speak for the consumer act upon the assumption that man is a rational animal. They assume that if he is told the "truth" he will make the proper logical deductions. They underestimate the human weakness for wishful thinking. The government can try to prevent misrepresentation and fraud. It can aid the consumer by fixing certain standards of quality. It can thus provide the means for thoughtful discrimination. The grading of goods thus far has been developed in the wholesale markets and from the producers' viewpoint.

At present what the consumer wants is determined to a great extent by what the advertiser, the stylist, or the high-pressure salesman tells him to buy. The demands of the market can be so stimulated or controlled that the individual purchaser has little to do with determining the grades, styles, or varieties of commodities offered. The fiction, moreover, persists that the consumer, through the barter of the marketplace, controls prices. For the articles manufactured by great corporations, prices are often set months in advance. As one economist states, "The concentration into great units has steadily reduced the control which the consumer can exercise over enterprise activity through the market place. The consumer is faced with administered prices, a take-it-or-leave-it policy and only a few sellers."[1]

Officials charged with protecting the consumer interest have found it necessary to search for the best method for administering their new responsibility. "Price" proved to be an unreliable criterion and quality standards were lacking. The Consumers' Advisory Board of the N.R.A. appointed a Committee on Consumer Standards to study the problem. The report of this committee contains proposals that are highly significant from the administrative viewpoint. It was clearly recognized that most of the existing agencies devoted to standardization reflected the viewpoint of the producer rather than the consumer. This applied to both public and private organizations. The committee took the view that the federal government should lead the way in developing consumer standards. The report stated:

Hitherto, the functions of the government in relation to its citizens in their capacity as consumers have been largely overlooked, while its services to industry have been steadily augmented. The spending of the national income is no less important to national welfare than the earning of that income through industry and commerce. In rendering this service to the American public as consumers, the federal government will be taking a

[1] Gardiner C. Means, "The Consumer and the New Deal," *Annals of the American Academy of Political and Social Science*, May, 1934, pp. 7–17.

first step toward redressing the balance of government service now weighted heavily on the side of production.[1]

The committee proposed that a Consumer Standards Board be set up, not to duplicate laboratory testing already being done, but rather to "provide for the first time in our governmental administration a central planning, coördinating and standards promulgating agency in the field of consumer standards." Ideally, a federal department under a secretary in the Cabinet is the most effective way of coördinating an interest in the administrative structure. But what if this seems politically impossible? The committee recognized the danger of placing a board concerned with a politically weak interest within a department dominated by a strong economic group. The report stated:

If placed under any existing bureau within one of the regular departments, it would be handicapped in its efforts to coördinate the work now being done in many different branches of the government by inevitable inter-departmental rivalries and prerogatives. . . . The Bureau of Standards is not recommended for the task because of its location in the Department of Commerce and the fact that the past history of its Commercial Standards division, its planned future close coöperation with the industrially affiliated American Standards Association, and the presence of research workers supported by industry in its laboratories, all give it a traditionally industrial approach.[2]

The Department of Agriculture offered no more suitable habitat because of its own concern with "the production and marketing rather than the use of agricultural products." It was hoped that the proposed board would in time win for itself a place independent of any of the departments closely identified with special economic interests. It would function through a technical staff made up of specialists in various commodities. In addition to this an inter-departmental coördinating committee would bring together representatives from the Bureau of Standards, the Federal Specifications Board, the Bureau of Agricultural Economics, the

[1] *Proposal to Develop Standards for Consumer Goods by Establishing a Consumer Standards Board and Funds for Basic Testing*, mimeographed report, Dec. 1, 1933, pp. 16254–16255. For some valuable comments on the work of the Consumers' Advisory Board, see the Brookings Institution study of the N.R.A., pp. 123–129.

[2] *Proposal to Develop . . .* , op. cit., pp. 16254–16257.

Bureau of Home Economics, the Food and Drug Administration, the Bureau of Fisheries, the Bureau of Chemistry and Soils, the Bureau of Mines, the Consumers' Advisory Board of the N.R.A., and the Consumers' Counsel of the A.A.A. The report stated that

. . . the duties of the Board should be to coördinate and make available in form for consumer use the existing work of public and private standardizing agencies; to determine the areas of most needed new work; to designate, after consultation with consumers and industry, the qualities to be considered in testing a given commodity; to arrange with appropriate federal or other laboratories for needed tests; to draw up standards based on the preceding; and to promulgate standards.

It is only through knowledge of what he is buying that the consumer can be protected. Only scientists and technicians are competent to tell the consumer what he needs to know. Only a government agency designed directly to give such information can be effective. There is a wealth of data in various federal bureaus; but there must be a bureau charged by law with the specific duty of interpreting and disseminating this material for the consumer.

Governmental responsibility is not limited to fixing a legal rule, but extends to safeguarding the conditions under which the law is administered. Whether these conditions are favorable or unfavorable is of the utmost significance to the successful attainment of the purposes of the statute. If, as a matter of national policy, the consumer is to be protected, then administrative devices capable of attaining this objective must be created. Legislators, as the responsible agents for formulating state purpose, must reckon with the fact that a certain web of interests enmeshes the execution of any law. The administrative process must be implemented to deal with this situation.

On July 30, 1935, the President by Executive Order number 7120 set up within the National Recovery Administration a Consumers' Division and instructed its officials "to stimulate interest in the problems of the consumer, to review public policy insofar as it relates to the consumer, and, in general, to suggest ways and means to promote larger and more economical production of useful goods and facilitate the maintenance and betterment of the American standard of living." This division superseded the consumers' agencies in the emergency council and the N.R.A. consumers' advisory board. This new agency at the abolition of the N.R.A. was transferred to the Department of Labor. It has condemned certain commercial products by name! Will it be able to continue this policy?

Our representative system places in a more advantageous position politically those classes that can be best represented upon a geographical basis. It places in a disadvantageous position those interests which are spread so thinly over the country that they cannot control congressional districts. It militates against classes that are economically weak. It discriminates against interests that are poorly organized and that do not have an immediate and substantial pecuniary stake in governmental affairs. The working of our present democratic machinery is rigged in favor of those interests that happen to fit in with the economic system.

A rationalizing of the services of the federal government runs counter to the economic and social forces that have grown up around the existing structure. The present framework of the administration is largely explained in terms of the efforts made by organized groups to secure agencies for serving their own peculiar needs. Interest groups focus their attention upon their narrow objectives and remain oblivious to the broader implications of their demands. The relative importance of a particular bureau often depends upon the aggressive activity of its supporters before Congress rather than upon its desirability for the administration, viewed objectively. In large measure, the standards as to what is right for a special interest have been the guiding criterion in determining bureaucratic development.

Where a special interest is identified with a certain bureau, officials often unite with allied forces on the outside in obstructing change. For them administration in the public interest means the promotion of the interests of a certain group. Their task is not regulation but service. They are not concerned with performing the traditional duties of the state, but in developing new fields of governmental activity. Here the scene is not dominated by diplomats, tax gatherers, soldiers, policemen, judges, and commissioners, but rather by entomologists, pomologists, bacteriologists, statisticians, physicists, economists, and engineers. The following chapters attempt to explore some of the problems that arise in public administration when officials are instructed to serve the interests of certain special groups.

Chapter XVI

HOW THE DEPARTMENT OF AGRICULTURE AIDS THE FARMER

"But I was thinking of a plan
To dye one's whiskers green,
And always use so large a fan
That they could not be seen."

THE Departments of Commerce, Agriculture, and Labor were established and developed in direct response to group demands. Many other groups have sought representation in the President's Cabinet. The American Engineering Council has led a systematic campaign to secure a National Public Works Department. The National Education Association has been most persistent and active in organizing the supporters of a Federal Department of Education. The American Exporters and Importers Association has advocated a Department of Foreign Trade headed by a secretary with a chair in the Cabinet. The organized scientists have urged a unification of research in a separate department; even the artists have requested a national Department of Fine Arts. It has obviously been impossible for Congress to go on increasing the group spokesmen in the President's Cabinet. When at first the federal government undertook new activities in response to group pressures, separate "departments" were added under the supervision of commissioners who were not Cabinet members. These so-called "departments" have been either elevated to the rank of executive departments or lowered to that of subordinate bureaus.[1]

When the question of changing the agricultural bureau to a major executive department was being debated in Congress, it was stated that "the creation of a cabinet officer at the head of a great department with numerous clerks will not increase the

---

[1] L. M. Short, *The Development of National Administrative Organization in the United States*, p. 418, Johns Hopkins Press, 1923.

agricultural productiveness of the country to the extent of a single hill of beans, it will merely create additional offices for politicians to fill."[1] Criticism of the proposed change was refuted, not by discussing the merits of the case, but rather by stating bluntly that farm organization all over the country wanted a Department of Agriculture. This was argument enough. The congressional attitude was put thus by one representative: "Mr. Speaker, I am in favor of the passage of this bill, in the first place because the farmers of my state want it; and, in the second place, because it is right." The very pertinent question was raised: if these farm organizations know exactly what Congress ought to do, why should not other interests be permitted to dictate their wishes to the legislators? The issue was scarcely disposed of by the rejoinder given: "Well, sir, the farmers of this country, throughout the length and breadth of the land, are above any other organization on earth."[2]

From the beginning the organized farmers have looked upon the Department of Agriculture as a service agency designed to answer their needs. Congress has supported scientific work designed to increase productivity through improved farming methods. It has further encouraged the farmer by assisting him in marketing his products, by curbing speculative practices on the grain exchanges, and by providing market reports. It has furnished various elaborate credit facilities that help farmers to carry a heavier overhead and conduct operations on a larger scale than would otherwise be possible. Along with this went the involved administrative machinery that paid the farmer to limit the production of crops while other agencies in the same department worked hard to improve the harvests. Officials and farmers were alike confused by the paradox of purposes within which they stood. Is the government to educate the farmers as to their own best interests or is it to supply them with scientific data and leave their financial welfare to the operation of the law of supply and demand?

Since the public interest can be realized only through promoting certain special interests, it is of fundamental importance that each department of the government have its purpose clearly envisaged. In what terms is the public interest to be given reality? What is

[1] *Congressional Record*, May 21, 1888, pp. 4477–4482.
[2] *Ibid.*

the true interest of the farmer, which is to guide the department? Most of the bureaus within the department are designed to promote various aspects of agriculture.[1] Their interpretation of the public interest is based upon their interpretation of the farmers' interest. To the extent that they promote the welfare of agriculture, they promote the general welfare. This is their guide for administration in the public interest. Their leader is the Secretary of Agriculture; he serves as the point about which official plans and opinions for agricultural promotion must crystallize. How is he to guide his department so as to forward the general welfare? He has under his charge bureaus that are not directly concerned with agriculture and bureaus that approach the farm problem from different viewpoints. Much of the departmental work is scientific research, much is regulatory, and some is simply administrative and informative. Much thought has been expended on increasing harvests; much administrative energy has gone into limiting production.

It is against such a background of different functions and divergent viewpoints that the Secretary of Agriculture must build up his view of the public interest. He must try to synthesize the activities of the various bureaus that Congress, in response to different group pressures, has established in his department. National agrarian policy has passed through various phases, but in each phase it has left behind bureaus whose purposes must somehow be harmonized with the work of the department as a whole. The secretary must at the same time retain the confidence of the farmers. Their interests must be identified with the department.

It is a great mistake to talk of farmers as though they were a unified class. They vary all the way from small cropsharers and truck gardeners to great wheat ranchers and fruit growers, and sharp economic rivalries divide those engaged in the same work. The poultry farmers and dairymen of the Middle West, for example, compete with the butter-and-egg men nearer the great

---

[1] They are as follows: Bureau of Agricultural Engineering, Bureau of Agricultural Economics, Bureau of Animal Industry, Bureau of Chemistry and Soils, Bureau of Dairy Industry, Bureau of Entomology, Office of Experiment Stations, Extension Service, Office of Information, Bureau of Plant Industry, Bureau of Plant Quarantine.

urban markets of the East. Their interests are very different. The citrus growers of California and the orange growers of Florida cherish a mutual jealousy. Beet-sugar growers in Utah must compete with the sugar-cane planters of Louisiana. Only dire distress can bring the cotton planter of the South into a political alliance with the wheat grower of the West. The agricultural class, so-called, is cut through by deep-seated social, political, and economic differences.

Nevertheless, farm organizations have appeared claiming to speak for several million members. Most influential has been the American Farm Bureau Federation. The leaders of this organization determined to bring together all those who could promote the farmers' interests. In 1923 to 1924, largely through the instrumentality of this organization, the farm bloc was organized.[1] The federation drew its strength from the local farm bureaus organized to work with the thousands of county agents over the country. Here is a national agency that ties in with Congress and with the great extension service of the Department of Agriculture and the state agricultural services. It has an able representative in the capital who has seen Presidents, Senators, and Secretaries of Agriculture come and go.

The American Farm Bureau Federation has its chief strength in New York, Ohio, Indiana, Illinois, California, Iowa, and Alabama. Bureaus are scattered through other states to attract the progressive farmer. There is little rivalry between this organization and the National Grange. Farmers often hold memberships in both organizations. The Grange is social, fraternal, and ritualistic; the farm bureaus are more concerned with fighting the farmers' legislative battles. Some competition has occurred in California where the local granges have become associated with a so-called "radical" element. The main strength of this old agricultural society is found in the northeastern part of the country and especially in New England. The Farmers' Union has attained its greatest strength in the South and has been a rival of the American Farm Bureau Federation there. The laws in some states give legal recognition to the county farm bureaus by prescribing that there must be a bureau if there is to be a county agent. In some

[1] See author's article on the farm bloc in the *Encyclopedia of the Social Sciences*.

instances the Farmers' Union has actually opposed agricultural extension work on this ground.[1]

The government cannot rely for its contacts with agriculture upon those farmers who happen to be organized. Officials must seek out the farmers if they are to serve them effectively. The Department of Agriculture has developed a remarkable system for keeping in touch with farming communities and ascertaining the needs of this class. The farm problem is, of course, far from solved. Its economic solution is dependent upon conditions which lie beyond the ken of scientists and which involve economic factors beyond the control of administrators. Within the field of routine administration, however, the Department of Agriculture has functioned with intelligence and diligence. The Department of Agriculture regards a close relationship with the farmer as a responsibility of primary importance. The department distributes annually 25,000,000 publications in printed form and the mass of mimeographed materials amounts to about 52,000,000 pages. Through the press service in the Office of Information, releases are prepared for farm journals, newspapers, trade publications, etc. Part of this material describes the activities of the bureaus and the discoveries of their scientists. To some extent this is publicity for the department. On the other hand, some of the information, because of its very nature, must be distributed speedily and accurately. Crop news and instructions concerning the regulatory work of the department must be sent quickly to those concerned in such matters.

Since 1926 the department, through its radio service, has undertaken to supply stations over the country with accounts of the department's work. More than half of the 600 stations over the country coöperate with the department every day to the extent of carrying weather reports or market news. About 250 stations, however, carry the educational and informational programs of the Department. The manuscripts are sent from Washington to the state agricultural extension office where an editor adds news of local interest and adapts the program to the listeners in his section. All but seven states have adopted this arrangement. Daily programs designed for housekeepers are

[1] For an account of recent rivalries among farm organizations, see Clifton Hicks, "Upheaval in the Corn Belt," *Harper's*, October, 1934, pp. 621–632.

mailed directly to local stations; there is also a weekly service for consumers which is sent by the Food and Drug Administration. The network broadcasting companies give the department time. Special evening programs as well as the regular series are presented.

There are more substantial ways of keeping in touch with the farmer. The Hatch Act of 1887 authorized funds to be used for the establishment of agricultural experiment stations at landgrant colleges. This experimental work was assisted by further grants made in the Adams Act (1906) and the Purnell Act (1925). From 1915 to 1931 the staffs of experiment stations increased by 84 per cent and the funds received by the stations by 240 per cent. Federal appropriations for this work increased threefold during this period.[1]

The Office of Experiment Stations in the Department of Agriculture is charged with general supervision of the expenditure of these funds. The stations report systematically on the progress of investigations and the Office of Experiment Stations acts as a clearinghouse for this information and as a general coördinating agency. In this fashion scientific work in the states is assisted and supervised by the federal government. Specialists in the bureaus at Washington and on the experimental farms over the country can thus keep informed and can coöperate.

It is through the extension service that the federal government endeavors to place the results of scientific discovery at the disposal of the farmer. The initiative in this work came from the Department of Agriculture. Dr. Knapp was the moving spirit in agricultural extension work. Education, he thought, should be by demonstration. He encouraged the farmer to try experiments. He urged the cotton growers to diversify their crops so that they would not be altogether dependent upon the success of one harvest. In 1907, in Smith County, Texas, the first county agent began his work. The movement spread to other states. The scope of the work expanded. Officials worked with the children on the supposition that, if Agriculus, Junior, succeeded in growing prize pigs or plants, his father might come around in time. Nor was mother forgotten. Demonstration work started in the kitchen soon after it was

[1] For a full summary of this development, see C. H. Wooddy, *Growth of the Federal Government*, McGraw-Hill, 1934, pp. 312 ff.

undertaken in the fields. Money was given by the General Education Board, by the states, and by the federal government to
develop the work thus modestly begun in southern cotton patches.

With the passage of the Smith-Lever Act in 1914, extension
work was undertaken systematically and on a nation-wide scale.
Several supplementary acts have broadened its scope. A permanent appropriation ensures the continuance of this work. In
the economy drive of 1934 this arrangement was questioned but
Congress refrained from cutting these funds for fear of arousing
a loud protest from the farmers all over the country. Federal aid
for extension activities now totals about $9,000,000 a year. Sums
are allotted to the states in proportion to their rural population
and on the condition that they match federal aid with state
appropriations.

The directors of extension work in the states prepare budgets
indicating the projects planned for the coming year. Each budget
must be approved in Washington. Representatives from the
department likewise audit the funds already expended. The state
directors are appointed by state authorities—usually by the
governor, subject to the approval of the Secretary of Agriculture.
Within the last twelve years only one such appointment has been
vetoed. This check from headquarters has protected the service
from incompetent men although it has not eliminated political
appointments. It does mean, however, that even a political
appointee must be properly qualified in the eyes of the federal
authorities before he can take office.

The Extension Service shows the farmers how to apply the
findings of the scientists in the Department of Agriculture.

In each State the Organization consists of a State administrative and
supervisory staff with headquarters in most cases at the State agricultural
college, and county extension workers who have their offices usually in the
county seats. County agricultural extension agents are employed in 2200
agricultural counties and home demonstration agents in 1250 counties.
Work with farm boys and girls is carried on in counties having extension
workers by the agricultural and home demonstration agents, by assistant
agents, or by club agents. There are 4605 county agricultural, home
demonstration, and club agents, 471 supervisory officers, and 1082
extension specialists.[1]

[1] *The United States Department of Agriculture, Its Structure and Functions,*
miscellaneous publication 88, 1934, p. 107.

DEPARTMENT OF AGRICULTURE AIDS FARMER

It is these officials who bring the services offered by the government to the farmers. They come into the barnyards and they go into the fields. The problems of the farmer's wife are discussed with her; his children are enlisted through the 4-H clubs. With head, heart, hands, and health they are encouraged to learn more about farming and to compete in raising prize stock and crops. The enrollment in these clubs is now over 925,000.

The extension service has proved a flexible device for taking from the great storehouse of information within the Department of Agriculture data of immediate usefulness to the farmer. At one time marketing problems may be more pressing than crop production. Contacts with the Bureau of Agricultural Economics then become of more importance than relations with the Bureau of Plant Industry. The extension service can switch the current of information from one agency to another. It is interesting to note that, despite the great increase in extension activities, there has not been a proportionately great increase in either the personnel or overhead expenses of this service.[1]

When we turn from the setup in Washington to that in the field, we find a very successful combination of consultation and coördination in public administration. The state director of extension work, after conferring with the county commissioners, makes out a list of those qualified to serve as county agents. The usual requirement is that a man be graduated from an agricultural college and have some practical farming experience. The county authorities then select their agent from this list. It is not the custom to name as agent a resident of the county. These agents, together with the women who act as home-demonstration agents, serve under the general direction of the state director and often under the supervision of district agents. The organization varies somewhat in different states. The work is always done, however, in close coöperation with the state agricultural colleges.

The county agent's task is to make himself useful to the farmers. He is the representative alike of the county, the state, and the federal government where anything pertaining to agriculture is concerned. The Department of Agriculture is careful not to place any regulatory duties upon the agent. He can advise but not dictate. State specialists on various phases of agriculture keep

[1] Wooddy, *op. cit.*, p. 318.

in touch with the agent and try to supplement his work. The county agent is one of the most significant administrative officials in the country today. In the eyes of many farmers he is the symbol of the public-service aspects of government. Here there is no question of whether state or federal, central or local authority is concerned; there is no bewildering maze of bureaucratic organization. The county agent makes government personal and understandable to the farmer.

Agents and home demonstrators alike, at the beginning of each year, hold meetings with farm men and women to discuss plans and projects for the next twelve months. They agree in these local soviets upon the problems to which they will give their attention. They choose the demonstrations they wish to try and farmers volunteer to coöperate in carrying on certain experiments. The vitality of the whole movement depends on these farm contacts. Successful administration is based on free coöperation. These details of administration are significant in that they show the close adaptation of bureaucracy to the individual. Yet a centralized supervision is maintained.

No expenditures of federal funds can be made until the state budgets are approved by the Secretary of Agriculture and certified to the Secretary of the Treasury, and no state director can be appointed without the sanction of the federal authorities. Here coördination is secured through the powerful sanction of fiscal control. Further coördination comes about in another fashion.

The extension service of the department is a channel for conveying the expert opinion of the scientific bureaus to the states and thence to the farms. Connected with the central office are specialists who have their offices in various scientific bureaus of the department. They serve as liaison officers between the bureaus concerned with research and the extension service. On the staff of this service are specialists on plant pathology, dairying, forestry, home economics, etc.

Officials find support in the local interests that profit directly by the department's work. The nation-wide system of land-grant colleges, the agricultural extension service, and the experiment stations constitute a great political machine that rallies to the support of the department whenever any curtailment or retrenchment is threatened. Farm organizations aid in marshaling this support. In the seventy-second Congress it was proposed to abolish the Federal Board for Vocational Education and to cut in half the appropriations for agricultural extension work. The Washington representatives of the farmers immediately got busy. They called upon the land-grant colleges to protest, the 4-H Clubs joined in, the county agents appealed to the farmers, and the educational interests concerned with vocational education came into line. The result was a tremendous nation-wide protest that showed Congressmen the strength and alertness of those supporting this federal activity. Over 60,000 letters of protest rained down upon the Hill. The outcome was only a 10 per cent reduction in the appropriation for vocational education and none at all for agricultural extension work. It has been demonstrated time and again that this political and economic combination of interests is too strong for any agrarian politician to defy with impunity. The farmers are frank and blunt in asserting their rights and they are the last to deny the efficacy of this political machine.

The spokesmen for agriculture have firmly established themselves in the capital. The American Farm Bureau Federation has taken an active interest in all legislation relating to agriculture, and has continued this interest in the administration of the laws finally enacted. For example, when the Gooding-Ketcham Seed Dyeing Bill was passed, neither the Department of Agriculture nor the organized farmers knew just how the provisions of this act were to be carried out. The law provided that all leguminous seeds unadapted to general agricultural usage in this country be dyed one-tenth red as a warning to the farmers. The problem as to how these seeds were to be dyed was one for the administrators to solve. What dye could be found that would carry out the purpose of the act? The American Farm Bureau Federation did not want to see the act wrecked by the technical difficulty of finding a proper dye. They kept urging the department to experiment and encouraged coöperation with the Du Pont Corporation in order that a suitable chemical might be found. It was only after considerable experimentation that the technical difficulties of this act were overcome and the law thereby made effective. A squirt gun was devised with a long snout, which could be injected into the sacks of grain to spray a light red fluid onto the grain.

When the Lenroot-Tabor Bill was passed at the behest of the farmers, it was necessary to set up sanitary standards for fluid milk imported into the United States. The purpose of this bill was to keep out Canadian milk, which was alleged to be impure and which was known to be in strong competition with American dairymen's products. The Bureau of Animal Industry had to formulate rules for putting this act into effect and the American Farm Bureau Federation was closely concerned in the rulings that set up standards governing the competing product.

Examples could be extended indefinitely demonstrating the concern that such farm organizations take in administrative problems. Officials in the Department of Agriculture are urged to explore every channel in order to solve the technical difficulties that occur in carrying out legislative mandates.

As a matter of routine, the farmers' representatives always attend the hearings held by the department. These hearings, however, have little more than a formal significance. Spokesmen for the farmers appear before administrators and read statements into the records. They have gathered their facts from the files of the department and the statements that they make are "old stuff" to the government officials. They seldom seek to collect new information because they recognize that they can add little factual data to that which the department already possesses. The significant contacts do not take place in these hearings provided for by statute, but rather through personal relationships existing between farm lobbyists and civil servants. Representatives of the farmers regard such hearings as a safeguard against arbitrary action on the part of the government rather than as an important avenue for the expression of opinion.[1]

Farm organizations take a lively interest in appropriations for the Department of Agriculture, and there have been occasions when certain interests have initiated new lines of endeavor and expanded administrative activities upon their own initiative. As a matter of fact, there are not many cases where a given bureau has initiated plans for the expenditure of funds. The urge more frequently comes from the outside. For instance, the cane-sugar interests secured a large appropriation from Congress to finance

[1] Interview with Chester Gray of the American Farm Bureau Federation, Washington, June 6, 1933.

research for their product. The variety of cane sugar grown in Louisiana is subject to a mosaic disease that greatly injures the crops. The sugar planters had no definite plans for expenditure of this money. They simply wished something done to improve sugar cane. They had the money appropriated and then instructed officials to find a cure for the disease.

Officials in the Bureau of Plant Industry not long ago were presented with a very substantial sum to be expended in conducting research on the sugar beet. They suddenly found themselves called upon to find the best means of expending a very large sum. In a word, the expansion of the administrative activities cannot fairly be charged altogether to the federal bureaucrat who seeks to increase his own importance. Nor have the organized farmers been entirely responsible for encouraging the expenditure of funds in agricultural research. The Chamber of Commerce of the United States of America thought that weeds ought to be studied. Businessmen were impressed with this problem. The farmers had been fighting weeds since Adam delved and Eve spun. The farm organizations were only too ready to lend their support to this ambitious project, and money was obtained for the study. The research might have grown with all the fecundity of its subjects had not the depression intervened.

The secret of the farmers' power lies in the way their great potential political strength has been focused by a few aggressive leaders upon the accomplishment of a series of definite objectives. A handful of farm leaders have kept aggressively on the job interpreting for the farmer the "content" of his self-interest and then marshaling support behind their proposals. They go before the appropriations committee and request the adoption of an itemized list of increased appropriations. Some of these leaders, after fighting the farmers' battles as lobbyists, later enter the administration as officials. The way in which agricultural opinion can be transmitted to the administrative authorities and through them transmuted into national policy is vividly conveyed in the account by the president of the American Farm Bureau Federation as to how the present farm-relief plan was created:

At the conference called by Secretary Wallace on March 10, attended by thirty-four farm leaders representing practically every national farm organization in the United States, views were frankly exchanged in an effort to work out an effective program. A committee was appointed, made up entirely of farm leaders, and within two hours it came back with a definite program, which, after discussion, was agreed upon by the group.

This statement of principles was presented first to Assistant Secretary Tugwell, and then to Secretary Wallace, both of whom approved it. They told us they would henceforth call this program "their baby," thus assuming full responsibility. On the next day, this program was presented to President Roosevelt by a committee led by Secretary Wallace, of which I was a member. The Department of Agriculture promptly drafted a bill which carried out these principles and submitted it to the President for his approval. We farm leaders were called in by Secretary Wallace and Assistant Secretary Tugwell to go over the bill, and we gave it our approval. President Roosevelt then promptly forwarded the bill to Congress with a brief message urging its early enactment.[1]

This statement gives an unusually direct insight into how officials and agrarian leaders worked together, but it leaves one basic question unanswered. Why did they coöperate? To answer this question fully would require a book on "the farmer as a political factor in American politics." It is well to remember, however, that agricultural discontent has been a persistent irritant in party politics from the Granger movement on down. The basic strategy of the Republican Party has for decades centered around maintaining the loyalty of the western farming states without unduly disturbing the industrial East. The problem of farm relief became more and more insistent in recent Republican administrations and at length could no longer be staved off by increased appropriations for scientific research in the Department of Agriculture. President Roosevelt's support from the South and West meant that it was politically impossible to postpone further a positive and far-reaching attempt to aid the farmer. The industrial areas had benefited in the boom of the 1920's but the plight of the farmers had steadily grown worse. Staple farm products in the great agricultural nations increased in volume about 50 per cent in the two decades after 1913. In the United States agricultural exports and farm prices had fallen greatly by 1932. The

[1] Quoted from E. A. O'Neal's nation-wide broadcast, Mar. 30, 1933, by Lawrence Sullivan in "Saving the Farmer," *American Mercury*, April, 1934, pp. 457–458. See also C. V. Gregory, "The American Farm Bureau Federation and the AAA," *Annals of the American Academy of Political and Social Science*, May, 1935, p. 152.

pressure of such economic conditions enforced political pressure in an imperative protest. Bold action was demanded.

The new plan for farm relief recognized that data on how to grow a bumper crop did not solve the farmer's problems. Nor were the special credit facilities provided by the federal government a solution to his difficulties. The Federal Farm Loan Board, the federal land banks, intermediate credit banks, and agricultural credit corporations have been established since 1914 to give the farmer the credit he needed. These efforts of the government were all directed toward assisting the individual farmer on his own farm. It was not until 1929, with the coming of the Federal Farm Board, that the emphasis shifted from bigger crops to better markets.

The average farmer cannot be expected to gather facts concerning the export demand for farm products, foreign and domestic tariffs, or acreage and yield probabilities for the coming years. Still less can he formulate an intelligent opinion based upon a study of such complicated factors. Agricultural problems today puzzle specialists who devote all their time to study and investigation. Piers Plowman today rides a tractor and listens to the radio, but his problems of crop production and marketing have been intensified rather than simplified by technological advances. How can a government by public opinion meet the question of farm relief? The A.A.A. attempted an answer. Regardless of its success or failure, it remains highly significant as an experimental attempt at reconciling democratic principles to the realities of modern economic life. On Jan. 6, 1936, the Supreme Court in a six to three decision declared this legislation unconstitutional. The merits of this case cannot be treated here. Constitutional obstacles may cause delay in bringing relief to agriculture but the farmers are too powerful to be long denied. The federal government is committed to helping agriculture.

The A.A.A. presented a novel development in democratic government. The usual process is agreement upon a law by the representatives of the people and then the enforcement of this law upon the community. Although the Agricultural Adjustment Act went through the formal steps of enactment, its significance is not found here. The act was the concoction of economists in the Department of Agriculture and officials in farm organizations. It was passed by Congress at the behest of the President and placed in the hands of the A.A.A. officials. It was at this point that the democratic process began. The successful administration of the act was dependent upon the winning of the coöperation of the farmers. If the law was to have any meaning, it had to receive the consent of those falling within its very terms. It became the task of the administrator, as part of the process of making the law effective, to convince the farmers of the validity of the Agricultural Adjustment Act.[1]

The administrators, aided by the great fact-gathering machinery of the government, drew up a program for building a favorable public opinion. This program was arranged in accordance with their interpretation of the public interest and they sought support for it in these terms. The administrators here acted upon the assumption that the issues were too complex and the cost of ignorance too high for the problem to be left to the farmer. The tenets of democratic fundamentalism were discarded. The farmer-citizen could not be left to gather the facts needed for an understanding of his economic predicament.

The situation is different in industry. A small group of business executives can exchange views quickly. They can afford to hire experts to prepare the data needed. It is part of big-business routine to examine impending economic developments. Large-scale industry is better equipped than agriculture to discover its own

---

[1] Assistant Administrator Stedman described the attitude of the officials thus: "We regard ourselves as an agency to facilitate coöperative activity of farmers, not one for economic research or fact-finding. Devising a program requires reasoning from the facts, and presenting a program to farmers involves interpretation and the placing of greater emphasis upon some facts than upon others, according to experience and judgment of their relative importance. Hence, while we try at all times to keep the facts conspicuously in the foreground, we do depart from the objective attitude by devising and supporting a positive plan of coöperative action which is intended to improve the economic condition of agriculture. We are not neutral about carrying out the purposes declared by Congress in the Adjustment Act." Address at the Round Table on Public Relations of Federal Administrative Agencies, annual meeting of the American Academy of Political and Social Sciences, Chicago, December, 1934.

This is a remarkably frank and intelligent view of a process which is common in some degree to many New Deal agencies, but which is nowhere better exemplified than in the A.A.A.

best interests. Facing the millions of discouraged farmers, the A.A.A. undertook to prescribe for the ills of agriculture.

The A.A.A. attempted to restore the purchasing power of American farmers to the level of the halcyon years, 1909 to 1914. To accomplish this end, the production of certain basic agricultural commodities had to be restricted by coöperative agreement among the farmers. In compensation for thus limiting their harvests they were paid a sum to make up for the difference. To finance the scheme a tax was levied on the industries that prepared farm products for the market. This brief explanation must suffice since we are concerned with the process of administering this law and not with the statute itself.

The first step was to collect factual data about a particular commodity. The Department of Agriculture is a vast repository of information, and the chief function of the A.A.A. was to collate the facts in order to formulate a program for action. The officials then placed before the farmers a definite plan. And therein lay the significant aspect of this process. A concrete proposal was offered; the farmers were asked to discuss and criticize its provisions. Under such conditions a consensus of opinion was possible. If a majority of those growing the commodity opposed, the plan was rejected; if opinion was so sharply divided that later coöperative action seemed unlikely, the project was laid aside. The practicability of the scheme rested upon the securing of consent. Hence it was to the advantage of officials to encourage discussion and to present arguments that carried conviction.

In 1934 the administration utilized a system of direct referendum voting on specific commodity programs. Over 1,500,000 cotton growers voted in the Bankhead Act referendum, and more than 500,000 others participated in the hog-corn referendum. The A.A.A. did not classify the ballots according to the returns from tenants, cropsharers, and landlords because of the pressure that the more powerful class might exert. The large proportion of farmers eligible to vote who actually participated in the referenda indicates the striking difference between the general vague interest of the citizen and the direct concern of the economic class. The farmers understood the issue and they saw their stake in the outcome. The A.A.A. recognized the limitations of public opinion at the same time that it acknowledged the fundamental importance of free consent. Here was an effort to make democracy work in the face of difficulties inherent in our social and economic system.[1]

Its success depended upon the acceptance of the program by the farmers. Unless they agreed to the scheme of restricting production and worked together in good faith, the purpose of the A.A.A. would have been defeated. Accordingly, publicity activities became of strategic importance. In countries under a dictatorial regime, consent to the government's program can be created through a skillful use of propaganda. Through appeals to hate, fear, greed, and pride, the emotions of the populace can be so manipulated as to produce a great mass support behind governmental policy. Under democracy an essential difference prevails. The opposition is not muzzled. Official publicity can be counteracted by a critical press or resisted by minority groups. The proposals of administrators are thus contingent upon a generally favorable reception by those groups affected.

The Secretary of Agriculture presented a philosophic explanation for his administrative technique. He recognized that the restriction of production necessitated strict control of farm activities: this did not mean "regimentation" by compulsion from above but rather "social discipline" on the part of the farmers themselves. Through the county control associations, the farmers helped to "make as well as to administer adjustment policy."

Thoroughly democratic in form and spirit, the associations are effective instruments in economic self-government. They began by adjusting county and individual allotments. They were concerned at first about getting Government checks out to farmers as quickly as possible. This pre-

[1] The department states that "when the Agricultural Adjustment Act was passed in 1933, all county, agricultural and home demonstration agents, Federal and State extension specialists, and administrative staffs were mobilized for the purpose of carrying on the educational work in support of the campaigns to control production of the various commodities. In carrying forward this responsibility in 1933, farmers were given, first, the fullest possible information on the current economic situation with reference to agriculture as a whole and to such basic products as wheat, cotton, tobacco, corn and hogs. This was followed by intensive campaigns to lay before farmers the provisions of the emergency plans which had been worked out to enable farmers to adjust their production in line with effective demand." Miscellaneous Publication 88, *The United States Department of Agriculture: Its Structure and Functions*, 1934, p. 110.

occupation soon gave place, however, to a deeper interest in the purposes of the whole undertaking. The committees now study crop supply and demand conditions, and price relationships. They bring general economic information to bear on local farm problems.[1]

These agencies could not carry the final responsibility in executing the law but they aided greatly in the preliminary steps of policy formulation. Without the help of these associations, the program could not have been made effective, according to Secretary Wallace. In thus decentralizing administrative work, and at the same time creating new channels through which farmer opinion might find expression, the Agricultural Adjustment Act promoted true democracy, the Secretary argued.[2]

The New Deal administrators took a broad view of the implications of their duties. To make their program effective, they found it necessary to penalize those who refused to coöperate. To the critics of bureaucracy, the Secretary had this answer: Economic distress is the greatest threat to democratic government. It engenders class strife which in turn paves the way toward dictatorship. Men are little concerned with abstract principles of liberty when they hunger for bread. Officials are acting on the theory that they can improve material conditions in agriculture under a national scheme of crop control and at the same time strengthen democratic institutions. "The exact methods of achieving economic democracy are by no means settled," the Secretary stated.

How far the principle of majority rule applies legitimately to the control of farm production is not yet established, either through experience or discussion. But we cannot rule it out in advance as being inconsistent with democracy. We should certainly give the benefit of any doubt to the voluntary principle, while not regarding that principle as absolute. And we should encourage discussion, far and wide. We should also consider every alternative to the present adjustment programs.[3]

Secretary Wallace was trying to right the wrongs of the economic order. He was trying to raise the price of goods while telling consumers that it was for their own good to pay more. Underlying the

[1] *Report of the Secretary of the Department of Agriculture*, 1934, p. 8.
[2] *Ibid.*
[3] *Ibid.*, p. 9.

A.A.A. was the theory that a balance must be struck between the income due the farmer and the price paid by the consumer. This balance must bring such a return to the farmer as to enable him to buy the products of industry. Economists in the Department of Agriculture stated: "Successful action in correcting the price disparities, in restoring farm incomes, and in preventing the recurrence of unbalanced agricultural production, will help to restore the proper functioning of the whole economic mechanism. It is greatly to the public interest that this be done."[1]

When the President urged Congress to pass the Agricultural Adjustment Act, he stressed the need for new means to meet the unprecedented farming crisis. "If a fair administrative trial of it is made and it does not produce the hoped-for results, I shall be the first to acknowledge it and advise you," he said. Here was experimentation on a huge scale, but officials could not serve in an attitude of tentative experimentalism. A project of this size, moreover, creates a huge political interest. It identifies the welfare of great numbers of people with a governmental institution. It establishes a giant bureaucratic machine. It creates loyalties that resent criticism of the organization that supports them. There comes into being a Leviathan that resists change. When difficulties were encountered, Secretary Wallace asked Congress for amendatory legislation increasing his authority. In the face of protest from dissatisfied farmers, he reasserted his belief in his experiment and charged those who urged repeal of the act with lacking the "proper spirit."[2]

The relations between the farmers of the nation and the officials concerned with their welfare demonstrate certain dangers as well as great potentialities for the future. If officials are really to promote the welfare of a class, they must develop a very close relationship with its individual members. They must awaken these people to their own best interests. They must arouse them to concerted action. This necessitates an elaborate organization It also means that officials must lead and initiate. It places the power of pressure groups behind the machinery of bureaucracy

[1] Mordecai Ezekiel and Louis Bean, *Economic Bases for the Agricultural Adjustment Act*, pamphlet, p. 20; both of these men are economic advisers in the Department of Agriculture.

[2] *Washington Post*, Apr. 5, 1935, editorial page.

in order to carry through a program for benefiting a particular class. Under such conditions, how can democratic control be preserved? The farmers themselves must make their own organization representative. Agricultural pressure groups must be managed by the rank and file.[1]

How can the general welfare be forwarded? A balance of interests within the administration must be preserved. The general administrative structure must reflect the relative economic importance and social significance of groups that contribute to the general welfare. Unless democratic government can develop such an organization, it cannot carry the burdens that it is at present assuming. In agriculture a tremendous experiment was cut short. The persuasive power of billions of dollars vastly assisted the process of showing the farmer that his own best interests lay in the A.A.A. program. A more crucial test of the government's effort to administer the public interest in positive terms will probably come in reconciling the interests of labor with those of industry.

Why does the federal government not provide services for the industrial worker that are comparable to the facilities provided for the farmer? Why are there not 4-H clubs for the urchins in mining towns and in mill villages? Why are not the wives of mill workers brought together and shown how to bake, to can foods, or to weave raffia baskets? Why does not the federal government undertake a campaign to educate the laborer and the artisan to the advantages of coöperative action? Why is it in the public interest to employ thousands of county agents to instruct the farmers in ways of improving their working conditions while similar aid has not been accorded other economic classes?

There are several answers. Improving the conditions of the wage earner is done most directly at the expense of the wage payer. Arousing the industrial worker to demand a higher standard of living would mean precipitating a class struggle. As a matter of fact, agrarian discontent is due to the demand of the farmer for a higher standard of living than the unregulated operation of the supply and demand of farm products will allow. If our far-

[1] A. D. Lindsay, *The Essentials of Democracy*, University of Pennsylvania Press, 1929, stresses the importance of preserving democracy within voluntary associations. See especially lectures 4 and 5, pp. 51–82.

mers were peasants, there would be much less of a farm problem. The present maladjustments would still exist, but the price of farm products would not have to be shifted so high to meet the demands of agriculture for a "fair share of the national income." The Department of Agriculture has worked hard to raise the standards of the farming population. The industrial community has acquiesced in this development on the assumption that raising the standards of the farmer increases the market for manufactured articles. Increasing the farmers' purchasing power is a stock argument in defense of moves to improve his efficiency and productiveness.

Special state aid to agriculture is also justified in terms of an economy of scarcity. Where the need is great for producing, in order to feed and clothe society, the community lends its sanction to all efforts for increasing production. This has meant helping the farmer out of the general coffers. It has also meant a general social sanction for those captains of industry who could produce and deliver the goods on the large scale demanded by the rest of the citizenry. The exploitation of labor, the spoilation of natural resources, and the reaping of huge private rewards by individuals were accepted by the rest of society as part of the price of production. The government, reflecting the general social temper, refrained from dictating to business and undertook to educate the farmer. An administrative organization built up in a society where the elimination of scarcity was the main objective must now be adjusted to a society where the regulation of production and the distribution of wealth are the major problems. To meet this situation becomes increasingly difficult under existing constitutional powers. The farmers now discover that they are not geared in with our governmental system as nicely as are some other special interests who experience no constitutional barriers to securing a high tariff rate or a generous bonus.

Chapter XVII

PROVIDING SERVICES FOR LABOR

"Take some more tea," the March Hare said to Alice, very
earnestly.

"I've had nothing yet," Alice replied in an offended tone: "so I
ca'n't take more."

"You mean you ca'n't take *less*," said the Hatter: "it's very easy
to take *more* than nothing."

WITHIN the federal administration there are various services designed to temper the harshness of a competitive
society and rectify to some extent the inequalities of the present
economic system. Regulatory agencies attempt to strike a balance
among the conflict of groups. Research bureaus are established to
study and analyze factors that relate to the welfare of particular
classes and interests. The Department of Labor has an especially
heavy responsibility: within its ambit falls the United States
Conciliation Service, the Bureau of Labor Statistics, the Immigration and Naturalization Service, the Children's Bureau, the Women's Bureau, and the United States Employment Service.
Officials on these agencies have not been able to greatly assist
labor's fight for a full dinner pail but they have offered statistics
from time to time to prove its emptiness.

Officials in this department must use their good offices to promote the peaceful settlement of industrial disputes; they must
collect and disseminate useful information on labor problems; and
they must develop a nation-wide system for employment. They
must deal with aliens and with those seeking citizenship. No
administrators have a task demanding greater skill in handling
human relations. In no department is wisdom, tact, and strength
of leadership more needed. The Secretary of Labor is charged with
the statutory duty of "fostering, promoting and developing the
welfare of the wage earners of the United States, improving their
working conditions and advancing their opportunities for profitable
employment." Can such an official walk the tight-rope of im-

partiality between capital and labor, fostering with a fine detachment the economically weak against the importunities of the politically strong? The Department of Labor must act as a representative agency if it is to fulfill its administrative function.

Labor leaders insist upon a voice in administration. They want to be present where the "rules of the game are determined." "Whether we can live a good, satisfying life, depends primarily on the administrative functions of government and upon those rules which prevail in industry," the President of the American Federation of Labor recently declared. "To the wage-earners of the country the department which we were especially instrumental in having established—the Department of Labor—has the greatest potential value."[1]

The potentialities of this department and its relations with labor can best be understood by exploring its past and by examining recent developments. The Knights of Labor wanted a federal bureau. By the Act of June 27, 1884, a Bureau of Labor was created and placed in the Department of the Interior under a Commissioner of Labor. Four years later Congress passed an act to establish an independent "Department of Labor," although the commissioner in charge did not have a seat in the Cabinet. Labor was not satisfied with this status. The American Federation of Labor pressed for a Secretary of Labor.

Commercial and manufacturing interests meanwhile were agitating for a Department of Commerce. With the increasing public interest in trusts following the great anthracite mining strike of 1902, President Roosevelt suggested a Cabinet Secretary of Commerce and Industries "to deal with commerce in its broadest sense." In the congressional debates that followed the spokesmen of organized labor expressed the fear that, should this joint department be established, labor would come to occupy "a subordinate and overshadowed position." "Any man that is fair in this House would see," Mr. Richardson of Alabama asserted, "if he would think of the matter for a moment, that the Secretary of this department of Commerce and Labor is in no wise likely to be a representative of labor either organized or unorganized. You may say that a Secretary ought not to represent the interests of any class,

[1] William Green, *American Federationist*, March, 1933, p. 231.

so did I say that. But can any man shut his eyes to the overwhelming possibilities, yea certainty, in this matter?" This fear that a secretary of the proposed joint department would represent the interest of the employer appears time and again in the discussion. Samuel Gompers stated: "There can be no question that the members of the President's cabinet are representatives of the employers and business men's side of industry, commerce and finance."

Labor leaders feared that a joint department would be dominated by business. The Manufacturers' Association of the United States, they asserted, would be more concerned with the aid that such a department might give to extending the export trade than to helping the worker. They questioned whether an association with such a point of view could possibly accept a representative of labor as a suitable man for a secretary of the Department of Commerce and Labor. They insisted upon the difference between employer and employee. They argued that each had a right to representation in the Cabinet of the President. They were willing to coöperate with business in the erection of separate departments, but they were most unwilling to reduce the independence of the Department of Labor by an allegiance with business and thus "put its light under a bushel in a department where the magnates of commerce and leaders of great industries would be the supreme rulers."[1]

Nevertheless, a joint Department of Labor and Commerce was set up in 1903. It lasted only ten years, giving way before the pressure of business and of labor for separate departments. The principle of class representation in the federal administration was definitely realized when in 1913 the Department of Labor was granted a status distinct from the Department of Commerce. "The influence of the federation in this result may not be doubted," Professor Harwood Childs writes. "In addition to the customary types of pressure brought to bear upon Congress, President Gompers extracted from President Taft a promise to sign the Department of Labor bill if the labor proviso of another bill was struck out."[2]

[1] *Congressional Record*, House, Jan. 15, 1903, pp. 864 ff.
[2] Harwood Childs, *Labor and Capital*, p. 221, Ohio State University, 1930.

The American Federation of Labor gained for labor the right to be included along with commerce and agriculture in the Cabinet. The original bill made no financial provision for establishing the department. More pressure was necessary before even a small appropriation was provided. The federation has continued to seek increased support for the department, and it is only within recent years that the funds provided have in any way met with the hopes of organized labor. The contrast between the slender administrative services granted to labor and the elaborate machinery that exists to serve business and agriculture becomes more marked upon analysis.

The Bureau of Labor Statistics formed the nucleus of the new department. During the period from 1915 to 1932 when so many governmental agencies expanded greatly, Wooddy reports that in the case of this bureau "the increase for the period as a whole is negligible."[1] The stimulus for building up the department was by no means supplied only by the American Federation of Labor. This organization fought for labor's right to a Cabinet seat. The federation also insisted upon bringing within this department those federal activities that related to the wage earner. For the forces behind the creation of some of the bureaus one must look elsewhere. The impetus came from social workers as much as from trade unionists.

The Women's Bureau was established through the urging of women's organizations. "Women always get what they want when they band together and go after it," the bureau states. "Uncle Sam himself is not proof against the wills and wants of determined women. Though he may meet their advances along certain lines with a frown and even a rebuff he usually capitulates in the end to their beseiging and beseeching."[2] Representatives of the following organizations were largely instrumental in securing the establishment of the bureau: the National Women's Trade Union League, the National League of Women Voters, the Young Woman's Christian Association, the National Consumers' League, along with the American Federation of Labor and the National Federation of Federal Employees.

[1] C. H. Wooddy, *The Growth of the Federal Government—1915-1932*, p. 366, McGraw-Hill, 1934.

[2] Typed memorandum of Apr. 19, 1930, sent to the author from the bureau.

PROVIDING SERVICES FOR LABOR

The inception of this bureau can be traced to a meeting where a group of social workers discussed the need for a federal investigation of the working conditions for women in industry. One of the group, Miss Mary McDowell of the University Settlement of Chicago, decided to act.

I had been eating dinner with them, and I said, "Why not?" As I walked home I thought it over. I recalled that Mr. Charles P. Neill, whom I knew when a student, who had helped back of the stockyards when he was taking his degree at the University of Chicago, had been made Commissioner of Labor Statistics by Mr. Roosevelt. I said: "Why he would listen to me, I believe." I called up Miss Jane Addams and said: "I believe Mr. Roosevelt knows you." "Well," she said, "I believe he does." "Would you ask him to have an investigation made of the women and children in industry?" "Well, why not?" That's what she always says, "Well, why not?" And I said, "Very well," and that was the way it began. We went to the National Women's Trade Union League meeting in New York. Then things began to move in the right direction, and after a while President Roosevelt said: "You will have to get all the sisters after this." So we got all the sisters after it. It was a long time before we made any impression on certain gentlemen up on the top of the hill, and we never made sufficient impression; in fact, we never really and truly got what we asked for, in spite of the fact that all of these non-voting ladies asked for it, until all the men's unions asked for it."[1]

The movement for the Children's Bureau can be traced back to its beginning among the social workers of New York City. The director states that the idea of a federal Children's Bureau originated with Miss Lillian D. Wald, head of the Nurses' Settlement in New York City. The project was discussed with Mrs. Florence Kelley, secretary of the National Consumers' League, who drew up an outline of the functions that should properly be performed by the bureau. These preliminary recommendations were taken over in large measure in the draft of the law as finally enacted. The sponsors of the measure persuaded the National Child Labor Committee to undertake a publicity campaign on behalf of the bureau and an office was accordingly opened in Washington. This office, the director of the bureau writes, "by wise and patient effort" aroused and organized the public interest which was the all-important factor in securing the law. The National Child Labor

[1] Typed memorandum sent to the author from the bureau.

Committee brought together the great associations willing to urge the enactment of the law.[1]

The interest and support of women's organizations is the best explanation for the existence of special bureaus for women and for children. Their activities necessarily involve work of an educational, statistical, or public-health nature. These two bureaus are based upon the assumption that women and children in industry have certain peculiar problems that demand special consideration. The agencies are manned and directed by women and they offer a unique opportunity for the professional woman bent upon a career in the public service.

The Women's and the Children's Bureaus are concerned with weak and underprivileged classes. The children of the poor and their working mothers and sisters have little political support to offer these bureaus. Grasshoppers and boll weevils are politically more significant than working women and children. No direct dollars-and-cents utility can be claimed in justification of the appropriations made to these bureaus. Their officials must secure the coöperation of manufacturers and businessmen. They must get the support of those women who have time and money to devote to public questions and social welfare.

The chief of the Women's Bureau in a letter to the writer described as follows the importance of private organizations in administration:

These organizations make intensive and extensive use of material sent out by the bureau, borrow its exhibits for display at conventions and conferences, call on members of its staff to speak at meetings and to give advice on many matters from time to time. It is these organizations which are largely responsible for the creation of the bureau in the first place and they form a network throughout the country for getting to the attention of certain groups of the public the facts which it collects and disseminates. Moreover, a number of important surveys have been undertaken at the request of these organizations of the hours, wages, and working conditions of women in industry.[2]

This bureau is a fact-finding agency. It has no mandatory powers. It must depend upon private organizations to undertake

[1] Julia C. Lathrop, chief of Children's Bureau, "The Children's Bureau," *American Journal of Sociology*, November, 1912.

[2] Letter of July 15, 1930.

reforms. The bureau regards the League of Women Voters as such a force. Officials liken the league to "a powerful dynamo sending currents of facts made available by the Women's Bureau over a national network of wires and starting activities necessary to effect the desired improvements."[1]

Organizations of women and of social workers are a significant environmental factor in the work of the Department of Labor. They help to give this department an air of "middle-class respectability" that is irksome to those who would have the Secretary of Labor aggressively champion the rights of the proletariat. The department's most important labor contacts are with the American Federation of Labor.

The federation has been chiefly concerned in getting its candidates named to the secretaryship of the Labor Department. The first two secretaries, W. B. Wilson and J. J. Davis, were approved by the American Federation of Labor. Samuel Gompers worked in harmony with the Wilson administration and the wartime conditions strengthened the leaders of organized labor. The postwar "deportation delirium" was succeeded by the placidity of the Coolidge era. It was not until President Hoover appointed W. N. Doak that a sharp dispute arose between the President and the federation. American Federation of Labor leaders had assumed that the chief executive would name his Cabinet aide from the panel of names that they offered. They insisted that the Secretary of Labor should be nominated from the ranks of the federation. They were criticized for attempting to coerce the President. The *New York Times* remarked editorially that "had the President agreed with Mr. Green's major premise, it would have been as much as to agree that a Secretary of the Treasury must always be a member of the American Bankers' Association."[2] The President was thus able to declare his independence of the American Federation of Labor by appointing Doak, who had aided in the presidential campaign, as chairman of the Republican Labor Division.[3]

The new secretary staunchly defended the policies of his chief. He predicted the early return of prosperity in numerous public

[1] Private memorandum from the bureau.
[2] Dec. 1, 1930, p. 20.
[3] W. S. Allen, "One of Mr. Hoover's Friends," *American Mercury*, January, 1932. This article presents an unfriendly but illuminating picture of Doak.

speeches; he supported the presidential veto of the Wagner Unemployment bill despite the protest of the unions. He announced that the figures of the Bureau of Labor Statistics indicated an increase of employment. When Ethelbert Stewart, the chief of the bureau, denied that his statistics substantiated any such optimism, he was forced from office. "I have had a tin can tied to the end of my coattail," he told newspaper men at the time of his "retirement."[1]

Secretary Doak was particularly assiduous in battling the "radical element." He continually stressed the menace of the alien agitator and assailed as un-American the groups who criticized his policy.[2] A special corps of investigators undertook to ferret out aliens who had illegally entered the country. Much ballyhoo accompanied this purge. The Secretary of Labor became a Secretary of Sedition. "It mattered little who filled this tail-end Cabinet job," the *Nation* stated. "In those gilded days A. F. of L. leaders sat at festive boards with bankers and magnates—indeed, became bankers and industrialists themselves—while the open shop and the company union, rechristened 'the American plan' flourished."[3] The Department of Labor carried on some investigations of interest to social-service workers and labor leaders, but only a small amount of its time and resources actually dealt with labor-employer relations.

The fight of organized labor for a department to foster the interests of the wage earner seems a hollow victory indeed when the predominate attention given to immigration and naturalization work is noted. The official at present in charge of this work states:

Only a few days after the inauguration, Miss Perkins told me that instead of finding a department concerned with the interests of labor she found one almost wholly preoccupied with matters concerning immigration. The Immigration Service alone absorbed 3,659 out of the 5,113 employees in the Department and nearly $10,000,000 out of the $13,500,-000 appropriated for the Department as a whole. Immigration and naturalization together represented 70 per cent of the total appropriations of the Department of Labor.

[1] *New York Times*, July 3, 1932, part 1, p. 3.

[2] See *New York Times* index of 1931 and 1932 for numerous entries under W. N. Doak bearing on these points.

[3] *Nation*, Feb. 23, 1933, p. 192.

PROVIDING SERVICES FOR LABOR

As might be expected under the circumstances, the activities of the Immigration Service had engaged the attention of most of the higher officials of the Department.[1]

Seven officials were exercising more or less independent authority in this field. Their respective functions were confused and responsibility was divided. Secretary Perkins consolidated the two Bureaus of Naturalization and Immigration and centered responsibility in Commissioner D. W. MacCormack.[2] This official has undertaken the task of reorganizing the bureaus and encouraging a better morale on the staff. The demands of economy and efficiency necessitated the removal of a large number of immigration inspectors, patrol inspectors, and naturalization examiners. How could the weakest men be weeded out without protests of unfairness or political favoritism? The commissioner set up special boards composed of representatives from the Civil Service Commission, senior representatives from the immigration and naturalization services, and representatives of the public. These lay members were nominated by the American Arbitration Association. The commissioner thought that their inclusion would provide an added assurance that neither influence, favoritism, nor prejudice would be permitted to affect the dismissals ordered. These boards sought out the able men as well as the defective and provided lists of those able to undertake heavier duties.

The new commissioner found that the service was feared and distrusted by the alien population and held in odium by many citizens.

There were constantly reiterated charges of extra-legal administrative methods [he states], of raids on assemblages of peaceful citizens, unfeeling and unnecessary separations of families, arrests and searches without warrant, unduly long jail detentions, demands for excessive bail, persecutions of labor leaders, and lack of consideration, discourtesy and even brutality on the part of individual agents.[3]

This was the heavy indictment that had accumulated against the predominant service in the department designed to foster the welfare of the worker. Most serious was the way in which deporta-

[1] Address of D. W. MacCormack, before the Chicago Bar Association, Oct. 25, 1933.
[2] See *Hearings* on Department of Labor Appropriation Bill for 1935 and for 1936.
[3] *Ibid.*

tion proceedings had been used to quell labor troubles. Many labor leaders are of foreign extraction and attempts have been made to brand them as alien agitators. In the past officials in the Department of Labor have been more concerned with uprooting false doctrines and policing the harassers of industry than in protecting the worker. They have readily responded to the cry: "Deport the alien labor agitator and his followers." "We find that most of those arrested as radicals are native born or naturalized citizens," the present commissioner states.[1] Even aliens, however, cannot be deported merely because they are radical in their political views. To come within the meaning of the statute they must be anarchists or advocates of violent revolution or members of organizations preaching the overthrow of the existing government.

"When I first began to go into these cases personally," the Commissioner states, "I found that we were deporting persons as Communists who were clearly not Communists. The theory upon which these deportations were based was as follows: These men had joined what are known as the "left-wing" labor unions—such as the National Miners' Union and the National Textile Workers' Union, not affiliated with the Federation of Labor, but affiliated with the so-called "Trade Union Unity League" which for these left-wing unions took the place of the Federation of Labor for the standard conservative unions. The Trade Union League was affiliated with the Red International of Labor Unions, and that in turn with the Third International and with the Communist Party in Moscow. Now, by that exceedingly tenuous thread they were connecting some poor miner, some poor textile worker, who had joined the union—perhaps the only union available to him—with the Communist Party at Moscow, and saying that he was subject to deportation as a Communist.[2]

On the other hand, the statute and judicial precedents bind immigration officials to order the deportation of any self-confessed alien communist. Some liberal organizations criticize officials for enforcing this law. Individual cases are dramatized and the bureaucrat is attacked. In the John Strachey case, for example, "official stupidity" was the charge of the critics.

Officials have borne the brunt of protest against conditions over which they have no control. The best the Secretary of Labor can do is to delay deportation proceedings. The case for or against

[1] Address at Conference on Civil Liberties, Dec. 8, 1934.
[2] *Hearings*, Department of Labor Appropriation Bill for 1936, House, p. 96.

a change in the present statute lies beyond the purview of this chapter. The significant point here is to note the reaction of officials in their difficult positions. They had either to commit obvious injustices in executing their legal duties or else secure an amendment to the statute. The present commissioner has thus been forced to assume the role of crusader.

The number and variety of statutes relating to immigration make their administration difficult. A codification of these laws is desirable. "The other day," the Commissioner reports, "I was quite seriously given a choice between two diametrically opposite decisions of Federal Circuit Courts to enable me to settle the question before me according to my own views and with ample legal authority."[1] The chief difficulty at the present time, however, is the lack of discretion in carrying out the law.

It has been borne in on me [the Commissioner states] that much of the protest directed against the administration of the alien laws has been misinformed and misdirected.

When the laws themselves are obscure, complicated, and confused—clarity cannot be looked for in their enforcement. When the laws are cruel, unfeeling and unyielding—the protest against the hardships involved should be directed to the law givers and not against the administrative agencies. When the laws permit of no discretion being exercised in their execution—the remedy lies in an appeal to the Congress for an amendment to the statutes rather than an appeal to the enforcement officers to violate their oath of office.[2]

National policy with respect to our treatment of the foreign born is usually approached with emotionalism and prejudice rather than with scientific deliberation. Societies representing racial groups take one view while organizations of professional patriots line up in opposition. Extremes of radicalism encounter the extremes of chauvinism and ancestor worship. Persons fearful for the purity of certain racial strains join hands with militaristic organizations. The official finds himself at the vortex of these conflicting elements.

The present chief of the service has cautioned his men in this fashion: "Our Service is one whose every problem is human—whose every act and decision affects the lives and welfare of human beings. We must, therefore, ever strive for that most difficult

[1] Remarks before American Arbitration Society, May 9, 1933.
[2] Address before the National Conference of Social Work, June 12, 1933.

ideal—technical accuracy informed by justice and humanity." Here are standards for directing administration in the public interest. They have been made specific in a series of printed lectures issued to all in the service. The immigration official exercises extraordinary powers. Aliens are not protected by the constitutional guarantees accorded citizens. Administrators collect the evidence, hold a hearing, and hand down their decision. Their decree may separate parents and children and banish the family breadwinner from the country. The present commissioner has attempted to train the members of his staff to realize their responsibilities. The reforms in this service demonstrate what can be done through internal reform and progressive administrative leadership.

The Department of Labor in all its branches has undertaken a more positive policy. Its lead comes from the White House and not from the American Federation of Labor. The present secretary was selected over the protest of this organization. The Secretary of Labor must stand for the President's labor policy. Organized labor as such cannot be represented in the Cabinet. The President must have secretaries in whom he has full confidence and who will contribute toward developing an administrative program for the general welfare. There is no place for the spokesmen of special interests. The Secretary of Labor must consider the 40,000,000 wage earners of the nation and the millions who are unemployed. The 2,500,000 workers affiliated with the American Federation of Labor are but a part of the broad picture. The administrative task of the officials in the Department of Labor is to study the conditions of labor and to relate their findings in this field to the general welfare.

Organized labor wants a department that is representative of the union wage earner. Many businessmen, on the other hand, are suspicious of a governmental agency that is "for labor and nobody else." They do not want a secretary with a partiality toward labor.[1] Secretary Perkins takes the view that the government should try to balance the interests of the employer and the employee. It should encourage coöperation and harmony. This is a doctrine of "sweet reasonableness." This viewpoint annoys those who stress the significance of the class struggle in labor relations.

[1] *Business Week*, July 2, 1930, p. 21.

PROVIDING SERVICES FOR LABOR

The only point pertinent to our discussion is the administrative effect of this policy. The very existence of a Department of Labor indicates that the state has assumed certain responsibilities toward certain of its citizens who are economically weak. That the federal government has a definite responsibility for the welfare of labor is a relatively new idea in this country.[1] The extent of this responsibility is as yet unexplored, although Secretary Perkins has taken some preliminary steps.

Much has been written of the government's recognition of collective bargaining and of the tribunals established to handle employer-employee relationships. These developments leave labor unions to take the initiative in organizing the workers and arousing them to fight for their rights. The tentative steps taken by the Department of Labor suggest more fundamental responsibilities. If the Secretary of Labor is charged with the statutory duty of "fostering, promoting and developing the welfare of the wage earners of the United States, improving their working conditions, and advancing their opportunities for profitable employment," it is incumbent upon the government to encourage workers to unite in protecting their own interests. If this department is to be administered in the public interest, it must become a rallying point for those concerned with the welfare of labor. It is not enough to rely upon labor unions. The department's responsibility extends to both organized and unorganized labor. Groups of wage earners intent upon forming a union appeal to the department for advice and information. Officials feel that they must assist such undertakings in order to build up a better relationship between employers and their employees. It is not enough to collect the facts relating to men, women, and children in industry. Their interests must also be represented in all governmental matters affecting them. It becomes an administrative duty to bring the viewpoint of labor into the process of government. Should this department become a "pressure unit" within the administration for the advancement of the labor interest?

[1] Professor A. N. Holcombe, *Government in a Planned Democracy*, p. 101, Norton, 1935, stated: "The institutions for the representation of labor need governmental aid more than those for the representation of capital in order to maintain the balance between the upper and lower classes and preserve the ultimate supremacy of the middle class."

The more positive the policy pursued by the department on behalf of labor, the greater becomes the possibility of conflict, not only with employers, but also with the vested interests of the labor world such as the American Federation of Labor. Shall the wage earner identify his welfare with the bureaucracy of the Department of Labor or the American Federation of Labor? Shall the representation of the interests of labor be a public or a private responsibility? If the government undertakes to balance the demands of labor against those of the employer, it must either rely upon the labor-union leaders or undertake its own positive interpretation of labor's welfare. Presidents have been able to avoid this dilemma in the past by making a labor-union candidate Secretary of Labor or by following a nugatory labor policy.

The present secretary has invited wage earners to write their own program. A number of regional conferences have been called by the department recently for the purpose of bringing together union officials, social workers, leaders in civic affairs, and specialists in labor problems. A national meeting was called in Washington. Here a basic scheme of labor legislation was drawn up by the delegates. This plan was not regarded as a blanket proposal for all the states, but rather as a statement of principle. The secretary stressed the importance of fitting the scheme to the conditions within the various states. In the development of adequate state labor departments she found the clue to the proper administration of those general principles laid down by the federal government.

A new Division of Labor Standards has been established in order to promote more uniform labor laws. The secretary has described this agency as "a rallying point for the efforts of interested persons and organizations, State departments of labor and Federal Government departments whose common object is to secure improvements in the working and living conditions of wage earners and their families."[1] Thus the department serves to coördinate those activities inside and outside the federal government that relate to labor problems.

Secretary of Labor Perkins regards education as another important administrative duty. Workers must be given information that will enable them to understand not only the conditions within

[1] News release, Department of Labor, Nov. 13, 1934.

their own industry, but also the larger problems of all labor and even of national welfare. She has stated:

As the Secretary of Labor, one of my duties is to make such information available to the 40,000,000 wage earners of the country. This function will be performed by the Labor Information Service just organized within the Bureau of Labor Statistics. This new division will issue each month a Labor Information Bulletin which will attempt to summarize briefly general labor and economic facts of interest to all workers.[1]

Here is striking evidence of the effort on the part of administrative officials not only to ascertain the best interests of wage earners, but also to marshal the forces of labor behind the program of the administration. The bulletin contains articles explaining new legislation that relates to labor and industry. The accomplishments of the New Deal are reported and economic conditions in various industries are described. The bulletin is apparently intended to awaken workers to a greater degree of class consciousness and to supply them with a better factual basis for defending their interests. It is a logical development on the part of a governmental agency established to serve the interests of a great economic class. At the present juncture the aspirations of this information service are doubtless far ahead of its accomplishments. Nevertheless its potentialities are far-reaching.

The federal administration is becoming very aware of the importance of proper public relations. In the Department of Labor this is especially important. If the data issued is to be used by wage earners, it must be easily understood. If the department is to succeed, its objectives must be sympathetically viewed by the public. In the past the newspapers carried little news of the department's activities. The Washington correspondents gave scant attention to its work and this neglect was largely justified. Secretary Perkins has brought her department before the public eye and the economic stress of the time has placed "labor" news on the front page.

One official (at a salary of about $5000) has been given the task of passing upon all publicity and of seeing that contradictory information is not given out by the bureau's chiefs in the department. This official prepares the annual report, and all reports

[1] *Labor Information Bulletin*, September, 1934.

emanating from the departmental bureaus pass through his office. Statistical information and similar technical data are put in a form suitable for public understanding.

The Department of Labor is being resuscitated. The raids on persons of foreign extraction have ceased. A system of national employment agencies is being organized. An able director has been placed in charge of the Bureau of Labor Statistics. Wage earners are being urged to think of plans for labor legislation within the states. The secretary stated in her annual report for 1934:

> The idea is now generally held that employers have a certain public social responsibility in the conduct of their industries. Wage earners as well as Government agencies should be a factor in formulating these policies of public responsibility and they should be invited and permitted to make constructive contribution in solving the economic problems that confront us on the industrial side of our national life.

The Department of Labor, if it is to discharge its duties in the public interest, must help to bridge the gap between the selfishly divergent aims of capital and labor. It must strive to get the facts that will make a rational settlement possible. It must seek to aid labor in presenting its case by providing the facilities for conciliation and the data for negotiation. The department can try to enlist the public on the side of justice. It can instruct both employer and employee in the ideal of adjustment through democratic agencies. It can urge a better standard of working conditions upon the state governments. It can urge federal support for low-cost housing and old-age pensions. It can promote state and federal coöperation toward a higher common level for the wage earner.

Officials in this department, however, are circumscribed in their legal authority. Their appropriations have never been more than a fraction of the amount allotted by Congress to the Department of Commerce or of Agriculture. The financial support they get will be largely determined by the policy of the President or of the majority party toward labor. The relations between employer and employee are of the very pith of politics today. The hostility of business has been one of the immediate reasons for the niggardly support granted the department.[1]

---

[1] *Business Week, op. cit.*, has stated: "Manufacturers have resisted any effort to build up this service, because they feel that during wartime, when they could not

Collective bargaining has now been accorded official recognition. The Wagner-Connery Labor Disputes Act outlawed any interference with the formation of unions or any discrimination against union members by their employers. A special board has been established to administer labor's new "magna carta." This development marks the most liberal policy toward labor thus far advanced. Its continuance will mean strengthening the "labor interest" in the federal administration.[1] Under such a policy this department may in time approach the Departments of Agriculture and of Commerce in size and importance.

In the past organized labor has sought little more than its right to an "ambassador" in the President's Cabinet.[2] It strove to promote its cause by collective bargaining or by state labor laws. The great part that the federal government is now undertaking in employer-employee relations opens up new fields for labor to explore. The significance of the Department of Labor must be sought in this wider realm. Whether federal officials can reconcile the conflicts between capital and labor under a broad mandate from Congress is perhaps the most crucial test for public administration in the public interest. The Department of Labor can vitally assist this process by providing the facts for an equitable adjustment and by assisting all wage earners in the promotion of their best interests.

---

protest without impugning their patriotism, the department was used against them to unionize labor."

[1] The constitutionality of the Labor Relations Board remains to be determined. A lower federal court declared against the board's authority in December, 1935.

[2] For further data on the federation, see Matthew Woll, *Labor, Industry and Government*, Appleton-Century, 1935; Lewis Lorwin, *American Federation of Labor*, Brookings Institution, 1933; David A. McCabe, "The American Federation of Labor and the N.I.R.A.," *Annals of the American Academy of Political and Social Science*, May, 1935, p. 144; Frances Perkins, *People at Work*, John Day, 1934. See also *Labor and Government*, edited by A. L. Bernheim and D. Van Doren, McGraw-Hill, 1935.

Chapter XVIII

THE DEPARTMENT OF COMMERCE RESPONDS TO BUSINESS

> Still she went on growing, and, as a last resource, she put one arm out of the window, and one foot up the chimney, and said to herself "Now I can do no more, whatever happens. What will become of me?"
> Luckily for Alice, the little magic bottle had now had its full effect, and she grew no larger.

THE opinion of the businessman should be brought to bear upon administrative activities affecting industry and commerce. Such relations should be broadly and intelligently studied by the officials and the entrepreneurs directly concerned. Businessmen will continue to talk of government interference so long as a wide gulf exists between them and those in official circles. It was neither conspiracy nor accident that built up the close and innumerable ties linking business with governmental activity; the relationship grew in response to specific needs and deliberate intent. That the relationship is often inefficient and clumsy no one can deny; but industrial practices necessitated both governmental service and regulation.

Standards for directing administrative action in accordance with the public interest cannot be left in thin air. Upon what assumption are such criteria based? The philosophy of the public interest dominating the administration in power has been reflected in the relations between businessmen and the Department of Commerce. Officials can greatly influence the attitude of those interests with whom they must deal. Shall administrators stress their possible usefulness to private firms? Or should businessmen be encouraged by the government to feel some responsibility for meeting the social problems engendered by industrial relations? Should the extent to which the government aids one class be correlated with efforts for providing services in other fields? The problems of administration raised by these questions are demonstrated in the relationship between industry and the Department of Commerce. The experience of this department shows the use to which consultative devices may be put. It illustrates how the conception of "public interest" prevailing at a given time directs the focus of administrative activities.

In the Department of Commerce, the Bureau of Foreign and Domestic Commerce is the great service agency for industry. When Mr. Hoover entered upon his duties as Secretary of Commerce in March, 1921, he immediately called representatives of business into consultation.[1] How could the department be organized so as to meet the needs of the industrial and commercial community? Long conferences were held and the sympathetic coöperation of businessmen was aroused. With the support of the business public behind him, Mr. Hoover then made his demands of Congress. In criticizing excessive expenditures, the essential fact is sometimes overlooked that no government official can spend public funds unless Congress continues to supply appropriations.

The personnel of the bureau increased over "900 per cent and expenditures nearly 1300 per cent between 1915 and 1931." The department reported that 505,661 commercial services were rendered in 1922; ten years later over 3,500,000 were reported. The Bureau of Foreign and Domestic Commerce, by devising elaborate ways of aiding private enterprise and of rendering service to businessmen, expanded at a rate out of all proportion to the growth of other bureaus in the Department of Commerce.[2] It collected data for the National Retail Dry Goods Association on methods of wrapping packages in department stores; it undertook a quarterly survey of radio dealers' and wholesalers' stocks and sales; it studied the marketing practices for the manufacturing jewelers and silversmiths; it conducted an annual checkup on the ultimate disposition of old copper and brass at the request of the National Association of Waste Material Dealers. If the Lord helps only those who help themselves, these interests received little aid from divine sources.

When, for example, organized druggists asked the Bureau of Foreign and Domestic Commerce to make a study of their mer-

[1] *New York Times*, Apr. 6, 1921, p. 14; Apr. 26, 1921, p. 27.
[2] C. H. Wooddy, *The Growth of the Federal Government*—1915–1932, p. 176, McGraw-Hill, 1934.

chandising methods, it apparently never occurred to them first to ask the question: Is this a function that the government should perform? Bureaucratic facilities were available that could be used for this purpose; public servants stood ready to undertake the work. Many trade associations have neither the personnel, the skill, nor the resources to carry through surveys of their industry so expertly as the Bureau of Foreign and Domestic Commerce, and, if the government will do this work for them at far below cost, why should they make the effort themselves?

As a result, the government undertook investigations that trade groups might have performed for themselves under the pressure of necessity. Their capacity for such tasks was never fully tested, since a federal agency stood at hand ever ready to help itself by helping them. Competitors feared to trust their association with confidential data; the need of an impartial medium was felt. But confidence among members of the trade was scarcely stimulated by the surrender of their problems of management, and methods are not best solved by government officials.

The expenditures of the bureau mounted from year to year as its activities became more varied and extended further afield. The world literally became its province. The most precocious child of Mr. Hoover's organizing genius, it took its place in the seventeen-million-dollar-eight-acre-seven-story office building of the Department of Commerce and spent $5,349,891 of public funds in 1932. Its appropriations had increased nearly sixfold since 1921.

A development of such proportions cannot be disposed of as a "mushroom growth" of bureaucracy taking place in the dark and put over on an unsuspecting public by selfish officials. On the contrary, the bureau grew in a great glare of publicity and was sponsored by many of those who are now its loudest critics. What factors account for this phenomenal growth?

To explain bureaucracy in terms of bureaucrats is too easy a solution. The entire responsibility cannot be deposited on the desk of the administrative official. The businessman and the politician must likewise be reckoned with if the case of the Bureau of Foreign and Domestic Commerce is to be fully stated.

It became the avowed policy of the Bureau of Foreign and Domestic Commerce to build up the closest possible contact with business organizations. Good judgment was used in the tactics employed. The bureau was reorganized. Sixteen commodity divisions were established. (This number was later raised to twenty.) As explained by Dr. Julius Klein, the director of the bureau: "The purpose of introducing this new system was to bring the bureau into more direct and vital contact with producers interested in foreign trade." Officials were selected to head each new division only after consultation with the industry concerned. A personal tie-up between industry and government was sought.

A further advance was made when men prominent in industry were asked to serve upon advisory committees connected with the commodity divisions. Working in conjunction with subdivisions under the commodity divisions were committees composed of the representatives of specific trades. For instance, under the Textile Division there was a Cotton Goods Committee that has coöperated in improving and expanding the import classifications of cotton goods. Within this same division the Committees of the International Association of Garment Manufacturers and the Association of Cotton Goods Manufacturers supplied funds and lent their support and approval to a study of prison-labor competition. Similarly, the commodity division dealing with crude rubber was guided in large measure by an advisory committee of the Rubber Association of America. In theory the industries chose their representative to head the commodity division and then used the advisory committee as a means of directing the attention of the bureau to their business problems.

In actual practice, these advisory committees often were little more than stalking-horses for the ideas of the commodity-division chiefs. The initiative and direction came from the bureaucrats. The committees became useful channels for aligning the support of a particular industry behind the proposals of the civil servants.

The advantages of these committees were summarized by the bureau as follows:[1]

1. Representative and properly appointed committees can act for a whole industry in laying out or putting through any program of interest to this department and the industry.
2. Committees can summarize for us the opinion of an industry. This is useful in (*a*) gathering information, (*b*) determining policy, and (*c*) avoiding mistakes.

[1] Private letter to the author.

3. Committees enable us to pass to the trades in a most effective manner any ideas that we may wish to spread. In this way we can prepare the way for new work.

4. In certain cases we do not feel that we can assume responsibility for determining policy or procedure; strong committees can share this responsibility.

5. Members of committees are in most cases enthusiastic about our general work and pass the word along. This helps to secure greatest use of our services.

In a word, the organization of the bureau was designed to reach the business public and to discover there new tasks that might be undertaken. If the bureau was to flourish, it must find work to do. Its organization provided the connections with important industries through which suggestions might be taken up and more services added.

The hundreds and hundreds of conferences called by Secretary of Commerce Hoover were designed not so much to secure advice and direction as to advance plans of which the department already approved as a result of its own investigation. Officials felt that the initiative had to come from the bureau, that the average business-man could not think in general terms, but that, once given a concrete problem, he could make recommendations. Advisory committees served to call the attention of businessmen to the broader questions within their industry.

The bureau demonstrated its ability in trade promotion by selling itself to American business. Its annual report for 1928 carried the admonition: "The work of the bureau is effective only in proportion to the number of persons who make use of its services."[1] If it was to succeed as a governmental bureau, it must advertise its wares and convince the public of its usefulness.

Businessmen were more than willing to avail themselves of this "free" service bureau which graciously supplied information that would otherwise be difficult or even prohibitively expensive for individual firms to obtain for themselves. Under the leadership of Dr. Julius Klein, a publicity campaign was begun for persuading business to make a greater use of the bureau's facilities. Speakers were sent about and close contacts were built up with trade-association executives.

[1] Page 7.

DEPARTMENT OF COMMERCE RESPONDS TO BUSINESS

The tendency, of course, was for the bureau to go farther and farther afield in its ambitious efforts to serve business. The official, anxious to justify his position and to increase the duties of his bureau, worked hand in glove with the trade-association secretary, who was equally desirous of proving his usefulness to the membership of his industry.

The service favored expansion and growth. The business community was sympathetic. Prosperity had not yet dodged around the corner out of sight. Appropriations were easily forthcoming. The bureau presented evidence that, in the profits its trade-promotion activities brought to business, it paid for its keep many times over. It regularly published in its annual report a section entitled: "Dollars and Cents Return to the Business Public." Here concrete cases demonstrated the usefulness of the information collected from near and far. Testimonial letters bespoke the good work of the bureau. Business firms wrote for information and often got much more than they asked for or expected. Trade information on almost every conceivable commodity in almost every imaginable spot was gathered. Five cents would bring a report on "The Proprietary and Ointment Trade in China" and for twice that sum one could obtain a discourse on the "Wearing Apparel of the Peruvians" or a dissertation on "Training for the Steamship Business."

Its responsiveness to the request of business firms carried the bureau into ever-increasing expenditures and into undertakings narrow and specialized in scope. But the close and well-organized relationship built up between trade associations and commodity divisions of the bureau encouraged this tendency. Businessmen learned that the ambition of the public official to be of service fitted in with the interests of industry. The Chamber of Commerce of the United States of America added the weight of its influence in encouraging this development.

The organization of the bureau not only harmonized with the economic background but with political factors as well. Members of Congress discovered that they would gain politically by supporting this bureau.

The establishment of district offices of the Bureau of Foreign and Domestic Commerce in certain important cities was one of Mr. Hoover's innovations. Smaller municipalities hankered for similar recognition and their manufacturers and exporters desired the services of such branch offices. A political plum was thus discovered. These new offices stirred up sectional rivalries. Certain Congressmen recognized the opportunity for winning the favor of commercial interests by securing a district office for their section. In 1921 there were seven district offices in the United States; by 1932 the number had increased to thirty-six. In 1933 the 235 employees in these offices cost the government $601,900 per annum in salaries and wages alone. This rapid increase is easily explained. Politicians came to the aid of ambitious job holders and the two worked together to mutual advantage.

If San Francisco had a district office, then why not Los Angeles? Accordingly an office staff of eight persons costing over $30,000 a year was set up in Los Angeles. If New York had an office, then why not Philadelphia, and Baltimore, and Norfolk? Was Charleston or Charlotte or Jacksonville to be overlooked? The demands of all were answered. Other places of minor importance made their pleas. The officials in Washington had started rolling a ball that gathered vast momentum. More district offices were created than the bureau wanted. Political expediency proved a stronger force than bureaucratic ambition. The officials found firm friends in Congress. A certain Texas Congressman became their enthusiastic spokesman. By 1932 Texas had district offices in Dallas, El Paso, Galveston, and Houston, and coöperative offices in San Antonio and Fort Worth.

Dr. Julius Klein explained that, through these outposts of the bureau, thickly dotting the country, a very real effort had been made "to teach those who knew nothing of the bureau to learn what it would do for them if their wants were made known." Here again, just as in the case of the commodity divisions, the structure of the bureau served to increase its strength and influence. The policy of advertising the bureau and convincing businessmen of its usefulness was actively applied in each locality. "This has been accomplished to a considerable extent," according to the annual report of 1922, "by means of direct and constant contacts between these offices and the men directing the policies of local trade organizations, banks, and foreign trade clubs, as well as with individual export managers and executives."[1]

[1] Page 132.

DEPARTMENT OF COMMERCE RESPONDS TO BUSINESS

Bureaucracy expanded, not in a covert fashion, but rather by applying the tactics of the modern advertising agency. It built up a great question-answering business. Steadily increasing demands were made upon the field offices for information and guidance in trade promotion.

In considering this Bureau of Foreign and Domestic Commerce it becomes clear that its growth cannot be attributed to the machinations of officials anxious to add to their own importance. The bureau grew because it was able, by skillful propaganda and persuasion, to enlist the support of businessmen. It succeeded in promoting foreign trade and it uncovered new opportunities for profit abroad. It created a field of usefulness, and business found new tasks that it might perform. Regional market surveys were undertaken for studying methods of distribution in various parts of the country. Congressmen saw that they might please certain commercial interests back home by having such surveys made in their regions, just as adding to the bureau's lists of offices might mean winning more votes in a given congressional district. As a result, new offices were added at the urging of certain localities and new functions that were unwarranted and wasteful were undertaken at the behest of special interests.

The success of the bureau in a sense proved the cause of its undoing. This is well illustrated by the work done by the bureau in the foreign field. Here its activities leaped the bounds of economy and efficiency. In the effort to answer fully every question upon foreign trade that businessmen asked, and in the quest for trade opportunities, more officials were sent about the world and more offices were opened in remote and distant countries. A remarkable system for discovering and transmitting commercial information was built up during the past ten years, but a large personnel was necessary and much money. By 1933 well over $1,250,000 was being spent each year to maintain the 466 employees in the fifty-three foreign offices. These agents were charged with the duty of reporting to Washington by letter and cable on economic and commercial conditions in their area, supplying American exporters with lists of foreign importers and investigating potential markets for American products, besides collecting data on tariffs, commercial laws, and foreign taxation. The qualifications of these officials have been criticized, because of their paucity of practical business experience. Their chief fault, however, lay in the fact that there were too many of them.

Offices were set up in Accra, Caracas, Guatemala, and San Juan, where their presence was scarcely justified by the volume of trade. Central Europe was thickly dotted with offices at Vienna, Warsaw, Belgrade, Budapest, Prague, and Bucharest. All these, of course, were in addition to the consuls and vice-consuls already on the scene, whose primary duties also related to the commercial interests of the United States. Friction occurred.

In 1930 the State Department and the Department of Commerce drew up an agreement for the coördination of the work of consuls and commercial attachés in Great Britain and northern Ireland. If the plan proved successful in this region, it was to be extended to other countries. From the instructions sent abroad at the time one can get a clear picture of the difficulties the new plan was intended to meet. The multiplication of reports and letters upon the same subject had proved wasteful of time and energy. It was evident that jealousy marred the relations between the two services. Under the new plan of coördination, the instructions stated:

Every Consular officer and every representative of the Department of Commerce will receive due credit in American commercial circles for his particular contribution. It contemplates that the consuls and commerce representatives shall really coöperate.

While the Commercial Attaché and the Consul General are under the plan to determine which service shall prepare a report or trade letter, it is not intended that either shall seek to prepare the work which is apt to procure the most reputation, but that the division shall be made solely to obtain the best result. . . .

Naturally any alteration in existing consular practice with regard to commercial activities might cause some apprehension lest consular officers might lose some of their standing and become mere instruments of another Department. Such apprehension is now unwarranted.[1]

Two years later the plan of coördination was revised and extended. A liaison committee was created to consider the operation of the plan and to agree upon instructions to be sent simultaneously to the officials of both departments. The Department of Commerce was given the right to "prepare comments upon the work

[1] Diplomatic serial 929, Department of State, file no. 166/590a, Mar. 24, 1930.

performed by consular officers in the discharge of their commercial functions." In July, 1933, a new coördination agreement was concluded whereby all communications with commercial attachés were to go through the State Department. The number of offices abroad was drastically reduced. Specialized aid to individual exporters was eliminated. No more could businessmen request that government officials abroad collect their bills, sell their merchandise, or call upon their customers. Officers were reminded that their function was providing "information of primary interest to the Government and to the American people as a whole."[1] This coördination agreement changed the entire focus of the bureau. It ceased to be a bureau of errand boys for the tired businessman. Administration in the public interest demanded a broader focus.

Bureaucrats cannot be blamed for the growth of this agency. Their course was charted by a conception of the national welfare that made the promotion of business prosperity a major public function. The dominant political philosophy of the time sped the bureau on its way. It was but one of a number of bureaus designed to serve a particular class. The group supporting this bureau happened to be the most powerful political and economic class in the nation. The officials, if they were to justify their existence, had to prove their usefulness. To survive they had to advertise their utility. Their desire to extend their activities was a healthy sign. It indicated that the officials in charge were alert and enterprising. The old type of bureaucrat, pictured as arbitrary, slow, dull, and enmeshed in red tape, was not the problem here. Here were adaptable and aggressive officials working in close touch with organized groups and ever seeking new fields of endeavor.

The elaborate structure, built up during the boom through the coöperation of businessmen and bureaucrats eager to discover and create new functions for the federal government, proved too expensive a piece of apparatus. The Bureau of Foreign and Domestic Commerce grew by rendering special service to special interests. Exporters and manufacturers were willing and glad to receive the functions offered by officials desirous of increasing the powers of their bureau. Here were organized minorities attracted by the

[1] Joint press release issued by Departments of State and Commerce, Aug. 25, 1933.

work that the bureau was willing to do for their benefit. If they were to secure advice from the government in running their business and if they were to have the errors in their particular industry discovered for them by public officials, then their Congressmen must supply the bureau with generous appropriations.

All the elements were harmonious. The bureau was especially organized to reach trade associations, chambers of commerce, and exporters' clubs. A definite policy of self-advertisement was directed from Washington. The bureau urged industries to avail themselves of its facilities. Organized groups in industries and in localities gave these public officials an ever-increasing collection of problems to solve.

Then the business crash came. Manufacturers and exporters realized that other organized groups had in their turn been building up their special service bureaus in the government. Trade groups acknowledged that their bureau had grown too large and that it was costing more than it was worth. They found that they had unwittingly helped to build a huge bureaucratic structure.

The bureau was criticized for inefficiency, for delaying reports, for compiling misleading statistics, for appointing incompetent officials. It was charged that years went by before the facts uncovered in investigations and surveys were published and that the findings were out of date and misleading when they finally appeared. It was charged that young graduates of business courses were sent out to counsel business leaders, and that political appointees were given jobs while the constructive work expected of the bureau was neglected. The old cry of "red tape" was raised by erstwhile supporters of the bureau.

When appropriation slashes were first proposed for the Department of Commerce, trade associations failed to present organized opposition to the move. At a meeting of trade-association executives held in New York, it was decided to preserve a neutral stand toward the reduction. They explained that their apathetic attitude was due to the conviction that "the one government department representing business men was content to let business flounder unaided at a time when a properly conceived program of direction and encouragement might have saved the day."[1]

[1] *New York Times*, May 1, 1932, II, p. 6, col. 7.

DEPARTMENT OF COMMERCE RESPONDS TO BUSINESS

However unwarranted such blame may have been, it was symptomatic of a questioning attitude on the part of businessmen concerning the problem of trade promotion. A more critical spirit developed on the part of business. Was the support of an elaborate governmental agency for the promotion of foreign trade a wise expenditure of public funds when world tariff maladjustment stultified the exchange of goods in the world market? Should not the government turn its attention to the more fundamental conditions of international trade and the problems of foreign exchange before sending agents abroad to seek trade opportunities amid the prevailing disorder?

It became clear that the functions and purposes of government bureaus needed correlation. Why should public funds be used and public servants engaged to aid the grocers in improving their merchandising methods when the whole economic structure of the nation demanded basic readjustment?

The American Manufacturers' Export Association circularized a questionnaire among its members regarding the proposed reorganization of the government's foreign-trade services. Although these firms widely used the facilities offered by the Bureau of Foreign and Domestic Commerce, they recognized the need for retrenchment. Among the many suggestions made, two appear of particular significance: (1) that each branch office of the bureau support itself by fees from firms in any designated territory that it can amply and economically serve; (2) that the possibilities of the American chambers of commerce abroad be further developed.[1] Many of those who once supported the bureau enthusiastically now viewed it skeptically.

It was recognized that prosperity could not be restored by propaganda and that business could not be prodded into activity. The problem of world trade was seen to involve more than beating one's competitor to the foreign market. A storehouse of trade information in Washington was of little avail in itself. In other words, the task of business recovery had to be related to the general policy of the administration in both economic and foreign affairs.

[1] *Overseas Trading Data*, American Manufacturers' Export Association, 401 Broadway, New York, May 27, 1933, pp. 1042–1049.

PUBLIC ADMINISTRATION

When we look back over the development of the Department of Commerce under the Hoover regime, we note that the department was concerned with providing the maximum of service to business. Industrialists were called into consultation to consider means of expanding trade, of effecting economies in manufacture, of increasing business efficiency. They were called to Washington in order to tell the Department of Commerce how best they could be served. The result was the rapid expansion of governmental services. A sense of proportion was lost. Business promotion was the end and aim of the department. Its implications for foreign relations were ignored. The broader implications of business activities as related to the rest of society were given little consideration. In an age of prosperity it was easy to identify the public interest with the profit-making interest of industry.

The Roosevelt administration faced a different situation. Administrative officials in the Department of Commerce could not continue on the assumption that their sole task was increasing the efficiency of business methods of management and production. They had to broaden their criteria for determining the public interest. In facing the depression, the new Secretary of Commerce had to consider what changes in the practices and policies of the department should be made. What could be more appropriate than consulting the heads of representative corporations and industries?

Secretary Roper consulted a number of prominent businessmen with whom he was personally acquainted and in whom he had confidence. Their response to his suggestion for an advisory council was so cordial that a preliminary conference was held on June 4, 1933. The names of other business leaders were proposed and three weeks later the first session of the Business Advisory and Planning Council brought all these men together. It was recognized that a representative group in any formal sense of the word was impossible, but in issuing invitations due regard was given to securing spokesmen (1) from the different industrial interests such as steel, textiles, lumber, etc., (2) from the different territorial divisions of the country, and (3) from the small as well as the large manufacturers. A considerable variety of industrial experience was represented on the council and its members were drawn from various parts of the country although the majority of the gen-

[308]

eral council members came from cities within easy reach of the capital.

The general complexion of the council was liberal. Among the businessmen serving were many well-known for their progressive attitude in labor relations and industrial management. They were frankly the spokesmen of business and predominantly of big business; but they were from that segment of the business community that was more rather than less sympathetic to the broad purposes of the New Deal. No one has been able to devise any basis upon which a council representative of economic interests can be objectively recruited. The problem certainly was not solved here, but the effort was made to bring together a group of intelligent industrialists who were willing to consider in broad terms the role of government in the nation's economic life. The council included the heads of the Chamber of Commerce of the United States of America, the National Association of Manufacturers, and the National Industrial Conference Board. The council appeared essentially an advisory rather than a representative device. The aim was a membership of sufficient diversity and prominence to give weight to the advice offered in the name of the council.

The leading spokesmen on this council have taken the stand that "if industry does not organize and govern itself, either the State or Federal Government will—with the consequent paralyzing effects on initiative and progress."[1] This assumption has been implicit in the work of the council and has been voiced time and again. It indicates that the businessmen on the council believe and even fear that democratic government can control economic enterprise. They have argued that it is to the best interest of businessmen, as well as to the public interest, to eliminate unfair trade practices. They supported the N.R.A. Through the Industrial Advisory Board they represented the viewpoint of business in the formulation of code authorities under the N.R.A.

The Council's committee on industrial relations reported: "In their united effort at recovery from the world-wide depression, the parties to American industry are confronted with some real conflicts of interest. Surely it is the part of wisdom to minimize these conflicts and to seek out the areas in which interests coincide

[1] Statement of Gerard Swope at meeting of council, Nov. 1, 1933.

and in which cooperative action is possible."[1] This council has sought a middle course. It is willing to compromise. Whether the terms of compromise will be in the public interest is for the administrators to decide. The council is today nothing more than a temporary expedient for bringing into "unified focus the manifold voices of business" in order to link sympathetic business leaders in coöperative contact with the New Deal program. Out of this emergency agency there may possibly develop an effective device for representing the "business interest" in federal administration. It is an experiment in administration that should be tested to the full.

Here is one device for confronting businessmen with the broad implications of a competitive industrial order. What can the practical man of affairs offer to the solution of public problems? Constructive suggestions should come from those having direct experience in commerce and industry.

The council reports directly to the Secretary of Commerce. It works through special subcommittees. Several committees were established to study departmental problems such as the foreign service of the department, the making of domestic commerce surveys, and the publication policy of the department. Other committees turned their attention to general business problems. For example, the council on Apr. 15, 1935, sent a report to the Secretary of Commerce on the credit and capital requirements of small industry. The council recommended that the Reconstruction Finance Corporation, the Federal Reserve Board, and the Securities and Exchange Commission, in coöperation with the investment bankers, consider ways of providing adequate credit facilities for the small industries of the country. This report was brought to the attention of all the administrative officials concerned with the problem. How effective this machinery will become remains to be seen. The council, at least, formulated the opinion of industrialists on an important public question and simultaneously directed the attention of federal officials to that problem.

Suppose that the chief of one of the commodity divisions of the Bureau of Foreign and Domestic Commerce is developing a project. He finds that his work relates to a field covered by one of the subcommittees of the council. He confers with this committee and

[1] W. C. Teagle, *Employee Representation and Collective Bargaining*, p. 9.

contacts the businessmen immediately interested in this subject. Working together they develop certain specific proposals. The subcommittee prepares a report which is passed upon by the Executive Committee. The recommendations sent on to the Secretary of Commerce represent an agreement between the departmental officials and the businessmen on the council. Thus a meeting of minds is secured at the very beginning of the administrative process. There is every likelihood that such proposals are practicable and administratively sound. Whether they are in the public interest remains to be determined by those ultimately responsible for general policy. Considerations of this sort can be made only at high administrative levels and they often involve presidential judgment. But before proposals are brought up for such consideration, it is essential that they be acceptable to the administrators and the "administrated."

How shall the council conduct itself with reference to the public? The answer to this lies in the publicity policy of the organization. The reports and recommendations of its various committees are submitted to the Secretary of Commerce. He is left to make public this data in such form as he sees fit. With very few exceptions the secretary has given the council's findings and proposals to the newspapers. This arrangement is hardly in keeping with the council's advisory character. It is not an agency for urging the acceptance of a particular policy. Those in control realize that they have not yet formulated their own basic concepts with sufficient clarity to defend a long-term consistent policy. Moreover, it is not within their province to arouse opinion and to urge that the entire business community support their proposals.

The council can only speak for the handful of business executives that compose it. The Secretary of Commerce must be left free to determine what consideration their advice deserves. If he disagrees with their conclusions, that is his own affair. Businessmen are organized in pressure groups through their trade associations and through the national chamber of commerce. These organizations by the skillful use of publicity attempt to win the support of business opinion for their proposals. They are prepared to fight Congressmen or administrative officials if their policies are unfavorably viewed. The Business Advisory and Planning Council should not become another pressure group. The folly of this was demonstrated in May, 1935. When the Chamber of Commerce of the United States of America criticized certain New Deal policies, some members of the Business Advisory and Planning Council hastened to assure the President that they supported him. Administration leaders used the reports of the council to show that businessmen approved of certain controversial legislation. This created dissension and a few weeks later several prominent members of the council resigned.[1]

The council has now decided against any publicity for its proceedings or recommendations. Functioning as a *confidential advisory body* of representative business leaders, the council may yet prove effective. Its significance lies in the fact that it has been taken into the administrative setup and given a job to perform. Will this device prove more or less effective than cruder lobbying methods? Here for the first time the federal government has recognized that businessmen have a peculiar responsibility to carry, that they have a special contribution to make, and that it is in the public interest that they be lined up with the administrative process.

Of course, the influence of bankers, manufacturers, and other business interests has always been present in the administration and in the legislature.[2] No other class has been more powerful. But the great political strength of businessmen has been directed toward the securing of immediate and particular ends. One manufacturer has connived to secure a higher tariff for his product; another has sought some service from a federal bureau. Or a whole industry has pursued its interests with little thought for the objectives of other industries. This must continue in any acquisitive society.

The Business Advisory and Planning Council, however, provides a means whereby a group of leading industrialists may take thought for business and consider the interests of the property-owning and labor-employing class with reference to the concerns of labor, of the consumer, of the farmer, and of the public generally. They will thus try to discover what is to the ultimate advantage of business. They are not directly concerned with the public interest.

[1] *New York Times*, June 27, 1935, p. 3; June 29, p. 7.
[2] For a timely discussion, see R. J. Swenson, "The Chamber of Commerce and the New Deal," *Annals of the Academy of Political Science*, May, 1935, p. 136.

DEPARTMENT OF COMMERCE RESPONDS TO BUSINESS

They are not trying to act impartially or unselfishly. The most that can be expected is enlightened selfishness. The Department of Commerce must operate on the tacit assumption that what is good for business is good for the country. But the department cannot fulfill its purpose under the law unless it can get a broad view of business welfare.

The Secretary of Commerce has his own subjective conception of what is in the "public interest." He feels a vague responsibility for the taxpayer and the consumer, but he cannot hope to obtain tangible criteria for judging these interests. Secretary Roper in organizing the Business Advisory and Planning Council acted in the hope of discovering some guide to the actual content of the "business interest."

The council has been unable to formulate clearly this interest. Disagreement among its members has reduced its effectiveness. In December, 1935, the council decided to consider thereafter only those questions brought up by the President or by the Secretary of Commerce. The council recognized the futility of volunteering opinions on controversial political issues. Its attention is now to be focused on administrative problems. This council may in the course of time discover a sphere of usefulness. Thus far it has been busy realizing its limitations.

It is a highly significant development for the federal government to undertake the public responsibility of ascertaining through consultative agencies the opinions of particular economic groups. It is a further indication of the inadequacy of our popular representative assemblies as devices for discovering what is in the general welfare. In the face of this administrative development, Congress becomes increasingly a body for reviewing the proposals of the administrative branch rather than a positive agency in the formulation of public policy. Government has become too much for the politicians. In a system that makes it possible for demagogues to win a vast popular following by mouthing specious remedies and making outrageous promises, the administrative branch becomes the strategic point for rallying the forces of intelligent resistance. Workable alternatives can at least be offered to offset impractical popular panaceas. Under a democratic government the simplifier and the popularizer tends to become a person of power. Yet the very abilities that bring him this power are not the abilities that make him competent to wield it intelligently. He wins a response by striking a popular chord; yet he has no grasp of the complexities of the problem he has simplified so attractively.

In increasing degree our administrators, through consultation with the appropriate experts and the interests most directly affected, are attempting to secure the views of those who are competent to speak with authority and understanding. Representative government cannot endure unless it represents those who think as well as those who feel. The ballot box makes no distinction and the politicians whose fate depends on the election count must use the most effective means of collecting votes. Sometimes the castigation of business is the best way to win elections; sometimes prudence suggests compliance with the dominant business interests in the state or congressional district. Nowhere in our representative system under the constitution is there any provision for discovering the best interest of the businessman, or of the farmer, or of labor, or of any other broad national interest.

The Business Advisory and Planning Council is an experiment. If it proves workable it offers an answer to our problem. It avoids the dangers of the extragovernmental pressure group. It supplements a representative system that is patently inadequate. It provides advice for the official who is seeking the substance of the interest that he is called upon to administer. If the federal government is to concern itself more and more in the affairs of industry, industry must be brought more directly into this process of government. The problem is not that of finding defenders of business rights. The average politician is only too anxious to serve those who hold the moneybags. Such representatives hold their ears so close to the ground that they get them full of grasshoppers even on the sidewalks of the financial district. Spokesmen are needed who recognize the social responsibilities as well as the rights of industry. Business needs spokesmen who stand firmly upon economic reality and look ahead to the long-range welfare of industry. Such men are more often found in the ranks of business than in the gangs of politics, but they have not been effectively drawn into the public service.

Much might be accomplished in establishing a closer tie between industry and the federal government in the states, the cities, and even smaller communities. French chambers of commerce offer

[314]

a lead.[1] These organizations of local businessmen are authorized by law and charged with the performance of certain governmental tasks. A vital relationship between industry and government should be developed from the smaller to the larger areas. In many communities a committee of representative businessmen could be selected to coöperate with officials. Such committees could watch the activities of federal officials in their community. They could weigh the effectiveness of regulatory laws as they actually worked. They could judge the value of projected public works and of relief for the unemployed. They could inform their business community as to how public funds were being used. Such local committees would be of invaluable assistance to a central business advisory board in its task of broad evaluation and constructive criticism.[2]

Administration in the public interest necessitates the clarification of group interest. Farmers, workers, and industrialists must all seek agreements upon the best interests of their respective classes. Administrative officials need guidance. Direction comes most authoritatively and clearly from the political appointees at the head of the great departments. The policy of such officials as exemplified by the Departments of Labor, Commerce, and Agriculture indicates that the relations of federal officials with these interests is vastly affected by the general political philosophy of the administration in power. Most striking is the relative neglect of the Department of Labor during the Hoover-Coolidge administrations and the great emphasis placed upon the activities of the Department of Commerce. President Roosevelt has had several difficulties with this latter department, while the Departments of Labor and of Agriculture have received fresh impetus under the New Deal.

The political climate under which officials function has a profound effect upon their activities. This is to be expected where departments touch the welfare of such politically potent interests

---

[1] E. Pendleton Herring, "Chambres de Commerce, Their Legal Status and Political Significance," *American Political Science Review*, August, 1931. L. W. Lancaster, "The Legal Status of Private Organizations Exercising Governmental Powers," *Southwestern Social Science Quarterly*, March, 1935.

[2] E. Pendleton Herring, "Where Does Business Come In?," *The Christian Science Monitor*, Aug. 20, 1935, p. 14.

as agriculture, labor, and business. Special interests cannot turn aside the general political trend dominating the administration as a whole. Where they are in harmony with this trend, they can accelerate moments for their own benefit and override other group interests less fortunately placed. This situation is illustrated by the experience of the Bureau of Standards as a subordinate agency within the Department of Commerce.

Chapter XIX

BUSINESS SUPPORT OF SCIENTIFIC RESEARCH

"Now, if you're ready, Oysters dear,
We can begin to feed."
"But not on us!" the Oysters cried,
Turning a little blue.
"After such kindness, that would be
A dismal thing to do!"

PURE science has no focal point in the federal government. Those interested in such research are in a relatively weak position. They must fight their battles on many fronts. They are, moreover, no match for the commercial interests that tend to identify their welfare with various governmental agencies. Since it is not the policy of the federal government to undertake scientific research as a major administrative function, there is no department that puts this purpose foremost and subordinates all other related activities. Scientific research thus remains one of the interests that cuts across the lines of the existing administrative framework. The position of the scientist as a member of the federal bureaucracy is clarified by considering the Bureau of Standards in the Department of Commerce.

This bureau was established primarily to maintain national standards of measurement and to carry on the research necessary to their development. A vast amount of scientific investigation has developed out of this original duty. After the World War, when the bureau came under the influence and direction of Mr. Hoover, the promotion of industrial standardization became a major activity. During the Hoover administration the Bureau of Standards was built up into an agency primarily concerned with assisting business. It was one thing to conduct scientific experiments as to properties of forces and substances and to test and safeguard measuring devices. It was quite another to become the preacher of a gospel of standardization for business.

Under the impetus of these new activities the bureau grew. A Division of Simplification and of Commercial Standards was created. The bureau was converted into a great service agency for business. This bureau during 1915 to 1932 was one of the most rapidly expanding agencies of the government.[1] When an administration came into power that was more concerned with the regulation of business than with providing free services to business, the Bureau of Standards was severely reduced. Its scientific work suffered. Businessmen at the time had enough to worry about without considering the Bureau of Standards. The scientists there were left to sink or swim.

The Bureau of Standards is a subordinate agency in a department designed to aid commerce. The Bureau of Standards has become an agency for *industrial research*. Its political support has come from industrialists and from the technicians employed by businessmen. Various ways have been developed for maintaining a close tie-up with industry. These contacts are graphic evidence of the way in which a scientific bureau has assumed the tone of the department that embraces it.

During the war the need for scientific investigators to help in the solution of problems arising in the process of manufacturing caused businessmen to turn to the experts on the staff of the Bureau of Standards. The result was that many highly trained civil servants were persuaded to leave the government service. The director of the bureau soon discovered that several of the scientific divisions in the bureau were seriously depleted and in some cases temporarily wiped out. In self-defense the bureau urged industrial interests to send their own specialists to the bureau under the "research associate plan." The result has been "a most happy one and beneficial to industry and to the bureau," the director reports. "The original scheme to maintain the integrity of the research groups at the bureau has been expanded to make provision for carrying out at the bureau fundamental investigations of interest to industry which are financed by industry itself."[2]

[1] C. H. Wooddy, *The Growth of the Federal Government—1915–1932*, p. 483, McGraw-Hill, 1934.

[2] For the full text of the actions by which Congress opened the way for the admission of qualified individuals to the use of federal research facilities, see 27 Stat. L., p. 395 and 51 Stat. L., p. 1010; George K. Burgess, "The Government Laboratory and Industry," *Journal of Maryland Academy of Sciences*, April, 1931.

BUSINESS SUPPORT OF SCIENTIFIC RESEARCH

According to the most recent survey, about forty-three associates are now maintained at the bureau by seventeen organizations that may be broadly classed as technical societies and trade associations. Other organized groups, committees, and firms sponsor thirty additional research associates at the bureau. If in the opinion of the director the nature of the investigation warrants the bureau's help, and the facilities can be arranged, the appointment of a research associate is allowed. Each proposed piece of research is outlined on a special form and submitted to the appropriate official who passes it on to the director for approval. When the project has been approved by the administrative officials and supporting group, a research authorization is drawn up and a copy filed.

The associate is subject to the same rules and regulations as a regular employee of the bureau. He must observe the same hours and conform to routine administrative practice. Reports to his supporting association are made through the director, but they are not for publication. The results of the investigation, while immediately available to the industry concerned, are published for general circulation, usually either as a bureau publication or in a technical journal. Devices developed in the course of the research cannot be patented for private gain.

The bureau places its equipment at the disposal of those working under this scheme, and government scientists also devote their energies to the problems of these industries. The aims of the research associate plan is explained by the bureau as follows:

. . . (a) To permit qualified workers to utilize the bureau's facilities and staff in conducting researches of mutual interest; (b) to afford training and experience in research in an institution where research is a most important part of its service to the nation; (c) to promote close-knit coöperation between the industries and the bureau; (d) to encourage the application of science to industry; (e) to lend the prestige of the government to research results in order to expedite the acceptance and application of such results in the industries.[1]

The extraordinary laboratory equipment of the bureau has been utilized by those sent in from private industry. All the services of a modern laboratory stand ready for use: precision

[1] *Research Associates at the Bureau of Standards*, Circular 29, 1926, p. 4.

time service, beating second signals through electric currents for making precise time-interval measurements; vacuum appliances; compressed air piped to the laboratories; electricity of wide range of voltage and current; refrigerating plants; liquid air and liquid hydrogen; freezing brine circuits; live and exhaust steam; air conditioning for the control of air humidity; provision for sound-proofing and lightproofing; and freedom from vibration. Few industries can afford such elaborate equipment. The bureau further contributes the services of special laboratories designed for many kinds of delicate measuring and testing. The heat of distant stars can be ascertained with one bit of apparatus, while another tests the strength of brick walls or structural steel. The bureau, however, boasts of more direct aids to industry. There are experimental mills for making textile yarn and fabric; papers and paper pulp; Portland cement; lime; gypsum products; clay products ranging from brick to fine porcelain, enameled ware, glazes, and glass; sugars; pure chemicals, alloys, and special metals; and rubber and rubber goods. There are a tannery, a foundry, a rolling mill, and numerous technical shops for instrument making.

Industrialists have welcomed all such opportunities. For example, the Portland Cement Association sent the bureau a group of specialists to study the chemical constitution and internal structure of cement. Another group sponsored by the American Electric Railways Association investigated the welding joints in rails. The rails themselves would last from fifteen to twenty years, but the welded joints failed within a year or two. The costliness of track maintenance prompted the railways to seek help from the bureau. A research program was agreed upon. The electric railways through their association supplied a specially designed impacting machine and a staff to operate it, together with welders and welding apparatus. It was thought that the impact of the wheels in passing over the joints impaired the welding. Various types of welding were accordingly tested by the impact machine and the most resistant type was discovered. Those in the dyeing and cleaning industry were particularly successful in their contacts with the bureau. Their research associates found a way for recovering a large proportion of the gasoline lost in cleaning clothes. In various ways many industries have profited by a direct dollars-and-cents return for their coöperation with the Bureau of Standards. Any industry confronted with perplexing problems may utilize the scientific resources of the government.

Not only have scientists employed by great industries and trade associations been given a place in the bureau under the research associate plan, but also the scientists employed in the bureau have been linked with industry. Bureau officials through their membership on committees of various kinds have built up numerous semiofficial bonds with outside organizations. The following analysis made a few years ago shows the extraordinary extent of such committee work.

RECORDS OF BUREAU PERSONNEL ON COMMITTEES OF VARIOUS ASSOCIATIONS

Name of organization	Listings	Individuals listed	Maximum listing of any individual
American Standards Association............	181	63	22
Federal Specifications Board..............	120	61	8
American Society for Testing Materials	304	55	24
National Fire Protection Association........	13	6	3
American Institute of Electrical Engineers...	45	19	7
National Research Council.................	74	26	22
American Society of Mechanical Engineers...	46	30	4
Miscellaneous societies (110)..............	329		
Total.................................	1112	155	24

In January, 1934, a report on the bureau stated:

Committee work constitutes a serious, though practically necessary, drain on the time and energies of the staff. At present there are 825 committee assignments for work of interest to the Bureau with scientific, engineering, testing and standardizing organizations, interdepartmental and international activities, etc. The number would be larger were not a strenuous effort made to cut down the number.[1]

Not only is the bureau lined up with business by this personal coöperation on the part of individuals; the standardization work

[1] *Report by Joint Committee of Science Advisory Board, Visiting Committee, and Business Advisory and Planning Council*, pp. 6–7.

prompting this contact also assures its continuance. The pages of the *Standards Yearbook*, the *Research Journal*, the *Technical News Bulletin*, and the *Commercial Standards Monthly* all indicate the interest that is taken by the bureau in the work of trade associations and technical groups. For example, the *Standards Yearbook* for 1930 outlines the activities of 375 associations that make standardization an important service to members.

Herbert Hoover, when Secretary of Commerce, used the bureau as a device for promoting coöperation among industrialists. His outstanding achievement was the simplified-practice procedure—a method for reducing waste by eliminating unnecessary variety in industrial products. The producer, distributor, and commercial consumer, under the auspices of the Department of Commerce, were urged to agree upon the kind of goods that could be conveniently discarded. It was pointed out that in many cases sales were made in about 20 per cent of the available varieties of the product. It was argued that a great diversity was not economically sound. The Department of Commerce[1] claimed that simplified-practice agreements, by reducing the inventory and storage space, would release capital investment, increase stock turnover, and tend to stabilize production, distribution, and employment. Mr. Hoover preached unceasingly the virtues of simplified practice and won many industries to the procedure.

The movement is traceable to conditions arising out of the World War. The War Industries Board urged that production be limited to a few varieties. In the depression of 1921 a reaction occurred. In the effort to break through the resistance of the purchaser, a superabundance of diversified articles appeared on the market. It became evident that some means for encouraging simplification was desirable. Herbert Hoover, at this time president of the Federated American Engineering Societies (now the American Engineering Council), appointed a committee to study prevailing conditions in industry. Its report was entitled *Waste in Industry*.[2] When he became Secretary of Commerce he estab-

---

[1] *Simplified Practice, What It Is and What It Offers*, Department of Commerce, Washington, 1929.

[2] *Waste in Industry, Report of Committee on Elimination of Waste in Industry of the Federated American Engineering Societies*, McGraw-Hill, 1921.

lished the division of simplified practice in the Bureau of Standards to eliminate waste.

Would industry accept the simplification scheme? Trade associations were appealed to by word and picture through the publicity bureau of the Department of Commerce. When a trade association became interested in the scheme, a preliminary survey was made and then a general meeting of producers, distributors, and users was held. The survey was considered and definite recommendations were formulated. The proposals resulting from this conference were then brought to the attention of all concerned with the problem and their adherence was requested. Efforts were made to convince them of the value of the changes. When formal written acceptances had been received from organizations representing 80 per cent of the total volume of the industry, the recommendations were endorsed by the Department of Commerce and published in its "Elimination of Waste Series."

Under the Hoover regime a vast ballyhoo accompanied all this activity. Great claims were made for the economies effected. Within recent years this enthusiasm has cooled and little is now being attempted. The simplified-practice work was not welcomed by scientists in the Bureau of Standards. It was looked upon as a commercial and not a scientific task. The varieties chosen for elimination were those that did not sell. The only standard applied was that of "dominant sales." Agreements were reached by a committee of businessmen. They might decide to eliminate a variety that was relatively unimportant and produced on a small scale, but which was nonetheless the principal product of some small manufacturer. The modest proportions of his undertaking could not be taken as a just index of its social utility. The bureau officials could not deny the wishes of the Secretary of Commerce, but they did not relish having such simplified practices promulgated in the name of their bureau. Moreover, they found that they had no means of enforcing these agreements and no effort has been made in recent years to check how carefully they are being kept. Officials believe that a census would disclose many infringements.

The Bureau of Standards has offered a further service to industry through its coöperation in promulgating commercial standards. Such standards set the "specific limitations below or beyond which the grade, quality, composition, or dimensions of a commodity shall not be allowed to fall," as agreed upon by those fixing the level. The request for the establishment of a commercial standard usually comes from trade associations, although private companies may initiate proposals. The Bureau of Standards acts as the general coördinating agency for informing and bringing together all those concerned with the project. No charge is made for this work. "Industry, through federal taxation, has already financed the work," it is stated.[1]

The Bureau of Standards designates an official as "project manager" and charges him with general supervision of the project. He surveys existing standards and examines all other pertinent data. This provides the basis for a tentative specification. A general preliminary conference is then held. Acting upon the recommendations of the preliminary conference or the survey committee, agenda are prepared for a general conference of producers, distributors, organized consumers, and allied interests. These agenda are then referred to the proper technical division of the Bureau of Standards for review. When this review has been completed and adjustments made, the agenda are submitted to the proponent group. A general conference of all interested parties is then held to consider what course is feasible with regard to the proposed standard. It may vote to make it a "recommended commercial standard" and appoint a standing committee to carry on future contacts between the industry and the division of trade standards.

The process, however, is not permitted to rest at this stage. Mere verbal approval at the general conference is not regarded as adequate. The Bureau of Standards seeks the formal written acceptance of the recommended standard. If the industry to the extent of 65 per cent of production or consumption by volume signifies its acceptance, and if no serious protest is raised, the bureau issues a circular letter announcing the success of the project and the date when the standard becomes effective. An adjunct to the above procedure is the certification plan.

This consists in the compilation and distribution by the Bureau of Standards of lists of manufacturers who are willing upon request to certify to purchasers that the products bought from them

[1] *The Commercial Standards Service and Its Value to Business*, Commercial Standard CSO-30, Department of Commerce, Washington, 1930, pp. 9 *ff*.

comply with all the requirements and tests set forth in nationally recognized commercial standards. This plan is also applied to certain specifications used by the federal government in its buying. These lists of manufacturers "willing-to-certify" are supplied to any prospective purchaser or group of consumers desiring them.

To what extent does the bureau attempt to be directly helpful to the public, *i.e.*, to those who do not stand in a special-interest relationship to the bureau? Industry, impelled by its own self-interest and possessing ample resources, is in a better position to cope with technical problems than the unorganized mass of individuals whose concern with the manufacturing process is quite remote, but whose stake in the quality of the product is very personal. What has the bureau to say for these?

The bureau assumes that the citizen is to benefit from the work of the bureau to the extent that advances in scientific knowledge bring improved appliances upon the market. As society as a whole is enriched, so the individual is aided.[1] There are those who remain unsatisfied with this rejoinder.[2] The findings of the bureau go directly toward helping business cut its costs, increase its efficiency, and presumably add to its profits. But the advice of the bureau is not given to the individual buyer to aid him in selecting the product that gives him the best value for his money. Improvements in method of manufacture do not necessarily guarantee that prices will be cut. The crude and none too certain workings of competition are the only means of forcing upon the market a better article at a lower profit. Why should a governmental bureau devoted to scientific investigation and the improvement of industrial processes serve the producer and ignore the user? The question has been put bluntly to the bureau: "Why does a service run by taxpayers' money refuse information covering competitive products to that same taxpayer?"[3] The bureau explains its position in this wise:

Being primarily a scientific and technical agency, the bureau must limit its service to technical aspects of quality performance or practice. In tests

[1] F. C. Brown, "Who Profits from Scientific Work," *Scientific Monthly*, December, 1924, pp. 655–660.

[2] F. J. Schlink, "Government Bureaus for Private Profit," *Nation*, Nov. 11, 1931, pp. 508–511.

[3] Stuart Chase and F. J. Schlink, *Your Money's Worth*, Macmillan, 1927, p. 203.

other than those applying to individual instruments the chief purpose is usually to give the manufacturers information which may aid them in improving their products or processes.

The bureau must not be drawn into advertising controversy, hence it makes no statement as to the relative merits of commodities on sale. With the bureau's limited facilities, it would be possible to test only a small part of the many varieties of products. Consequently, bureau reports could not be made on all similar products and an unfair advantage would be given to those who might receive them. Furthermore, the quality of output might vary so that the test of an individual article or sample cannot apply to an entire output and in such case results so applied would mislead the public.

Experience has shown that the use of the bureau's name cannot be safeguarded so as to avoid complaints from competitors, and if results of tests of commercial articles appeared frequently in competitive advertising with the bureau's name attached, we would be limited in the kind of tests we could undertake. It appears therefore that the bureau can on the whole, render the best service by keeping its name out of such advertising.[1]

Officials have learned by past experience that to discriminate between competing commercial products will bring the wrath of one party down upon them.

On more than one occasion the bureau has published reports indicating the relative merits of one product over another. The effect of such incidents has not encouraged repetition. A scientific bureau cannot hold itself removed from the currents of politics and of interest groups. Some years ago the bureau reported its findings on wool and cotton blankets. Under certain conditions cotton blankets were said to be as efficient as woolen blankets. Several Senators from the wool states called to see the director of the bureau and gave him *their* opinion. The bureau has discovered that its reports upon storage batteries, sand-lime brick, and other commodities have been a bit too frank to suit the parties affected. Hence scientists protected by civil-service rules and acting for the public interest in entire good faith learn that there are some discoveries that should not be reported too exhaustively. The recent investigation of the bureau into the qualities of therapeutic glasses brought forth protests from the manufacturers that resulted in the alteration of the final report on the subject issued by the bureau.

[1] From a mimeographed release of the Bureau of Standards.

BUSINESS SUPPORT OF SCIENTIFIC RESEARCH

Of course, it is a difficult matter to secure documentary proof upon such a topic. The government officials are chary of talking and the manufacturers do not wish to tell of their coercive tactics.

In general, those in the bureau have not been disturbed in their purely scientific work, but their testing and specifications work have sometimes occasioned difficulties. For example, the Navy Department asked the bureau to test a consignment of electric light bulbs from the General Electric Company. The bureau reported that the bulbs were not up to specifications. The sales manager of the General Electric Company came down to Washington and demanded that the bureau change its findings. The bureau refused and the Navy Department supported its stand. When the time for appropriations came around, the Bureau of Standards discovered that it had created an enemy. The rag paper interests have fought the bureau's conclusions that wood-pulp paper properly made has superior lasting qualities.[1]

It is inevitable that from time to time the bureau will incur the displeasure of some industry whose products are adversely affected by the tests of the bureau. Since the bureau must make its peace with competing manufacturers, distributors, and large-scale buyers, it is not to be wondered at that the ultimate consumer gets slight consideration. He is simply not a participating factor in the situation. If he is to be taken into account, he must organize and present his case along with the other spokesmen of pressure groups.

While the bureau is doubtless justified in regarding its harmonious relations with business as an administrative asset and an incentive toward the further development of service to industry, still the bureau was not organized to serve as the handmaid of business. Its original purpose was scientific.[2] It was concerned

[1] For further illustrations, see F. J. Schlink, "What Government Does and Might Do for the Consumer," *Annals of the American Academy of Political and Social Science*, May, 1934, p. 38.

[2] The act to establish the Bureau of Standards states: "That the functions of the bureau shall consist in the custody of the standards; the comparison of the standards used in scientific investigations, engineering, manufacturing, commerce, and educational institutions with the standards adopted or recognized by the Government; the construction, when necessary, of standards, their multiples and subdivisions; the testing and calibration of standard measuring apparatus; the solution of problems which arise in connection with standards; the determination

with the custody and testing of standards rather than with smoothing obstacles from the path of mass production.

The services that the bureau performs for industry must be taken as part of the policy of Herbert Hoover. The experience with war economies under the War Industries Board doubtless inclined business toward the acceptance of such a policy. Scientific investigation, simplification, and standardization accord with mass production. The Bureau of Standards, as a subordinate agency in a department that is chiefly concerned in promoting the interests of business, has developed in accordance with this major function. The bureau under these circumstances could not very well bend its energies either toward protecting the consumer or toward devoting all its time to basic scientific research. Where the emphasis should be is a matter of public policy.

Bills have been introduced in Congress from time to time authorizing the Bureau of Standards to determine and report upon the relative merits of competing commodities [the director of the bureau states], but Congress has not looked with favor upon this proposed expansion of the bureau's activities, which would necessarily involve an enormous expense if a comprehensive, reliable and up-to-date service were to be maintained.[1]

From the nature of its equipment and personnel the Bureau of Standards might logically be placed in a Department of Science, a Department of Commerce, or a Department of the Consumer. It might conceivably be removed from under the supervision of any one department. The National Advisory Committee on Aeronautics, for example, attributes its remarkable success to "its status as an independent establishment, giving it complete administrative control of its own laboratories."[2] Unless the government is to be composed of an indefinite number of independent units, bureaus must be made subordinate to departments. Disagreement turns upon the major functions of the government with which subordinate bureaus shall be associated. No scheme of reorganization can eliminate such disagreements. The logic

of physical constants and the properties of materials, when such data are of great importance to scientific or manufacturing interests and are not to be obtained of sufficient accuracy elsewhere."

[1] F. J. Schlink, "What Government Does and Might Do for the Consumer," *op. cit.*, p. 154.

[2] Wooddy, *op. cit.*, p. 496.

of one plan of reorganization rests upon a scheme of values that might be anathema to a planner with a different set of values. The aspect of a bureau's activities that will receive most emphasis is the work most directly related to the major function of the department under which the bureau is placed as a subordinate unit. How is it possible to protect those activities of the bureau that do not directly accord with the dominant goal of the department?

The scientist in the Department of Commerce or the Department of Agriculture is working in a vast organization wherein research is merely one of a number of important activities. Within the same bureaus and often over the same desks must be performed regulatory, educational, and purely administrative activities. The pursuit of scientific truth must often be subordinated and coördinated to other and more immediate ends. Research cannot be conducted upon the assumption that administration in the public interest means the development of science for its own sake. Scientific work is directed to the solution of certain definite practical problems.

It is an academic question as to whether this arrangement is desirable or not. As a practical matter, these bureaus are supported by the government on such a wide scale because they answer certain pressing needs of the farmer and businessman. The Bureau of Chemistry and Soils, for instance, must advise the farmer on the utilization of waste products such as straw, stalks, and hull. It develops improved insecticides and fumigants. It studies methods of combating soil erosion. The practical focus of the bureau is illustrated in its very organization. The Division of Physics and Physical Chemistry is a subdivision of the fertilizer-investigations section.

No bureau is more deeply concerned with scientific research than the Bureau of Plant Industry. Botany, genetics, and biophysics are subdivisions of the bureau along with the subdivisions on Egyptian cotton breeding and Western irrigation agriculture. The major function of this agency is the introduction of new plants, the development of disease-resistant varieties, and general crop improvement through the selection, breeding, and proper cultivation of useful plants. Officials state: "In common with other agricultural research institutions in this country and abroad, it has been the experience of the Bureau of Plant Industry since its inception that the problems eventually of the greatest value to agriculture are those dealing with fundamental research."[1] Yet the support for such agencies comes from farmers who want help in meeting immediate problems and from Congressmen who want to see practical results for the money they appropriate.

The significance and value of scientific work cannot be left to the judgment of farmers and businessmen alone. Scientists can be adequately judged only by scientists. Seldom do scientists outside the federal government have a personal stake in the work of their bureaucratic colleagues. The members of the American Chemical Society are interested in the work of the Bureau of Chemistry and Soils in the Department of Agriculture. But their interest is professional. They are interested in any significant contributions to the sum of chemical knowledge. Such discoveries offer them little opportunity for personal gain. If the salaries of government chemists are reduced, the American Chemical Society in a fraternal spirit protests to Congress. But there is not in this relationship of scientific society to governmental scientist the impetus bred of self-interest that brings other groups to Washington demanding concessions or appropriations from Congress. It is not comparable to the interest that a businessman has in the tariff. The scientist in the federal government finds himself tacked to the kite tail of business and agriculture.

The government carries on scientific activities in forty federal bureaus, and eighteen of these are primarily scientific in nature. But in all these bureaus research is a function incidental to the chief purpose of the administrative superior. Certain interests of great importance in any broad view of the public welfare are very weak politically. In some cases this may be due to the nature of our structure of government. Or the weakness may be due to the economic organization of society under a competitive system. Whatever the reason, the fact remains that such interests, if they are to contribute their share to the general welfare, cannot be left unaided.

It is, therefore, the responsibility of the government to foster within the federal administration itself the representation of certain viewpoints that are socially important but politically weak.

[1] The United States Department of Agriculture, Its Structure and Functions, 1934, *Miscellaneous Document* 88, p. 150.

BUSINESS SUPPORT OF SCIENTIFIC RESEARCH

There is need for some agency that can take a broad view of the relative importance of scientific activity in various parts of the government and can advise Congress and the President as to what bureaus need increased appropriations and what departments can take a reduction without dangerous results. A recent experiment in administrative organization suggests one way of meeting the problem.

The Science Advisory Board was created by executive order in July, 1933, when the President named a board of nine members. By a later order the membership was increased to fifteen. The board was vested "with authority, acting through the machinery and under the jurisdiction of the National Academy of Sciences and the National Research Council, to appoint committees to deal with specific problems in the various departments." The National Academy of Sciences was incorporated by Congress in 1863 to advise the government upon scientific problems whenever called upon; the National Research Council was set up in 1916 as the "operating arm" of the academy. Representatives of all the important scientific associations are members of the council.

The Science Advisory Board undertook "not only a study of the functions, relationships and programs of the several scientific bureaus, but also the place of science in the Government structure." Working through its committees, the board made a survey of various federal agencies engaged in scientific work. Answers were sought to questions such as the following: "Is the organization adapted to the best fulfillment of its objectives? Are its objectives of distinct importance for the public welfare? Is its program planned with vision and keen appreciation of needs and opportunities? Are old projects dropped when their objectives have been attained? Is the personnel competent and alert? Is there proper coördination and coöperation with non-governmental agencies?"[1]

This last question was one of the problems considered by the Science Advisory Board in connection with its investigation of the Bureau of Standards. One of the economies of the Roosevelt administration was to cut the appropriations of the bureau nearly 50 per cent. The new Secretary of Commerce requested the American Standards Association to relieve the bureau of as much of

[1] *Report of the Science Advisory Board*, 1934, p. 12.

the simplified-practice procedure, the commercial-standards works, and the building and safety codes as it could. Scientific, commercial, and technical associations raised a howl of protest at this effort to cripple the bureau. The Science Advisory Board was requested to investigate the merits of the case in coöperation with the Visiting Committee of the Bureau of Standards and a special committee from the Business Advisory and Planning Council.

The joint committee that visited the Bureau of Standards represented those who were interested both in scientific research and in the promotion of industry. The personnel of this committee was interlocking; several of the men who represented business also spoke for the Science Advisory Board. Their report showed that they regarded the primary purpose of the Bureau of Standards to be that of *industrial research*. They were concerned with the scientific research of the bureau as it related to industrial problems. The report of the joint committee did not, therefore, reflect the viewpoint purely of science, but it was useful. It gave the director of the bureau support in his contention that the appropriations cut so drastically should be restored. The fact that the Business Advisory and Planning Council was a favorite child of the secretary did not make the report of its subcommittee any the less convincing. Appended to the recommendations of the joint committee were resolutions condemning the appropriation slash from such technical societies as the American Association for the Advancement of Science, American Chemical Society, American Institute of Electrical Engineers, American Physical Society, and American Society of Mechanical Engineers. The joint committee helped to focus this supporting opinion and so preserve the scientific work of the bureau from too drastic a budget cut.

By 1935 the Bureau of Standards had practically returned to "normal." The director had succeeded in having appropriations restored to their previous level. The retrenchment at the present time is no greater than the general curtailment of activities because of depressed business conditions.

An agency such as this Science Advisory Board tends to guide administration in the public interest because it is able to view the research activities of the government in broad terms.[1] The members

[1] It is interesting to note that in the British government the Department of

of the board had the prestige of presidential appointment. They were not identified with any federal scientific bureau. They could be authoritative, expert, and objective. The board offered advice only where requested and its recommendations were not made public until the secretary of the department concerned gave his sanction. The board tried "to look beyond details of program, procedure and personnel, toward the great social objectives of science, to see which of them are the necessary part of government and how each bureau can contribute toward them."[1]

The official life of the Science Advisory Board was terminated in December, 1935. The National Academy of Sciences then created a governmental Relations and Science Advisory Committee to continue some activities of the former official board. The numerous federal scientific activities will probably never be placed under a department devoted to the major function of research, but some measure of coördination is nonetheless desirable. This an Interdepartmental Science Board or a Science Advisory Board might supply. It could help to retrieve the balance for those bureaus that are dominated by industry, by agriculture, by labor, or by other organized and politically effective interests.

There are a number of significant developments within the federal government today that seem likely to advance administration in the public interest. They are not panaceas. All are susceptible to grave abuses. None has been perfected. Some may be soon abandoned. Properly understood and directed, however, they may go far toward meeting in a realistic fashion the practical day-to-day needs of officials and of citizens who have business with them. The following section will consider the possibility of building up some unified conception of the public interest within the administrative services through (1) a more harmonious administrative structure, (2) a more extensive use of consultative agencies, (3) a better understanding of administrative objectives by the public, and (4) a more deliberate attempt to formulate in positive terms a program for advancing the general welfare.

Scientific and Industrial Research conducts practically all governmental research except that in agriculture, medicine, and the war services. H. M. Treasury Committee on Civil Research, *Report of the Research Co-ordinating Sub-committee*, 1928.

[1] Report of the Science Advisory Board, 1934, p. 15.

Chapter XX

IS REORGANIZATION THE SOLUTION?

"I want a clean cup," interrupted the Hatter: "let's all move one place on."

He moved on as he spoke, and the Dormouse followed him: the March Hare moved into the Dormouse's place, and Alice rather unwillingly took the place of the March Hare. The Hatter was the only one who got any advantage from the change; and Alice was a good deal worse off than before, as the March Hare had just upset the milk-jug into his plate.

FROM our experience with the Departments of Agriculture, of Commerce, and of Labor, it is clear that the scope and character of administrative services are determined by the relative political strength of various classes. It has often been stated by students of administration that the federal departments should be organized in accordance with the major functions of the government. This is a sound principle; but what constitutes a major function? This is a question of national policy.

The major functions undertaken by the government will be those duties necessary to the continuance of the government itself and those activities supported by the most effective political demand. The conduct of foreign relations, national defense, taxation and fiscal control, the administration of justice, the postal service, promoting the interests of commerce, agriculture, and labor: these federal functions are given primary recognition. As an agency of home affairs, the Department of the Interior has been a general dumping place for various miscellaneous duties. Besides the traditional duties of the government and those activities supported by strong economic groups, there are a number of administrative services striving to win positions of greater relative importance in the bureaucracy.

Art, education, science, and health are admittedly important in any view of the public interest. In 1935 a bill was proposed for establishing a Department of Science, Art, and Literature with a secretary in the President's Cabinet. The comic spirit in which this proposal was received by the press reflected its triviality from the viewpoint of practical politics. Yet is the federal government to ignore matters that are socially important because they are politically insignificant? How, as a practical matter, can we bring into public administration those interests that do not have an effective political backing? How may a problem of obvious social importance but of little political significance be so placed as to contribute most effectively to administration in the public interest? Within the federal establishment various functions are incidental to the major purpose of the existing departments. Many of these functions cut across departmental lines. Sometimes they may represent interests that conflict with the chief purpose of the department. Often they are activities that require technical skill or special knowledge as well as sympathetic understanding.

Congress has decided that it is in the public interest to support scientific research, to develop roads, to protect the consumer, to guard the public health, to conserve natural resources, and to foster education. Yet these functions fill subordinate places in the administrative hierarchy. Of course, each of these activities has its special proponents who are not content to see their special interest relegated to a position of secondary importance. There is much to be said for elevating any one of these interests to a position of major importance. The outcome, however, will not turn upon the intrinsic worth of these subjects, but rather upon the political support each can attract.

The organized educators have faced this situation frankly. Under the generalship of the National Education Association they have fought for years to secure a federal Department of Education with a secretary in the President's Cabinet. They have had bills introduced into Congress; they have agitated in congressional districts; and they have lobbied before Congress. They have a foe worthy of their strength in the Catholic Education Association. It will require a long fight before their opponents are overcome. The issue has been a thorn in the side of more than one politician. In an effort to win the support of the National Education Association, Herbert Hoover appointed the National Advisory Committee on Education to investigate the matter. This committee represented all phases of education. Its report simply intensified the existing differences of opinion. The majority of the committee, much to the discomfiture of the President and his Secretary of the Interior, strongly urged a separate Department for Education. They stated:

> The peculiar nature of the many educational services performed by the Federal Government requires their distribution through many departments, but their effective performance also requires among them a degree of coöperation and coördination which only the Chief Executive can insure. Without an educational officer of equal status with the heads of all other Departments concerned, it would be impossible to secure that voluntary coöperation from all departments needed to integrate the educational resources of the Government. No bureau chief or head of a detached or independent establishment can have that equal access to the Chief Executive and equality of approach to the heads of all departments concerned essential to the effective total operation of education in the government.[1]

To attain coördination in the administration of educational activities, the National Education Association and its allies are ready to face the racial and religious animosities that arise when a federal Department of Education is proposed.

Such a campaign may be undertaken when an aggressive organization is willing to lead the movement. But administrative reforms cannot be left to pressure groups in all fields. Some more peaceful way of promoting coördination must be found. Public-health work, for example, is a governmental responsibility of great social importance. There is no politically powerful segment of the population that identifies its interests directly with those of the Public Health Service. The whole community benefits by the effectiveness of its work. To a peculiar degree its work is for the *general welfare*. Yet there seems to be little likelihood that the promotion of public health will ever assume an importance comparable to the promotion of agriculture or commerce. Everybody has an interest in health, but few realize its value until they become ill. Health matters can seldom be linked with the immediate interests of a politically effective group.

The Public Health Service is under the Secretary of the Treasury. It is composed of a professional corps of physicians and scientists under the direction of the Surgeon General. Its work by its very

[1] Report of the committee entitled *Federal Relations to Education*, p. 94.

nature cannot be directed by the lay mind. The officials in this service can thus enjoy a considerable degree of freedom from outside interference. The Surgeon General has stated:

The highly specialized professional personnel of the Public Health Service is segregated into a compact unit for administrative purposes and is so organized that it can be drawn on for expert help whenever it is needed in any other branch of the Government. This plan of organization involves a minimum of expense and insures uniformity and accuracy of method. The further development of this system would place at the command of the Government one source from which each requirement for such service could draw, and would obviate the building up of new professional units in the various departments at large overhead expense and with inevitable duplication of work and lack of coordination.[1]

Coördination in such terms means coöperation and advice. It means examining aliens for the State Department prior to the granting of visas; advising with the Department of Justice in the administration of quarantine laws; assisting the Department of Agriculture in the enforcement of the Pure Food and Drug Act against the adulteration of shell fish or the spread of typhoid fever through impure milk; aiding the Office of Public Buildings in the sanitary inspection of government office buildings, etc. To list its coöperative activities would be to call the roll of the departments and some of the independent establishments. But the point is clear. Coördination may be brought about through gathering together a great number of related bureaus under a single head or it may be secured through a bureau that specializes in one function which it interjects into the administrative process where required.

It has not been necessary to add a secretary to the President's Cabinet. The necessary administrative reform has been secured through the passage of an "Act Coördinating Federal Public Health Activities."[2] This statute provides "that upon the request of the head of an executive department or an independent establishment which is carrying on a public health activity the Secretary of the Treasury is authorized to detail officers or employees of the Public Health Service to such department or independent establishment in order to coöperate in such work." This measure was successfully urged by the federal public-health officers, state

[1] Dr. Hugh S. Cumming, "Coöperative Health Activities," *United States Daily*, June 29, 1929, index, p. 1035.

[2] *Public Health Reports*, Vol. 45, No. 17, pp. 920–924, Apr. 25, 1930.

boards of health, and organizations such as the National Tuberculosis Association, the Red Cross, the American Public Health Association, the American Medical Association, and the Association of State Health Officers.[1] In this instance a group of organizations worked to secure a reform that was clearly needed. These organizations kept within the bounds of the politically possible. No question of prestige was involved. They sought coördination by the simplest and most direct method.

Consider the parallel question of combining the War and Navy Departments in a single ministry of National Defense. Logical arguments of great weight supporting such a move have resulted simply in arousing jurisdictional rivalries and personal jealousies. Those urging such a combination have been so absorbed in the theoretical advantages of their scheme that they have lost sight of the real reason for uniting these departments. The real goal should be to promote a high degree of coördination between the military and naval establishments. To consolidate the departments would presumably result in a more logical organization. Such symmetry could be bought only at the cost of bitter protest. The effect that this change would have upon the morale of the services might well outweigh the benefits derived by the structural unity achieved. Relatives do not live in greater harmony because they are put under the same roof.

Coördination may be secured by devices less drastic than consolidation. Behind the army and behind the navy there are political machines of no mean strength. When either department is meddled with, these machines swing into action. They have resisted all efforts toward combining the departments. As a matter of fact, *esprit de corps* within the services is highly desirable and this traditional loyalty is heightened by a feeling of rivalry between the two services. The loyalties and traditions among the rank and file have not prevented administrative coöperation. The army knows what the navy is doing and vice versa. This contact is implemented by a number of coördinating agencies. There is the Joint Board, the Joint Economy Board, the United States Council of National Defense, and the Aeronautical Board. These devices serve to bridge the gap between the two departments.

[1] *Hearings* before a Subcommittee of the Committee on Interstate and Foreign Commerce, House, 69th Congress, Second Session, Feb. 24–25, 1927.

IS REORGANIZATION THE SOLUTION?

It is evident that the problem of coördination may be approached from various angles. A secretary at the head of a federal department coördinates the activities of the bureaus that are under his jurisdiction. Interdepartmental activities may be linked by joint boards. This might be called structural coördination in contrast with the functional coördination exemplified in the Public Health Service. This latter method seems very effective. Except where an important group definitely conscious of its own interests brings about the establishment of a special agency to unify all governmental activities that relate to its welfare, coördination should be promoted by making a corps of officials responsible for certain functions that cross departmental lines.

Thus an administrative agency was recently created to formulate a national planning program. Here was a definite job. The general welfare rather than the pressure of special groups dictated the task. The National Planning Board undertook to coördinate all planning activities within the federal government and to stimulate further planning in the states and cities. State planning agencies responded to the invitation of the national board. Consultant experts were sent into the field. These district chairmen tried to stir up interest in state and municipal planning.

This movement was put under way by an executive order. It marked one of the most positive efforts on the part of administrative officials acting under orders from the President to give substance and form to their conception of the public interest. The pressure of privately interested groups apparently had no place in this development. The scheme was the creation of the New Deal bureaucracy.

The National Resources Board created in 1934 absorbed the three members of the National Planning Board and added the Secretary of the Interior, the Secretaries of Agriculture, of Labor, of Commerce, and of War, together with the Federal Emergency Relief Administrator. Here was an attempt to relate the interests of various agencies in terms of conserving and developing the natural resources of the nation. In its brief experience the National Resources Board[1] has already demonstrated the difficulties and the possibilities of coördinating administrative action.

[1] On June 7, 1935, the National Resources Committee was established in place of the National Resources Board.

It has discovered that the evils of departmentalism remain if the lines of communication between officials in different departments must pass through the heads of these departments. Even where the secretaries are personally willing to coöperate, they are not in a position to deal directly with specific questions. In actual practice their administrative job is largely that of assuming responsibility for the proposals of their subordinates. They spend their days signing papers they have not written and scanning reports of topics they have not studied at first hand. As the responsible heads of their respective departments, they must think of the best interests of their own department. They must defend it from political attack. They must consider its relations with Congress and the President. They take the "expedient" into account and weigh it against what is "ideal."

Coördination can be better obtained at the level of the bureau chief. These officials have a direct grasp of the technical operations that are taking place in their bureaus. They have immediate contacts with specific problems. Their range is somewhat limited but within their field they can speak with the authority of experience and understanding. These officials can make a substantial contribution to problems that fall within their field of competence. That is to say, coördination among a certain group of bureau chiefs can be secured only when they can be united by their common concern in a question that impinges at various points upon their respective fields of jurisdiction. We can coördinate activity only with respect to some problem that possesses aspects of concern to several bureaus. The possibilities of coördinated action cannot be explored unless we recognize its limitations as well.

These generalizations are corroborated by the experience of the National Resources Board. Special studies were authorized by this board and carried out by various committees. One subject was tackled by a group of experts recruited from outside the government. Another problem was turned over to a committee of technical experts in the federal service. A third topic was committed to a group of bureau chiefs. In contrasting the reports made by these three committees, the National Resources Board found that the most concrete and practical proposals were offered by the bureau chiefs. The other groups wrote reports which displayed a broad grasp of the philosophic implications of their problem or which exhibited brilliant and original interpretations of their subject. But the report of the greatest usefulness was the one which squarely faced the administrative issues and which offered definite proposals for attaining a specific end.

Coördination can best be attained by the coöperative efforts of those directly interested in a particular subject. These are the people who are in a position to discuss a problem in accordance with its substantive merits and to consider concrete ways of approaching a solution. Their authority, however, must stop here. Theirs is not an executive function. It must be reiterated that coördination is at best an advisory function. A committee created to study and report upon a problem should not be retained to carry its recommendations into effect. Such a group cannot presume to dictate to any one of its members as to how he should administer his bureau. Friction would inevitably result. A coördinating agency has accomplished its purpose if it has secured a meeting of minds upon the proper policy to pursue and the steps that should be taken to reach a common goal. The recommendations of the committee can then be used as a guide for subsequent action by bureau chiefs acting in this capacity. They can take the committee proposals to their departmental superior and seek his sanction. They can thus counteract the effects of departmentalism by bringing into their isolated domains a common plan of action that cuts across structural lines in its pursuit of a broader interest.

The Central Statistical Board is a case in point. Many bureaus and commissions are engaged in statistical work. Yet there must be some planning and direction if such services are to be administered in the public interest. This activity cannot be extracted from various agencies and placed in a single bureau; but coördination is possible through the Central Statistical Board. This illustrates a mode of administration that has great possibilities.

The Central Statistical Board is a coördinating device and not a statistical agency. Its task is not the collection of statistics. Statistics are tools. They are significant to the extent that they prove useful. Their use is determined by the purpose of the bureau that collects them. If there is uniformity in the method of collection and compilation, their usefulness is enhanced. The figures collected in one department should be arranged so that a comparison can be made with the statistics on related subjects in other departments. The Central Statistical Board, acting as a clearing-house, can bring about uniformity of method. But the board is not designed to gather under one roof all the statisticians in the federal government. If statistical work is to remain vital, it must be kept in close contact with the work of the officials who use the statistics. Piling up figures should never become an end in itself. This decentralization is all the more important in the federal government because most administrators have had little economic training and many of them have difficulty in using statistics effectively. The collection of such data has little justification if it cannot be integrated with the administrative process and used effectively in daily work and in future planning.[1]

The board was set up by executive order on July 27, 1933. The chief executive, the Governor of the Federal Reserve Board, the erstwhile Administrator for National Recovery, and the Secretaries of the Interior, of Agriculture, of Labor, and of Commerce have each designated a member to the board. The Committee on Government Statistics and Information Services of the Social Science Research Council also named a member.[2] The members thus designated have coöpted five full members and four associate members. The board has an executive secretary with three assistants. Most of the work is done by committees composed of board and nonboard members.

The chief significance of this agency lies in its coördinating efforts. Here is an agency to which Cabinet officials may refer statistical problems. Such questions can thus be examined from the technical point of view. The board provides a vantage point

---

[1] Among the tasks undertaken by the board are the following:

"(1) Recommendations to provide for filling major gaps in our existing information.

(2) Assistance in the organization of new statistical units and services.

(3) Efforts to coördinate different inquiries and to avoid unnecessary duplication and unnecessary solicitation of information by different agencies from the same persons.

(4) Suggestions for the improvement of inquiries by new organizations and for the curtailment of plans for inquiries that were too ambitious, too burdensome, or likely to yield inaccurate or biased results." *Interim Report of the Central Statistical Board*, 1934, p. 1.

[2] This unofficial advisory committee was largely responsible for the establishment of the Central Statistical Board.

from which all the economic statistical work of the government may be examined. This agency should be able to increase efficiency and preserve standards of technical competence. At the present time its existence is precarious and its influence slight. It exemplifies an approach to the problem of coördination that seems practical and effective. The need for such an agency has been felt for years. Theodore Roosevelt favored a central statistical agency; the War Industries Board had such a division; the Institute for Government Research drew up a bill to authorize a federal statistical council. The greatly increased statistical work of the government and the multiplication of agencies made some coördinating device imperative under the New Deal. Administrative necessity rather than external pressure brought this new board into existence.

Much of the present confusion in the federal administration is due to the lack of coördination between the general purpose of an executive department and the aims of the bureaus subordinate to it. Services are added at the behest of certain interests and then placed in departments serving another special class. Especially within the past twenty-five years has the federal administration developed in response to group needs. No effective force for general coördination in the administrative services has counterbalanced this tendency toward particularism. Each group is concerned with its own affairs and wishes to forward them without consideration of their bearing on other interests. Obviously the dictates of these conflicting classes cannot result in an efficient administrative organization.

The administrative structure of the federal government cannot be rationalized in accordance with any a priori scheme. It is bound to the inequalities of our economic order and to the inconsistencies of popular government. This was a matter of no great moment so long as the federal government took a relatively negative role in industrial and social affairs. It becomes of vast importance as the federal government assumes more positive functions. If the government is properly to discharge its responsibilities, it has need of administrative machinery that will elevate its officials above the immediacy of special interests and give them a view of the general welfare.

The federal machinery of administration has been beaten out on the anvil of Congress by the hammer and tongs of selfish forces, which shape matters, now one way and now another, in the heat of conflict and controversy. That the finished product is not a well-articulated structure, but rather a distorted and lopsided maze, is the inevitable consequence. As the activities of the federal government have rapidly grown during the past two decades, the absence of any national plan of development has meant that organized minorities freely and capriciously have used governmental resources for their own ends. Perhaps this was inevitable under the changing conditions of the time; however, the period of experimentation is past. Twenty years has shown the results of leaving administrative development to the dictation of special interests.

The growth of the federal government cannot, of course, be explained entirely in terms of pressure groups, but certainly they have vastly influenced the arrangement of bureaus and department. National associations have provided the impetus for the great extension of special governmental services during the past two decades. Governmental facilities for aiding commerce, industry, and agriculture in the pursuit of their private aims have expanded enormously. According to the Committee on Recent Social Trends, "the most striking changes of the period [1915–1932] are found in agencies performing services of this character." This trend can be closely linked with the demands of national organizations upon the federal government. Pressure rather than merit has determined the services that the federal government has undertaken. There has been no united or consistent concept of the proper limits of governmental activity. Congress has not established any principles as to the proper scope and nature of federal services.[2] A bureau can tempt the support of Congress through the jobs it makes possible and it can coerce the legislators through its powers of propaganda. The procurement of apparent popular support through skillfully conducted publicity may so

---

[1] C. H. Woody, *The Growth of the Federal Government—1915–1932*, p. 554. McGraw-Hill, 1934.

[2] Representative McSwain from South Carolina has stated: "Members denounce the extravagance and red tape and unbusiness-like methods of bureaucracy, but when the particular issue is made they usually succumb to the propaganda and social influence and patronage persuasion of the bureaucrats in the seats of the mighty and the bureaucrats win." *Congressional Record*, Feb. 19, 1926, p. 4289.

fortify its position that Congress would hesitate to abolish the bureau or reduce its appropriation.

The need for a reorganization in the federal administration has been urged for over two decades. Remedial action has been recommended through presidential messages, the reports of congressional committees, and the careful study of experts. In 1910, $100,000 was appropriated to discover what reform was desirable. In vain did President Taft urge Congress to accept the proposals of the expert commission specially authorized to suggest changes. About ten years later, the Joint Committee on the Reorganization of the Administrative Branch, after elaborate hearings, drew up a report that was not even seriously considered by Congress.[1] It was all very well to investigate reorganization, but acting upon such findings was something else. The congressional maxim seemed to be: Upsetting the apple cart never butters political parsnips.

Herbert Hoover, however, on becoming President, was determined that Congress should face the issue. He stated in his message to Congress of December, 1929:

This subject has been under consideration for over 20 years. It was promised by both political parties in the recent campaign. It has been repeatedly examined by committees and commissions—congressional, executive, and voluntary. The conclusions of these investigations have been unanimous that reorganization is a necessity of sound administration, of economy, of more effective governmental policies, and of relief to the citizen from unnecessary harassment in his relations with a multitude of scattered government agencies.

Congress was not impressed, but two years later conditions had changed. The billion-dollar deficit of 1931 made the legislators receptive to plans that promised to reduce expenses. But could the need for economy and efficiency override the obstacles that had delayed reform for a score of years? It was recognized that futile bargaining with bureaucrats and special interests would be the

[1] For an authoritative treatment of the whole problem, see W. F. Willoughby, *The Reorganization of the Administrative Branch of the National Government*, Johns Hopkins Press, 1923; Peyton Hurt, "Who Should Reorganize the National Administration," *Political Science Review*, December, 1932; R. L. Duffus, "The Washington Jig-saw," *Harper's*, June, 1933. For other aspects of the problem of coördination, see S. Lyle Post. "Coördination of National Administration," *American Political Science Review*, April, 1935.

result if the task were left to Congress. Senator Vandenberg summed up the situation in these words: "This process of reorganizing the fundamental structure never in the world is going to be achieved by congressional effort on the floor of the House. It is absolutely impossible to get a meeting of minds when there are 531 minds that have got to meet. It must be an executive function."[1] The Economy Act of June 30, 1932, empowered the chief executive to regroup and transfer bureaus by executive order subject to a sixty-day veto by the legislature. President Hoover was not to enjoy this power. The Democratically dominated Congress tossed his recommendations into the discard to gather dust along with the earlier proposals of Taft and Harding.

The reorganization awaited from the days of the Square Deal was to be realized with the coming of the New Deal. Six weeks after President Roosevelt assumed office the newspapers reported that Secretary of Commerce Roper and Budget Director Douglas were preparing a list of sweeping changes for the federal bureaucracy. But what actually happened? There were rumors at first of drastic retrenchment in the Departments of Agriculture and Commerce; but the President's program of crop control and industrial regulation soon gave these services more to do than ever before. A few shifts were made, the most striking elimination in the name of economy and efficiency being the abolition of the Bureau of Efficiency!

Reorganization, it appears, has been indefinitely postponed. Judged by the actual changes made in the federal departments, little progress toward reorganization has resulted from the efforts of the past two decades. Nevertheless, highly important advances of a less tangible sort have been made. We have come a long way since President Taft declared: "This vast organization has never been studied in detail as one piece of administrative mechanism." The thought and study of the last twenty years have established the basic principles for administrative reform. Each decade has marked a step forward.

It is now agreed that reorganization is needed, that the federal bureaus should be distributed in accordance with the *major purpose* of each executive department, and that the chief executive should undertake the task. President Roosevelt has the legal

[1] *Congressional Record*, Mar. 11, 1932, p. 5946.

authority to reorganize the bureaucracy, but does he dare use it? In a word, we have today a consensus of opinion as to what *should* be. We have some highly significant theories, but very little application of these principles. Why? President Hoover put the situation very succinctly in a special message to Congress in 1932 He stated:

We may frankly admit the practical difficulties of such reorganization. Not only do different factions of the Government fear such reorganization, but many associations and agencies throughout the country will be alarmed that the particular function to which they are devoted may in some fashion be curtailed. Proposals to the Congress of detailed plans for the reorganization of the many different bureaus and independent agencies have always proved in the past to be a signal for the mobilization of opposition from all quarters which has destroyed the possibility of constructive action.[1]

The question raised is this: What can be done toward the clarification of the public interest within the bounds set by our political framework? Schemes for reorganization cannot be superimposed without consideration of the political and economic factors that are affected thereby. Experts have burned the midnight oil in devising Utopian plans; in vain have they rubbed their student lamps looking for an almost magical reordering of the bureaus and departments. Major changes must come slowly and even indirectly. The possibility of reorganizing the federal administration depends upon an understanding of the social forces and group pressures that stand in the way.

As a practical matter, what the theorist might regard as ideally best in administrative organization must be reconciled with what is politically possible. Democracy means that our federal structure shall be the product of what politically effective individuals and groups are able to get. If the government is to act as an impartial arbiter among all groups and if the administration is to serve all classes and interests, how can this be accomplished in the face of our political structure?

Congress has displayed little understanding of such problems, but an enlightened bureaucracy and constructive presidential leadership can do much toward improving administrative conditions. The conflict of political forces must determine the ultimate

[1] *Ibid.*, Feb. 17, 1932, p. 4238.

fate of administrators, but they do not have to be passive victims. The developments reviewed in this chapter show that coördination in the federal administration is not altogether dependent upon the pressure of interested groups. Officials can seek to clarify the interests of those classes that are represented by important bureaus and departments. Through coördinating devices they can mobilize those elements that are of intrinsic social import but meager political strength. These agencies will enable officials to look beyond their limited jurisdictions and participate in the pursuit of common objectives. This is one way toward administration in the public interest.

Chapter XXI

EXPERIMENTS AT CONSULTATION

"And can all the flowers talk?" "As well as *you* can," said the
Tiger lily. "And a great deal louder."
"It isn't manners for us to begin, you know," said the Rose, "and
I really was wondering when you'd speak! Said I to myself, 'Her
face has got *some* sense in it, though it's not a clever one!'"

ADVISORY committees are being put to the test in the
federal administration. As officials are given more discretion, the need for keeping some check upon their activities
becomes all the more urgent. Yet the broadening of administrative
authority is an indication that the legislative body has reached the
periphery of its own competence. The advisory committee provides
a means of introducing the opinion of the governed at a highly
strategic point. It is a device for encouraging democracy in administration. At the same time it aids officials in carrying their heavy
burdens by offering counsel and criticism. It brings bureaucracy
into closer accord with those it must govern. The very intimacy
of this contact increases the need for impartiality and integrity on
the part of administrators. Here is an institutional contrivance that
holds potentialities for good or evil. Its significance lies in the fact
that it is suited to a society increasingly technical and specialized
and to a government increasingly regulatory and encompassing.
Officials are discovering that, if they take the initiative, they can
secure a ready response from those under their jurisdiction.

With legislators looking to officials for much of the substantive
formulation of bills, it is desirable that the framing of such legislation be done in close touch with those of experience in the fields
affected. Through such consultation administrators and legislators
alike can win the support of the parties directly concerned and
the confidence of the public. Government must be aware in
advance of the practical consequences of its edicts. The habit of
prior consultation is an obvious safeguard. Advisory committees,

[349]

while providing a means of securing pertinent opinion, should not be used as a way of escaping responsibility.

The use of numerous advisory agencies in the administrative services shows that we are no longer content with the crude instrument of the ballot as a means of measuring consent, but are cognizant of the need for more efficient methods of discovering the opinions of the governed. This development, as Professor MacMahon points out, carries with it certain dangers. "It daily sharpens the need for administrative authorities who are skillful in consultation, vigilant in arranging representation that is reasonably comprehensive, sympathetic but wary, above all independent. Only by careful use of advisory boards will the danger of compromising administration at its core be avoided."[1]

Advisory committees have their weaknesses and dangers, but they do suggest a way of introducing the informed and vital views of citizens into the governing process. They provide a channel for bringing in fresh currents of opinion from technical societies and trade groups. They can be set up close to the source of opinions. They can be used by administrators before the professional politician has an opportunity to muddy the waters. The advisory committee is a highly flexible device. These committees have not hardened into any one form. They come and go, created for many different ends and established by diverse authorities. To attempt a complete picture of this shifting scene would be a futile undertaking.

Advisory committees have been established in various bureaus as a means of securing outside support or expert advice. The purpose here is simply to note the extent of this development and its possible significance.

There is a great variation in the status of these advisory agencies. The Federal Advisory Council is made a part of the Federal Reserve System by law. Composed of a member from each of the twelve federal reserve districts, the council confers with the Federal Reserve Board on general business conditions and makes recommendations on the policies and activities of the board. The National Advisory Health Council of the U. S. Public Health Service is legally authorized to advise the Surgeon General with

[1] Article on "Advisory Boards" in *Encyclopaedia of the Social Sciences*.

respect to his various duties.[1] On this council, a model of its kind, are found the leading authorities in public hygiene and preventive medicine. The National Advisory Committee for Aeronautics has done notable work. The President names two representatives each from the Navy and War Departments, one each from the Weather Bureau, the Smithsonian Institution, and the Bureau of Standards, and eight others who are skilled in the science of aeronautics.[2] Other advisory agencies resting upon statutory authority are the Advisory Board of the Inland Waterways Corporation,[3] the Advisory Committee to the Bureau of Fisheries,[4] and the Advisory Council to the National Arboretum.[5] These boards are all designed by statute to introduce lay advice and opinion into the administrative process.

Other important consultative agencies have been created by administrative authority. The Business Advising and Planning Council of the Department of Commerce has already been discussed as a most ambitious effort to link business opinion with administration. The significance of the Science Advisory Board must also be recalled. A National Advisory Committee composed of representatives of business, agriculture, education, labor, and youth has been authorized to assist the director of the National Youth Administration.[6] The Advisory Council to the Committee on Economic Security brought together men who were prominent in business, labor, and social welfare.[7] The Veterans' Administra-

[1] Code Supplement, 1926, Title 42.

[2] 45 Stat. 1451.

[3] The law provides for a board composed of six members appointed by the Secretary of War "from individuals prominently identified with commercial or business interests in territory adjacent to the operations of the corporation. But no member of the board shall be an officer, director, or employee of, or substantially interested in, any railroad corporation. U. S. Code, Title 49, 154.

[4] The advisory committee under the statute is made up of men from certain sections who are "prominently identified with the various branches of the fishery industry, qualified in aquatic research and experienced in fish culture." U. S. Code, Title 16, 749.

[5] The Secretary of Agriculture is empowered under the act creating a national arboretum to appoint an advisory council to assist in its planning and development. Public 799, 69th Congress.

[6] *U. S. Government Manual*, p. 129, 1935. Issued by National Emergency Council.

[7] For the membership of this committee, see *ibid.*, p. 495. With regard to the Social Security Bill: "The experts called in to draft the bill were sequestrated, their

tion has had the assistance of a Legal Advisory Council and a Medical Advisory Council since 1927. These committees meet annually. The legal committee has been especially helpful in promoting a uniform guardian law throughout the country.

When the Blue Eagle was in its heyday, the advisory committees for the consumers, the industrialists, and the workers performed essential work. The utility of this kind of agency has won definite recognition within recent years. Officials have not awaited statutory authorization to avail themselves of advice and support from outside the government. Other advisory committees, less conspicuous than those already mentioned, have proved their value to bureau chiefs in several departments.

The advisory board to the U. S. Bureau of Mines brings together representatives from the various coal producers, eastern and western, bituminous and anthracite, the mining employees, and all associated industries. Copper, silver, lead, zinc, gold, iron, steel, petroleum, gas, and the nonmetal industries are all represented. The Bureau of Mines has functioned for over twenty-five years as a fact-finding body for the mining industries. The success of its work has depended upon the coöperation of the mine owners. In bureaus of this sort a close tie-up with industry is essential. Unless the bureau can show that it is of genuine usefulness to the mine operators, its days are numbered.

The advisory board can guide the bureau chief along the lines of maximum usefulness and incidently can support him when Congress threatens to cut appropriations. The minutes of this board show that its members encourage officials to increase their services to the industry through educational and safety work. Proposals that the Bureau be given certain police functions, including the legal right to enforce its safety recommendations, have met with a less enthusiastic reception.[1] The board also urges

findings and advice ignored. Even the council of industrialists, scholars, welfare workers and A. F. of L. leaders who were asked to represent the public as advisers took a too progressive view to suit the New Deal's creator, and so did his Cabinet committee, which after passing down the advisory council's recommendations, found its own recommendations still further whittled by the President." Paul Ward in *Nation*, Sept. 11, 1935, p. 296.

[1] Advisory Board to the U. S. Bureau of Mines, minutes of meeting, Apr. 15, 1935, Washington, D. C. Supplied by American Mining Congress.

that all statistical work relating to the mining industry be centered in the bureau.

Advisory committees find their most congenial habitat in bureaus concerned with research and statistical work. Such bodies have been most extensively used in the Bureau of Standards, the Bureau of Foreign and Domestic Commerce, and the Census Bureau. They marshal support behind their parent bureau and they keep officials in close contact with the needs of the groups they are supposed to serve.

Advisory committees have served a more positive purpose, however. The advisory board to the National Park Service, for example, has brought to this bureau the recommendations of a number of leading scientists.[1] These men have endeavored to promote the educational possibilities of the national-park system. They meet once or twice a year; their sessions are private and they issue no reports to the public. Their deliberations are guided by agenda that are circulated beforehand although any topic can be raised at the meeting itself. The members come together for definite business. They consult with officials from the field. This small body of experts has had great influence in developing our national parks and in keeping a critical eye upon their administration. This advisory committee brings in men who would not be recruited directly to the service. It opens an opportunity for public service without imposing a heavy burden on those undertaking the work.

The recent advisory committee instituted in connection with the Patent Office suggests another important field of usefulness for such bodies. Criticism of the cumbersome procedure of the Patent Office prompted the Secretary of Commerce to appoint a special committee of several patent lawyers and officials to investigate the problem. The body was continued later with a membership of fifteen composed entirely of patent lawyers and manufacturers. The term of office is brief and thus a larger number can be given the educational experience of serving on the committee. Through this committee critics of the Patent Office find an official forum for their complaints. Officials can benefit by the suggestions of those technically competent to judge their activities and concerned in promoting efficiency within the government. This

[1] *United States Daily*, Apr. 18, 1929, index, p. 391.

committee demonstrates the value of having administrative procedure scrutinized by a group of technically competent critics.

This is not the first time that the Patent Office has called upon outside assistance. In 1929[1] the Secretary of the Interior invited several patent-law associations, the Chamber of Commerce of the United States of America, the National Manufacturers' Association, and the American Engineering Council to select representatives to serve on a committee on Patent Office procedure. Two engineers nominated by the American Society of Mechanical Engineers were later added to the committee at the suggestion of the Secretary of Commerce. The secretary instructed the committee to study the methods employed in the Patent Office with a view to increasing efficiency and urged them likewise to suggest improvements in the patent laws if need be.

A very extended report was drawn up covering the whole problem of the administration of the Patent Office. No consideration apparently was too minute for their attention. They recommended a building adequate for the needs of the Bureau of Patents; they suggested the creation of important new positions; they advised sweeping changes in the existing routine. Their interest ranged from such matters of general policy down to minor details. They suggested, for example, that a special kind of envelope with a brass fastener be substituted for the folder then in use. They gave their opinion as to the best way to make use of the office space available, to employ the energies of the workers in the most efficient fashion, and to expedite the handling of the business. If, on the one hand, they suggested improved equipment, increased salaries, and additional technical or clerical aid, they also in some instances recommended that certain employees be discharged, that labor-saving devices be substituted, that procedure be simplified, that routine be rearranged, and that a further division of labor be introduced.

Their investigation was to all appearances thorough and complete. The committee took occasion to commend the administration of the Patent Office for the good work already done. The committee stated that the recommendations contained in its report were based mainly upon information obtained from the

[1] *Ibid.*, Nov. 16, 1929, index, p. 2363.

Patent Commissioner and his staff, and represented in a measure contemplated action that the office for various reasons had been unable to undertake. The report of this volunteer committee of outside experts thus reiterated the suggestions of the Patent Office officials and added a commendation of their work. The committee procured the services of four individuals through the courtesy of the Department of Commerce, the Chamber of Commerce of the United States of America, and the Bureau of Efficiency, who reported back to the committee after making "a limited but thorough study" of the internal operations of the Patent Office.

A question that arises in connection with an investigation of this character is the extent to which the committee acted solely upon its own initiative. The possibility, at least, suggests itself that the Patent Office officials, in seeking support for changes that they deemed necessary, made use of this outside agency in order that an air of disinterestedness and of *expertise* might surround the suggested changes. In other words, it is conceivable that this committee was useful for obscuring, as a screen, the source of recommendations for further and substantial aids necessitating appropriations from the public treasury.

Whatever the inspiration of these changes may have been, the fact remains that a considerable number of them were rapidly put into effect. An appropriation was secured for new accommodations, into which the Patent Office moved about a year ago. Complete reorganization took place in some divisions, modern facilities for filing and storing were procured, and adequate stenographic assistance was provided. The suggested increase in force was carried out in part. The work in arrears was greatly reduced. Salaries of their principal examiners were increased and many other minor changes in the interest of efficiency were brought about. The Patent Office undoubtedly profited by the use of such outside help. Whether used for the strategic purpose of securing support or in good faith to obtain expert advice, the investigating committee of private experts representing important interests proved its usefulness.

In 1923 Secretary Work called together those concerned with the Indian. As a "Committee of One Hundred," these persons met, discussed Indian affairs, and at the conclusion of a two-day session made a report containing recommendations and suggestions for improving the Indian service.[1] The secretary brought this report to the attention of Congress. This conference came at a time when the Indian bureau had been subjected to rather violent denunciation by outsiders. An excellent way to disarm critics is to listen respectfully to their talk.

The Office of Education has attempted an interesting experiment in decentralization. A number of regional councils have been set up to study the planning of school buildings in different parts of the country. Each regional council has seven members: school superintendents, members of the school board, and an architect. The National Advisory Council on School Building Problems is composed of the chairmen of the regional councils.[2] This arrangement has worked well. The problems in each region have been faced by a board of experts and administrators. Questions of import to all are cleared through the national council. It is essential that the members of advisory councils confine their attention to a sphere that is of genuine interest to them. Decentralization may meet the requirements in some cases while the use of subcommittees assigned to special problems may be more suitable under other conditions.

Advisory bodies have served to deflect from the shoulders of officials the full impact of disagreement among outsiders on the interpretation of the law. The experience with the advisory board of the Migratory Bird Treaty Act is a case in point.[3] This board is composed of state game wardens, representatives of naturalist

[1] *Annual Report of the Board of Indian Commissioners*, 1929, pp. 20–21.

[2] Department of Interior Pamphlet 7, July, 1930, p. 3.

[3] In a private memorandum to the author the Biological Survey reports:

"In all lines of its scientific, educational, regulatory, conservation, and control work, the Biological Survey enjoys friendly and helpful coöperative relationships with a large number of national, State, and local organizations and individuals. Resolutions have been passed by many such organizations endorsing the Bureau's work and their representatives have taken an active part in presenting the wishes of their membership before budget officials and legislative bodies. Much financial assistance has also been furnished by coöperators in support of various lines of work in which they were interested. Coöperators have in some instances provided practically all of the funds for prosecuting special investigations and in publishing reports thereon. Among the more notable of such reports the following may be mentioned:

"'The Conservation of the Elk of Jackson Hole, Wyoming,' a Report to Honorable Dwight F. Davis, Secretary of War, Chairman of the President's Commit-

and conservation organizations, writers, and sportsmen. As might be expected, strong differences of opinion have appeared between sportsmen and the conservationists. The board meets in Washington annually in order to consider proposed changes in the regulations of the bureau. Hearings are held. After considering the evidence, the board tries to agree upon recommendations to the bureau. The administrators can thus escape the conflict of opinion between groups and accept or reject the final recommendations of the board. "Those in a position to know state that most, if not all, of the recommendations made by a majority of the Committee or by those members of that body who represent a majority of the sportsmen of the country, are sure to find their way into the regulations of the Secretary," Professor Comer writes.[1]

Where an administrator is open to attack, an advisory committee acts as a protective buffer to criticism. During the days of national prohibition the drys were highly desirous that no alcohol intended for industrial uses leak out for beverage purposes. The industrialists on the other hand did not wish to be irked by an overrigid supervision. The Commissioner of Internal Revenue appointed the Alcohol Trades Advisory Committee to represent the interests of these businessmen in the administration of the law. The industrialists could appeal to this body over the decisions of the prohibition commissioner. When the drys tried to place responsibility upon the Commissioner of Internal Revenue for alleged failure to enforce the National Prohibition Act, the advisory committee came to the rescue. The American Drug Manufacturers' Association, the American Chemical Society, the American Pharmaceutical Association, the National Association of Retail Druggists, the Proprietary Association, the American Manufacturers of Toilet Articles, the Flavoring Extract Manufacturers' Association, the Manufacturing Chemists' Association, and the National Paint Oil and Varnish Association were the chief interests that banded together to offset the influence of the

---

tee on Outdoor Recreation, and Honorable Frank C. Emerson, Governor of Wyoming.

"'Report on Cooperative Quail Investigation: 1925–26; With Preliminary Recommendations for the Development of Quail Preserves,' by Herbert L. Stoddard, Division of Food Habits Research, Bureau of Biological Survey."

[1] *Legislative Functions of Federal Administrative Agencies*, p. 236.

organized drys.[1] An advisory committee of this sort can be expected to reach some agreement.

How should these committees be composed? The Bureau of Marine Inspection is launching a committee that brings together widely divergent interests. Shipping associations and seamen, inland water carriers, and ocean-going lines are all represented upon a newly organized council. This is a deliberate effort to recognize officially all elements of the shipping industry as advisers to the federal government.

Since advisory committees are capable of fulfilling a variety of functions, no general rule can be set for their selection. Where these agencies are used to acquaint those outside the government with the problems and difficulties in executing the law, it is desirable to include a wide variety of interests and to provide for a frequent change of members. When officials are seeking technical advice, a small body of experts is clearly preferable. When a committee offers advice, the official must be free to either take it or leave it. Its recommendations should be made in confidence. Final responsibility for any action taken must rest with the administrator.

All goes well when advisory committees follow the lines set forth by the administration and when harmony prevails among those consulted. But if these committees are to be representative of all the parties concerned, they will often include members with sharply conflicting points of view. The Director of the Woman's Bureau of the U. S. Department of Labor some years ago invited six women to serve on an advisory committee and aid the bureau in investigating the effects of laws regulating the employment of women. Violent disagreement soon appeared. Representatives of the American Federation of Labor, the National Women's Trade Union League, and the National League of Women Voters found themselves in fundamental disagreement with the Woman's Party. They accused this organization of disrupting the hearings and they resigned from the committee. The spokeswoman for the American Federation of Labor stated that the Woman's Party was using the investigation to secure publicity and to forward its own propaganda. The Woman's Party representative retorted that the American Federation of Labor delegates made "repeated

[1] Senate, 68th Congress, First Session, Document 44.

use of officials on the Women's Bureau to further its opposition to efforts toward equalizing the position of women in industry and the professions."[1] There is, of course, always the danger that private interests may use official contacts to further their own aims.

During the Hoover administration several advisory committees were created for special purposes.[2] The advisory committee to the unemployment relief organization attracted considerable attention. In addition to the prominent politicians, philanthropists, and businessmen on the board, officers were invited from the following associations: the American Railroad Association, the National Conference of Social Work, the Association of Community Chests, the Knights of Columbus, the American Legion, the National Manufacturers' Association, the Association of Welfare Officials, the Family Welfare Association of America, the American Federation of Labor, the National Grange, the Chamber of Commerce of the United States of America, and many, many others. The list in its contradictory variety completely belies any significance to its title of "advisory." It would be farcical to expect any consensus of opinion to arise from this ill-assorted crowd. That the committee accomplished nothing of importance is hardly surprising. If positive recommendations are sought from an advisory committee, this body should be composed of experts rather than representatives.

The individuals on these committees must be drawn directly from industry or the professions. Their fundamental purpose is to do away with that middleman, the politician. If the partisan politician who waves the flag and kisses the babies is merely supplanted by a trade association or labor-union politician, nothing has been gained. The representative factor is of little consequence except as an indication of the expert qualifications of the committeeman, the breadth of his experience, and his close touch with a profession or industry. When an economic or social interest has the vitality to sustain a responsible organization, this agency should be taken

[1] *New York Times*, May 10, 1926, p. 39.

[2] President Hoover's Committee on Conservation and Administration of the Public Domain brought together twenty-one prominent citizens to gather facts and make recommendations for the preservation of the public domain. *United States Daily*, June 9, 1930, index, p. 1130.

into account when spokesmen for this interest are selected. This connection, however, must be taken as indicative of the appointee's competence to advise rather than of his authority to represent.

A uniform system of consultative agencies would not be a practical scheme to impose all at once, but certainly steps should be taken in this direction, and the deliberate development of more systematic relations should be encouraged. Some might argue that, if such committees are to have any vitality, they should grow in response to an imperative need felt by these groups themselves. Such an impetus is unlikely. Distrust of bureaucracy must be allayed by the efforts of our administrators. They are in a better position to see the broad implications in problems confronting an industry than those immersed in the day-to-day struggle of making their own businesses pay. Those in private life for their part can bring a realistic and practical viewpoint to bear on administrative problems. This is sometimes lacking in official circles. Such an interchange is of prime importance to the successful administration of public affairs under a democracy. The situation surveyed in this chapter indicates that inventiveness is not wanting in devices for bringing bureaucrat and citizen together.

National conferences, *ad hoc* committees, and special commissions of inquiry are useful for calling attention to particular problems, but they remain temporary and limited. The systematic development of advisory committees has much more to offer for the future.

Where economic or social groups are organized into a representative association, their *expertise* and coöperative impulses should be joined to the bureaucracy by clearly defined ties.[1] Consultative committees should be made up from panels proposed by those organizations whose members fall directly within the jurisdiction of the bureau concerned. In order to achieve the most

[1] W. F. Willoughby has suggested "the creation for each of the great fields of a council that would embrace, on the one hand, the heads of representatives of the government services working in that field, and, on the other, representatives of the private organizations, the members of which are directly interested in that field of endeavor." *Principles of Public Administration*, Johns Hopkins Press, 1927, p. 171. For some very interesting comments on the use of advisory committees in France, see Walter R. Sharp, *The French Civil Service*, pp. 35, 393, 507, 547–560, Macmillan, 1931.

effective exchange of informed opinion, it will be desirable in some cases to create subcommittees under the same bureau. It is impossible to set forth a detailed plan of organization since conditions vary too widely in different departments. The principle to be followed, however, is to place on consultative committees spokesmen for those interests most directly and frequently affected by the activities of any given federal agency.

Our haphazard experimentation with such advising agencies offers evidence to substantiate Laski's eloquent justification of this device:[1]

Here, at least, is a real way of preventing the atmosphere of administration from degenerating into the issue of orders, on the one hand, and their indifferent acceptance on the other. It provides means for utilizing the services of men who now avoid public life, either because they are unwilling to undergo the process of election, or because their interest is not in the general complex of governmental functions, but in a single aspect of that complex. The system popularizes the administrative process by widening the area of persons who are competent to scrutinize it. It provides for a constant interchange of opinion between the center and the circumference of government. Because the system is advisory and not executive in character, it leaves simple and intelligible the ultimate institutions, and it does not make authority degenerate into anarchy by the indefinite division of power. It prevents it from becoming autocratic by subjecting it, at each stage, to the pressure of an opinion usually specially competent, and always specially interested; and it assures a hearing for that opinion. It brings the organized interests of men, their churches, their trade-unions, their chambers of commerce, into a definite relation with the central and local governments. It makes it possible for those activities to bear the impress of external opinion by subjecting them to a constant stream of criticism and inquiry. It multiplies, in a word, the sources through which the citizen's personality may be made significant. That after all, is the purpose of democracy.

[1] *Dangers of Obedience*, pp. 80–81, Harper, 1930.

Chapter XXII

PUBLICIZING ADMINISTRATIVE ACTIVITIES

"It's long," said the Knight, "but it's very, *very* beautiful. Everybody that hears me sing it—either it brings the *tears* into their eyes, or else—"

"Or else what?" said Alice, for the Knight had made a sudden pause.

"Or else it doesn't, you know."

POPULAR government rests on the assumption that the people are capable of passing a verdict for or against the administration in power. The accuracy of this verdict depends upon the public's knowledge of what the government has done or has failed to do. The judgment of many voters will turn upon some direct experience in dealing with the government. Their special interest in a limited phase of governmental activity may determine their opinion of the whole. The devices for bringing the individual into the governing process are limited, however. Despite the enormous growth of administrative agencies and services, the government is viewed by most people as a thing apart.

Official relations with the "public" turn largely upon the use that is made of the press and the radio. By the public is meant the populace viewed as a great undifferentiated mass. It was to that audience that President Roosevelt directed his fireside radio talks. Here, likewise, are the millions of newspaper readers who have been so sedulously courted by politicians and officials.

It is no accident that "public relations" have been a matter accorded great consideration during the Roosevelt administration. This problem is intimately linked with administration in the public interest. A government with positive objectives inevitably creates areas of hostility. The regulation of economic enterprise disrupts certain vested interests. The establishment of new services breaks into old habits, often introduces unwanted competition, and frequently incurs the misunderstanding of those to be served. As the government advances into new fields, it must be supported by general approval. This public sanction must more than out-weigh the accumulation of petty irritations that official activities arouse among the interests that are dislodged. An administration that undertakes to interpret the general welfare in concrete terms must do two things: it must endeavor to win popular approval for its policies and it must watch the reaction to its proposals. One striking evidence of the effort made to reach the public is the extensive use that the New Dealers have made of the radio. The following table shows broadcasts over the National Broadcasting Company network from Sept. 1, 1933, to Aug. 31, 1934:

Speaker	Number of broadcasts	Time	
		Hours	Minutes
Roosevelt, F. D.	25	11	05
Farley, J. A.	18	8	22
Wallace, H. A.	21	6	25
Ickes, Harold	11	5	35
Roper, D. C.	10	5	13
55 Senators	151	40	57
85 Representatives	153	30	58
74 administrative officials	190	79	23

The care with which this administration watches the newspapers is indicated by the *Press Intelligence Bulletin*. This is a mimeographed publication prepared by the Division of Press Intelligence for the use of the important federal executives. It contains a condensation of newspaper articles and editorials clipped from journals all over the country. The entries are listed under the federal agency with which they deal. The name of the paper is given, its party affiliation, and the date. An index number enables any official to call for the original clipping should he deem it of sufficient importance. This is the most systematic effort on the part of federal officials to find out what the country is thinking.

This relationship between the government and the public in actual practice is narrowed down to contacts between a small group of officials and a small group of newspaper correspondents. Except when the President or other officials speak over the air, the public relations of national administrative agencies are little more than the relations between 200 or so of the abler Washington correspondents and 200-odd public-relations officials in the federal employ. For the run of routine news this is the picture. It must be modified on occasion to include the direct conferences of journalists with the President and leading administrators, but in the main the view of the government presented to the public is the product of official publicity men within the government and the newspapermen stationed in the capital. To the latter governmental problems are all part of "the great game of politics," and it is the brilliant plays, the dodges, the fumbles, and the dramatics of conflict that they regard as most significant. The nature of political news is conceived in much the same terms as events in the world of sports.

Reporting must be a selective process. All the facts in any case can never be presented. Reporting "what really happened" means selecting the elements that seem significant to what the reporter believes is a "full understanding" of any given situation. What the public gets is determined by the subjective hunches of newspapermen as to what they think will titillate the reader's jaded interest. There is in Washington little conscious misrepresentation of fact, but there is the tendency to play up one aspect of certain events and to tone down another. This is natural and even inevitable. Official publicity men recognize this and act accordingly. Necessarily there is a relationship between the general policy of a bureau and the kind of news that is disseminated. Every federal bureau has its staff of experienced publicity men who determine the manner of presentation and the form of news concerning their bureau's activities.

The railroads learned years ago that it was better to give plenty of the "right" kind of news about a train wreck than to attempt to disguise the fact that a serious accident had occurred. Thus they scotched rumors. News now comes out of the federal bureaus in a flood. Today's mistake is washed away by the plans of tomorrow. Sifting out the news from the mass of prepared official statements is a task that discourages further curiosity regarding detail on the part of the busy journalist.

The present system makes for a generally favorable presentation of all news concerning the departments. For the newspapermen, the easy course is that of acceptance without further investigation.

PUBLICIZING ADMINISTRATIVE ACTIVITIES

If a Washington correspondent questions an official statement and wants more information, his questions will be answered. The government bureaus are careful to avoid any appearance of deception or secrecy relating to their activities. In fact, the press representatives are taken into the confidence of officials to an extraordinary degree. This trust is very rarely violated and the success of this relationship is recognized. But it is perhaps more useful to the government than to the press or to the public. To lock up news in a newshawk may disarm the reporter's suspicions, but it does not do the newspaper reader much good. To an extraordinary degree the bureaucracy has taken the newspaper men into its own camp.[1] Presidential secretaries under Wilson and Coolidge were lawyers and politicians, but Hoover saw the value of newspaper experience and F. D. Roosevelt apparently considers it the best training for his White House secretaries.

Kent says that the newspapermen outnumber the professors in the New Deal by nearly two to one.[2] The public relations of federal administrative agencies depend predominantly upon the relationship between newspapermen speaking for the government and their erstwhile fellow journalists. It is said that one great metropolitan newspaper has had its bureau stripped twice of every man except the chief. The intimacy of this relationship is significant because of the great faith the public must perforce place in Washington correspondents for the data upon which to base opinions. As one observer has stated:

> The work of the Executive Departments is performed, to a large extent, behind closed doors. . . . It is to the Washington correspondent that our newspapers must look to resist the bureaucratic interferences with a free Press. The precise degree of support which the Press, as a general proposition, should lend to the Government is difficult to determine, but it can at least be said that in the United States the Press gives too much, rather than too little.[3]

[1] For data on individuals, see William E. Berchtold, "New Deal Press Agents," *New Outlook*, July, 1934; also Elisha Hanson, "Official Propaganda and the New Deal," *Annals of the American Academy of Political and Social Science*, May, 1935, pp. 176–186; J. F. Essary, "Uncle Sam's Ballyhoo Men," *The American Mercury*, August, 1931.

[2] *Baltimore Sun*, Oct. 22, 1934.

[3] For a discussion of the relations of the press with the federal government, see *Conference on the Press*, Princeton University Press, April, 1931, p. 71.

Inquiry among a wide variety of Washington correspondents, columnists, and press-association heads disclosed very little dissatisfaction with existing arrangements. Arthur Krock of the *New York Times* condemns the present system because:

. . . it robs the newspaper correspondents of opportunities to know the Federal staff and thus help the public to understand their actions by acquaintance with their mental processes and approaches to public questions. The channel system would completely substitute the dead printed leaflet—what we call the hand-out—for the warm and living speech of public men. Since governments are made up of men and not of acts, the system defeats to this degree the legitimate will of the people to know the kind of men and women to whom they have entrusted the conduct of affairs.[1]

Newspapermen, however, are not denied access to officials. Information is given out through one official, chiefly because this is a more efficient arrangement. Systematic contacts with the press and the public under the direction of competent and specially designated officers are a necessary and inevitable aspect of administration.

The extent and rapidity of the expansion and multiplication of administrative agencies have made the task of reporting so complicated that the average correspondent cannot cope with the problem. Only news agencies such as the Associated Press are able to designate special reporters to special beats. As Kent has written, "Such a thing as really 'covering' Washington in the old newspaper sense is now out of the question. The press agents alone make it even relatively possible."[2]

The nature of the news is often of such a technical character that it must be interpreted and explained if it is to be reported accurately and understandingly. The increased importance of experts in the government increases the need for publicity experts to interpret the technicians. Administrators well qualified for their special work may be very poorly qualified for dealing with the press. The public-relations divisions within the federal bureaus are welcomed by the press, but they are also useful from the purely administrative viewpoint.

[1] "The Press and Government," *Annals of American Academy*, July, 1935, p. 164.
[2] *Ibid.*

PUBLICIZING ADMINISTRATIVE ACTIVITIES

Official publicity men promote administrative efficiency by relieving other officials of the task of coping with reporters. Where an interview is sought, the journalist can be sent directly to the appropriate official without wasting the time of others in aimless inquiry. Important officials are available only at prearranged times. Subordinate officials are often frightened into silence by an inquiring reporter or stimulated into making unwise remarks for which the whole bureau is held responsible. Statements of policy, if they are to be authoritative, should come through a responsible source. Otherwise a bureau would find itself in an embarrassment of self-contradictions. The present confusion would be worse confounded if the existing divisions of information and public relations were abolished.

In examining official publicity the fact is evident that the federal government does not present a unified front. Its many-sided activities are clearly reflected in the many aims sought through its publicity agencies.

As a tentative analysis, the publicity activities of the federal government may be classified according to the purpose for which the propaganda is intended, as follows:

1. To advertise the services offered by a particular bureau.
2. To create support not only for the bureau but also for the policy with which it is concerned.

1. To many of the bureaus and offices in the federal establishment, well-managed publicity is essential for their existence. Agencies such as the Bureau of Home Economics or the Bureau of Agricultural Economics have their chief reason for being in the fact that they are sources of information. If they are not used widely, they lose their justification for support from Congress. These bureaus must advertise their usefulness to the citizen and to the special interests that they may serve. Their "tax-supported advertising" raises no particular issue save that of expense and expediency.

2. To most federal bureaus advertisement of their function and services is not essential to their continued existence. Publicity is necessary, however, in order to secure the active support or a favorable attitude on the part of the general public or of some particular group. The publicity work of such bureaus may then be directed toward attaining an immediate objective of

policy or toward creating a better understanding of the work or policies of the bureau.

These preliminary considerations point to the thesis that under present-day conditions an office for the management of public relations is one of the essential devices of successful administration. In other words, good government in a modern democracy demands well-handled publicity for the purpose of winning public support and for the purpose of defending the administration from the counteragitation of opposing groups.[1] No longer is official propaganda confined entirely to war time. The positive character of governmental functions and their multifarious and intimate connection with the economic and social interests of the citizen make understanding and coöperation essential to efficient administration.

Much of the work of modern administration is providing services to the public. "Is the user satisfied with these services?" becomes a pertinent question for officials. It has been suggested that government enterprises should follow the lead of public-utility corporations in cultivating friendly public relations.[2] The intelligent use of advertising has been recommended. Certainly much could be done toward stressing the need of courtesy in official relations with the public. Officers in the Immigration and Naturalization Service have recently received definite instructions on this point. The problem of public relations is not entirely a matter of explaining administrative action to the voters. Attending to complaints and creating a friendly atmosphere is also very important.

Deliberately and legally establishing agencies for the creation and stimulation of favorable opinion seems to vitiate the basic concepts of popular government. Can one speak of government by consent when this consent is manufactured by official propagandists? It has been only too well demonstrated that mass persuasion through appeals to prejudice and through outright misrepresentation can be made the basis of dictatorial power. Sir Henry Maine years ago pointed out the danger for democratic

[1] The same view is taken by G. E. G. Catlin, "The Role of Propaganda in a Democracy," *Annals of American Academy*, May, 1935, p. 219.

[2] Marshall E. Dimock, "Selling Public Enterprise to the Public," *National Municipal Review*, December, 1934. Two doctoral dissertations have been announced as follows: James L. McCamy, *Public Relations in Governmental Administration*, University of Chicago; E. S. Wengert, *The Public Relations of Administrative Agencies*, University of Wisconsin.

government that lay in generalizations, "the trick of rapidly framing and confidently uttering general propositions on political subjects, for producing not indeed agreement but the semblance of agreement, in a multitude of men." In his day he lamented that "men ambitious of political authority have found out the secret of manufacturing generalities in any number."[1] In our day the process has been extended and developed to the character of an art, if not to the proportions of an industry. Framing generalizations, selecting facts, and naming slogans is a profession for an increasing number of men. And many of them are employed in the service of the federal government.

If such activities are inevitable because of political conditions and economic forces, what criteria can be discovered for guiding the publicity work of the government? The appearance of possible abuses is to be expected. Certain situations such as the following may be assumed as possibilities:

That certain government departments are identified with special interests and that official propaganda is used to forward these interests under the guise of the "general welfare."

That official propaganda may on occasion create opinion which it uses to secure increased appropriations from Congress, a larger staff, or more authority.

That officials through their prestige and position skillfully exploit the channels of publicity open to them for their partisan advantage.

That publicity handled with ineptitude or hostility may vitiate the program of even an able and conscientious administrator.

As a matter of actual fact, there is little ground for criticizing the conduct of publicity work at the present time. Agreement seems general that our federal official publicity agents do their work efficiently, supply all the facts whenever possible, and act with great candor.

The administrators, following the President's example, talk freely. But the absence of any general conscious effort to build a

---

[1] *Popular Government*, essay 2, p. 107, John Murray, London, 1886: "All generalization is the product of abstraction; all abstraction consists in dropping out of sight a certain number of particular facts, and constructing a formula which will embrace the remainder; and the comparative value of general propositions turns entirely on the relative importance of the particular facts selected and of the particular facts rejected."

united public support would indicate that the government, if attempting propagandist tactics, was failing badly. The administrative leaders appear to have no clear objective and hence official publicity cannot be concerted toward indoctrinating the terms of a national political creed or program. The floodlight of publicity has not sent a guiding beam ahead, but has rather diffused abroad a blinding glare.

The White House is the great publicity office and the public-relations officials take their cues from the President. They attend the press conferences of the chief executive and report any developments of importance to their respective chiefs. In the opinion of W. M. Kiplinger: "There's too little coördinating among these multitudinous government publicity agents. There's need for a coördinator, attached to the White House, maintaining contact with all government agencies, ironing out their contradictions and confusions, thinking always in terms of helping the average reader."[1]

Edward L. Bernays has gone so far as to suggest that

. . . the United States Government should create a Secretary of Public Relations as [a] member of the President's Cabinet. The function of this official should be to interpret America's aims and ideals throughout the world, and to keep the citizens of this country in touch with governmental activities and the reasons which prompt them. He would, in short, interpret the people to the government and the government to the people.[2]

The establishment of such an office would introduce a false appearance of harmony and consistency within the administration. The coördination of public policy cannot be left to a publicity office. Unity of interpretation is desirable, but only when it reflects a genuine unity of purpose. Official publicity becomes dangerous when it hides the true conditions. If there is confusion in high places, the public should know it.

The proper function of the public-relations official is very well explained by Mr. Alfred D. Stedman, assistant administrator of the A.A.A.:

To the press, we attempt in many ways including distribution of mimeographed announcements to make available accounts of events as

[1] W. M. Kiplinger, "What Can You Believe?" *Today*, Nov. 24, 1934, p. 22.
[2] Edward L. Bernays, *Propaganda*, p. 114, Horace Liveright, 1928.

they occur. It is up to these informational agencies to do as they please with this information. Sometimes, to our temporary discomfiture, some of these agencies are ahead of us. Newspapermen particularly provide frequent instances of individual initiative in anticipating events, new policies and programs. We do not conceive it as part of our function to interfere with enterprise of this sort, but rather to help it along, so far as we can possibly do it consistently with an even break to the press. Genuine reporter interest, which goes beneath the surface of the day's news grist into the elements of important economic situations, is the greatest kind of an asset. Hence we try whenever possible to give reporters access to original sources of information. Sometimes misinformation of consequence becomes general. But eventually when that happens it usually stirs up so much interest as to enhance the news value of correct information, finally calling widespread attention to the facts when they can be announced.

On the basis of our experience thus far, it is possible to believe that programs of action, depending for their success upon growing public understanding of the facts, have an exceptional chance to succeed in this country. Our experience is such as to buttress rather than to weaken faith in the working of democracy, which depends upon honest information widely distributed.[1]

The chief effect of the systematized effort to explain the administration to the public has been to place the executive branch in a favored position. Where is the power within the government that has comparable facilities for reaching the minds of the multitude? If the democratic state is to function, both sides of public questions must be presented to the public. Dictatorship by systematic public persuasion is characteristic of fascism and communism. Propaganda is the weapon of dictatorship for marshaling a mass movement behind a few leaders. We cannot view with equanimity a development that places great powers of persuasion in the administrative branch and brings no countervailing force on the other side.

The mark of a democracy is the existence of a loyal opposition and the discussion of public questions before the tribunal of the public. Our democratic institutions must be those suitable to the developing needs of our society. Our task is to encourage within our system those tendencies which, if further developed, might restore in some measure the equilibrium in democratic control.

[1] Address at Round Table on Public Relations of Federal Administrative Agencies, December meeting of American Political Science Association, Chicago, 1934.

Our opposition bench must be in accordance with American traditions and prevailing trends. It has been frequently suggested, for example, that Cabinet members be allowed to take part in the debates of Congress. There they could be subjected to questioning by the opposition. This proposal has some merit. Fiery verbal combat between Congressmen and Cabinet members holds the elements of drama that attract popular attention to public problems and put the news on the front page. Broad problems of policy might thus be aired and even details of administrative behavior explained.

The pressure for time during the session is already overwhelming and getting through the mass of business has left the legislators little time or energy for thoughtful debate on policy. Lawmaking is a task for specialists. The ablest members of Congress are competent to deal with legislation upon only the few subjects that they have studied. Debates between such Congressmen and the appropriate administrative officials can be well handled in committee hearings.

On several occasions within the last few years proposals for broadcasting the proceedings "on the hill" have been made. Fortunately these suggestions were not acted upon. Nothing would be gained by such a step. The wiles for holding the attention of a radio listener are not the best methods of discussing the merits and details of pending bills with fellow legislators. The problem comes down to one of publicity technique. Politicians and statesmen have much to learn about the potentialities of the radio, the press, and the talking movies.

The floor of Congress is no longer the place where national issues can best be brought to public attention. The tactics of political debate are unsuited to modern devices for wide communication. Issues must be dramatized, arguments simplified, situations clarified, and discussion condensed. The manner suited to the forum is not appropriate to present needs.

The congressional investigation is a device of greater effectiveness in focusing prolonged public attention on the work of the legislative branch. It is very doubtful whether much useful information is uncovered in the actual hearings. The committee members have files of evidence gathered by their own agents and their chief task is to get the offenders on the carpet and force an admission of guilt. This process holds the sustained interest of newspaper readers. As Paul Mallon stated recently in the *New York Times*, if all data developed in the munitions investigation had been offered in a Senate speech by Senator Nye, it would have received comparatively little attention. The drama arising from procedure by "investigation" would have been lost. The *process* of disclosing the information excites public interest as much as the data itself.[1]

Generally speaking the activities of Congress are reported in a reasonably adequate and accurate fashion. The progress of legislation is noted and debates are summarized. But Congress is not *presented* to the public in the sense that the administrative branch is interpreted by its own professional spokesmen. It is the technique of the alert public-relations expert to forestall criticism, to present the best side of the case, to dramatize events, and to arrange situations that generate favorable news. This the administration is doing.

In a word, the deliberate and intelligently planned system for building up a favorable public opinion has developed greatly in the administrative branch and has been left to chance in the legislative branch. Especially during the period of economic crisis was criticism of the President often interpreted as obstruction to recovery.

Since the administrative branch is developing systematized and efficient publicity services, since this public-relations work is an inevitable outgrowth of social and technical advances, and since it is essential to efficient administration, it must be seriously reckoned with as a significant governmental development. Its power is great and its purpose generally justified. But its effect is to give the administration a disproportionate amount of influence in the formulation of public opinion. To restore a balance, the views of those in opposition should be brought clearly before the public.

[1] Paul Mallon, *New York Times*, Dec. 9, 1934, magazine section: "On big hearings days now one telegraph company has as many as eleven operators on duty. The biggest day's business at the munitions hearing a few months ago was 21,000 words for that company. This was the day the du Ponts were on the stand. Now a Senator could talk himself blue in the face on the Senate floor saying exactly what he may say in a Congressional investigation, yet people outside the sound of his voice might never know he spoke."

This is a task that cannot be left entirely to those controlling the mediums of communication. They are the mere purveyors of what happens. They can be held to no definite responsibility for disclosing all sides of an issue. The press has not met the need. In fact, it is misleading to talk of the "press" as an entity that can be held responsible for intelligent criticism and leadership. There are thousands of newspapers, large and small, urban and rural, good and bad, according to individual value judgments. The despatches of Washington correspondents must go through the hands of an editorial staff bound by their owners' policies and their own conceptions as to what is news. The press is a great business for the merchandising of facts, rumors, banalities, and ideals. The problem is one of building up somewhere within the government an opposition bench. What are the possibilities? One way to meet the problem is to organize systematic counterpublicity.

In the publicity division of the minority party is the starting point for developing an agency capable of at least meeting on their own grounds the publicity agencies of the federal administrative offices. Here the needed expert opinion in public-relations management could be joined to the essential democratic duty of maintaining an opposition.[1] It is neither possible nor desirable that congressional activities officially pass through a formally designated publicity office. But those critical of the administration and distrustful of bureaucratic activity should have facilities for

[1] Thomas S. Barclay has written: "Observers of the American political system have long recognized the difficult position of the opposition party as an effective critic of the legislative and executive policies of the party in power, especially in the interval between campaigns. Our constitutional practices result in the nomination of 'available' men for the presidency, and in the rather complete elimination of the defeated candidate from a position of acknowledged party leadership. The methods and traditions which govern and control the procedure of Congress are hardly adapted to produce party leaders who can speak authoritatively for the minority. It is rare that the party out of power is cohesive, united, and ready to present and support an alternative program. It is decidedly difficult, under normal conditions, to arouse public interest in the minority's position, save in the period which precedes an election. On the other hand, because of the great prestige attaching to the presidential office, and because of the elaborate methods of favorable publicity so highly developed by recent chief executives, the party in power is able to direct continuous attention to its policies and program." "The Publicity Division of the Democratic Party 1929–30," *American Political Science Review*, February, 1931, p. 68.

reaching the public that are comparable in quality, though not in size, to those enjoyed by the party in power.

The mistakes and abuses of the administration as well as the achievements and triumphs should be called strikingly to general attention. Coördinated criticism might ultimately lead to the presentation of a clear alternative and a constructive program on the part of the opposition. Intelligence and professional skill today characterize the public relations of federal administrative agencies. Before our official publicity work is developed further, it is highly desirable that the other side of the picture be presented to the public with something approximating the efficiency with which the administrative branch reports its accomplishments to the press and to the public.

The proviso that there be an active opposition in no way weakens the argument that organized publicity is essential to administration in the public interest. As the federal government shoulders the task of economic recovery and the reform of abuses in the business world, the people must be made to understand what is happening. These responsibilities of government are too complex for the mass of voters to grasp in detail. But the principles must be made clear. Administrators will meet with misunderstanding unless the President and his politically responsible aides explain in clear and simple language the objectives of the administration.[1]

In attempting, then, to administer in positive terms for the public welfare, officials must likewise assume the additional responsibility of keeping the voters informed. This is constantly being done through the issuance of pamphlets and reports and through the contacts that bureaus have with various interest

---

[1] Raymond Clapper, *Washington Post*, June 15, 1935, p. 2: "In Washington officials read the large newspapers which carry accounts of national developments at Washington. But the vast majority of persons out in the country read newspapers in which accounts of proceedings at Washington are less complete. New measures go to Congress in bewildering array. It is difficult enough for a newspaper correspondent, who is paid for doing it, to keep abreast of all that the Administration is doing. How much more difficult it is then for a busy person, driven by the day's business of earning a living, to sit down and analyze the A.A.A. amendments, the holding company bill, the Eccles banking bill? He hears that some professor has worked out a new idea. Somebody says it sounds like a crazy idea, and that Roosevelt is socialistic; and thus another person turns suspicious and sour, and so the thing spreads."

groups. Over and above these special relationships there must be a broad and inclusive view of the general interest. The President must endeavor to formulate his goals and explain his purposes to the mass of voters. If the federal government is to answer the needs of all important groups in the community, then some general accounting of this stewardship is necessary. Such a general view is very difficult unless the administration is an integrated whole directed toward commonly held objectives.

Chapter XXIII

AN ADVANCE TOWARD ADMINISTRATION IN THE PUBLIC INTEREST

She very soon came to an open field, with a wood on the other side of it: it looked much darker than the last wood, and Alice felt a *little* timid about going into it. However, on second thoughts, she made up her mind to go on: "for I certainly wo'n't go *back*," she thought to herself, . . .

A DEMOCRACY inclines toward chaos rather than toward order. The representative principle, if logically followed, leads to infinite diversity rather than ultimate unity. The counting of noses is significant only to the extent that this regiments popular consent and distributes responsibility among the people for decisions made by the rulers. Since the "voice of the people" is a pleasant fancy and not a present fact, the impulse for positive political action must be deliberately imposed at some strategic point, if democracy is to succeed as a form of government.

Accordingly, the tests appropriate for judging democratic institutions are these: Is responsible leadership made possible? Can the varied interests of the community exert their influence in governance? Meeting these criteria means reconciling stability in executive control with flexibility in representation. Thus the democratic state is basically set in a position of straddle that recalls the heroic posture of the Colossus at Rhodes and the usual attitude of the average politician today.

The task of government in a democracy, we assume, is the adjustment of warring economic and social forces. The public interest is the standard that supposedly determines the degree to which the government lends its forces to one side or the other. Without this standard for judgment between contenders, the scales would simply be weighted in favor of victory for the strongest. So long as the "natural" (*i.e.*, the unregulated) operation of economic forces was thought to result in the ultimate well-being of the community, political intervention in the "public interest" was seldom demanded. The persuasiveness of such conceptions depended upon the persistence of the basic conditions that occasioned their acceptance in the first place.

It now appears that these economic conditions under which democracy emerged are changing. A choice is offered between a planned society, which means governmental leadership in economic activities, or a competitive system, which under modern capitalism results in cyclical depressions and widespread distress. With the respective merits of either horn of this dilemma we are not concerned, but its implications for democratic institutions are pertinent here. Can a workable adjustment be made?

The freedom of a competitive economic order is not proving compatible with the security of the individual. His position is even more endangered by monopolistic capitalism. Yet if a guarantee of economic security is demanded of the government, it must be forthcoming at whatever price. Otherwise representative institutions would be false to their own tenets. It is politically impossible to deny this demand and retain democracy. But can a degree of discipline sufficient to protect the individual be imposed in the economic realm without placing business enterprise under a control so irksome that businessmen will immediately repudiate such a policy in the next election?

It may be that a dictatorship for business will be prescribed by the agencies of democratic government, but it does not seem likely so long as the channels of political propaganda and popular persuasion are open to the banker, merchant, and industrialist. To advocate a planned society under our system of capitalism and democracy is to urge a leopard to change his spots. A new social pattern may be desirable, but such a design cannot be stamped upon an unwilling democracy, even for its own good. Yet, unless a workable political adjustment is discovered which will deal with the new forces of modern capitalism so that the regime is tolerable to all important elements in the community, the whole structure will topple and crash. The primary purpose of the liberal democratic state is to reconcile particularistic interests in such a way that the regime may continue. If capital and labor reach an impasse and decide to war to the death for political control, either fascism or communism may emerge. Democracy would be knocked unconscious early in the struggle. The modern democratic state must head off such a conflict if it is to survive.[1] It cannot afford to await the survival of the fittest. The exigencies of the age demand positive state activity in order that democracy itself may continue.

This situation, while generally recognized, is outlined here in order to clarify the problem of practical administration confronting the democratic state. How can this definite and positive responsibility of the present-day state be carried into execution? Can this essential objective be realized under a form of government basically designed to liberate the opinions and powers of the multitude of particularistic social and economic groups that form the community? The spokesmen of special interests have a place in the government; the problem for modern administration is to allow them to state their case but not to coerce the official. The agencies for formulating and carrying into effect that authority which is supposed to promote the general welfare have multiplied enormously. There is no provision, however, for unity or consistency in the interpretation of the public interest. A remote system of checks and balances between Congress and the President and between House and Senate has proved a device for stalemate and delay rather than unity or responsibility of control.

The parliamentary system demonstrates a truism of government that our system has tried to ignore, namely, that co-equal powers cannot wield authority over the same jurisdiction and escape conflict. The Cabinet is the government in Great Britain; the Chamber of Deputies is the determining power in France. The fiction of checks and balances and a separation of powers does not dispose of the conflict under our system. Party discipline, popular enthusiasm, personal magnetism of leaders—intangible and uncertain factors such as these are relied upon to make our system work. Judicial review is a limited and belated method of preserving a dubious degree of consistency and order. The constitution provides restrictions upon power, and leaves the dis-

[1] For a discussion of the crisis of capitalism and democracy from various viewpoints, see H. J. Laski, *The State in Theory and Practice*, Viking, 1935; John Strachey, *The Coming Struggle for Power*, Covici-Friede, 1933; Walter Lippmann, *The Method of Freedom*, Macmillan, 1934; Lewis Douglas, *The Liberal Tradition*, Van Nostrand, 1935 and James P. Warburg, *It's Up to Us*, Knopf, 1934.

covery of leadership to the ingenuity of the politician or the personal magnetism and influence of the statesman.

Unless we are to rest resigned with this situation upon the supposition that this is the inherent nature of the democratic state, there is need for promoting a purpose of the state over and above the purposes of the medley of interests that compose it. The preservation of the democratic process itself demands that some means be found for preventing the domination of organized minorities. The democratic state, to be consistent with its own principles, must preserve conditions under which a clear conception of the public interest can be formulated and presented to the voters. The general will of the social-contract philosophers has never materialized and we are left with a governmental apparatus of eighteenth century design whose obsolescence becomes the more striking in the light of present-day demands. Only through persistent alteration has the machinery been preserved at all and today its original parts are greatly obscured by the changes of the last few decades.

As the federal government has undertaken more activities, the need for responsibility and integration has increased, but at the same time social groups and economic classes, being now more closely affected, exert a greater influence on the government. Congress is torn by blocs and dominated by organized groups. Sectionalism disrupts its national character and the demands of political expediency make its members unable to raise their eyes to those matters that transcend their own political fortunes.[1] We make the political lives of our representatives narrow and precarious by binding them to sections. The direct primary and the modern technique of campaigning render the individual aspirant for office dependent upon an extensive organization in order to reach the voter. The political machine or the backing of a well-financed interest group is essential unless private funds are available. The political party has been the means of establishing a working relationship between the constitutionally separated

[1] The author has discussed some of these problems in the *American Political Science Review*, "First Session of the Seventy-second Congress," October, 1932; "Second Session of the Seventy-second Congress," June, 1933; "First Session of the Seventy-third Congress," February, 1934; "Second Session of the Seventy-Third Congress," October, 1934; "First Session of the Seventy-fourth Congress," December, 1935.

legislative and executive branches. It has provided an extra-official allegiance that has made it possible for the President and a majority in Congress to act together. However, as an agency for formulating a program and standing responsible for its consummation, the political party has proved inadequate.[1] The fundamental need is a governmental institution that will join the disparate economic forces of society behind a unified political program.

This problem has been faced directly in Europe. Parliaments of industry were instituted in many countries as a device for giving a more vital basis to the representative system and for introducing expert opinion. Through these assemblies of economic-class spokesmen it was thought a consensus of opinion might emerge and the sharp rivalries induced by capitalism might be welded together. But such hopes were disappointed.[2]

Political assemblies were unwilling to tolerate rival economic parliaments. Moreover, the representative principle could not be applied to occupational groups without the establishment of a dogmatic standard as to the relative importance of various economic classes; this vitiated *ab initio* the very object sought. Such assemblies were the creations of constitution makers unmindful of custom and of politicians seeking to placate protesting minorities. Economic parliaments had no foundation in the institutions or practices of the country. They were not the product of broad and gradual development. They were created at the top and they withered for lack of substantial support from those they purported to represent. Yet most of the nations of the world dallied with this theory of economic representation in the years of readjustment following the World War.

These experiments, despite their failure, are eloquent evidence of the general need for synthesizing the economic and political forces within the state to the end that the public interest may be interpreted, not merely in terms of factional compromise, but in accordance with the wisdom and experience of the whole com-

---

[1] For an analysis of this point see the author's article, "For Them on the Fence," *North American Review*, November, 1933.

[2] See the author's "Legalized Lobbying," *Current History*, February, 1930, and "Czeckoslovak Economic Advisory Council," *American Political Science Review*, May, 1930. See Lewis Lorwin, *Economic Advisory Councils*, Brookings Institution, 1931.

munity. Great Britain has perhaps come closest to succeeding in devising political implementation suitable to its national needs. The British Cabinet, as John Dickinson has written "is independent enough, and occupies a post of sufficient prestige, to promote adjustments which an ordinary representative, concerned mainly with the narrow affairs of his own constituency might hesitate or fear to do. At the same time its proposals are subject to the double check of being rejected by the assembly and repudiated at the polls."[1] Integrated with an intelligent and trained civil service, the Cabinet brings together power and *expertise* in governance based upon responsibility to the people.

While the success of cabinet government in Great Britain demonstrates the possibility of combining these essentials of modern democracy, it does not follow that these British institutions have a general application. The operation of such governmental forms in a different setting is quite unpredictable and would necessarily lead to a train of unforeseen adjustments. In the United States the inescapable fact of federalism is a bar to rule by a single committee of political leaders. Sectional and economic interests are too well defined and too staunchly held to be easily brought under the sway of a national cabinet. The simple fact that the United States is not Great Britain is enough to rule out as impracticable the hope that we could enjoy the benefits of British government by copying the outward forms.

We must perforce seek a solution to our problems in terms of our own institutions. Concrete suggestions for reform are more likely to be practical and hence more likely to be readily adopted if they are based upon existing trends. Through the selection and combination of certain tendencies, emphasis and support may be given to the forces that seem to hold promise for the problems of the state. It is hardly to be expected that any final solution can be found, but at least an impasse may be avoided. One set of factors, if supported and developed, can prevent certain difficulties, while another selection from the current forces about us would lead in turn to even greater problems.

[1] John Dickinson, "Democratic Realities and Democratic Dogma," *American Political Science Review*, May, 1930, p. 297. British writers are inclined to stress the danger of bureaucracy under their system. See, for example, Ramsay Muir, *How Britain Is Governed*, R. R. Smith, 1930.

AN ADVANCE TOWARD ADMINISTRATION

The events of the Roosevelt administration have often been interpreted as being so colored by emergency conditions as to be of little general significance. Actually these critical conditions have served to show more clearly problems of persistent importance that obtained, but in lesser degree, in previous administrations. The economic crisis made the demands of special interests for relief more insistent and more numerous. The need of presidential control and leadership was thereby greatly emphasized and hence more widely recognized. In the past, however, the President has time and again been better able to uphold the public interest than a Congress controlled by blocs and organized minorities.[1] While the increased power of the chief executive is open to abuse, it seems an almost inescapable result of congressional weakness in coping with pressure groups. The problem must be met by bringing about a stronger working relationship between the President and Congress rather than by insisting upon a separation of powers and a jealous delimitation of functions.

The need of attempting to formulate an official program in the public interest by a responsible administrative agency arises from the experienced strength of minority groups in pressing their case by propaganda and organized agitation and from the now-recognized inability of the public to formulate opinion. The fact that a spontaneous and coherent public opinion cannot arise to solve political problems does not mean that popular government is impossible. It means rather that our governmental institutions must be fitted to the limited capacity of the citizen to participate in political decisions. If the public can do no more than indicate assent or dissent, the clear presentation of alternatives becomes of the utmost importance. The offering of positive proposals by a responsible administration is then the first goal to seek. Especially during the Roosevelt administration has the office of the chief executive acted as a clearing office for new theories and proposals.

---

[1] W. H. Taft makes some pertinent remarks in *Our Chief Magistrate and His Power*, Columbia University Press, 1916. President Hoover once undertook a deliberate counteroffensive against organized minorities, *New York Times*, Sept. 26, 1931, p. 1. President Coolidge has stated: "It is because in their hours of timidity the Congress becomes subservient to the importunities of organized minorities that the President comes more and more to stand as the champion of the rights of the whole country. . . . " *American Magazine*, August, 1929, p. 146.

Suggestions have come from hard-headed and often socially near-sighted men of affairs and from imaginative and often entirely impractical men of theory. The President has picked up items here and there and, working with an informal group of advisers, official and unofficial, has drawn up legislation for congressional action.

The increased power of the President means, of course, an increase in the importance of the bureaucracy. Consistency in the formulation of presidential policy involves an intelligent and efficient arrangement of the whole administration service. This is recognized by the greatly increased demand during the last decade for administrative reorganization and civil service reform. During the last few years especially has the need for a properly qualified bureaucracy and a responsible administrative hierarchy been recognized.[1] The increased professionalization of those in the government service and the greater scope for the expert have been concomitant trends. These developments are now so apparent to all that they require no elaborating here, but they are significant as indicating the sphere within which the present and future problems of the democratic state must be met. Another objective of modern democracy, then, is the development of a competent bureaucracy.

If the existence of the democratic regime rests upon the assumption that the state exists not for the welfare of any one class but for the benefit of the people as a whole, this great and growing bureaucracy must be guarded from domination by economic groups or social classes. On the other hand, it must be kept free of the abuses of aloof, arbitrary, and irresponsible behavior to which public servants are so often prone. In short, it must not develop a group interest within itself that will become its *raison d'être*. Every political institution has within it potentialities for good or evil, but its susceptibility to abuse is no conclusive argument against its more positive aspects. A strong executive at the head of a powerful administrative service may constitute an implicit danger, but such a situation is necessitated today by the more immediate and compelling conditions which call for unity and leadership.

[1] L. D. White, *Government Career Service*, University of Chicago Press, 1935; Luther Gulick, *Better Government Personnel*, McGraw-Hill, New York, 1935.

AN ADVANCE TOWARD ADMINISTRATION

Since the element of consent is the first essential of the democratic state and is the very foundation stone of our popular assemblies, we must rule out as incompatible with the principles of representative government the domination of the chief executive over Congress through a constitutional grant of authority that would establish his unquestioned authority for a fixed time. But a unified, integrated authority in the state can be created only by improving our administrative machinery and personnel, and by bringing the executive and legislative branches into closer accord. To follow the full implications of such a union would go beyond the purview of this study. We can only note in passing the repeated efforts made of late to bring administrators and legislators together at the White House. The use of a Presidential "contact man" for reaching Congressmen is significant. The clumsy device of patronage is another means of winning support. More direct and effective means are yet to be discovered.

One of the most striking characteristics of our government is the chasm that exists between the administrative and the legislative branches. Here is separation not merely of powers but also of sympathies and viewpoints. Those who man the two branches do not speak the same language. They think in different terms. Congressmen look upon the bureaucracy with more suspicion and distrust than understanding and respect. It is the rare legislator who knows much about the actual operations of our departments and bureaus or who appreciates their problems.

The Congressmen who have served for years upon certain committees in the course of time learn about the administrative agencies that come within the province of these committees. But theirs is a partial view and it is not shared by the changing rank and file of the House and Senate. To maintain his seat a legislator must know his constituency and the needs of his section; he has little time left for a study of the federal administrative offices. Moreover, the Congressman strives to meet the demands for legislative action made by his constituents. As a representative, this is his job. Suggestions, however, coming from such interested parties have little connection with the broad needs of the country and little understanding of the administrative task of carrying the proposal into effect. We cannot afford to enact a mass of sporadic and uncoördinated legislation.

Laws are now more and more frequently formulated in the administrative offices. They are sponsored by Congressmen and Senators who have more faith than understanding. This shift makes a responsible bureaucracy all the more urgent. It also makes it highly desirable that the representative factor be introduced into the administrative process. The compromise of group interests and the formulation of the actual terms of the legislation should be worked out largely in negotiation between administrators and the interested parties and then submitted to the legislature for criticism and discussion. Of course, the committees of Congress provide an opportunity for experts and lobbyists to testify, but the work of these committees is unrelated. There is no assurance that bills will receive the attention commensurate with their importance in the general program of the session. Political animosities often intrude in the hearings. The degree of intelligence with which a problem is handled depends upon the caliber of the committeemen. And the committees are composed in accordance with the dictates of political expediency, the operation of the seniority rule, and the personal ambitions of Congressmen. The committee system has nothing to offer in our search for integration and responsibility in political affairs.

Administrators are in a more secure position than the elected representatives, however. They can cope with lobbyists on a relatively secure footing. Moreover, their special knowledge enables them to understand the merits of proposed legislation in terms of what is possible of enforcement and of accomplishment. Neither special interests nor the bureaucracy are able to decide the major question of policy—should this bill be passed? This must remain a legislative problem. But the form of the enactment and the pros and cons of the issue can best be understood by those directly in touch with the problem under consideration.

If the expert knowledge of special-interest representatives and that of the bureaucrat are combined, some workable solution can generally be found. Agreement at this point forestalls opposition later in Congress. Private parties in consultation with experts in the government must agree upon a course of action. The detailed and technical provisions of a bill can thus be discussed by those most competent to deal with these questions. The difficulty at present is that measures drawn up by administrators in consultation with outside experts and interested parties are opened up for amendment in Congress by legislators seeking to curry political favor. Such activities would be discouraged by placing more directly the responsibility for formulating legislation in the administration and by seeking to disarm the conflict of sections and of classes by compromise in advisory committees.

Of course, differences will remain, and the right of opposition will mean that democratic government continues. Our goal is not the eradication of all disagreement but rather the expression of a state purpose by a responsible agency expert in character and in close touch with the realities of the situation that must be met. If Congress wishes to go its own way, it remains free to do so, but it is thereby put on the defensive and its decisions are open to the suspicious scrutiny of the administration, the public, and the special interests allied with the presidential program.

The opposition which arises in Congress and which not infrequently becomes hardened into blocs is the result of underlying group antagonisms. Only too often the lawmaking process becomes a matter of swap and barter between minority interests. In this situation the proposals of the administration have great weight, especially when they combine the recommendations of the President as party leader with those based upon bureaucratic experience.

The federal government now has a heavier task of law enforcement than ever before. The wider area of administrative discretion makes greater demands upon the bureaucrat. His task of discovering the public interest is no longer guided by statutory provisions that set clear limits to his activities. With this greater degree of discretion has gone a very much broader field of jurisdiction. The problems are more complex technically. All these duties have been placed upon an administrative machinery that was not designed to carry such a burden. It is woefully lacking in coördination. This means that it is more difficult for the official to measure his activities against the decisions of other officials in related fields. He lacks proper terms of reference.

How can a program be formulated for the promotion of the general welfare and carried into effect consistently and justly? There is no final answer to this problem. Sweeping constitutional changes may be necessary.[1] The partial answer offered in this book points to the contribution that might be drawn from the administrative branch. The lines that may be followed are summarized in these four words: clarification, consultation, coöperation, and coördination.

Clarification stresses the administrative duty of collecting pertinent facts, relating them to the task to be met, and then presenting these findings to the public. It is, for example, the duty of the State Department to study foreign affairs and to explain its decisions clearly. The Coördinator of Transportation studied his problem thoroughly and then presented his conclusions so that all might read. The graphic reports of the recent Committee on Economic Security showed a commendable effort to place the need for old-age pensions and unemployment insurance before the public. Research and publicity for this research must go hand in hand.

Consultation with the persons and groups most directly concerned must likewise become a regular feature of administration. This is the greatest safeguard against arbitrary or ill-considered action. The practice of hearings and conferences is fairly general. Such contacts should be made more systematic. Official recognition of lay interests should be carried further. The Business Advisory and Planning Council is a hesitant step in the right direction.

As consultative agencies are developed, a greater degree of coöperation between the government and private organizations is made possible. The National Advisory Committee on Aeronautics shows how experts inside and outside the administration can join forces. Officials, by deliberately developing close contacts with the groups under their general jurisdiction, can maintain public confidence and act for the best interests of the parties concerned.

To realize the public interest in public administration, however, it is necessary to coördinate the activities of officials. Under any system of administrative organization there will always be activities that cut across the established lines. A thorough reorganization of the federal government would reduce but by no means eliminate these interdepartmental lines. The need persists, then, of finding some point for coördinating these activities that escape integration

[1] For a penetrating discussion of this situation, see W. Y. Elliott, *The Need for Constitutional Reform*, McGraw-Hill, New York, 1935.

within their respective departments. Under our present illogical arrangement this need is especially pressing. As already noted, a few federal departments serve to coördinate the interests of those classes politically strong enough to secure such departments. For other interests special agencies such as the Central Statistical Board or the Science Advisory Board suggest another means.

The hope for the future lies in first clarifying the issues in special fields, then consulting with all parties concerned, and finally bringing together all governmental agencies with a stake in the outcome of a given issue. Administrative devices must be developed to meet these needs. For example, The National Advisory Health Committee, the National Crime Conference, and the Power Policy Council approach this end, each in its own fashion.

How can coördination be secured in the broadest sense? An immense gain in integration and control of administrative activities came about through the creation of the Bureau of the Budget under the Budget and Accounting Act of 1921.[1] Our fiscal affairs had hitherto been handled in a hit-or-miss fashion by congressional committees acting largely independently of one another in the consideration of separate departmental appropriations. Not until the committee reports were all in did Congress know the total sum of appropriations requested. Under the presidential budget system, estimates are compiled by a central agency and then revised after consultation with the departments and independent establishments. The Budget Bureau has representatives in the various services who make it their business to understand the needs and functions of their respective fields. These liaison officers try to smooth out the disagreements and bring the estimates down within the limit set by the President for all expenditures for the ensuing fiscal year. As a coördinating agency, however, the Budget Bureau is hardly adequate.

The chief executive cannot grasp the relative merits of the many demands for federal funds. As Congressman Beck has written:

. . . he has neither the time nor the opportunity to make any first-hand examination of the needs of the far flung activities of the various departments and 150 bureaus [sic] under his control; the most that any President can, or has done since 1921, is to order the total of the items contained in the Budget to be held at a certain amount. This involves a more or less

[1] W. F. Willoughby, *National Budget System*, Johns Hopkins Press, 1927.

arbitrary deduction from such items as may have been requested by the various departments and subsidiaries.[1]

The estimates do not receive a more discerning treatment at the hands of Congress. Generally the House reduces the appropriations slightly. The members of the committee ask many questions of a very detailed sort. Why does the furniture in our embassies cost so much? Where are the towels used in the offices of internal-revenue agents sent to be laundered? Is the official sure that he is not buying rebuilt typewriters and paying the price for new ones? Congressmen conduct such inquisitions in a conscientious manner and the hearings of the appropriations committees are a valuable storehouse of information as to the conduct of the federal departments. The work is all done by subcommittees, however, and hence no clear general picture of the activities of the administrative services is obtained. The Committee on Appropriations pools the work of the subcommittees and brings together a report that is submitted to Congress. The same general procedure is followed in the Senate. Usually this body slightly loosens the purse strings that have been tightened by the House.

There is no place where a broad comparative view is taken of the various administrative activities of the federal government. Within the departments the situation is no better. The officials in charge of divisions send to the chiefs of their respective bureaus estimates to cover expenses for the coming fiscal year. The bureau chief takes as his guides the competing demands of his subordinates, the needs of the various groups served by his office, and the possible limits that his departmental superior may have set upon his bureau's share of the total appropriations for the department. In this system estimates are distributed so as to meet the many cries for funds, but with no evaluation of the relative importance and significance of the activities of bureaus when compared on an *interdepartmental* basis. The framework of the department provides the terms of reference in the drawing up of estimates. But since a bureau may be concerned with an interest that is not directly related to the major concern of the department within which it is a subordinate division, the bureau chief may be forced to play politics in order to secure adequate appropriations.

[1] James M. Beck, *Our Wonderland of Bureaucracy*, p. 200, Macmillan, 1932.

AN ADVANCE TOWARD ADMINISTRATION

The coördination of federal administrative activities brought about by the Budget and Accounting Act is confined to securing economies of operation and encouraging uniform business methods. The correlating machinery that has been set up under the office of the chief coördinator in the Budget Bureau has been useful for securing coöperation in purchasing supplies, lending and exchanging transportation facilities, drawing up specifications and contracts, utilizing to better advantage government real estate, etc. This work is important, but it does not go far enough. There is coördination of effort in the printing, binding, and distributing of government publications. It is only within the last year or so that the necessity has been recognized for concerted administrative action in transportation, communications, water-power development, etc.

The administrative service has lacked and still lacks adequate machinery for bringing together the officials engaged in closely related work. Congress, on occasion, or the chief executive may decide that a certain service is receiving a disproportionate share of federal funds. The Budget Bureau may insist upon some economy in business practice, but it is generally agreed that the Bureau of the Budget does not suffice as a coördinating agency. Officials have learned that, if they can create the need for financial support, they can eventually get funds. We must have an administrative agency that is competent to consider federal activities in terms of their relative importance.

The National Emergency Council was recently established as a general coördinating agency.[1] The council has a field representative in every state. This official acts as chairman of a state council which brings together all the field officers in charge of federal activities in the states. This comprises a group of from ten to thirty officials, depending on the number of federal agencies at work in the state. The state council is supposed to coördinate the

---

[1] "Purpose—The functions of the National Emergency Council are: (a) To provide for the orderly presentation of business to the President; (b) to coördinate interagency problems of organization and activity of Federal agencies; (c) to coördinate and make more efficient and productive the work of the field agencies of the Federal Government; (d) to coöperate with any Federal agency in performing such activities as the President may direct; and (e) to serve in an advisory capacity to the President and the Executive Director of the National Emergency Council." *U. S. Government Manual*, p. 479.

work in the field and to consider local problems. From each state council a report is sent to Washington every two weeks telling of local problems and progress. These reports are combined with the Washington reports.

The council thus circulates among all the member agencies a composite report which shows biweekly the developments that are taking place in the departments at Washington and in their various field agencies. From time to time special reports are prepared on major projects. It is the duty of the executive director to shape the general program upon the basis of the mass of material collected. The National Emergency Council has proceeded on the assumption that a lack of information is the explanation for the present lack of coördination. There are of course other factors. The officials in the council content themselves with trying to find out what all the administrators in the government are doing. Then they pass this data on to the members of the council. They assume that, if officials know of duplication and waste, they will try to eliminate such abuses. The officials in the council realize that they cannot superimpose from without their own ideas of harmony in administrative methods or activities.

The council has not functioned as an organic whole. It has been little more than a clearinghouse for information. Any coördinator other than the President encounters inevitable opposition. Department heads will not submit to direction from anyone less than the President. Precedence is a powerful factor and infringements of such rights have aroused violent disputes in the past. It may be foolish that men insist upon sitting at the Cabinet table in a certain order or that officials value the prerogatives of their position and want their rank recognized. It is nonetheless a fact and cannot be ignored in any scheme for coördinating administrative activities. Donald Richberg soon discovered that in his capacity of "coördinator-in-chief" he could exercise little authority.

In this three-ring circus of our government the President rules in administrative circles and strives for general harmony in all three branches. Certain traditions have been built up protecting departments and independent bureaus from outside interference. The practical problem of administration is how best to secure the maximum degree of coöperation within the government as it exists. Ideally a much more harmonious and symmetrical arrangement could be devised. But a giant bureaucracy cannot be remade without inviting a period of chaos. It seems wiser to use the materials at hand and to test the soundness of our structure point by point. Suggestive of how a coördinating board can function is the experience of the Advisory Council of the N.R.A. This council was recognized in Washington as one of the more successful parts of the Blue Eagle brood. It was composed of two representatives each from the Industrial Advisory Board, the Labor Advisory Board, and the Consumers' Advisory Board, and one representative each from the National Industrial Recovery Board, the Planning and Research Division, and the Legal Division of the N.R.A. The Advisory Council of the N.R.A. is significant because it fills on a smaller scale the role that an administrative coördinating council might occupy. Without getting involved in questions of policy, we can still evaluate the council in terms of its administrative effectiveness.

This council was an intermediary between the policy-determining board, the National Industrial Recovery Board, and the three representative advisory boards. It demonstrated its usefulness as a coördinating device. Its members were recruited at a level sufficiently high for them to speak with authority for their respective divisions, but not sufficiently high for them to speak the final word of command for the N.R.A. This made their advisory function the more significant. Officials who make the final decisions must often bow as a matter of practical necessity to what is politically expedient. This council, however, did not have to consider such extraneous factors. Its terms of reference were set by the broad terms of the statute within which a mass of administrative questions accumulated for decision. Its task was to build up a line of policy consistent with itself and flexible enough to meet the situations that arose in the execution of the law.

The members of the council thus dealt with internal administrative policy. They developed a body of precedents. Their decisions were ground from the grist brought in by day-to-day problems. They tried to dispose of these issues as they arose in such a fashion as to keep the whole administration consistent. As the council grew in experience, its decisions became broader and less dogmatic. They tended more and more to be explanations of policy.

With this agency concentrating its attention upon the internal aspects of administrative action, the National Industrial Recovery Board was left free to consider its recommendations with reference to external problems of politics. What will Congress say? What is the reaction of the press? What does the President want?

The council was not executive but advisory. While representative of several points of view, its members were not delegates dependent for instructions upon the interests for whom they spoke. Their task was not to speak the will of industry or of labor or of the consumer. It was their duty to clarify problems that involved the interests of all three classes. They came together to discuss those issues in which they all had a common stake and to reach a compromise agreement if possible. Their goal was to suggest a policy, not to carry it into effect.[1]

An administrative advisory body with a membership embracing all the interests falling within the jurisdiction of the federal government might be developed gradually. It would serve as a means of harmonizing administrative action within the statutory terms set by Congress. It could discover contradictoɪy purposes. It could evaluate the relative importance of various bureaus. It could pass upon the projects offered by the research and planning agencies in the various departments or commissions. It could include officials and laymen in its membership. The latter would be selected by the consultative agencies allied to the government to give expert advice on questions relating to health, education, transportation, labor, industry, etc. The former would speak as experts for their respective departments or commissions.

The council would be occupied chiefly in considering internal administrative problems and in integrating the work of the various bureaus. It might be used as a recruiting ground for the formation of interdepartmental committees to study special problems. Special subcommittees might be formed to investigate and report confidentially to the President. Building up an administrative council in the future would mean little more than encouraging a process that is already under way. The parts of the whole are scattered here and there in various departments. Where advisory committees do not actually exist, still the practice of informal consultation is generally established. As the powers and duties of

[1] Interview with Willard Thorp, chairman of advisory council.

administrators develop, they must arrange in more substantial fashion their relations with special interests. To this end administrative advisory committees should be extended more systematically throughout the federal services.

These committees would be composed of representatives from the special interests with which a particular bureau is concerned. These committeemen would be technically competent to advise, but not legally authorized to commit their industry or profession to the support of any governmental policy. Such spokesmen might be selected from a panel made up by the appropriate organizations of interests having regular contacts with a particular bureau. These committees would form part of an administrative advisory council. Its chief usefulness would be in coördinating the work of various branches within the administrative services and in coöperating with private interests.

The council in plenary session would serve as an open forum for the exchange of viewpoints and the discussion of problems submitted to it by the President. Administrators could thus learn what their fellows are doing and planning. *Ad hoc* committees might be appointed from this body to consider special problems and offer confidential advice to the bureaus immediately affected. Above all, the council should avoid any appearance of duplicating the duties of Congress. Its first responsibility would be to discover how the laws passed by Congress could be most effectively and harmoniously executed.

Some device for "grasping this sorry scheme of things entire" is certainly needed. Our experiments with emergency councils, advisory councils, and consultative committees all points to the possibility of developing these agencies further. A general administrative council, closely joined to the White House secretariat and aided by consultative committees in special fields, could be readily realized.

Some sort of administrative council or general staff for the federal government has won wide acceptance in theory and in principle.[1] Opinions differ as to its precise composition and

[1] W. Y. Elliott, *The Need for Constitutional Reform*, pp. 101, 203; W. J. Shepard, "Democracy in Transition," *American Political Science Review*, February, 1935, pp. 16–17; A. N. Holcombe, *Government in a Planned Democracy*, pp. 152 *ff*, Morton, 1935; C. E. Merriam, "Planning Agencies in America," *American Political Science*

duties. Specific suggestions as to organization and function are given in the final report of the National Planning Board. This study recommends a body of five members to be appointed by the President for an indeterminate tenure. They would be assisted by experts selected from a rotating panel. This panel would include "men or women from various groups able to contribute to national planning—as governmental bureaus, labor, agriculture, industry, the home, technical and scientific societies, and other groups directly concerned with the sound formulation of the lines of our national progress."[1] This board would initiate inquiries on emerging national problems; it would seek to coördinate various planning activities of other federal agencies and provide information on all planning projects. The report makes this very important point:

It cannot be too strongly emphasized that the function of such a board as proposed is not that of making final decisions upon broad questions of national policy—a responsibility which rests firmly upon the elected representatives of the people of the United States. Such a board would be useful in proportion as it was detached from immediate political power and responsibility, as a general staff gathering and analyzing facts, observing the interrelation and administration of broad policies, proposing from time to time alternate lines of national procedure, based upon thorough inquiry and mature consideration, constantly preparing and presenting to the authorities its impressions, findings, conclusions, and recommendations for such disposition as those entrusted with governmental responsibility may deem appropriate.[2]

Review, April 1935; establishment of National Economic Council, *Hearings* before Subcommittee of Committee on Manufactures, 72d Congress, First Session, 1932, *passim*. W. F. Willoughby in *Principles of Public Administration*, pp. 52–58, Johns Hopkins Press, 1927, stresses the need for a "bureau of general administration." David Lawrence in *Beyond the New Deal*, McGraw-Hill, 1934, emphasizes the advantages of giving the chief executive a real secretariat. There was talk of this during the Hoover administration. *United States Daily*, Mar. 16, 1929, index, p. 113. See the provocative article by Lindsay Rogers, "Putting the Cabinet to Work," *The New Republic*, Feb. 8, 1933. Professor Rogers states: "The proper articulation of expert advice from extra-governmental persons with the expert advice of permanent officials is one of the most important but as yet one of the most neglected problems of efficient public administration."

[1] *Report of the National Planning Board*, 1934, p. 35.
[2] *Ibid.*, p. 37.

A planning council, if it is to be a body for deciding policy, must either supersede the President and Congress as formulators of policy or become a fifth wheel on the governmental machine. We discard as chimerical and impractical a super-planning board that will tell the country what to do. As Bernard Shaw has said: "The great purpose of democracy is to prevent your being governed better than you want to be governed." At the beginning of this book we frankly accepted the limits on government set by the assumptions of democracy. Yet to make democracy workable, a clarification of objectives is needed. A planning board could indicate alternative courses. An administrative council could check up on the actual operation of the course pursued.

The public must know "where it stands." Do we fully realize the difficulties of attempting a positive and official interpretation of the public welfare under our present form of government? Democracy has meant laissez faire in the political realm. Can we bring social and industrial activities under state regulation without submitting to an ever-increasing political regimentation? An extraordinary willingness to coöperate will be necessary if coercion is to be avoided. An efficient machinery of coördination is essential. Such a machinery could at least indicate the need for coöperation and suggest possible directions to follow.

The government of the democratic state reflects inescapably the underlying interest groups of society, but the very fact that the state exists evinces a basic community of purpose. National rivalries or the operation of economic forces imperfectly comprehended may result in conditions that threaten the livelihood of certain classes. In guarding their own self-interest these classes may be willing to sacrifice that form of government whose keystone is toleration. Those seeking self-preservation are little concerned with guarding the democratic ideal. If a strong class interest can be identified with the continuance of democracy, so much the better.

The bureaucracy of the future should have as its most immediate interest the preservation of the democratic regime. The higher the intelligence, the training, and the devotion of this corps, the greater will be the likelihood of its fulfilling the essential duty of making the democratic state function. Of course, the danger remains that possibly the bureaucracy may ally itself with capital or with labor and so bring about the rule of fascism or communism. But this is by no means an inherent defect. There is no reason for thinking that governmental servants are bound together by an inner necessity that predisposes them to any one economic or social interest.

A responsible and integrated administrative service is a basic necessity in the continued existence of the democratic state under modern conditions. The town pump did well enough as a focal point in simpler days. But what remains now? Our representative institutions stress the confusion and conflict of special wills or succumb to the dictation of a party machine more concerned with power than with principle. If democracy means the peaceful adjustment of social conflicts, it thereby involves a willingness on the part of all concerned to make substantial sacrifices in order that this process may continue. This is basic to the acceptance of democracy as a method. But the democratic process must be implemented to cope with the demands of the present and of the future.

The government must undertake the coördination of its numerous activities and the planning of further developments in such clear and unequivocal terms that the citizen can perform his elementary duty of voting yea or nay. In the executive branch lies the task of confronting the people generally with an interpretation of the public interest that they can accept or reject through the established channels of representative government. It is thus that a positive view of politics can be attained by the man in the street.

The essence of democracy lies in the freedom it allows all citizens to voice an opinion concerning how and by whom they shall be governed. It recognizes the right of all to consider the welfare of all. What is in the public interest is thus a common problem.

For some years to come the voter will have to consider what aspects of the general welfare the federal government should properly take under its jurisdiction. The administrative aspects of this shift cannot be ignored. Whether the federal government should assume more or less responsibility for the general welfare is a highly debatable point. But what cannot be gainsaid is the necessity of accommodating the administrative machinery to its burden. At the present time this machinery is inadequate in many ways. Many of its imperfections are due to weaknesses inherent in democracy itself.

The immediacy of special interests makes improvements for the general welfare more difficult to realize. The situation is not hopeless, however. Within the federal administration much significant experimentation is taking place. The results will indicate how far the federal government can carry the administration of economic activities in the public interest. Such governmental interference seems an inescapable tendency; aiding one group awakens the desires of others.

More bureaucracy does not necessarily mean the death of democracy, but it does involve some essential readjustment. In recent years changes have been accelerated by economic stringency. It has been difficult to see clearly the direction of many trends. Old phrases have been used to discredit developments that deserve more careful analysis. No solution lies in damning bureaucracy while at the same time increasing the administrative duties of the federal government. The litter in Washington must be examined piece by piece. Are we ready to pay the price for federal participation and control?

The New Deal has not invented this question, but recent events have sharpened the issue. It is an issue designed to raise the devil politically; but such demons cannot be exorcized by the mumbo-jumbo of slogans. Forms of government must accord with social needs. Constitutionalism is not an end in itself. In this country it is a method of government upheld by a grave weight of tradition and the merits of great accomplishment. The ultimate justification of the United States Constitution lies in this—that its specific provisions harmonize with the high purpose expressed in its preamble.

Index

INDEX

Bureau of Agricultural Economics, and Food and Drug Administration, 249
investigations by, 40
and publicity, 367
and Standard Container Act, 37
Bureau of Biological Survey, 356n.
Bureau of the Budget, 389–391
and Federal Power Commission, 145
and Interstate Commerce Commission, 199
Bureau of Chemistry and Soils, 227–229, 329, 330
Bureau of Foreign and Domestic Commerce, and advisory committees, 299–300
bureaucracy and, 305–306
criticism of, 306–307
curtailment of foreign work by, 305
establishment of branch offices by, 301–303, 307
establishment of foreign offices by 303–305
publicity work of, 300, 302, 306
rapid expansion of, 297–298, 301, 306
reorganization of, 298–299
Bureau of Home Economics, 14, 250
opposition to, 247–248
publicity and, 367
Bureau of Immigration and Naturalization, 286–290
Bureau of Internal Revenue, 44–68
administrative problems of, 53–54
field work of, 64–65
history of, 46–47
investigation of, 53–58
organization of, 47–48
personnel problems of, 54–57, 61–63, 65–66
popular interest in, 53
regulatory powers of, 51–53
responsibilities of, 61–62
Bureau of Labor Statistics, 282, 286, 294
Bureau of Marine Inspection, advisory council to, 358
Bureau of Plant Industry, 329–330

Bureau of Standards, 250, 317–333
and business, 317–325
and the consumer, 325–328
and interest groups, 326–327
purpose of, 327n.
research associate plan of, 318–329
restoration of the appropriation of, 331–332
service work of, 318–325
and the simplified-practice movement, 323
standardization work of, 323–325
Bureau chiefs, and the budget, 390
and coördination, 340–341
Bureaucracy, and Andrew Jackson, 17–18
and Bureau of Foreign and Domestic Commerce, 305–306
competent, need for, 384
congressional opposition to, 12–13
criticism of, 10–15
danger of overexpansion of, 39–41
defense of, 14–15
democratic government and, 3–16
early opposition to, 10
emotional aversion to, 12–13
and the public interest, 8–9
and special interests, 7–9, 11, 14–16
Bureaus, and departmental subordination, 328–329
and outside support, 37–38, 41–42, 344–345
program for proper administration of, 43
and special interests, 257
Burgess, G. K., 318
Burgess, W., 97–98
Business, and administration, 296–297, 312–315
and Bureau of Standards, 317–325
and Department of Commerce, 296–316
and Department of Labor, 290, 294, 294n.
and Federal Trade Commission, 115–117, 125–126, 129–133, 135
and foreign policy, 78–88

INDEX

European experiments in economic representation, 381
Ex officio boards, failure of, 217
Excess-profits tax advisers, 48–49
Extension Service of the Department of Agriculture, 263–267
Ezekiel, M., 276

F

Farm Bloc, 261
Farm credit, 271
Farm organizations, 261–262, 266–270
Farm prices, and the public interest, 275–276
Farm problem, 270–271
Farm referenda, significance of, 273–274
Farmers, and the Constitution, 278
  and Department of Agriculture, 258–278
  and Interstate Commerce Commission, 195–196, 198
  and the New Deal, 270–278
  and the public interest, 277–278
Farmers' Union, 261–262
Federal Advisory Council of the Federal Reserve System, 350
Federal Communications Commission, 158–159
Federal Power Commission, 139–157
  administrative problems of, 145–147
  changing policies of, 142–143, 148–150
  creation and organization of, 139–140
  criticism of, 151–152
  investigation of, 147–150
  and the New Deal, 152–155
  and the power interests, 142–144
  and Roosevelt, 223
Federal Radio Commission, 158–178
  abolition of, 223
  criticism of, 161–162
  and Department of Commerce, 161–162
  and education, 164–165, 175
  and labor, 164
  policies of, 166–173
  and the public interest, 167–178

Federal Radio Commission, and sectionalism, 162–163
  and special interests, 163–165, 167–178
Federal Reserve Board, 216
Federal Trade Commission, 108–138
  changing policies of, 122–124, 129–133
  and Congress, 115–119, 127–128
  and the courts, 112–113, 120–123, 130, 137–139
  creation and early work of, 110–112, 115, 118–120
  investigation of, 119
  and the packers inquiry, 118–121
  and politics, 115–117, 156–157
  and the public interest, 112–113, 124, 133–134
  and Roosevelt, 222–224
  and self-regulation of business, 127–135
  weakness of, 138–139
Federal Trade Commission Act, 111
Federal Trade Commissioners, tenure of, 114
  varying aims of, 114, 122–124, 133
Federated American Engineering Societies, report of, 322–323
Ferguson, H., 14*n.*
Finer, H., 10, 20
Fletcher, H. P., 101
Food and Drug Administration, and Bureau of Agricultural Economics, 249
  and the consumer, 240–241
  criticism of, 238–239, 241
  decentralization of, 233
  and Department of Agriculture, 228–229, 239–240
  organization of, 226–227
  personnel of, 241
  service work of, 232–238
  weakness of, 231–232
Foote, W. A., 77
Foreign Bondholders Protective Council, 87
Foreign loans, and State Department, 79–88

[407]

INDEX

INDEX